MW01118579

HISTORICAL DICTIONARIES OF INTERNATIONAL ORGANIZATIONS SERIES
Edited by Jon Woronoff

The Pan American Union Building, 1954.
Credit: OAS. *1954 THE PAN AMERICAN UNION BUILDING*

The cornerstone of what is now the Organization of American States (OAS) was laid at an elaborate and formal ceremony on May 11, 1908, in Washington, D.C. President Theodore Roosevelt made the keynote address and others such as U.S. Secretary of State Elihu Root, Brazilian Ambassador Joaquím Nabuco, Cardinal Gibbons, Mexican Ambassador Francisco León de la Barra (speaking for Latin America), Andrew Carnegie, and Director General John Barrett of the International Bureau of American Republics (IBAR) were also present. The Governing Board of the IBAR had authorized construction of a headquarters building in Washington, D.C., in 1903, which was approved by the Third International Conference of American States meeting in Rio de Janeiro in 1907. An architectural firm in Philadelphia won the design competition and a construction contract was awarded to a company in Worcester, Massachusetts. The project got underway on April 13, 1908. The cost of what became known as the "House of the Americas" (plus annex and grounds) was $1,115,387, most of which came from a $853,174 contribution from the Carnegie Fund.

The building was dedicated and inaugurated on April 26, 1910, by U.S. President William H. Taft. With the exception of U.S. Secretary of State Philander Knox and President Theodore Roosevelt, the same individuals who attended the cornerstone ceremonies also spoke at the inaugural dedication. Over the next fifty years the organization (and building) would go through two more name changes. At the Fourth International Conference in 1910 (Buenos Aires, Argentina), the name of the building was changed from "International Bureau of American Republics" to that of the "Pan American Union" (shown above the three portico arches in the photo), which the Secretariat of the OAS retained until 1970 when it adopted its present name of Organization of American States.

The two statues that adorn the front of the building are designed to symbolize the geography of Panamericanism: the one on the right (north side of building) has "North America" carved at its feet (top of the base); the one on the left (south side of building) represents "South America," and the center portico represents the Central American republics. The Commonwealth Caribbean states are not represented on the facade of the building since none were independent until the 1960s and they were therefore ineligible for OAS membership at that time. The tall statue in the center-foreground is a representation of Queen Isabella of Spain, donated by the Spanish government.

Source: John Barrett, *The Pan American Union: Peace, Friendship, Commerce.* Washington, D.C.: PAU, 1911.

Historical Dictionary of Inter-American Organizations

Larman C. Wilson and David W. Dent

*Historical Dictionaries
of International Organizations, No. 14*

The Scarecrow Press, Inc.
Lanham, Md., & London
1998

SCARECROW PRESS, INC.

Published in the United States of America
by Scarecrow Press, Inc.
4720 Boston Way
Lanham, Maryland 20706

British Library Cataloguing in Publication Information Available

Library of Congress Cataloging-in-Publication Data

Wilson, Larman C. (Larman Curtis), 1930–
    Historical dictionary of inter-American organizations / Larman C. Wilson,
David W. Dent.
        p.   cm.—(Historical dictionaries of international organizations ; no. 14)
    Includes bibliographical references.
    ISBN 0–8108–3381–6 (cloth : alk. paper)
    1. International agencies—America—Handbooks, manuals, etc. I. Dent,
David W.   II. Title.   III. Series.
JZ5331.W55 1998
341.24'5'0257—dc21   97–24787
                                                                            CIP

ISBN 0–8108–3381–6 (cloth : alk. paper)

♾ ™ The paper used in this publication meets the minimum requirements of
American National Standard for Information Sciences—Permanence of Paper
for Printed Library Materials, ANSI Z39.48-1984. Manufactured in the United
States of America.

TO
NAOMI JOHANNA GILBERT WILSON,
mother, homemaker to provider-educator,
for her independence and strength of character,
dedication to three sons, and for her constant loving
support and trust.
—her son, L.C.W.

THERESA AND DENISE,
for their love, enthusiasm, and support
—D.W.D.

Contents

Maps

Editor's Foreword

Cooperation among the diverse countries in the Americas has a very long and impressive history, far more so than in Africa, Asia, or the Arab nations. The Latin American region has been particularly successful at conflict resolution and the peaceful settlement of disputes. But this cooperation has never come easy to a region with many differences, including language, economic position, and culture, to say nothing of philosophy and, on occasion, political ideology. There is also the recurrent theme of asymmetries in power and hegemony, with a massive and sometimes menacing United States, the larger Latin American countries (Argentina, Brazil, and Mexico) and their neighbors, or, more generally, the larger states and some quite small but no less independent nations. These imbalances explain why more has not been accomplished and why any progress has been hard won. At the same time, it is clear that working away persistently at the problems, many of them have been significantly reduced—and some resolved—by a bevy of inter-American organizations.

This dictionary presents these organizatons in all their complexities and variety. Some cover only part of the Americas; others encompass the entire region; and several link the Americas with the rest of the international community. Some have a broad range of activities, while others are limited to one or a few fields. Their origin and history, membership, scope and functions, and leadership and operation are fully explored. Of particular importance are the discussions of essential issues and problems highlighting some of the more serious controversies and trouble spots in the region. Naturally, the dictionary also introduces persons who have played a significant role in the government and operation of inter-American organizations. In addition to numerous dictionary entries a useful chronology and introduction summarize the past and present relations. For those who want to know more about specific aspects of inter-American organizations, there is a comprehensive bibliography with many current citations for further exploration. To enhance the dictionary, there are several important appendices, including the Charter of the Organization of American States (OAS).

This *Historical Dictionary of Inter-American Organizations* was written by two leading specialists on inter-American organizations. Larman C. Wilson is Professor Emeritus of International Relations at American University, and David W. Dent is Professor of Political Science at Towson University (formerly Towson State University). Both have lectured and written extensively on many of the organizations and issues dealt with here. Professor Wilson was a member of the OAS Inter-American Juridical Committee's Third International Law Course in Rio de Janeiro. Professor Dent has prepared university students to participate in the Model OAS exercise, a simulation of the activities of the General Assembly of the organization, for the past 17 years. The authors' experience and united efforts provide a valuable and unique overview of the field. This volume comes at a very propitious moment, when older organizations are reforming and refocusing, and new ones are emerging. One inter-American organization—the Organization of American States—will celebrate the 50th anniversary of the signing of its Charter in 1998. This work is a particularly welcome addition to the growing series of Historical Dictionaries of International Organizations.

Jon Woronoff
Series Editor

Acknowledgments

I undertook this challenging project in the early 1990s while still a full-time faculty member, but I soon found that my ability to make what would be considered normal progress was stifled by my teaching duties, including research supervision and a multitude of committee responsibilities. It was largely due to these commitments that I was not able to devote myself fully to writing this dictionary until I retired (the Spanish word —*jubilación*—is much more apt under these circumstances) in 1995. After several months of composing entries and a bibliography, however, I was still far behind in producing a finished manuscript. At this point I decided to invite David W. Dent, fellow Latin Americanist and expert on the Model Organization of American States, to join me as a co-author of this project. Special thanks are due to him for his dedication to bringing this dictionary to a more rapid completion.

Before turning to our joint expressions of appreciation, I want to thank a number of individuals at American University, first, in the School of International Service and second, in the University (Bender) Library. In the former, my thanks to Dr. Nanette S. Levinson, Associate Dean, for her general support; James Benseler and Laurie Walsh, Faculty Services, for helping with the appendixes; Rebecca Saxe, Faculty Services, for helping with the bibliography; to Monica Wells, my final Graduate Fellow, who also assisted with the bibliography; and to Tom DeLorme, Program Manager, for invaluable computer assistance. In the library, my thanks go to the various persons providing reference and ALADIN assistance who cheerfully and efficiently responded to my requests for information so that I could complete numerous bibliographical entries.

David W. Dent wants to extend our joint appreciation to three individuals at the Hispanic Division of the Library of Congress. Dr. Everett E. Larson (Head, Reference Section), Dr. Juan Manuel Pérez (Senior Bibliographer), and Tracy R. North (Program Assistant) were friendly and provided assistance in locating various published sources of information, especially those found on the Internet. Without the Hispanic Division of the Library of Congress, a marvelous repository of information for Latin Americanists, we would not have been able to produce a dictionary of this caliber.

A special debt of gratitude is also owed to a number of persons at the Organization of American States for their cooperative and professional assistance. First, to Enrique Lagos, Assistant Secretary for Legal Affairs, for providing information about the legal dimension, identifying important documents, and arranging important referrals (Larman Wilson notes his valuable assistance over many years, as well as that of Dr. Alberto Tolosa, now retired, former Senior Legal Advisor and Dr. Domingo Acevedo, Principal Legal Advisor). Second, to Juana Olmos, Information Specialist in the Office of Public Information, for providing numerous documents, assistance with the entry for the OAS, and important referrals to other critical materials. Next, our special thanks to four individuals affiliated with the Columbus Memorial Library at the OAS: Dr. Virginia A. Newton, Director, for her general support; René L. Gutiérrez, Librarian, for verifying numerous sources of information and providing current OAS documents; Stella Pérez de Villagrán, Documents Librarian, for locating critical OAS documents; and finally, Miguel Angel Rodríguez, Photographer, for making available the photograph collection. We thank also Anne-Marie Blackman, Senior Specialist, Unit for the Promotion of Democracy, for providing documents.

Finally, we appreciate the advice, aid and encouragement of several close friends and others at different stages of the project. G. Pope Atkins, professor emeritus, U.S. Naval Academy, offered insights on different aspects of the inter-American system related to inter-American organizations. Issac Cohen, Director of the Washington office of the United Nations Economic Commission on Latin America and the Caribbean (ECLAC), offered critical advice in improving the quality of the dictionary. Jack Child, Professor at American University, helped to clarify different aspects of the inter-American security system. Thomas W. Mullen, Professor of Political Science at Dalton College, provided us with clippings on current Latin American affairs from a wide variety of newspapers and magazines that we were able to use to update the constantly changing nature of inter-American organizations. Jon Woronoff, Editor of the International Organizations series, made a better dictionary with his careful editing and commentary at critical stages of the writing process, for which we are most grateful.

Abbreviations and Acronyms

AACC	Anglo-American Caribbean Commission
AALAPSC	Afro-Asian Latin American Peoples' Solidarity Conference
AC	Andean Community
ACEDELA	Atlantic Community Development Group for Latin America
ACJ	Andean Commission of Jurists
ACP	African, Caribbean, and Pacific Countries Group of States
ACS	Association of Caribbean States
AD	Acción Democrática
ADC	Andean Development Corporation
ADELA	Atlantic Community Development Group for Latin America
AFL-CIO	American Federation of Labor-Congress of Industrial Organizations
AFTA	American Free Trade Area
AG	Andean Group
AIOEC	Association of Iron Ore Exporting Countries
ALADI	Asociación Latinoamericana de Integración
ALALC	Asociación Latinoamericana Libre de Comercio
ALCA	Area de Libre Comercio de las Américas
ALIDE	Asociación Latinoamericana de Instituciones Financieros de Desarrollo
ANAS	Asociación de Naciones del Asia Sudoriental
ANASE	Association des Nations l'Asie du Sud-Est
AP	Andean Pact
APEC	Asia-Pacific Economic Cooperation Forum
APEF	Association des Pays Exportateurs de Fer
APNWLA	Agency for the Prohibition of Nuclear Weapons in Latin America and the Caribbean
APP	Alianza para el Progreso
ARLABANK	Arab Latin American Bank
ARPEL	Asistencia Recíproca Petrolera Estatal Latinoamericana

ASEAN	Association of Southeast Asian Nations
ASG	Assistant Secretary-General (OAS)
ATCPG	Antarctic Treaty Consultative Party Group
BCIE	Banco Centroamericano de Integración Económica
BLADEX	Banco Latinoamericano de Exportaciones
CABEI	Central American Bank for Economic Integration
CAC	Caribbean Aid Council
CACJ	Central American Court of Justice
CACM	Central American Common Market
CADC	Central American Defense Council
CAF	Corporación Andina de Fomento
CAIS	Central American Integration System
CAJ	Comisión Andina de Juristas
CAMC	Central American Monetary Council
CAP	Central American Parliament
CARIBCAN	Caribbean-Canadian Cooperation Agreement
CARICOM	Caribbean Common Market
CARIFTA	Caribbean Free Trade Association
CBI	Caribbean Basin Initiative
CC	Caribbean Community
CCIA	Comisión Consultivo Internacional del Algodón
CDB	Caribbean Development Bank
CEAP	Coopération Economique Asie-Pacifique
CECLA	Comisión Especial de Coordinación Latinoamericana
CECON	Comisión Especial para Consultación y Negociación
CEESI	Comisión Especial para Estudiar el Sistema Interamericano
CEMLA	Centro de Estudios Monetarios Latinoamericanos
CEPAL	Comisión Económica para América Latina y el Caribe
CERDS	Charter on the Economic Rights and Duties of States
CG	Contadora Group
CGCED	Caribbean Group for Cooperation in Economic Development
CIA	Central Intelligence Agency
CIAP	Comisión Interamericana de la Alianza para el Progreso
CIAV	Comisión Internacional de Apoyo y Verificación
CICAD	Comisión Interamericana para el Control del Abuso de Drogas

CICEC	Intergovernmental Council of Copper Exporting Countries
CIDI	Comisión Interamericana de Desarrollo Integral
CIECC	Consejo Interamericano para Educación, Ciencia, y Cultura
CIES	Comisíon Interamericana Económica y Social
CIFLA	Commission for Inland Fisheries of Latin America
CIM	Comisión Interamericana de Mujeres
CINDER	Centro Interamericano para el Desarrollo Regional
CIP	Comisión Interamericana de Paz
CIPEC	Conseil Intergouvernemental des Pays Exportateurs de Cuivre
CIS	Commonwealth of Independent States
CIT	Consejo Internacional del Trigo
CLAD	Centro Latinoamericano de Administración para el Desarrollo
CLAMS	Center for Latin American Monetary Studies
CMC	Consejo Monetario Centroamericano
COAS	Charter of the Organization of American States
COMECON	Council on Mutual Economic Assistance
CONDECA	Consejo de Defensa Centroamericano
COPESCAL	Comisión de Pesca Continental para América Latina
CWC	Commonwealth Caribbean States
EAI	Enterprise for the Americas Initiative
EC	European Community
ECADB	Eastern Caribbean Development Bank
ECCB	Eastern Caribbean Central Bank
ECCM	Eastern Caribbean Common Market
ECLAC	Economic Commission for Latin America and the Caribbean
ECOSOC	Economic and Social Council
ELN	Ejército de Liberación Nacional
EPTA	Expanded Program of Technical Assistance
EU	European Union
EZLN	Ejército Zapatista de Liberación Nacional
FAO	Food and Agriculture Organization
FCPA	Foreign Corrupt Practices Act
FFDRPB	Financial Fund for the Development of the River Plate Basin
FIP	Fuerza Interamericana de Paz
FMI	Fondo Mundial Internacional
FMI	Fonds Monétaire International
FMLN	Frente Farabundo Martí de Liberación Nacional

FONDESCA	Fund for the Economic and Social Development of Central America
FONPLATA	Fondo Financiero para el Desarrollo de la Cuenca del Plata
FSLN	Frente Sandinista de Liberación Nacional
FTAA	Free Trade Area of the Americas
GA	Grupo Andino
GA	General Assembly (OAS, UN)
GATT	General Agreement on Tariffs and Trade
GDP	Gross Domestic Product
GEACP	Groupes des États d'Afrique, des Caraïbes, et du Pacifique
GEPLACEA	Grupo de Países de Latinoamericano y el Caribe para la Exportación de Azúcar
GLACSEC	Group of Latin American and Caribbean Sugar Exporting Countries
GLIN	Global Legal Information Network
G-8	Group of Eight
G-15	Group of Fifteen
G-14	Group of Fourteen
G-77	Group of Seventy-Seven
G-3	Group of Three
HLAS	*Handbook of Latin American Studies*
IACAC	International Cotton Advisory Committee
IACAP	Inter-American Committee for the Alliance for Progress
IACESC	Inter-American Council for Education, Science, and Culture
IACHR	Inter-American Commission on Human Rights
IACI	Inter-American Children's Institute
IACID	Inter-American Council for Integral Development
IACtHR	Inter-American Court of Human Rights
IACO	International Civil Aviation Organization
IACRD	Inter-American Center for Regional Development
IACW	Inter-American Commission of Women
IADACC	Inter-American Drug Abuse Control Commission
IADB	Inter-American Defense Board
IADB	Inter-American Development Bank
IAECOSOC	Inter-American Economic and Social Council
IAICA	Inter-American Institute of Agriculture
IAII	Inter-American Indian Institute
IAJC	Inter-American Juridical Committee
IAMS	Inter-American Military System
IANEC	Inter-American Nuclear Energy Commission

IAPC	Inter-American Peace Committee
IAPF	Inter-American Peace Force
IAS	Inter-American System
IASS	Inter-American Security System
IATC	Inter-American Telecommunications Commission
IATRA	Inter-American Treaty of Reciprocal Assistance (Rio Treaty)
IATTC	Inter-American Tropical Tuna Commission
IBA	International Bauxite Association
IBAR	Inter-American Bureau of American Republics
IBRD	International Bank for Reconstruction and Development (World Bank)
ICCEC	Intergovernmental Council of Copper Exporting Countries
ICCO	International Cocoa Agreement
ICJ	International Court of Justice
ICO	International Coffee Organization
IDA	International Development Association
IDB	Inter-American Development Bank
IELAR	Institute for European-Latin American Relations
IFA	International Finance Corporation
IGO	International Governmental Organization
IIC	Instituto Interamericano da Criança
IIDH	Instituto Interamericano de Derechos Humanos
IIN	Instituto Interamericano del Niño
IL	International Law
ILO	International Labor Organization
IMF	International Monetary Fund
INGO	International Nongovernmental Organization
INTAL	Institute for Latin American Integration
IO	International Organization
IOBE	International Organization of Banana Exporters
IPC	International Petroleum Company
IRELA	Instituto de Relaciones Europeo-Latinoamericanas
IS	International System
ISA	International Seabed Authority
ISI	Import Substitution Industrialization
ISO	International Sugar Organization
IWC	International Wheat Council
LAADFI	Latin American Association of Development Finance Institutions
LAECP	Latin American Energy Cooperation Program
LAEO	Latin American Energy Organization
LAES	Latin American Economic System

LAFTA	Latin American Free Trade Association
LAG	Latin American Group
LAIA	Latin American Integration Association
LC	Library of Congress (Washington, D.C.)
MCC	Mercado Común Centroamericano
MERCOSUR	Mercado Común del Sur (Southern Cone Common Market)
MFN	Most Favored Nation
MMFA	Meetings of Consultation of Ministers of Foreign Affairs
MNC	Multinational Corporation
MNR	Movimiento Nacional Revolucionario
MOAS	Model Organization of American States
MRTA	Movimiento Revolucionario Túpac Amaru
NAFTA	North American Free Trade Agreement
NAM	Nonaligned Movement
NATO	North Atlantic Treaty Organization
NGO	Nongovernmental Organization
NIEO	New International Economic Order
NJM	New Jewel Movement
OAS	Organization of American States
OAU	Organization of African Unity
OCAS	Organization of Central American States
ODECA	Organización de Estados Centroamericanos
OEA	Organización de Estados Americanos
OECD	Organization of Economic Cooperation and Development
OECS	Organization of Eastern Caribbean States
OIC	Organización Internacional del Cacao
OIC	Organización Internacional del Café
OIS	Organización Internacional del Azúcar
OIT	Organisation Internationale du Travail
OLADE	Organización Latinoamericana de Energía
OLAS	Organization of Latin American Solidarity
OMC	Organización Mundial del Comercio/Organisation Mondiale du Commerce
OMS	Organización Mundial de la Salud/Organisation Mondiale de la Sante
ONUCA	Organización Naciones Unidas en Centroamerica
ONUSAL	Organización Naciones Unidas en El Salvador
OPANAL	Organismo para la Proscripción de las Armas Nucleares en la América Latina y el Caribe
OPEC	Organization of Petroleum Exporting Countries
OPS	Organización Panamericana de la Salud

ORIT	Organización Regional Interamericana de Trabajadores
OSPAALA	Organization of Solidarity of the Peoples of Africa, Asia, and Latin America
OTAS	Organización del Tratado del Atlántico Sur
PA	Pacto Andino
PAHO	Pan American Health Organization
PAIGH	Pan American Institute of Geography and History
PAM	Pan American Movement
PARLACEN	Parlamento Centroamericano
PAU	Pan American Union
PC	Permanent Council (OAS)
PDF	Panamanian Defense Force
PLACE	Programa Latinoamericano para Cooperación en Energía
PNUD	Programa de las Naciones Unidas para el Desarrollo
PRI	Partido Revolucionario Institucional
RG	Rio Group
RSS	Regional Security System
SAFTA	South American Free Trade Association
SAPs	Structural Adjustment Programs
SATO	South Atlantic Treaty Organization
SC	Security Council (UN)
SCCN	Special Committee for Consultation and Negotiation
SCLAC	Special Committee on Latin American Coordination
SCSPMSIAS	Special Committee to Study and Propose Measures for Strengthening the Inter-American System
SCT	Special Committee on Trade
SELA	Sistema Económico Latinoamericano
SG	Support Group (Contadora)
S-G	Secretary-General
SHAPE	Supreme Headquarters of Allied Powers in Europe (NATO)
SICA	Sistema de Integración Centroamericano
SIECA	Secretaría Permanente del Tratado General de Integración Económica Centroamericana
SL	El Sendero Luminoso
SLACC	Special Latin American Coordinating Committee
SUNFED	Special United Nations Fund for Economic Development
TC	Trusteeship Council
TNE	Transnational Enterprise

TNO	Transnational Organization
UBEC	Union of Banana Exporting Countries
UKHCEC	United Kingdom High Commissioner for the Eastern Caribbean
UN	United Nations
UNCED	United Nations Conference on Environment and Development
UNCLOS III	United Nations, Third Conference on the Law of the Sea
UNCTAD	United Nations Conference on Trade and Development
UNDP	United Nations Development Program
UNEP	United Nations Environmental Program
UNESCO	United Nations Educational, Scientific, and Cultural Organization
UNHCR	United Nations High Commissioner for Refugees
UNO	Unión Nacional Opositora
UNSC	United Nations Security Council
UPD	Unit for the Promotion of Democracy
UPEB	Union de Países Exportadoras de Banano
URL	Uniform Resource Location
URNG	Unidad Revolucionaria Nacional Guatemalteca
USAID	United States Agency for International Development
USMLOEC	United States Military Liaison Office in the Eastern Caribbean
VTF	Venezuelan Trust Fund
WB	World Bank
WHO	World Health Organization
WIC	West Indian Commission
WIF	West Indies Federation
WINBAN	Windward Islands Banana Growers' Association
WISA	West Indies Associated States
WTO	World Trade Organization

Chronology of Inter-American Organizations and Events

1804	Haitian independence from France.
1823	Monroe Doctrine declared.
1826	Congress of Panama begins Spanish-American phase of Movement.
1844	Dominican Republic declares independence from Haiti.
1846	Mexican-American War begins (ends in 1848).
1848	First Congress of Lima (Peru) meets.
1856	Continental Congress of Santiago (Chile) meets.
1861	U.S. Civil War begins (ends in 1865).
1862	Mexican Empire of France under Maximilian established (ends in 1867).
1864	Paraguayan War begins between Argentina, Brazil, and Uruguay (ends in 1870).
1864–1865	Second Congress of Lima meets.
1868	Calvo Doctrine enunciated.
1870	Paraguayan War ends.
1877–1879	Third or Juridical Congress of Lima meets.
1879	War of the Pacific begins (ends in 1884).
1888–1889	First South American Congress on Private International Law (Montevideo, Uruguay) meets.
1889–1890	First International Conference of American States (Washington, D.C.) begins inter-American phase of Pan American Movement. International Union of American Republics and Bureau of American Republics established.
1898	Spanish-American War begins and ends.

1901–1902	Second International Conference of American States (Mexico City) meets.
1902	Pan American Health Organization is established.
	Drago Doctrine enunciated.
1906	Third International Conference of American States (Rio de Janeiro, Brazil) meets.
1907	Central American Court of Justice is established (lasted until 1918).
	Tobar Doctrine is enunciated.
1910	Fourth International Conference of American States (Buenos Aires, Argentina) meets.
	Bureau of American Republics becomes Pan American Union.
1911	Mexican Revolution begins (ends in 1940).
1912	U.S. military continues intervention in and begins occupation of Nicaragua (ends in 1932).
August 1914	World War I begins (ends in 1918).
August 15, 1914	Panama Canal opens.
1915	U.S. military intervention in and occupation of Haiti begins (ends in 1934).
1916	U.S. military intervention in and occupation of the Dominican Republic begins (ends in 1924).
1918	World War I ends.
1920	Covenant of League of Nations approved and League established.
1923	Fifth International Conference of American States (Santiago) meets.
1928	Sixth International Conference of American States (Havana, Cuba) meets.
	Chaco War begins (ends in 1935).
1928–1929	Extraordinary International Conference of American States on Conciliation and Arbitration (Washington, D.C.) meets.
March 1933	President Roosevelt proclaims Good Neighbor Policy.
December 1933	Seventh International Conference of American States (Montevideo) meets.
1935	Chaco War ends.

1936	Inter-American Conference for the Maintenance of Peace (Buenos Aires) meets.
1938	Eighth International Conference of American States (Lima) meets.
September 1, 1939	World War II begins in Europe (ends in May 1945).
September-October 1939	First Meeting of Consultation of Foreign Ministers of the American Republics (Panama City) takes place.
July 1940	Second Meeting of Consultation of Foreign Ministers of the American Republics (Havana) takes place.
December 8, 1941	United States enters World War II in Asia (ends in August 1945) and in Europe.
January 1942	Third Meeting of Consultation of Foreign Ministers of the American Republics (Rio de Janeiro) takes place.
July 1944	International Monetary Fund established.
February-March 1945	Inter-American Conference on the Problems of War and Peace (Mexico City) meets.
April-June 1945	San Francisco Conference drafts United Nations Charter.
October 1945	United Nations established.
December 1945	International Bank for Reconstruction and Development established.
1947	Cold War begins (ends in 1989).
August-September 1947	Inter-American Conference for the Maintenance of Continental Peace and Security (Rio de Janeiro) meets: Inter-American Treaty of Reciprocal Assistance (Rio Treaty) prepared and signed.
February 1948	Economic Commission for Latin America is established.
March-May 1948	Ninth International Conference of American States (Bogotá, Colombia) meets: Charter of the Organization of American States is prepared and signed.
December 1948	Inter-American Treaty of Reciprocal Assistance (Rio Treaty) goes into effect.
1950	Inter-American Tropical Tuna Commission founded.
June 1950	Korean War begins (ends in July 1953).

March-April 1951	Fourth Meeting of Consultation of Ministers of Foreign Affairs (Washington, D.C.) takes place.
October 1951	Organization of Central American States established (in effect in 1955).
December 1951	OAS Charter goes into effect and OAS established.
July 1953	Korean War ends.
March 1954	Tenth International Conference of American States (Caracas, Venezuela) meets.
June 1954	U.S. initiates covert intervention in Guatemala to remove Arbenz.
Summer 1954	Ecuador seizes U.S. tuna boats in coastal waters.
1958	West Indies Federation established (ends in 1962).
1959	Inter-American Nuclear Energy Commission established.
January 1959	Castro replaces Batista and launches the Cuban Revolution.
August 12–18, 1959	Fifth Meeting of Consultation of Ministers of Foreign Affairs (Santiago) takes place.
September 1959	Inter-American Commission on Human Rights established.
December 1959	Inter-American Development Bank established.
1960	Latin American Free Trade Association established.
	Organization of Petroleum Exporting Countries established.
	Central American Common Market agreement signed.
August 16–21, 1960	Sixth Meeting of Consultation of Ministers of Foreign Affairs (San José, Costa Rica) takes place: approves sanctions against the Dominican Republic (lifted in January 1962).
August 22–29, 1960	Seventh Meeting of Consultation of Ministers of Foreign Affairs (San José, Costa Rica) takes place.
March 1961	President John F. Kennedy announces Alliance for Progress.

April 1961	U.S. sponsors invasion of Cuba (Bay of Pigs).
June 1961	General Treaty of Central American Economic Integration ratified, formalizes the Central American Common Market.
August 1961	Alliance for Progress approved ("Charter of Punta del Este") at Inter-American Economic and Social Council Meeting in Uruguay.
January 1962	Eighth Consultation of Ministers of Foreign Affairs (Montevideo) takes place: Cuban participation in OAS suspended.
November-December 1962	Cuban missile crisis increases threat of nuclear war.
1963	International Coffee Organization established.
January 1964	OAS creates Inter-American Committee for the Alliance for Progress.
July 1964	Ninth Consultation of Ministers of Foreign Affairs (Washington, D.C.) takes place: sanctions against Cuba approved.
December 1964	First Special International Conference of American States (Washington, D.C.) meets.
April 1965	Dominican civil war begins and U.S. military intervenes.
May 1965–1970	10th Meeting of Consultation of Ministers of Foreign Affairs (Washington, D.C.) takes place: creates Inter-American Peace Force for the Dominican Republic (withdrawn in September 1966).
January-April 1967	11th Consultation of Ministers of Foreign Affairs (Washington, D.C.; Buenos Aires; Punta del Este) takes place.
1967	Treaty of Tlatelolco signed.
	Trinidad and Tobago becomes first Commonwealth Caribbean state to join OAS.
	Organization of Latin American Solidarity established.
February 1967	Third Special International Conference of American States (Buenos Aires) meets: approves protocol of amendments to OAS Charter.

1968	International Sugar Organization established.
April 1968	Organization for the Prohibition of Nuclear Weapons in Latin America established.
May 1968	Caribbean Free Trade Association established.
June-September 1968	12th Meeting of Consultation of Ministers of Foreign Affairs (Washington, D.C.) takes place.
July 1969	Soccer War between El Salvador and Honduras initiated.
July 1969-November 1970	13th Consultation of Ministers of Foreign Affairs (Washington, D.C.) takes place.
October 1969	Andean Group established.
November 1969	Inter-American Specialized Conference on Human Rights (San José) meets: American Convention on Human Rights is prepared and signed (goes into effect in July 1978).
1970	Caribbean Development Bank established.
1970–1971	Tuna War between Ecuador and the United States continues.
1972	Cuba joins Soviet Council for Mutual Economic Assistance.
February 1973	Venezuela joins Andean Group.
July 1973	Caribbean Common Market established.
1974	International Bauxite Association is established.
	Group of Latin American and Caribbean Sugar Exporting Countries established.
	Union of Banana Exporting Countries established.
	UN Security Council meets in Panama during Canal crisis.
February 1975	Lomé I is approved (in effect in April 1976).
July 1975	16th Consultation of Ministers of Foreign Affairs (San José) takes place: Freedom of Action resolution on relations with Cuba approved.
1976	Chile withdraws from Andean Group.

1977	Suriname becomes member of OAS. Panama Canal Treaties signed at OAS (in effect October 1978).
July 1978	American Convention on Human Rights goes into effect and American Court of Human Rights established.
September 1978-June 1979	17th Consultation of Ministers of Foreign Affairs (Washington, D.C.) takes place.
1979	Lomé II established (in effect in 1981).
1980	Latin American Integration Association established (replaces Latin American Free Trade Association).
July 1981	Organization of Eastern Caribbean States established.
1982	Javier Pérez de Cuéllar becomes secretary-general of UN.
April-May 1982	20th Consultation of Ministers of Foreign Affairs (Washington, D.C.) takes place.
April 2,-June 14, 1982	Argentina and Great Britain involved in South Atlantic War.
January 1983	Contadora Group formed.
November 1983	U.S. military invades Grenada.
January 1984	U.S. President Reagan's Caribbean Basin Initiative goes into effect.
April 1984	Nicaragua brings case against the United States before the International Court of Justice (Court rules against the United States in November).
December 1984	Lomé III is approved (in effect March 1985).
July 1985	Contadora Support Group formed.
December 1986	Rio Group formed.
1988	Canada and the United States approve a Free Trade Agreement.
November 1989	UN Security Council approves creation of UN Observer Group for Central America for Nicaragua.
December 1989	Lomé III is approved (in effect March 1990 for 10 years). U.S. military invades Panama to capture Noriega.
1990	Cold War ends with collapse of the Soviet Union.
January 1990	Canada becomes member of the OAS.

June 1990	U.S. President Bush announces Enterprise for the Americas Initiative.
December 1990	UN Security Council approves creation of UN Observer Group for El Salvador.
December 16, 1990	Haiti elects Aristide elected in first free elections in Haitian history.
January 1991	Persian Gulf War begins.
	Belize and Guyana become members of the OAS.
March 1991	Southern Cone Common Market established.
June 1991	OAS approves Santiago Resolution on Representative Democracy.
October 1991	Ad Hoc Meeting of Foreign Ministers approves sanctions against military government in Haiti.
December 1991	Central American Integration System established (replaces OCAS).
	Peace accord signed to end civil war in El Salvador.
1992	Ecuador drops out of the Organization of Petroleum Exporting Countries.
December 1992	Joint OAS-UN effort begins against Haiti.
June 1993	UN Security Council-approved oil embargo against Haiti initiated.
August and October 1993	Joint OAS-UN sanctions against Haiti lifted and reimposed.
April 1994	Uruguay Round of GATT negotiations signed.
May 1994	UN Security Council approves total embargo against Haiti with naval enforcement.
July 1994	UN Security Council authorizes U.S. to organize a multinational military force for action in Haiti.
September 1994	César Gaviria Trujillo becomes seventh secretary-general of OAS.
September 19, 1994	U.S. military units land in Haiti.
October 15, 1994	Deposed President Aristide returns to Haiti.
December 1994	North American Free Trade Agreement approved by the United States.
	Economic crisis in Mexico occurs.

December 8–9, 1994	Presidential Summit of the Americas (Miami, Florida) meets.
January 1995	North American Free Trade Agreement goes into effect.
February 1995	U.S. and International Monetary Fund arrange $50 billion aid package for Mexico.
August 1995	Association of Caribbean States established.
January 1996	World Trade Organization established.
March 1996	U.S. President Clinton signs Helms-Burton legislation.
April 1996	Inter-American Convention Against Corruption approved by OAS foreign ministers.
June 1996	Helms-Burton bill becomes law, tightening U.S. embargo against Cuba. Chile joins Southern Cone Common Market.
October 1996	José Arnoldo Alemán defeats Daniel Ortega in Nicaraguan presidential election. World Trade Organization begins judicial hearing on European Union claim against the U.S.'s Helms-Burton Act.
December 1996	Guatemalan government and leftist guerrillas, with help of United Nations, sign accord ending 35 years of conflict.
January 1997	Bolivia joins the Southern Cone Common Market. Andean Pact changes name to Andean Community.
July 1997	Mexico's dominant party suffers major losses in national elections.

Maps

Mexico

Gulf of
Mexico

Cuba

North

Atlantic

Ocean

Caribbean Sea

Venezuela

Colombia

Ecuador

B r a z i l

Peru

Pacific

Ocean

Bolivia

Paraguay

Chile

Uruguay

Argentina

South

Atlantic

Ocean

LATIN AMERICA

| 0 | 400 Nautical Miles |
| 0 | 400 Kilometers |

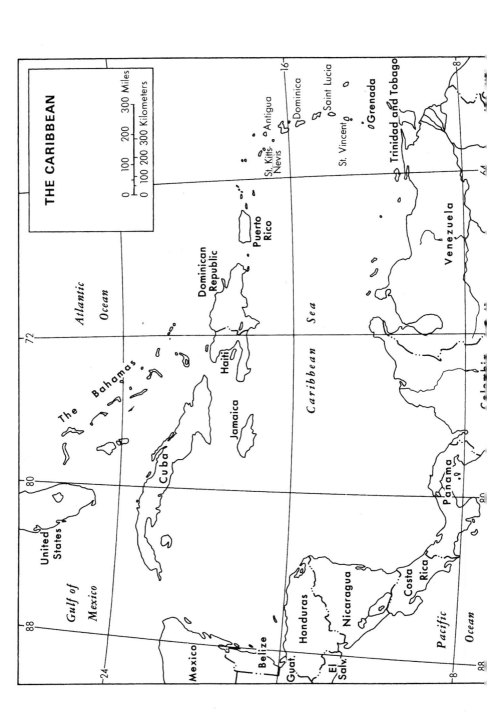

THE CARIBBEAN

300 Miles
300 Kilometers
0   100   200
0   100   200   300

Atlantic Ocean

Gulf of Mexico

United States

The Bahamas

Cuba

Jamaica

Haiti

Dominican Republic

Puerto Rico

St. Kitts-Nevis
Antigua
Dominica
Saint Lucia
St. Vincent
Grenada
Trinidad and Tobago

Caribbean Sea

Venezuela

Mexico

Belize

Guat.

El Salv.

Honduras

Nicaragua

Costa Rica

Panama

Pacific Ocean

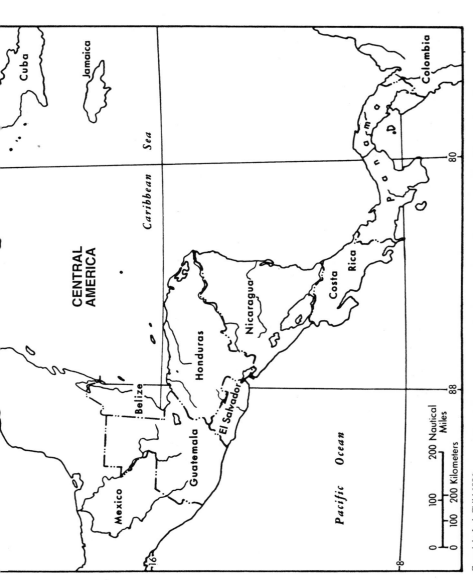

CENTRAL AMERICA

Cuba

Jamaica

Caribbean Sea

Colombia

Panama

Costa Rica

Nicaragua

Honduras

Belize

El Salvador

Guatemala

Mexico

Pacific Ocean

16

80

88

8

| 0 | 100 | 200 Nautical Miles |
| 0 | 100 | 200 Kilometers |

SOUTH AMERICA

Caribbean Sea

North
Atlantic
Ocean

Panama

Venezuela

Guyana

Suriname

French Guiana

Colombia

Ecuador

Brazil

P e r u

Bolivia

South
Pacific
Ocean

Paraguay

Chile

South
Atlantic
Ocean

Uruguay

Argentina

| 0 | 500 | 1000 Kilometers |
| 0 | 500 | 1000 Mile |

Introduction

Since the late 1800s, international organizations have been a central part of inter-American relations and diplomatic history, often serving as important political mechanisms for confronting the many multilateral issues affecting the United States and the other American and Commonwealth states that constitute the Western Hemisphere. This book is designed to describe the growth and vitality of inter-American organizations and their importance in hemispheric affairs since World War II. At the regional and subregional levels over 100 inter-American organizations are examined, with basic information on their history, functions, location, and significance for inter-American relations. Key political and economic leaders, events, controversies, and policy themes are also entries in the dictionary. The reader will also find a comprehensive bibliography of over 1,200 items, organized for future research and investigation.

The most important inter-American body is the Organization of American States (OAS), the major institutional component of the inter-American system, the first regional organization accepted by the United Nations, and, today, the oldest and most complex regional governance system in the world. Although the OAS can trace its organizational lineage to the First International Conference of American States in 1889 and the period from 1911 to 1948 when it was known as the Pan American Union, its current institutional structure dates from the creation of its official charter in early 1948. Meeting in Bogotá, Colombia, the United States and 20 Latin American countries met to codify the purposes and objectives of hemispheric cooperation, conflict resolution, and procedures for collective security. The creation of the OAS was indeed a watershed event in the history of inter-American relations, since it established rights and duties under international law that constituted a more equal relationship between the United States and the Latin American States. For example, enshrined in the OAS Charter are such important rights and principles as equality, national sovereignty, and nonintervention. After 1948, the OAS would be headed by a secretary-general from Latin America, not a U.S. representative handpicked by the president of the United States.

Since 1948, OAS membership has grown from 21 to 35 formal members and 40 permanent observers from all parts of the world. Over the past fifty years the OAS has been joined by over 100 regional and subregional organizations throughout the hemisphere, created to address economic, social, political, and security matters of concern to their member states. It is the content, complexity, and significance of these regional and subregional organizations—now such an important part of the process of economic and political development of the hemisphere in the aftermath of the Cold War—that make up the majority of this dictionary.

Over the past fifty years, a wide variety of institutions—universal, regional, and subregional—have been established by states to improve and regulate their relations. At the regional level, most of these state efforts have focused on some aspect of economic and/or political organization. The major organizations that now function exclusively within the inter-American arena include the Organization of American States (OAS), the Inter-American Development Bank (IADB), the Economic Commission for Latin America and the Caribbean (ECLAC), a regional agency under the United Nations, the Latin American Economic System (LAES in English; SELA in Spanish), the Latin American Integration Association (LAIA), and the Rio Group (RG). They operate along with a myriad of subregional organizations, such as the Amazon Pact, the Andean Community, the Association of Caribbean States (ACS), the Caribbean Common Market (CARICOM), the Cartagena Group, the Central American Common Market (CACM), the Organization of Central American States (OACS), and the Southern Cone Common Market (MERCOSUR).

Characteristics of International Governmental Organizations

The following discussion is taken from Clive Archer, *International Organizations* (2nd edition, 1992), the leading book on classifying and defining international organizations (IOs). This section examines the key characteristics—classification schemes, functions, and definitions—of international governmental organizations (IGOs) with emphasis on the international governmental organizations that operate in the Western Hemisphere. Such an organization can be defined as any formal, continuous structure, established by agreement between members (governmental and/or nongovernmental) from two or more sovereign states, whose central purpose is the pursuit of the common interest of its membership. Inter-American organizations can also be classified as international organizations (IO) based on 1) *membership*—international governmental organizations (IGOs), international nongovernmental organizations (INGOs), and transnational organizations (TNOs) and regional versus universal organizations; 2) *aims and activities*; and 3) *major structural characteristics*. Emphasis in this book will be on IGOs that function at the regional or subregional level within Latin America and the Caribbean. It will not include TNOs or "international regimes," organizations that are more fluid and less formal than IGOs or INGOs.

Membership

The members of IGOs are the official representatives of states (e.g., as in the UN) in contrast to INGOs, whose representatives come from nongovernmental groups (e.g., human rights organizations and labor organizations). IGOs function solely according to the will of their individual members, a view expressed about the OAS in the 1950s by its first secretary-general, Alberto Lleras Camargo. The Organization of American States has no authority to act beyond the will of its member states, therefore it has little organizational autonomy. The *extent* of membership distinguishes a regional from a universal (i.e., global or international) organization. The OAS is a regional organization with 35 member states in the Western Hemisphere, from Canada in North America to Argentina in South America and including the small island states in the Caribbean. The *universal* category includes the UN, an international organization with 185 members (1996) representing almost all of the world community of nations.

This same regional-universal division could be applied to international law, for there are certain regional approaches or schools that deal with certain issues differently than within the universal or global context—first exemplified by the League of Nations and then by the UN. It was Chilean jurist Alejandro Álvarez who first made a case for the existence of an American or regional school of international law, developed mainly as a counterpoise to U.S. intervention in Latin America. The principle of nonintervention thus became more absolute and restrictive in inter-American organizations, eventually constituting the cornerstone of the Inter-American System (IAS), than within the context of universal international law.

Goals and Activities

Inter-American organizations carry out a wider variety of functions in their day-to-day activities. The more common goals and activities can be classified as economic (development and integration), political (democracy promotion, security, and human rights protection), legal and juridical (international law), and environmental and health-related. It is worth noting that the functions of some international bodies change over time, for example the 1985 Support Group (of eight Latin American states plus the secretaries-general of the OAS and UN) originally formed to back the Central American peace process later evolved into the Group of Fourteen and finally became the much larger Rio Group, concerned primarily with economic and environmental issues.

Structural Characteristics

Most IGOs are designed to include the following structural characteristics: permanent headquarters, employees made up of international bureaucrats, the existence of policy-making organs (plenary and nonplenary) and secretariats, voting formulae (sovereign equality or weighted), and quota systems for financing. While the OAS operates upon the basis of sovereign equality in voting, other international agencies that lend money, such as the IMF and the World Bank, have weighted voting systems that recognize different levels of economic power. The OAS is administered by a secretary-general whose authority oversaw 620 employees and an annual budget of $111 million in 1996. Its key policy-making structures include the General Assembly, which meets once every year, and a Permanent Council that meets more frequently to deal with issues of importance to the member states.

The Importance of Inter-American Organizations

Why are inter-American organizations—either at the regional or subregional levels—an important subject of investigation? The following discussion attempts to answer this question by focusing on five critical reasons for the growth and significance of the matrix of international organizations and associations now operating in the Western Hemisphere.

The End of the Cold War and the New Integration Trade Initiatives

The Cold War period (1940s through the 1980s), with its emphasis on security, has been replaced by a new paradigm (or theoretical framework) that has put economic cooperation and integration, democratic development, and privatization at the forefront of hemispheric concerns. Although economic integration efforts reach back to the 1940s in inter-American relations, the end of the Cold War accelerated economic development and emphasized integration strategies in the Latin American and Caribbean countries. Their leaders began to realize that structuralist theories of economic growth advocating import substitution industrialization—driven by a large state apparatus and the production of goods for the internal market—must now give way to neoliberal economics in which the state is reduced in size and scope and national economies redirected to promote the expansion of exports, free-market allocation practices, and a more open policy toward the acceptance of foreign capital. This economic development strategy, however, has not been without its strains on domestic tranquility, civil-military relations, and the ability to sustain democratic forms of governing.

Throughout the Cold War period, the United States worried more about the encroachment of communist forces than solutions for solving basic economic development problems of the Latin American and Caribbean states. For example, in 1961 the Kennedy administration announced the Alliance for Progress, a bold and expansive aid initiative, which publicized the importance of economic development and integration strategies, but more as a means of achieving political stability and countering the Cuban Revolution than correcting Latin America's economic and social malaise. Throughout the Cold War there was regular interplay between the differing priorities of Latin America and the United States, the former stressing economic development and the latter emphasizing the importance of anticommunist stances and national security. These economic, political, and security differences regularly manifested themselves in the activities and decisions of the Organization of American States (OAS), resulting in the first set of amendments (1967 Protocol of Buenos Aires) to its 1948 charter. Several years later this divergence in how best to promote hemispheric initiatives led to a challenge to U.S. dominance with the formation in 1975 of the Latin American Economic System (LAES), a major bargaining group with headquarters in Caracas, Venezuela. With economic development the major goal of the Latin American and Caribbean countries, common markets and import substitution industrialization policies began losing adherents, while assembly-for-export free-trade zones increased in popularity during the 1970s.

The role of the International Monetary Fund (IMF) became increasingly important and its standby loan arrangements necessary in aiding Latin American and Caribbean development strategies. This factor, and the substantial increase in the price of petroleum, led to the so-called "Lost Decade" of the 1980s, when several Latin American governments, unable to service their excessive foreign debts, defaulted on payments to foreign creditors. Economic development goals remained paramount throughout this period, but new means of solving these problems began to take hold, including, after rescheduling and reducing the debt payments, a shift to privatization, revival of regional integration efforts, and new stress on free trade associations. The end of the Cold War also prompted a U.S. shift to regional integration efforts, including President Bush's 1990 Enterprise for the Americas Initiative (EAI), which advocated less debt, more trade and investment, environmental protection, and free trade. In 1994 Mexico joined Canada and the United States in the creation of the North American Free Trade Agreement (NAFTA), a comprehensive agreement that would almost totally eliminate trade and investment restrictions over a fifteen-year period.

This trend continued into the 1990s among the Latin American and Caribbean states with the formation of the Southern Cone Common Market (MERCOSUR), integrating the economies of Argentina, Brazil, Paraguay, and Uruguay, and later Chile and Bolivia; the creation of the Central American Integration System; and the 1995 formation of the Association of Caribbean States (ACS). As the end of the century approaches, further measures to achieve greater economic integration and cooperation are being planned among regional and subregional bodies.

New Issues of Regional Concern

New issues of growing importance to all 35 states that comprise the Western Hemisphere have given international organizations an indispensable role in solving economic, political, and social problems at the supragovernmental level. These new issues that are helping to define the nature of inter-American relations include trade expansion and economic integration, mechanisms for protecting human rights and combating terrorism, a reinvigorated effort to provide clean government by attacking official and unofficial corruption, promotion of democracy, regulation of immigration flows, protection of the environment, and the ongoing fight against narcotics trafficking and the corrosive effects of drug cartels. Two issues of particular concern to the United States— relations with Castro's Cuba and the future of the Panama Canal—also affect, in one way or another, the rest of the member states in the hemisphere. The democratization of Latin America over the past decade is another issue that has been taken up by regional and subregional organizations. For example, democratic forces inside Paraguay, members of MERCOSUR, and the OAS rallied to thwart a military coup there and support a democratically elected president in 1996.

A Diminution of U.S. Hegemony in Hemispheric Affairs

The increasing role of inter-American organizations has served to dilute the historical hegemony of the United States in inter-American relations and hemispheric affairs, raising new questions about how best to conduct hemispheric relations in what some have called "an age of uncertainty." Others argue that the United States still retains a predominance of influence within the hemisphere, and that influence is growing on account of the North American Free Trade Agreement (NAFTA). Nevertheless, the quest for hegemony remains a constant in U.S. policy toward Latin America, but at the same time it is becoming increasingly difficult to engage in unilateral and interventionist behavior in the region. From the Monroe Doctrine in 1823 to the end of the Cold War in 1989, one of the primary goals of the United States was to prevent extrahemispheric powers—Great Britain, Germany, Japan, and the Soviet Union—from establishing a counterweight to U.S. hegemony in the region. This attitude, sometimes referred to as "strategic denial," has diminished with the end of the Cold War and the growing importance of economic and political integration.

A Growing Process of Globalization

For more than a century, the world has been changing through a process whereby events, decisions, crises, and activities in one region have come to have significant repercussions for individuals, governments, and communities in distant parts of the globe. Globalization is considered by some to be the key characteristic of the modern economic system, contributing to the proliferation of international organizations. It has also given way to the realization that older regional organizations, for example, the Organization of American States (OAS), need to be periodically overhauled, while at the same time new organizations will be created to meet the needs of member states. What is now evident in the prevailing inter-American system is that organizations and associations that were created to meet the needs of member governments in one era have either failed or turned out to be ill-designed when times and circumstances take a dramatic turn. This has been one factor in the proliferation, and alteration, of inter-American organizations over the past several decades.

The Changing Role of the OAS

Over the past ten years the OAS has changed from an organization of often moribund status from the late 1970s through the 1980s to one with more vitality and importance in the 1990s. Throughout most of the Cold War, the OAS, whose effectiveness historically reflected the health of U.S.-Latin American and Caribbean relations, was often either neglected or marginalized. The OAS did serve as an effective "anti-communist alliance" against Cuba and the Dominican Republic from the early 1960s until the mid-1970s. This pattern was epitomized by two major events in the 1980s: revolutionary upheavals in El Salvador and Nicaragua and the 1982 war over the Falklands/Malvinas Islands.

The problems confronted by the OAS were compounded by the increasing arrears of many of its members, especially the United States, which refused to accept its originally mandated quota of two-thirds of the regular annual budget for the organization. This eventually led to a dramatic shortage of funds for the OAS budget, restrictions on the expansion of new issues on the inter-American agenda, acute reductions in staff at Organization headquarters in Washington, D.C., and the termination of important publications such as *The OAS Chronicle*. Unlike the 1960s, when research attention on the OAS and other inter-American organizations increased significantly, scholars and doctoral candidates for the most part avoided the OAS as a topic of investigation from 1970 until the end of the Cold War.

With the end of the Cold War, the "new" OAS began to again emphasize important economic and political issues largely neglected during the 1970s and 1980s, best illustrated by the 1993 Protocol of Managua, which has replaced two of its existing councils with the new Council for Integral Development. The 1994 Presidential Summit of the Americas further strengthened the economic development role of the OAS—in addition to linking economic development with democracy, human rights, and the environment—by assigning it the duty of overseeing the various integration and free trade agreements, which are eventually to culminate in the formation of the American Free Trade Area by the year 2005.

Inter-American Relations: Terms and Concepts

Since the Inter-American System (IAS) and most of the inter-American organizations comprising it are the result of some aspect of the historical interplay of U.S.-Latin American relations, it is important to clarify the meaning of key terms associated with inter-American relations. For example, the term *American* is not synonymous with being a citizen of the United States. The *Americas* are divided into North American, Central American, and South American areas, and when referred to as a whole, the term *Western Hemisphere* (or *American continent*) is commonly used, including the islands in the Caribbean Sea. Thus, an *American* is a citizen of any country in this hemisphere, whether North, Central, or South. *North America* includes Canada, the United States and Mexico; *Central America* commonly includes Belize, Costa Rica, Guatemala, Honduras, Nicaragua, El Salvador, and Panama; and *South America* consists of Argentina, Bolivia, Brazil, Chile, Colombia, Ecuador, Guyana, Paraguay, Peru, Suriname, Uruguay, and Venezuela. The *Caribbean* is divided into the *insular* Caribbean, meaning the island states in the Caribbean Sea—Antigua and Barbuda, the Bahamas, Barbados, Cuba, Dominica, the Dominican Republic, Grenada, Haiti, Jamaica, St. Kitts-Nevis, St. Lucia, St. Vincent and the Grenadines, and Trinidad and Tobago—and the *maritime*, composed of the island states of the Circum-Caribbean area as well as those along the Caribbean Sea in both Central and South America. (See map, page xxxiv)

Two other common terms—*Latin American* and *Commonwealth Caribbean (CWC)*—are historical-cultural in orientation and derived from their respective colonial masters. The citizens of the *Commonwealth Caribbean* (English-speaking territories and independent states of the Circum-Caribbean area with historic ties to Great Britain) countries reject the designation *American* and prefer to be categorized by individual citizenship, e.g., Jamaican or Trinidadian, or as from the CWC. The *Latin American* countries are those that were at one time colonies of Portugal (Brazil) or Spain, whose former possessions include Mexico, the Central American republics (except Belize), Cuba and the Dominican Republic, and all of South America except Guyana, Suriname, and French Guiana. Canada can also be considered part of the Commonwealth, and the United States Anglo-American, which means that, along with the Commonwealth Caribbean states, they all have the Common Law domestic legal system, while the Latin American states possess legal arrangements based on the Civil or Napoleonic Code. Therefore, inter-American relations are those between all states in the Western Hemisphere: American (North, Central, and South), Anglo-American, Commonwealth Caribbean and Latin American.

The *Inter-American System (IAS)* and *Organization of American States (OAS)* are similar terms but are not synonymous and should be viewed separately. The former constitutes the wide array of juridical principles, political policies, and administrative arrangements that have evolved among the American republics over the past 50 years as the accepted bases for international conduct among the member states. The latter is more narrow in scope, the principal multilateral organization through which the system operates.

Another way to illustrate the difference between the two is in terms of *membership*. Canada, for example, has been a member of and participant in the IAS for a long time, but it preferred not to join the OAS until 1990, after the end of the Cold War. While both provide the primary regional contexts for inter-American organizations, the UN, the major multilateral organization through which the International System (IS) operates, provides another since some of its organs, such as the Economic Commission for Latin America with headquarters in Santiago, Chile, operate regionally.

Subregional Organizations

Subregional organizations pursue their primary goals and activities in a particular geographical region. Most of those in the Western Hemisphere are concerned with economic integration, although there are others that relate to security, finance, culture, and conflict resolution. For two of the integration bodies, the 1960 Central American Common Market (CACM) and the 1973 Caribbean Common Market (CARICOM), successor to the 1968 Caribbean Free Trade Association (CARIFTA), there is a very high membership correlation with the previously discussed subregions of Central America and the Commonwealth Caribbean (CWC). From its founding, the CACM included as members all the Central American states except Panama, and Carifta/Caricom was originally, and until recently, limited exclusively to the CWC states (the former territories of Great Britain) due to the Lomé Accords with the European Community (EC). South America is another common subregion, one subdivided into the Southern Cone (Argentina, Brazil, Chile, Uruguay, and Paraguay) and the Andean area (Chile, Bolivia, Peru, Ecuador, Colombia, and Venezuela).

Another subregion, the Amazon basin, became prominent after a 1978 treaty among its members—Brazil, Bolivia, Peru, Ecuador, Colombia, Venezuela, Guyana, and Suriname. Other subregion, economic integration-geographical correlations can be identified: the 1960 Latin American Free Trade Association (LAFTA)—South American and Latin American states plus Mexico; the 1969 Andean Group (AG)—all the Andean countries until the mid-1970s; and the 1991 five-member MERCOSUR—Argentina, Brazil, Paraguay, Uruguay, and Chile—which is expected to evolve into a Southern Cone Free Trade Association.

Universal Organizations

United Nations

As the principal multilateral organization of the International System, the United Nations (UN) has played an important economic and political role in Latin America, and the Latin American and Caribbean states, mainly as a bloc, have played an important role in the UN. The Latin American states have been particularly interested in the economic development role of the UN, the development models of ECLA (after 1984, ECLAC—Economic Commission for Latin America and the Caribbean), and aid provided by the UN Development Programme and by certain specialized agencies, the IMF, and the World Bank. The UN has also served an important political function by acting as a counterpoise to the United States (either in the OAS, one of the "Regional Arrangements" coordinated with the UN, or outside the OAS) and to the Northern/developed states in the North-South axis that emerged in the 1960s. The Latin American states have exercised their increasing influence in the UN primarily through membership in the South/developing bloc in the General Assembly (GA), in the Economic and Social Council (ECOSOC), and in UNESCO (UN Educational, Scientific, and Cultural Organization), and also in the International Court of Justice (ICJ), where they have two seats, and in the Security Council (SC), where they hold two non-permanent, rotating seats. Through their influence in the GA, the Third World states were successful in passing resolutions in the 1960s for the creation of the UN Conference on Trade and Development (UNCTAD), obtaining approval for the Charter on the Economic Rights and Duties of States (CERDS), and in the 1970s calling for a New International Economic Order (NIEO) and the third UN Conference on the Law of the Sea (UNCLOS III). Given their preoccupation with economic development, the Latin American and Caribbean states have been especially interested in the role of the IMF and the World Bank. Throughout the history of the Inter-American system (IAS), they have been strong supporters of international law and the role of the International Court of Justice (ICJ).

International Monetary Fund and the World Bank

These two UN agencies were founded to assist in the reconstruction of European countries (both allies and ex-enemies) in the aftermath of World War II; several years passed before they turned their attention to economic development, particularly in Third World developing countries. The World Bank's official title, International Bank for Reconstruction and Development, reflected its initial role in funding projects for the reconstruction of Europe. Following in the wake of UNCTAD, CERDS, and NIEO, these two financial institutions increasingly became a part of the North-South axis as a result of weighted voting (the United States was in first place) and their development models and loan policies. There was mounting Third World opposition in the 1970s, reinforced by the economic problems of the 1980s, the "Lost Decade," and criticism focused on the requirements of conditionality and structural adjustment and those for standby arrangements.

International Court of Justice (ICJ)

The Latin American states were in support of decolonization and ending intervention and racial discrimination and did not favor the refusal of the ICJ, on legal and technical grounds, to deal with these issues until the early 1970s (involving the Republic of South Africa). This refusal resulted in the ICJ being viewed by the Third World states, particularly the African members, as a "politicized" court serving the interests of the North and ex-colonial powers. The first case of direct concern to Latin America came much earlier and dealt with asylum (the 1950 *Haya de la Torre* case between Colombia and Peru, in which a Latin American judge wrote a famous dissent). The most important and controversial case, because the United States ignored a ruling against it, was *Nicaragua v. United States of America* (1984), which was a response to the Reagan administration's intervention in that country.

Inter-American and European Organizations

The first principal transatlantic linkage was an early Commonwealth one between Great Britain and Canada, and then with the former's territories in the Caribbean through the unsuccessful 1958 West Indies Federation, which was to oversee their independence process. The second linkage was provided by the Lomé Convention (Lomé I took effect in 1976) of the European Community (EC), giving the exports of the CWC states (along with the ex-colonies in Africa and the Pacific) special access to the EC. In 1985, the EC established the Institute for European-Latin American Relations (IELAR) in Madrid, Spain. IELAR has overseen the creation of a whole series of EC (now European Union, EU) and Latin American organizations and processes, the oldest with Central America and the most recent with various economic (Group of Three and MERCOSUR) and political (Rio Group) bodies.

Inter-American and African, Islamic, and Middle Eastern Organizations

The major organization in this category is OPEC, the Organization of Petroleum Exporting Countries, most of whose members are outside Latin America. Venezuela is the one hemispheric member and originator of OPEC, established in 1960. Ecuador became a member of OPEC in 1972 but dropped out in 1992. In 1973, the Arab members of OPEC instituted an unsuccessful oil embargo against the United States in particular and other supporters of Israel in that year's war. In response to the U.S. government's punitive legislation against all OPEC members, the Latin American states formed the Latin American Economic System (LAES) in 1975, a multilateral economic integration association consisting of 27 Latin American and Caribbean members and excluding the United States.

Inter-American and Asian Organizations

There are two relevant organizations, the Association of Southeast Asian Nations (ASEAN) and the Asia-Pacific Economic Cooperation Forum (APEC). The earlier, ASEAN, was formed in 1967 among five states (two others joined in the 1980s) for the purpose of facilitating their economic development and industrialization. After severe economic problems in the 1970s and 1980s, a free-trade policy was endorsed in the early 1990s, along with a new peacekeeping role based on the organization's Treaty of Amity and Cooperation. ASEAN was unsuccessful as a peacekeeper in the UN effort to resolve the conflict in Cambodia. ASEAN has established links with the Rio Group and the Andean Group. The second body is APEC, more recent (1989) and informal, with 18 members. Four American states and two Latin American are included: Canada, Chile, Mexico, and the United States. As the Asian trade link with the Western Hemisphere grows, further activity within the inter-American organizations of the region can be expected.

Nongovernmental Organizations

International nongovernmental organizations (NGOs) have been important players in a variety of fields for a long time—especially in agriculture, economic development, and health—and their numbers have increased steadily along with their scope of activities. In the 1980s, they became increasingly active in confronting governments on issues of democratization and human rights, resulting in conflicts with member states faced with international condemnation for violating these principles. More recently, the environment and the human rights of indigenous peoples have become subjects of concern and focus. One trend is that NGOs are working more and more with IGOs, the OAS, and the UN. The OAS is in the process of giving official status to and establishing formal working relations with NGOs working in the important fields of democracy, human rights, and the environment.

Historical Overview of the Inter-American System

Inter-American organizations operate today within a context of political, juridical, economic, and strategic considerations that have deep historical roots in the relationship among states in the Western Hemisphere. Therefore, it is important to treat the historical context in which the multitude of organizations—regional and subregional—in this dictionary have emerged and operate. The following discussion traces the major historical themes in the development of the Inter-American System (IAS) through five periods, beginning with the Monroe Doctrine in 1823 and ending with the transformation of the Organization of American States (OAS) in the 1990s and the dramatic growth in free trade and regional integration movements after the end of the Cold War.

One of the key elements in this historical process—reaching back to the nineteenth century—is the development of the United States as the preeminent regional power (a status largely won in the Spanish-American War in 1898) and its ensuing relationship with the Latin American states. Throughout the past 100 years of inter-American relations, there was not one consistent pattern that defined the relationship but a history of symbiotic, cooperative, competitive, and conflictual interactions. Relations have favored the United States, whose regional power increased by gradually eliminating foreign competitors from its sphere of influence in the Western Hemisphere. This interesting historical interplay between a large and powerful United States and the mostly small and weak states in the Latin American region produced the asymmetries that would eventually produce what is frequently referred to as the Inter-American System (IAS).

As the United States transformed itself from a world power in the aftermath of World War I to a superpower after World War II, a regional system of inter-American organizations developed in an effort to handle a wide assortment of hemispheric problems on a collective basis. The regional system that we examine in this book was institutionalized in the early Cold War period and quickly became, like the U.S.-led Western alliance in the UN, a U.S. instrument in that global struggle. The Cold War dragged on for over 40 years, and global economic and political changes developed in which other states such as Japan and a group of European states (the EC) also became economic superpowers, while the United States struggled to maintain its role as the world's only military superpower.

The end of the Cold War has brought forth a new array of forces, influences, and interests impacting on inter-American relations and are currently altering the structure and focus of the regional system. These historical features that resulted in a regional system with an increasing number of inter-American organizations have contributed to the development of new goals and interests, often leading to important controversies and debates. For example, a common and persistent concern of the Latin American and Caribbean states has been their independence and sovereignty under international law combined with the important corollary of sovereignty—the nonintervention principle—in addition to their other commitments, such as promoting democracy, protecting human rights, and managing structural adjustment programs for economic development.

The Establishment of U.S. Hegemony: From the Monroe Doctrine to the Spanish-American War (1823–1898)

President James Monroe's proclamation in 1823 indicated a major U.S. interest in ending European control and influence in the Americas and in supporting the independence of the Latin American states. In most cases, it had the approval of the latter—although this positive attitude changed after the British seizure of the Malvinas Islands in 1833 and the Mexican-American War between 1846 and 1848—but the reality of Monroe's message was that the United States lacked the necessary power to enforce the doctrine. Around the same time the Spanish-American phase of the Pan American Movement began, initiated by Simón Bolívar, beginning with the Congress of Panama in 1826. The United States was also interested in expanding its territory and protecting what it considered to be its interests in the Caribbean and Central America, with frequent references to Manifest Destiny and the Monroe Doctrine as justifications. The territorial issue was accomplished by a short war with Mexico in the 1840s, and a treaty in 1850 that temporarily resolved the historical rivalry with Great Britain over land and transportation routes in Central America. During the U.S. Civil War, anti-European policy could not be pursued; Spain returned to certain parts of the Caribbean, and a joint European intervention in Mexico resulted in France setting up a Mexican empire under Austrian Archduke Ferdinand Maximilian Joseph.

The problem of European intervention was addressed by Argentine jurist Carlos Calvo after the U.S. Civil War, and it was soon declared illegal, a stance that later became a major American legal doctrine. Two South American wars—the Paraguayan War, 1864–1870, and the War of the Pacific, 1879–1884—resulted in a developing American interest in peaceful settlement of regional disputes. While the conferences of the Spanish-American phase of the Pan American Movement—all held in Latin America—focused on the problems of European intervention and peaceful settlement, it was the American phase of the movement that laid the basis for what evolved into the OAS. This began with the first International Conference of American States (1889–1890), which was noteworthy because it was the first to be held in the United States. At this conference, the United States stressed its primary economic interest in exporting manufactured goods to Latin America, and Argentina, also an exporter and the dominant Latin American power at the time, challenged the United States for leadership of the emerging regional system. The U.S. military victory over Spain in the 1898 Spanish-American War finally put an end to Spain's hemispheric influence, established the Caribbean as a U.S. sphere of influence (with a right to intervene in Cuba and a new possession in the case of Puerto Rico), and clearly crowned the United States the dominant regional power.

From Intervention to Cooperation (1898–1934)

The United States actively pursued its goal of economic and political control in the Caribbean and in Central America by means of blatant intervention and occupation during this period. U.S. presidents from Theodore Roosevelt to Calvin Coolidge used an assortment of corollaries to the Monroe Doctrine to justify and legitimize intervention. However, these repeated intrusions provoked mounting Latin American unity in opposition, and the meetings of the International Conference of American States became the arenas for those opposing the United States's hegemonic behavior. A 1902 joint European intervention in Venezuela prompted first the application of another Argentine-authored legal doctrine, by ex-Foreign Minister Luis Drago, proscribing economic interference, and second the famous Roosevelt Corollary to the Monroe Doctrine. The latter resulted in the United States taking over the collection of customs in the Dominican Republic and becoming the debt manager (often referred to as being "receivership") of a number of governments in the area. British influence in the isthmus came to an end, and U.S. control was established with the "independence" of Panama in 1903, the purchase of the bankrupt French canal company, and the signing of an extremely favorable treaty with the new state that paved the way for the U.S. completion and future control of the Panama Canal. Prior to World War I and before U.S. entry, U.S. gunboat diplomacy in the name of establishing economic responsibility and political stability resulted in military interventions in and occupations of three countries: Nicaragua, Haiti, and the Dominican Republic.

After World War I, a number of the Latin American states joined the League of Nations, a potential counterpoise to U.S. intervention, but the failure of the United States, now a world power, to join and the league covenant's recognition of the Monroe Doctrine rendered it ineffective. The Latin American states had been using the regular international conferences to challenge U.S. intervention by stressing principles of international law and by developing and applying their own legal doctrines, those of Calvo and Drago. Chilean jurist Alejandro Álvarez also wrote that a regional school of American International Law existed with non-intervention as its major rule. Since the criticisms of its interferences and occupations were particularly strong at the 1928 Sixth International

Conference in Cuba, the United States realized that the continued development of an effective regional system that would serve its increasing economic, political and security interests depended on its becoming less intrusive in the affairs of the Latin American states. The Hoover administration laid the basis for the Good Neighbor Policy which was formally announced and popularized by Franklin D. Roosevelt when he became president in 1933. The policy was effectively implemented when the United States accepted the nonintervention principle, first at the 1933 Seventh International Conference in Uruguay and next at the 1936 Inter-American Conference for the Maintenance of Peace in Argentina. With subsequent ratification without reservation by the United States, nonintervention became the cornerstone of the IAS. The Good Neighbor Policy assured positive cooperation and a stronger regional system, and it provided the impetus for advancing a multilateral policy on the "Principles of the Solidarity of America," in response to the war in Europe, approved at the 1938 Eighth International Conference in Peru.

Building the Foundations for Collective Security (1939–1945)

The three Meetings of Consultation of Ministers of Foreign Affairs (MMFA, see dictionary, "OAS, 3. Organs and Structure")—in Panama, 1939, Cuba, 1940, and Brazil, 1942—were prompted by the outbreak of World War II and early U.S. involvement in the European conflict. These meetings were notable for their creation of regional machinery and agreements that were reached on collective security, breaking relations with the Axis powers, and economic and military cooperation. These meetings also resulted in the establishment of a United States-led Inter-American Military System. At the 1942 meeting the United States announced that it would suspend for the duration of the war all tariffs and trade barriers, and it promised economic assistance to the Latin American states after the war in exchange for their current aid and support. Most Latin American states (Argentina was the one exception) strongly supported the United States in breaking relations and declaring war, offering the use of their airports and harbors and increasing exports of foodstuffs and strategic raw materials. As the war progressed, plans were made for a new postwar international organization, one that could deal with both the economic and political dimensions of the international system. In preparation for the San Francisco Conference, there were two 1944 conferences in the United States: the UN Monetary and Financial Conference (Bretton Woods Conference) and the Dumbarton Oaks Conversations. At the former, the Articles of Agreement were approved for two UN specialized agencies that were created to rebuild and manage the postwar economy: the International Bank for Reconstruction and Development (IBRD) and the International Monetary Fund (IMF).

The United States, by this time a new superpower, would dominate both of these agencies. At the latter conference, the Big Five powers approved the Dumbarton Oaks Proposals, which was essentially a draft of the UN Charter later drawn up at the San Francisco Conference in 1945.

The Latin American states resented their exclusion from this meeting and were critical of its proposals. The stage was now set for the last wartime American conference before the UN was established in San Francisco. The 1945 Conference on the Problems of War and Peace in Mexico was used by the Latin American states to strengthen the regional approach and to prepare a united front for protecting the autonomy of the IAS at San Francisco. The Latin American bloc, now joined by the United States, was in a good bargaining position and was successful in coordinating the regional and global approaches, evidenced by the addition of a chapter on "Regional Arrangements" to the UN Charter. They also won permanent representation in the International Court of Justice and the Security Council.

The Cold War (1947–1989)

From the onset of the Cold War, the United States became the leader of the Western alliance in the East-West struggle and was preoccupied with protecting and rebuilding Europe and containing the Soviet bloc by economic (Marshall Plan) and military (North Atlantic Treaty Organization, NATO) means. The United States, primarily interested in maintaining the status quo in Latin America, largely neglected the area and soon forgot its World War II promises. Nevertheless, the permanent building blocks of the IAS were laid in this early period: the first, a collective security arrangement strongly supported by the United States, was the Inter-American Treaty of Reciprocal Assistance (Rio Treaty), approved at a 1947 conference in Rio de Janeiro, Brazil. The second was the OAS Charter, approved at the 1948 Ninth International Conference in Bogotá, Colombia, which set up a juridically complete and integrated regional system incorporating the major earlier principles, especially nonintervention. But there was a major disagreement over economic assistance, the Latin Americans wanting multilateral public aid while the United States favored a bilateral and private capital approach. In 1951 the UN established the Economic Commission for Latin America (ECLA; in 1984 it changed its name to ECLAC, adding Caribbean) which has since been a dominant force in dealing with regional economic issues.

The U.S. interpretation of the Cold War made it difficult for its policy makers to see how its national interests could be protected through the multilateral machinery that was now in place and ready for testing in a region such as Latin America. The Korean War, 1950–1953, and developments in Guatemala in 1953–1954 prompted the United States to begin trying to convert the OAS into an anticommunist alliance on the basis of the Rio Treaty. In 1959, Fidel Castro came to power and initiated the Cuban Revolution, and the Inter-American Development Bank (IADB) and the Inter-American Commission on Human Rights (IACHR) were approved. During this period, ECLA's Raúl Prebisch's ideas about economic development in Latin America resulted in the formation in 1960 of the Central American Common Market (CACM) and the Latin American Free Trade Association (LAFTA). These changes in economic developmental strategy gave rise to the dependency school, embraced by the developing states, which prompted a dialogue with the developed nations. A related debate took place between the structuralists and monetarists over the policies of the IMF and World Bank in the development process. At this time another controversy developed, called the Tuna War, over the legal right—one opposed by the United States—of three developing coastal South American states to claim a 200-mile fish conservation zone.

Intervention, nonintervention, democracy, and communism all became issues with events of the 1960s: the 1960 attempt of Dominican dictator Trujillo to kill a Venezuelan democratic president; the 1961 U.S.-sponsored exile invasion of Cuba; the 1962 OAS suspension of Cuba and the missile crisis; Cuba's export of revolution; and the 1965 U.S. intervention in the Dominican Republic. Trujillo's attempt resulted in the first OAS collective sanctions against a member, the first use of the OAS as an antidictator alliance. A long-term debate began about how best to promote democracy and protect human rights without violating the nonintervention principle of the OAS Charter. U.S. President Kennedy's Alliance for Progress, which became an OAS program, also dealt with democracy and human rights but had little measurable success in meeting its overall goals. The failed U.S.-sponsored invasion of Cuba hastened Castro's turning to and becoming economically and militarily dependent on the Soviet Union. Because of this dependence and its nondemocratic government, the OAS suspended Cuban participation and imposed collective sanctions in 1962, making itself an anticommunist alliance. Later that year the OAS approved the U.S. embargo against Cuba as a means of forcing the withdrawal of Soviet missiles. In 1965, fearing a communist takeover, the United States intervened in a civil war in the Dominican Republic; and the OAS followed up with its first Inter-American Peace Force (IAPF). The increasing importance of human rights was indicated when a 1969 conference approved the Inter-American Commission on Human Rights (IACHR).

A Third World-initiated movement, one directed against the East-West axis and struggle, resulted in a new North-South alignment among the developed and developing states, outside but mainly in the UN. Most of the Latin American states (and the newly independent Commonwealth Caribbean states joining the OAS) became active members of this new bargaining axis. The first resultant group was the Nonaligned Movement, followed by one that became an important part of the UN in the mid-1960s, the UN Conference on Trade and Development (UNCTAD). From UNCTAD emerged the important bargaining alliance the Group of Seventy-Seven (G-77), which expanded to over 100 members by the 1990s.

The 1970s witnessed an increasing divergence between the Latin American and Commonwealth Caribbean states and the United States over the latter's policies toward the Chilean government of President Allende, Cuba, economics and trade. This regional, inter-American North-South divergence became related to the accelerating global East-West axis. In response to U.S. policy, the OAS rescinded the binding nature of its sanctions against Cuba in 1975, and soon the Latin American Economic System (LAES) was formed. The North-South axis was becoming increasingly important, and some Latin American leaders were using it as a forum against the North, U.S. foreign policy, the policies of the IMF—particularly its stand-by arrangements, which were viewed as interventionary—and the World Bank. Mexican President Luis Echeverría's proposal at an UNCTAD meeting became the UN General Assembly's Charter on the Economic Rights and Duties of States (CERDS). The same UN session also approved a resolution for the establishment of a New International Economic Order (NIEO). Related both to CERDS and NIEO was a UN debate between the North and the South about whether a code of conduct for multinational corporations (MNCs)—now transnational enterprises or TNEs—should be voluntary or compulsory. The best example of the new axis at work (now transcending the East-West one), especially the increasing influence of the South, was the Third UN Conference on the Law of the Sea (UNCLOS III), which held its second session in Venezuela in 1974 and did not conclude until 1982.

There were important economic developments affecting the Commonwealth Caribbean (CWC) states in the mid-1970s. First, the Caribbean Free Trade Association (CARIFTA) was replaced by the Caribbean Common Market (CARICOM), and the European Community (EC) approved Lomé I, which gave CWC exports special access to the EC. During this period four more CWC states joined the OAS, thereby increasing the influence of the Caribbean bloc. Relations between the United States and the Latin American and Caribbean states were affected both positively and negatively by key foreign policies of the Carter administration, particularly its stress on human rights, which alienated several states with military governments while giving new impetus to the status of human rights in the IAS; for example, the Inter-American Court of Human Rights (IACHR) began operation, and the new Panama Canal treaties were very popular. There was also a debate about the U.S. vote—and that of other states—being used in the IMF and the World Bank to further the human rights agenda.

There were six principal developments in the 1980s that had a significant impact on the inter-American system: the 1982 UN Convention on the Law of the Sea was approved by the developing but not by the developed states (the United States opposed it); the OAS became marginalized during the South Atlantic War and Central American peace process; the UN became a primary actor in Central America, first with and then in lieu of the OAS; a Latin American recession (called the "Lost Decade") in which several Latin American countries found it impossible to service their large foreign debts; the Reagan administration's 1984 Caribbean Basin Initiative (CBI); and the beginning and acceleration of the transition to democracy throughout the region. During the 1982 war between Argentina and Great Britain over the Falklands/Malvinas a debate ensued between Latin America and the United States over the proper peacemaking forum, the regional (OAS) or global (UN), with the former preferring the OAS and the latter favoring the UN.

In Central America, there was a clash between U.S. intervention against the Sandinista government of Nicaragua (it brought a case against the United States before the International Court of Justice and won) and the multilateral peacemaking efforts of neighboring states, beginning with the 1983 Contadora Group (CG) and becoming the Central American peace process. The latter finally prevailed, and UN involvement was made possible by EC support and Soviet-U.S. agreement. The "Lost Decade" brought major foreign debt defaults, beginning with that of Mexico, which presented a major challenge to the financial and monetary polices of the IMF. In response, the policies were changed U.S. cooperation, reflected in the plans named after two U.S. Secretaries of the Treasury—James A.Baker, III and Nicholas F. Brady. Privatization became an important new requirement and practice. The first major example of the beginning of the transition to democracy was the 1983 election of civilian Raúl Alfonsín as president of Argentina. Brazil followed with the end of its military rule in 1985. In 1986, the Uruguay round of negotiations of the General Agreement on Tariffs and Trade (GATT) began. The Caribbean bloc within the OAS gained importance with the addition of four new CWC member states.

The Post-Cold War Era: The 1990s

The end of the Cold War and the collapse of the Soviet Union led to speculation about the future course of U.S.-Latin American and Caribbean relations and of the IAS and the OAS in the 1990s. Canada and two other CWC states joined the OAS. A debate ensued over a new definition of regional security, building on the Latin American proposed but rejected concept of collective economic security for development in the mid-1970s. The emerging reformulation by the OAS Committee on Hemispheric Security is called "cooperation for hemispheric security" and includes promoting democracy, human rights, and integral development and dealing with migration and drug trafficking. There was continued inter-American support of the Central American peace process, but a new focus on free trade and regional integration also came to the fore. In fact, human rights and economic development have become interdependent in the aftermath of the Cold War.

Two relatively new areas of concern, especially for the regional system, backed by the UN were the environment and indigenous peoples. The OAS further strengthened its commitment to democracy and human rights when it approved a resolution on representative democracy and the Protocol of Managua (see dictionary, "OAS, 1. Charter of the OAS and Amendments") and implemented the former in 1992 by imposing economic sanctions against Haiti (see dictionary, "Aristide") after a military coup. A UN-approved 1994 military intervention there helped somewhat to restore democratic rule. This provoked a debate about sanctions, using economic means to restore a democratically elected president, and the human rights of the people who bear the brunt of such economic coercion. The human rights issue was also raised in terms of continuing U.S. sanctions against Cuba. A peace accord was reached by the UN Observer Group in El Salvador (ONUSAL) in 1992. A new 1990 U.S. foreign policy focus was indicated when President Bush proposed the Enterprise for the Americas Initiative (EAI). This was followed by a Latin American initiative forming the Southern Cone Common Market (MERCOSUR) and a major free trade accord among Canada, Mexico, and the United States, the North American Free Trade Agreement (NAFTA), was approved and became effective in 1995. Brazil now appears to be taking the lead—with strong support of past rival Argentina—in organizing, as an alternative to NAFTA, a merger of MERCOSUR and a revived Andean Pact to form a South American Free Trade Association (SAFTA). Chile, one of South America's fastest-growing economies, signed a separate trade pact with Canada in November 1996 and hopes to eventually negotiate membership in NAFTA.

Although the UN Convention on the Law of the Sea went into effect in 1994 and the United States became a party, the Summit of the Americas worked out a new American agenda. The agenda stressed economic development, was designed to revitalize the OAS through new economic duties, and set the year 2005 for the creation of an American Free Trade Area (AFTA); the environment and indigenous peoples were also covered. A new integration group, the Association of Caribbean States (ACS), was formed in 1995, and the Uruguay round of GATT (General Agreement on Tariffs and Trade) completed its negotiations and created the World Trade Organization (WTO), which began operation in 1996. The formation of NAFTA has divided the members of CARICOM, most requesting a "parity" agreement with the United States for their exports, although two have argued that they can negotiate separately with the United States without the approval of CARICOM—as a condition for joining NAFTA.

As the 21st century approaches, the Latin American and Caribbean states appear to be ready to apply new ways of solving collective economic and political problems, although the legacies of past struggles still haunt the inter-American system. Nevertheless, there is little doubt that the myriad of inter-American organizations that now operate will be active in defining the new relationships. Moreover, the inter-American balance is increasingly one in which the United States—once the preeminent hegemonic power in the region—must bend to pressures exerted by the Latin American and Caribbean states, as well as by Canada.

How to Use This Book

This reference book is designed to provide the reader with a set of useful tools to better understand the role of international organizations at the regional and subregional levels in the Western Hemisphere over the past fifty years. It contains two core parts: the dictionary and a comprehensive bibliography. The dictionary consists of inter-American organizations (e.g., the Organization of American States), subregional organizations (e.g., the Caribbean Common Market and the Southern Cone Common Market), international bodies such as the United Nations and the International Monetary Fund (IMF) that have had a direct impact on organizations, governments, and activities in the Western Hemisphere, and a number of international groups that link inter-American organizations with Europe, Asia, and the Middle East. In addition to these organizational entries, the dictionary contains others that pertain to significant political and economic leaders, diplomacy, international law, international political economy, wars and revolutions, and some historical events pertaining to inter-American relations.

The dictionary is heavily cross-referenced: within each entry, related terms are cross-referenced using the Latin abbreviation for "which see": q.v. (singular cross-reference) and qq.v. (plural cross-reference). Organizations that function in more than one language are listed in each along with their corresponding acronym, e.g., Central American Common Market (CACM)/Mercado Común Centroamericano (MCC). To enable the reader to locate each acronym and full title more easily, a separate section on abbreviations and acronyms is included in the front matter of the book. At the end of each entry in the dictionary, where appropriate, additional related organizations or terms are also cross-referenced. Headquarters addresses and electronic addresses of over 50 of the most significant organizations are included in appendix IX.

In addition to the dictionary entries, this book also features a bibliography with over 1,200 items (books, monographs, journal articles, government and organization documents) that correspond to the major organizations and themes associated with the role of inter-American organizations in the hemisphere. The bibliography is not annotated, but it does contain an introduction that selectively highlights key works in several major areas, and a section that provides instructions for using the Internet to track down electronic sources of information. Although we have been forced to be selective in choosing citations for the bibliography, the elaborate taxonomy, organized around the major entries in the dictionary, should prove to be extremely useful for those who seek more information on the subject. Bibliographic entries are alphabetized within each area of the taxonomy rather than as a whole, the more common pattern in reference books.

The Organization of American States (OAS) is given a considerable amount of attention in this book, primarily because of its long history of dealing with inter-American issues and its important new role in confronting a myriad of concerns in the Americas. The dictionary contains a lengthy entry on the history, Charter (and amendments), membership, organizational structure, and roles and functions of the OAS, emphasizing the recent changes in the organization in the aftermath of the Cold War. Of the nine appendices in this book, five focus on important aspects of the OAS: all the secretaries-general and assistant secretaries-general (and the dates of their respective terms in office) that have provided leadership for the organization, a complete list of member states and permanent observers, structural charts showing organizational functions and lines of authority, and a complete version of the most recent (1996) OAS Charter. Other appendixes include information on the United Nations and membership in international commodity organizations such as the Union of Banana Exporting Countries and the International Coffee Organization.

The up-to-date factual information in the dictionary and the extensive bibliography should provide a clear guide to the way politics and economics are organized at the international level. The dramatic changes in the magnitude and complexity of inter-American organizations over the past 50 years is a subject of increasing importance to scholars and policy practitioners; this book should help to better illuminate these multilateral bodies that feature so prominently in current inter-American relations.

The Dictionary

A

AFRICAN, CARIBBEAN, AND PACIFIC COUNTRIES GROUP OF STATES (ACP)/GROUPES DES ETATS D'AFRIQUE, DES CARAIBES, ET DU PACIFIQUE (GEACP). Ex-colonies of European powers that are connected with the European Community (EC, q.v.) under the terms of the Lomé Conventions (q.v.). Since 1975 the ACP has served as a forum for negotiation and discussion to enhance export earnings from agricultural and manufactured goods sold to member states of the European Community. In July 1989, the European Union (EU, q.v.) replaced the Lomé Conventions with a five-year trade and aid pact that would compensate the original 66 members for losses in commodity export earnings due to fluctuations in world market prices. With headquarters in Brussels, Belgium, the ACP has a Council of Ministers, a Committee of Ambassadors, a Consultative Assembly, a Secretariat, and a Center for Industrial Development. The preferential treatment allowed Caribbean members that export bananas to Europe has led to a number of diplomatic confrontations with the major Latin American exporters of bananas, such as Ecuador and Costa Rica. *See also* European Union (EU); Lomé Conventions.

AFRO-ASIAN LATIN AMERICAN PEOPLES' SOLIDARITY CONFERENCE (AALAPSC)/TRICONTINENTAL CONFERENCE. Meeting for the first time in Havana, Cuba, in 1966, it led to the founding of the Organization of Solidarity of the Peoples of Africa, Asia, and Latin America (OSPAALA) and the Organization of Latin American Solidarity (OLAS), both headquartered in Havana, the former having a secretary-general. The conference stressed the coordination and encouragement of national liberation movements and its opposition to foreign (meaning developed, northern and western states) intervention (q.v.) and racism. OSPAALA grew to include revolutionary organizations in 82 countries. OLAS held its first meeting in Havana in 1967, where it made a commitment to "armed struggle" as a strategy for achieving national liberation. Thereafter, OLAS attempted to coordinate the activities of revolutionaries in certain states throughout the region. Venezuela became one of the major arenas for pursuing the objectives of national liberation with emphasis on a rural guerrilla vanguard organization as a superior weapon to that of existing communist parties. Many leftist groups and political refugees from right-wing dictatorships in Latin America received OLAS sanctuary in Cuba during this period.

AGENCY FOR THE PROHIBITION OF NUCLEAR WEAPONS IN LATIN AMERICA AND THE CARIBBEAN (APNWLA)/ORGANISMO PARA LA PROSCRIPCIÓN DE LAS ARMAS NUCLEARES EN LA AMÉRICA LATINA Y EL CARIBE (OPANAL). Founded in 1969 to ensure compliance with the 1967 Treaty of Tlatelolco (q.v.), prohibiting all nuclear weapons within the application zone, OPANAL also promotes general and complete disarmament and the prohibition of all testing, use, manufacture, acquisition, storage, installation, and any form of possession of nuclear weapons. Members include 28 states that have ratified the treaty—Antigua and Barbuda, Argentina, the Bahamas, Barbados, Bolivia, Brazil, Colombia, Costa Rica, Dominican Republic, Ecuador, El Salvador, Grenada, Guatemala, Haiti, Honduras, Jamaica, Mexico, Nicaragua, Panama, Paraguay, Peru, Saint Vincent and the Grenadines, Suriname, Trinidad and Tobago, Uruguay, and Venezuela. Two additional protocols have been added to the original treaty: the first signed by France, the Netherlands, the United Kingdom, and the United States; the second signed and ratified by China, the Commonwealth of Independent States (CIS), France, the United Kingdom, and the United States. *See also* Treaty of Tlatelolco.

ALFONSÍN, RAÚL (1926-). President of Argentina (1983–1989) who came to power after the humiliation of the Argentine military in the Falklands/Malvinas War (q.v.) in 1982. After defeating the Peronists (their first presidential loss) on the Radical Party ticket, Alfonsín proceeded to introduce new economic policies to address Argentina's huge foreign debt, rampant inflation, stagnant growth, and pressures from the International Monetary Fund (IMF, q.v.) to meet its debt obligations. To assuage a public angry over the military's conduct in the Dirty War (1977–1981) and its humiliation by the British in the Falklands/Malvinas War, Alfonsín overturned the recently enacted Amnesty Law and organized the first human rights (q.v.) trials in Latin America. This caused civil-military relations to deteriorate rapidly as the military staged three unsuccessful uprisings against Alfonsín because of his human rights efforts. Argentina's faith in the effectiveness of international organizations was seriously weakened by its inability to assist in the long-standing dispute with Britain on the Falklands/Malvinas issue. Under Alfonsín a more Third World (q.v.) orientation in foreign policy developed that included closer ties with Latin American nations and the Nonaligned Movement (q.v.) and a concomitant coolness toward the United States over Reagan (q.v.) administration policies in Central America. Alfonsín was instrumental in finding a diplomatic solution to the Beagle Channel Islands dispute (q.v.) with Chile but made little progress in settling the Falklands/Malvinas imbroglio with Great Britain. In 1989, Alfonsín was forced to leave office six months early, due to hyperinflation and spreading social unrest, and handed over the office of the presidency to the Peronist victor in the elections, Carlos S. Menem (q.v.). *See also* Beagle Channel Islands Dispute; Falklands/Malvinas War; Human Rights; Perón, Juan D.

ALIANZA PARA EL PROGRESO (APP). *See* Alliance for Progress.

ALLENDE, SALVADOR (1908–1973). Marxist president of Chile (1970–1973) who, as part of a coalition of leftist parties, tried to move the country rapidly toward socialism through the acceleration of agrarian reform efforts and extensive nationalization of major sectors of the economy. Multinational corporations whose property was confiscated pressured the Nixon administration to use the CIA and its clout with international lending agencies such as the Inter-American Development Bank (IADB, q.v.) and the International Monetary Fund (IMF, q.v.) to weaken the legitimacy of the Allende government. The resulting efforts and policies were referred to as the "invisible blockade" of Chile. Despite a successful first year in office, Allende's Popular Unity government soon encountered substantial opposition from domestic and international forces that would eventually contribute to the military coup of 1973 that led to his death and 16 years of repressive rule under General Augusto Pinochet (q.v.). The Nixon administration's policy of destabilization and open hostility toward Allende's "revolution in liberty" served to undermine the credibility of the United States in its support for democracy (q.v.) in Latin America. After Chile's return to civilian rule in 1990, Allende's corpse was exhumed and given a state funeral to honor him as a president of a democratic Chile. *See also* Cold War; Human Rights; Pinochet Ugarte, Augusto.

ALLIANCE FOR PROGRESS (AP)/ALIANZA PARA EL PROGRESO (APP). An ambitious U.S. policy for Latin America during the Kennedy administration that included a massive assistance program tied to U.S. economic aid, a concerted effort to build democratic institutions, and a partially veiled hope that such actions would undermine Castro's (q.v.) radical revolution in Cuba (q.v.). However, it was under-funded, and many of its reform efforts were based on faulty assumptions about the relationship between revolutions and poverty in Latin America. To avoid future Cubas in the hemisphere, the United States argued that it would have to use its vast economic power and democratic principles to change Latin America. After years of neglect of the development needs of Latin America, the Alliance offered hope of achieving substantial economic growth, democracy (q.v.), and a needed reinvigoration of the Inter-American system (IAS, q.v.).

The Alliance for Progress was formally established by the Charter of Punta del Este (Uruguay) within the framework of Operation Pan America (q.v.), a precursor program advocated by Brazilian President Juscelino Kubitschek in 1958. Premised on a "takeoff theory" of political development heralded by Walt W. Rostow, an MIT economics professor who wrote *The Stages of Economic Growth: A Non-Communist Manifesto* (1960), it called for a peaceful revolution throughout Latin America that would serve as a counter to Fidel Castro's revolution underway in Cuba. With an initial promise of $1 billion, President Kennedy told Latin America it could reasonably expect to receive $20 billion in external sources over the next ten years. Alliance planners estimated that $100 billion would be required to succeed, with approximately $80 billion to be generated within the Latin American countries themselves. Foreign and domestic private capital was supposed to flow into Latin America at the rate of $1 billion per year, but few investors possessed the confidence to invest due to political instability, inflation, and the fear of expropriation. In exchange for funding promises from the United States, Latin America was expected to carry out needed changes, including tax reform, economic integration, agrarian reform, encouragement of private financing of development projects, new monetary and fiscal policies, improvement in health and education, and the building of democratic institutions. President Kennedy's pledge of an estimated total of $20 billion was to be channeled through appropriations to the World Bank (q.v.), Inter-American Development Bank (IADB, q.v.), and through its own government lending agencies, such as the Agency for International Development (AID) and the Export-Import Bank. Thus, the Alliance for Progress served an important role as a catalyst for the creation and development of many inter-American organizations during the turbulent 1960s.

After the assassination of President Kennedy, efforts to support social reform and economic growth to provide political stability were hampered by the Latin American armed forces' emphasis on internal security and counterinsurgency, which included civic action programs pushed by the United States. As more military governments came to power, diminishing the hopes for democratic development, and Castro's efforts to "export" revolutions elsewhere weakened, enthusiasm for the reform efforts of the Alliance for Progress waned in Latin America. Throughout the administration of Lyndon B. Johnson (q.v.), Washington, plagued with its own internal difficulties—declining interest in public investment, the costs and controversy over the war in Vietnam, and expensive "Great Society" programs such as the War on Poverty—soon lost interest in helping to bring democratic reforms and representative government to Latin America. Many of the reform proposals were also blocked by conservative political forces inside Latin America.

By 1963 the Alliance had fallen far short of its goals and seemed to be drifting into oblivion, since no single inter-American organization existed to give it direction. At a meeting in São Paulo in late 1963, a new Inter-American Committee for the Alliance for Progress (IACAP) was established to serve as a clearing house between the United States and its Alliance partners. The purpose of the IACAP was to transform the Alliance into a more truly multilateral organization by giving Latin American governments a greater say in, and responsibility for, Alliance affairs, but the results were nevertheless disappointing. The U.S. Congress terminated the Alliance for Progress in 1972 after realizing that its economic and social objectives had not been achieved. *See also* Johnson Doctrine.

ÁLVAREZ, ALEJANDRO (1868–1960). A Chilean jurist and diplomat who was the leading exponent of a regional school of international law, *el derecho internacional americano* (American international law). Although the concept had been presented in a resolution at the first International Conference of American States in Washington, D.C., 1889–1890 (and rejected by the United States), he first made his case for American international law in a 1910 book published in France, arguing that it would dilute the intrusiveness contained in the Monroe Doctrine (q.v.). Judge Álvarez also advocated the right to political asylum, based on practice (custom), not consent. While he continued to espouse the school's existence, other Latin American writers developed the nonintervention (q.v.) principle as the major characteristic of the American school, mainly as a counterpoise to U.S. intervention (q.v.). By the time of World War II (q.v.), supporters of the regional legal approach were a minority view. In the *Haya de la Torre* case (*Colombia-Peru Asylum* case, 1950), in which the Peruvian Haya, the head of the opposition party, escaped from the dictator in power and was given asylum in the Colombian Embassy, the International Court of Justice (ICJ, q.v.) denied the existence of political asylum as an American rule. Álvarez, a member of the ICJ, wrote a major dissent in the case. *See also* International Court of Justice (ICJ); International Law; Tuna War; United Nations, Third Conference on the Law of the Sea (UNCLOS III).

AMAZON PACT. The Treaty for Amazon Cooperation, signed in 1978 by most states with territory in the Amazon Basin—Bolivia, Brazil, Colombia, Ecuador, Guyana, Peru, Suriname, and Venezuela—is designed to provide a framework for collaboration on conservation, use of natural resources, and economic development among the countries of Amazonia. Joint efforts to develop and manage the basin were originally based on an effort to curtail foreign influence. However, because their development projects often required substantial foreign investment, the isolationist rationale could not be maintained, particularly in meeting the environmental demands of international economic lending agencies. Foreign ministers of the eight member countries meet every two years to create common development strategies and programs, and each member has a national commission to implement decisions reached at the biannual meetings. Current efforts to expand regional projects that emphasize sustainable development (q.v.) and more ambitious economic integration plans have benefitted from the groundwork laid by the Amazon Pact signatories. *See also* Environment; Sustainable Development.

AMERICAN INTERNATIONAL LAW. *See* Álvarez, Alejandro.

ANDEAN COMMISSION OF JURISTS (ACJ)/COMISIÓN ANDINA DE JURISTAS (CAJ). Made up of jurists from Bolivia, Chile, Colombia, Ecuador, Peru, and Venezuela, the ACJ was founded in 1982 to protect human rights and promote democracy (qq.v.) among its six members through counseling and education on legal and human rights issues. The ACJ also maintains consultative status within the United Nations Economic and Social Council.

ANDEAN COMMUNITY (AC). *See* Andean Group (AG).

ANDEAN GROUP (AG) or ANDEAN PACT (AP)/GRUPO ANDINO (GA) or PACTO ANDINO (PA). A subregional common market agreed to in 1966 and set up in 1969 to improve its members' bargaining power within the Latin American Free Trade Association (LAFTA, q.v.) with headquarters in Lima, Peru. Officially known as the Acuerdo de Cartagena (from the site where the treaty was signed in Cartagena, Colombia), its membership includes Bolivia, Chile (withdrew in 1976; rejoined in 1990), Colombia, Ecuador, Peru, and Venezuela (joined in 1973). Its original goals were to create a common market that would advance industrialization, tighten control over multinational corporations operating within the market, and offer special concessions to poorer members to stimulate economic progress. In May 1987, representatives of the six-member group signed the Quito Protocol, modifying the Cartagena Agreement by relaxing the strict rules on foreign investment contained in Decision 24. From 1971 to 1985, in accordance with a commission directive (Decision 24), foreign investors were required to transfer 51 percent of their shares to local investors within 15 years in order to qualify for preferential trade arrangements. Decision 24 deterred foreign investors and accelerated foreign indebtedness, thus eventually leading to the annulment of the directive in 1987 and greater liberalization of foreign investment from the end of the 1980s onward. In 1989, the Andean Group expanded its goals to include nuclear nonproliferation, regional development, and low levels of political integration. In 1991, the Andean Group, meeting in Caracas, Venezuela, established the framework for an Andean common market (Caracas Declaration), to start full operation by 1995. The Caracas Declaration also included provisions for the election of an Andean Parliament by universal suffrage and an "open sky" agreement giving airlines equal rights to airspace and airports within the Andean Group region.

The Andean Group consists of a number of organizational components, including a Commission, Council, Junta, Parliament (Parlamento Andino), Court of Justice, Reserve Fund, and a Development Corporation, that carry out its activities. Substantial increases in regional trade and industrial growth were evident in the first decade of the group's existence; however, these positive trends were reversed by the 1980s due to the heavy costs of import substitution industrialization programs, the international economic crisis, conflicts of national interest over tariffs, a boundary war between Ecuador and Peru, and poor enforcement of basic group policies. In 1997, the Andean Group became known as the Andean Community, a move that the members hoped would hasten joint negotiations with MERCOSUR (q.v.). The Andean Community's new approach to integrating with the more powerful economies to the south is a vindication of the Brazilian approach to integration, which envisages a much broader free trade area of the Americas emerging from subregional integration efforts already under way.

ANGLO-AMERICAN CARIBBEAN COMMISSION (AACC). A joint body created by Great Britain and the United States in 1942 for the purpose of taking wartime security measures in the Caribbean where the British had military bases. It became the Caribbean Commission (q.v.) in 1946, which in turn became the Caribbean Council in 1961.

ANTARCTIC TREATY CONSULTATIVE PARTY GROUP (ATCPG). Established when the Antarctic Treaty was signed in 1959 to protect the environment (q.v.) of the frozen continent by banning nuclear tests, military activity, economic exploitation, and all territorial claims. The consultative parties to the agreement include seven claimant states (Argentina, Australia, Great Britain, Chile, France, New Zealand, and Norway) with full voting rights and five nonclaimant states. Since it went into effect in 1961, ATCPG has allowed other states to join the consultative group for purposes of conducting "substantial research" in accordance with the treaty. The original treaty, renegotiated by 33 nations (1991–1992), now includes the Madrid Protocol on Environmental Protection, which bans oil exploration and mining for 50 years. There are now 40 parties to the original treaty. In 1996, an agreement was signed for dealing with the disposal of nuclear waste and other toxic material that were regularly stored or dumped in the Arctic by the Soviet Union. *See also* Environment; United Nations, Third Conference on the Law of the Sea (UNCLOS III).

ARAB LATIN AMERICAN BANK (ARLABANK)/BANQUE ARABE LATINOAMERICAINE/BANCO ARABE LATINOAMER-ICANO. After being founded in Lima, Peru, in 1977, its headquarters moved to Manama, Bahrain, in 1983. The Bank's parent company is Alabank International EC, with branches in the Caribbean and in South America. Its goal is to serve as a financial bridge between the Middle East and Latin America through banking activities in the region. Its members are shareholders in banks, companies, and financial bodies in 18 countries, including ten in Latin America (all are in South America except two in Haiti and Panama).

AREA DE LIBRE COMERCIO DE LAS AMÉRICAS (ALCLA). *See* Free Trade Area of the Americas.

ARGENTINA. *See* Alfonsín, Raúl; Beagle Channel Islands Dispute; Falklands/Malvinas War; Human Rights; Perón, Juan D.

ARIAS, OSCAR (1940-). While president of Costa Rica (1986–1990), he presented a peace plan (*una hora para la paz*) at a summit meeting of Central American presidents in his country in February 1987. His plan, as part of the ongoing Central American Peace Process (q.v.), replaced the failing first phase, called the Contadora Process, with the successful Esquipulas II phase. (Esquipulas was the name of the city in Guatemala where a prior commitment was made to follow Arias's plan.) For his proposal and determination to end the conflict in Central America, President Arias was awarded the 1987 Nobel Peace Prize. *See also* Central American/Contadora Peace Process.

ARISTIDE, JEAN-BERTRAND (1953-). Haitian religious leader and president (1991; 1994–1996) who played a key role in Haiti's efforts to democratize and demilitarize in the 1990s. He received his elementary education from the Catholic order of the Salesian Brothers and graduated from a local seminary in Port-au-Prince. Upon his return from foreign study in 1982, he was ordained a Catholic priest. However, his critical views of the dictatorship of Jean-Claude Duvalier and of Church policies contributed to the necessity of further study outside of Haiti and his eventual rise to prominence as a charismatic leader embracing the doctrine of Liberation Theology. By 1985 he had returned to Haiti and quickly became one of the foremost, and most courageous, critics of the Duvalier regime. Despite government attempts to kill him and efforts by the Church to suppress his radical sermons or force him into exile, he gradually became a hero of the poor masses and at the same time a growing threat to the survival and legitimacy of the dictatorship. His ability to mobilize opposition to the repressive Duvalier regime contributed to its collapse and removal in 1986.

Aristide announced his candidacy late in the presidential campaign of 1990 but still managed to win a large majority of votes in Haiti's first free and honest election. Inaugurated in February 1991, he was overthrown by the Haitian military in late September of the same year. He remained in exile for three years, mainly in the United States, while the OAS (q.v.) and the UN applied sanctions against the military government and militarily intervened in September 1994 to bring about his return to office. He was restored as president in October and finished his interrupted term in February 1996, when the winner of the December 1995 presidential election—René Préval—was installed in the first democratic succession in Haitian history. *See also* Clinton, William J.; Haiti, Sanctions by the OAS and the UN, Military Intervention by a UN Force.

ASIA-PACIFIC ECONOMIC COOPERATION (APEC)/COOPÉRA-TION ECONOMIQUE ASIE-PACIFIQUE (CEAP). A multilateral forum established in 1989 in Canberra, Australia to provide for regular discussion of regional trade issues and economic cooperation, with particular emphasis on means of enhancing cooperation between developed and developing countries. APEC's primary goals include the reduction of trade barriers on goods, services, and technology, the creation of a lobby group to press for changes in the global trading system, and the reduction or elimination of protectionist trade policies. APEC also focuses on human resource development, micro entrepreneurship, and infrastructure development at its various meetings and working groups. APEC's organizational structure includes ministerial meetings (annually), working groups and committees, and a Permanent Secretariat headed by an executive director and deputy executive director, both of ambassadorial rank. Its 19 members include Canada, Chile, Mexico, the United States, and fifteen other Pacific Rim countries. At its November 1996 meeting in Manila, APEC leaders endorsed a U.S. proposal to lower tariffs on computer technology in Asia. The APEC member nations account for 50 percent of total goods and services produced in the world and more than 80 percent of global trade in information technology, an economic sector worth over $500 billion annually. Global trade in technology is a major factor in generating export-related jobs worldwide.

ASISTENCIA RECÍPROCA PETROLERA ESTATAL LATINOAM-ERICANA (ARPEL). *See* Mutual Assistance of the Latin American Government Oil Companies.

ASOCIACIÓN DE NACIONES DEL ASIA SUDORIENTAL (ANAS). *See* Association of Southeast Asian Nations (ASEAN).

ASOCIACIÓN LATINOAMERICANA DE COMERCIO LIBRE (ACLADI). *See* Latin American Free Trade Association (LAFTA).

ASOCIACIÓN LATINOAMERICANA DE INTEGRACIÓN (ALADI). *See* Latin American Integration Association (LAIA).

ASOCIACIÓN LATINOAMERICANA DE INSTITUCIONES FINAN-CIEROS DE DESARROLLO (ALIDE). *See* Latin American Association of Development Finance Institutions (LAADFI).

ASSOCIATION DES NATIONS DE L'ASIE DU SUD-EST (ANASE). *See* Association of Southeast Asian Nations (ASEAN).

ASSOCIATION OF CARIBBEAN STATES (ACS). The charter creating the ACS was signed by a group of Circum-Caribbean states (q.v.) at a meeting in Cartagena, Colombia, in late July 1994, and it had enough ratifications to become effective at the first ACS meeting in Port of Spain, Trinidad and Tobago, in August 1995. The purpose of the ACS is to assure a regional role in protecting its members' economic interests in dealing with the United States and the North American Free Trade Agreement (NAFTA, q.v.). The ACS brought together 26 states as full members in early 1996: the 14 members—Commonwealth Caribbean (q.v.) plus Suriname—of the Caribbean Community (CC, q.v.); the six Central (Latin) American states; the members of the Group of Three (q.v.); and the three Greater Antilles nations (Cuba, the Dominican Republic, and Haiti). The three associate members at that time were Anguilla, Guadeloupe, and the Turks and Caicos Islands. A number of other dependencies (of Great Britain, France, the Netherlands and the United States) are eligible to become associate members. The headquarters of the ACS is in Port of Spain, and its secretary-general is a Venezuelan diplomat, Simón Molina Duarte.

ASSOCIATION OF SOUTHEAST ASIAN NATIONS (ASEAN)/ASSOCIATION DES NATIONS DE L'ASIE DU SUD-EST (ANASE)/ ASOCIACIÓN DE NACIONES DEL ASIA SUDORIENTAL (ANAS). A regional body, with vast international governmental organization (IGO) and nongovernmental organization (NGO) links to the rest of the world, that was established in 1967 by five noncommunist states (Indonesia, Malaysia, the Philippines, Singapore, and Thailand) to protect themselves from being drawn into the Vietnam conflict and the Cold War (q.v.) in Asia. Since the early 1980s, however, it has expanded its membership (Brunei joined in 1984, and in 1992 Laos and Vietnam were given observer status) and functions to include economic growth policies, regional peace and security, and economic, social, cultural, technical, and scientific collaboration at the regional and international levels. Over the past twenty years ASEAN has forged links with the United Nations Education, Scientific, and Cultural Organization (UNESCO), United Nations Development Program (UNDP, q.v.), European Community (EC, q.v.), Rio Group (q.v.), Caribbean Community (q.v.), European Union CC (EU, q.v.), Latin American Economic System (LAES, q.v.), and the Latin American Association (LAIA, q.v.). With ASEAN's organizational links to IGOs in the Western Hemisphere, many Latin American policymakers are pushing for deeper trade ties to the prosperous economies of Asia through this international organization.

ATLANTIC COMMUNITY DEVELOPMENT GROUP FOR LATIN AMERICA (ACEDELA or ADELA). Founded in 1956 by more than 50 firms to stimulate private foreign investment in Latin America, the group is a private multinational consortium, funded by financial contributions from European, Japanese, and U.S. companies.

B

BAENA SOARES, JOÃO CLEMENTE (1931-). A Brazilian ambassador and diplomat who served as the sixth OAS (q.v.) secretary-general. He is one of the few in this position to publish a memoir at the end of his two five-year terms (1984–1994), a book published by the OAS in 1994. *See also* Appendix II; bibliography.

BALAGUER, JOAQUÍN (1907-). Important political leader in the Dominican Republic whose original power base stemmed from his role as dictator Rafael L. Trujillo's (q.v.) presidential secretary. Due to his links to the brutal dictatorship, Balaguer was exiled in 1961 but eventually returned and was elected president in 1966, three years after the election of Juan Bosch and the U.S. intervention (q.v.) and occupation of 1965–1966. With the backing of the Dominican military and the United States, Balaguer served three terms as president from 1966 to 1978. In the election of 1978, however, the Carter administration turned against him because of its stress on honest elections. During the counting of ballots, the Dominican army took over and stopped the process (either at Balaguer's direction or on its own) in order to assure his reelection. This improper action prompted immediate public censure by the United States, Venezuela, and the Organization of American States (OAS, q.v.), demanding the resumption of ballot counting. Their actions were dubbed "electoral intervention" by some observers of the process. Balaguer succumbed to the pressure and was not reelected, the victory going to the leader of the opposition party, Antonio Guzmán Fernández.

Four years later Balaguer was defeated by another opposition leader, Salvador Jorge Blanco. Balaguer was elected in 1986 and then reelected in 1990 and 1994. His 1994 narrow margin over Francisco Peña Gómez provoked a controversy about fraud and resulted in a political agreement that he would serve only two years and would be prohibited from running again in a special election to be held in 1996. That election was won by Lionel Fernández, a leader with close ties to New York's large Dominican community. Balaguer's exit from Dominican politics in 1996 marked the end of his long, corrupt, and ruthless rule. *See also* Democracy; Dominican Republic, Intervention in by the United States and OAS Peace Force; Trujillo Molina, Rafael L.

BANCO ARABE LATINAMERICANO. *See* Arab Latin American Bank (ARLABANK).

BANCO CENTROAMERICANO DE INTEGRACIÓN ECONÓMICA (BCIE). *See* Central American Bank for Economic Integration (CABEI).

BANQUE ARABE LATINOAMERICAINE. *See* Arab Latin American Bank (ARLABANK).

BARCO, VIRGILIO (1921-). President of Colombia (1986–1990) whose term was marked by political violence propagated by left-wing guerrillas, right-wing death squads, and drug traffickers. Colombia's drug cartels (q.v.) killed thousands of judges, journalists, and public officials during Barco's tenure. He cooperated with the United States in dealing with drug trafficking by continuing to extradite Colombian drug traffickers to the United States for trial and imprisonment based on the Colombian-U.S. 1979 Extradition Treaty. For his government's cooperation, Colombia received $65 million during the first year of the Bush administration. Barco helped to bring the M-19 guerrilla movement into legal politics in 1990, but the success of this alteration in the political landscape was short-lived. *See also* Betancur, Belisario; Drug Cartels.

BARRIOS DE CHAMORRO, VIOLETA (1929-). President of Nicaragua (1990–1996) who led the anti-Sandinista coalition (National Opposition Union) in 1990 and won 55 percent of the vote, thus preventing the reelection of President Daniel Ortega (q.v.). In her campaign Barrios de Chamorro promised to end the war with the Contras (q.v.) and to revive the Nicaraguan economy. The widow of Pedro Joaquín Chamorro, the late owner of the country's leading newspaper *La Prensa*, she became one of the foremost opponents of Anastasio Somoza Debayle after the assassination of her husband in 1978. Once the Sandinistas (Frente Sandinista de la Liberación Nacional, FSLN) won the insurrection against Somoza in 1979, she was appointed to the five-member ruling body but soon resigned because of disagreements over the direction of the Nicaraguan revolution (q.v.). Thereafter, she used her powers as editor of *La Prensa* to oppose the Sandinista government. As president, she devoted her time to reversing the Sandinista revolution, pushing for national reconciliation and struggling for ways to achieve economic recovery. During most of her presidency she dueled with the Bush and Clinton administrations (and the conservative U.S. Congress) over the strings attached to aid promised to Nicaragua: the United States wanted the return of private properties and the removal of Sandinistas from the security forces in exchange for the promised economic assistance. She was succeeded in 1996 by Arnoldo Alemán, a rightist candidate who defeated Daniel Ortega who again ran on the FSLN ticket. *See also* Nicaraguan Revolution; Somoza Dynasty/Family.

BATISTA, FULGENCIO (1901–1973). A military and political leader of Cuba from the 1930s to his overthrow by Fidel Castro (q.v.) and the 26th of July Movement on January 1, 1959. Despite having been elected president of Cuba in the 1940s, Batista seized power in a bloodless coup in 1952 and proceeded to establish a repressive dictatorship until national revulsion against corruption (q.v.), greed, and violent countermeasures against his opponents drove him into exile. In the early stages of the Cuban Revolution (q.v.), Batista's followers and supporters, particularly his hated secret police, who engaged in torture and assassination prior to 1959, were subject to criminal prosecution. After a brief stay in the Dominican Republic, Batista fled to Portugal and finally Spain, where he lived in comfortable exile until his death in 1973. *See also* Castro, Fidel; Cuban Revolution.

BEAGLE CHANNEL ISLANDS DISPUTE. Major international border dispute between Chile and Argentina that brought the two countries to the brink of war in 1978. It centered on whether the ownership of three key islands would enable Chile to extend its sovereignty into the South Atlantic, thereby inhibiting Argentina's ability to project its influence in that region. An unsuccessful arbitration effort by the British crown ruled in favor of Chilean sovereignty over the islands in 1977, was quickly rejected by Argentina on narrow technical grounds, and led both countries to prepare for possible conflict. Vatican mediation efforts in 1978 prevented the outbreak of war and eventually led to the 1984 Treaty of Peace and Friendship in which the two parties agreed to allow Chilean control over the islands without the right to claim sovereignty or an economic zone in the South Atlantic region. Argentina's transformation from military to democratic civilian rule under President Raúl Alfonsín (q.v.) was an important factor in gaining Argentine acceptance of the ruling engineered by the mediators.

BELAÚNDE TERRY, FERNANDO (1912-). President whose two terms (1963–1968; 1980–1985) symbolized the recent end and restoration of democracy in Peru. Belaúnde was overthrown by the Peruvian military in 1968 primarily because of his involvement with the International Petroleum Company (IPC), a U.S.-based corporation known for its deep interference in Peru's internal and external affairs since its arrival there in 1913. The IPC's high profit repatriation, supposed illegal manipulation of Peruvian politicians, and other questionable business practices often generated nationalist resentment. Belaúnde's complicity in these abuses contributed not only to his overthrow but also to the subsequent nationalization of the company in 1968 by the military government. His association with the IPC influenced the strict controls on foreign investment built into the Andean Pact (q.v.) in the late 1960s. Belaúnde managed to maintain vestiges of legitimacy while in exile in the United States and returned to power on the wave of democratic change sweeping Latin America in the 1980s. *See also* Andean Pact.

BETANCOURT, RÓMULO (1908–1981). A popular Venezuelan politician and statesman who was known for his commitment to enlightened democratic reforms and opposition to both Marxist and rightwing authoritarianism. Founder of Venezuela's political party Democratic Action (Acción Democrática, AD), Betancourt served as president on two occasions: 1945–1948 and 1959–1964. His second term coincided with the Cuban Revolution (q.v.), the Alliance for Progress (q.v.), and President Kennedy's Latin American policy. As symbol of democratic values and practices and as hemispheric leader, Betancourt and Kennedy developed a warm friendship, and Venezuela quickly became one of the key targets of Alliance for Progress goals and ideals. Betancourt played a crucial role in expanding Venezuela's involvement in hemispheric affairs and managed to keep the country on a democratic path despite efforts from the left and right to replace him. Economic reforms were enhanced by Venezuela's leading role in the founding of Organization of Petroleum Exporting Countries (OPEC, q.v.) and a new international petroleum policy. After a failed assassination attempt against him in June 1960, Betancourt charged the Dominican Republic's dictator, General Rafael L. Trujillo (q.v.), with the crime and sought sanctions from the Organization of American States (OAS, q.v.). When an arms cache that originated in Cuba was discovered on a Venezuelan beach in 1963, Betancourt severed relations with Fidel Castro's government and pushed for sanctions against Cuba in the OAS. Betancourt died after suffering a stroke on a visit to New York City in 1981. *See also* Balaguer, Joaquín; Cuba, Collective Sanctions and Suspension by the OAS; Trujillo Molina, Rafael L.

BETANCUR, BELISARIO (1923-). Conservative Colombian politician who served as president from 1982 to 1986. To fight domestic violence, he negotiated truce agreements with three of Colombia's four largest guerrilla groups in 1984; and to deal with drug-trafficking terrorism he implemented for the first time (after his minister of Justice was assassinated by a member of one of the drug cartels [q.v.]) the Colombian-U.S. Extradition Treaty. But these peace efforts failed, and the use of the treaty provoked the M-19 guerrilla movement's seizure of the Palace of Justice in Bogotá in late 1985. The government's fiery retaliation led to the killing of over 100 hostages, including 11 Supreme Court judges. While president, Betancur defended a more active role for Third World (q.v.) countries in the United Nations, and his role in the Central American peace process (q.v.) brought him wide acclaim throughout the hemisphere. *See also* Drug Cartels.

BIG STICK POLICY. U.S. policy using forceful diplomatic measures and occasional landing of military forces to preserve U.S. strategic and economic interests in the Caribbean and Central American regions developed during the presidency of Theodore Roosevelt (q.v.). Roosevelt's philosophy—"speak softly and carry a big stick"—of dealing with Latin American governments he felt were unable (or unwilling) to carry out their obligations of safeguarding American lives and property generated considerable criticism from Latin Americans who perceived the "big stick" as nothing more than a facade for solidifying an informal empire in the Caribbean. Blatant intervention (q.v.) by the United States in the Caribbean region between 1895 and 1930 later contributed to the strongly worded nonintervention principle (q.v.) that is contained in the Charter of the Organization of American States (q.v.). *See also* Intervention and Nonintervention.

BISHOP, MAURICE. *See* Commonwealth Caribbean Leaders.

BLAINE, JAMES GILLESPIE (1830–1893). Politician, presidential aspirant, and two-time secretary of state who played a major role in U.S.-Latin American relations and the role of inter-American organizations during the last two decades of the nineteenth century. He helped to mediate the War of the Pacific (q.v.), stressed his own brand of Pan Americanism, pushed for economic expansion under the Monroe Doctrine (q.v.), and argued strongly that any canal across the isthmus should be built in Panama, but only under U.S. control and domination. As secretary of state in the Garfield administration, Blaine sought to mediate the War of the Pacific by demanding that Chile relinquish territory to Peru, a maneuver that many interpreted as an indication of his bias toward Peru, where he was promoting U.S. economic interests to counter those of Great Britain in Chile. As secretary of state under Benjamin Harrison (1889–1893), Blaine became the prime mover in the first Inter-American Conference held in Washington, D.C. in 1889–1890, a serious effort to establish firmer commercial links with Latin America.

Blaine was known in diplomatic circles for his heavy-handed policies and imperialistic attitude toward Latin America. Dubbed "Jingo Jim" by the press at the time, Blaine possessed a strong aversion to European involvement in the Americas. At one point he told the Colombians that the Clayton-Bulwer Treaty was obsolete and did not apply to Panama after they tried to engineer a new joint treaty for the neutrality of the planned canal. His efforts to further U.S. hegemony in the Western Hemisphere reflected vestiges of Manifest Destiny and the economic imperialism spawned in post-1870 Europe. Many modern historians argue that Blaine merely reflected the chauvinistic and militant foreign policy of the United States that took hold in the 1880s and 1890s and played a positive role in converting the United States from a regional to a world power.

At the first Inter-American Conference held in Washington, D.C. in 1889–1890, Blaine pushed for U.S. expansion and domination of the Western Hemisphere. His planned tour of the major industrial centers of the United States by the conferees and market-oriented approach to the conference, made it clear that Blaine was more interested in the economic well-being of the United States than Pan Americanism. In any case, Blaine's Washington conference is significant because it served as the genesis of the Pan American Union (1910–1948, q.v.) and the eventual establishment of the Organization of American States (q.v.) in 1948.

The Washington conference is also important because it began a period of U.S. domination of Pan American conferences in which meetings were often carefully orchestrated to preclude sensitive "political" topics that might lead to confrontation and enmity. Until the 1930s, the United States preferred to deal with economic, cultural and scientific topics at inter-American meetings. In contrast, the Latin American participants tried to use the conferences as a vehicle for promoting principles of equality, state sovereignty, international law, and nonintervention (q.v.). While Blaine was often criticized at home and abroad for his blatant political opportunism and big business orientation, he does seem to have been a genuine advocate of international peace and Pan Americanism.

Blaine's role in constructing a Latin American policy for the United States expanded the meaning of the Monroe Doctrine at the end of the 19th century. He reinterpreted it as an injunction against any kind of meddling by European powers in the Western Hemisphere, including ownership of strategic resources such as nitrates or an isthmian waterway. Blaine also emphasized the military importance of the Monroe Doctrine in controlling transit across the isthmus, thus converting the Caribbean Basin (q.v.) into an American sphere of influence. Ultimately, he believed that the Monroe Doctrine should preserve the region for U.S. penetration, not simply keep European powers out. In his role as U.S. secretary of state, James Blaine played a pivotal role in the country's Latin American policy, setting the stage for the era of intervention that would commence in the 1890s, and in the formation, evolution, and character of inter-American organizations during the following century.

BOLÍVAR, SIMÓN (1783–1830). Venezuelan Creole aristocrat and politician who played a major role in the liberation of northern South America from Spanish control between 1808 and 1824. After the wars of independence, he pursued efforts to create a permanent defensive alliance among Spanish American nations as a shield against future attacks by European powers. This was to be accomplished through a conference in Panama in 1826. However, in his invitation to the conference, Bolívar made no mention of Monroe's message and only at the last minute agreed to accept two representatives from the United States, one dying en route to the meeting and the other arriving after the conference ended. Although it had sold arms to the rebels and joined ranks with some, Bolívar believed that the United States had contributed little to their victory and its presence at the conference would only antagonize Great Britain.

The Panama Conference of 1826 contained the seeds of future Pan American conferences, but it failed to produce a true Pan American organization or movement since it did not bring all of the Spanish American states and the United States together. Sometimes referred to as the Bolívar Conference, it ultimately reflected the liberator's ambivalence toward the United States—he admired its political institutions in principle but believed they were unsuitable for Latin America—and his deep admiration for the British. In Bolivar's view, the British system of constitutional monarchy was better suited to the Latin American condition (although independent, at the time Brazil was ruled by a monarch) and Great Britain's friendship was a key ingredient for the region's security and future economic development. In the end, the Bolívar Conference revealed both the differing views held by the United States and Latin America and the weak sense of commitment among the new republics to a common approach to defending the Western Hemisphere. By assuming ownership of the Monroe Doctrine (q.v.), and using it as a justification for imperial expansion and control from 1823 until the end of the Cold War (q.v.), the United States weakened Bolívar's dream of unity throughout the hemisphere.

BOLIVIAN REVOLUTION. One of Latin America's most profound social revolutions that marked a watershed in Bolivian history during the 1950s. Led by Víctor Paz Estenssoro's Revolutionary Nationalist Movement (Movimiento Nacional Revolucionario, MNR), composed of Bolivian tin miners, peasants, and displaced members of the middle sectors, the revolution managed to destroy the old order, nationalizing 80 percent of the nation's mining industry, approving a broad agrarian reform program, declaring universal suffrage, and downgrading the old armed forces. Despite the fact that the old power structure was mostly dismantled, the Bolivian revolutionaries were unable to create a viable new order and thus the revolution remained incomplete after 12 years. They were inspired by the social welfare components of the Mexican revolution and its corporatist components of rule that they hoped would lead to the kind of stability and economic growth evident in Mexico since 1940. Using a state-capitalist development strategy after 1960, Bolivia's revolutionaries found that they had to compromise their programs in order to receive funds through President Kennedy's Alliance for Progress (q.v.). Despite suspicions of the political ideology of the MNR leaders and a two-month delay, the United States formally recognized (q.v.) the revolutionary government, but not until it was assured that compensation would be paid for the expropriated mining properties and that the government was not communist.

By committing the government to reimburse for the expropriated mines and assuring the United States that the nationalization program was not aimed at private property or foreign investors, the revolutionary leaders were able to lay the foundation for a close collaboration between the two countries. During the Kennedy years, for example, U.S. military and economic assistance to Bolivia expanded dramatically, due in large part to the threat of communist influence and the close ties between President Paz (then on a second term from 1960 to 1964) and President Kennedy. In a strange twist of events, the Bolivian revolution did not reduce the country's dependence on the United States or U.S. influence in its internal affairs. Bolivian reliance upon U.S. grants and loans, markets, and officials quickly superseded its earlier dependence on the tin mines, mine owners, and British markets. With a revitalized army, General René Barrientos overturned the MNR regime and consolidated power through an arrangement with peasant leaders who promised to remain loyal to the military as long as the generals did not threaten their interests.

After resigning from government posts in Cuba, Latin America's most celebrated revolutionary—Ernesto "Che" Guevara (q.v.), an Argentine by birth—chose Bolivia as a country ripe for a guerrilla takeover in 1965. In 1966, he organized the National Liberation Army (Ejército de Liberación Nacional, ELN), but it failed to recreate Castro's earlier success in the Sierra Maestra mountains of Cuba for three basic reasons: Bolivian peasants were not interested in joining a guerrilla campaign after the land reforms of the MNR; the Bolivian Communist Party was not interested in Guevara's efforts; and the United States mounted a counterinsurgency campaign that involved training and advising the Bolivian Army to track down Guevara's forces in the jungles of eastern Bolivia. In a disastrous campaign doomed to failure, Guevara was captured and executed by the Bolivian army in 1967. *See also* Guevara, Ernesto "Che."

BOSCH, JUAN (1909-). Popular Dominican politician who returned after a 25-year exile and was elected president in 1962 but was overthrown by the military in 1963. Supporters' efforts to recall him from exile resulted in a military coup, civil war, U.S. intervention (q.v.), and Organization of American States (OAS) (q.v.) creation of an Inter-American Peace Force (IAPF) in 1965. As the foremost political opponent of Joaquín Balaguer (q.v.), Bosch returned to compete in the 1966 presidential election but lost to the ex-Trujillista Balaguer by a margin of 18 percent. Throughout the long periods in which Balaquer served as president, Bosch remained his foremost opponent. *See also* Dominican Republic, Collective Sanctions by the OAS; Dominican Republic, Intervention in by the United States and the OAS Peace Force.

BRAZIL. *See* Agency for the Prohibition of Nuclear Weapons in Latin America and the Caribbean (APNWLA); Alliance for Progress; Cardoso, Fernando Henrique; Treaty of Tlatelolco; World War II.

BURNHAM, FORBES (1923–1985). *See* Commonwealth Caribbean Leaders.

BUSH, GEORGE (1924-). Former ambassador to the UN, U.S. Central Intelligence Agency director, vice president (1981–1989), and president (1989–1993) who was widely regarded as an astute foreign policy maker. He worked closely with Colombian President Virgilio Barco (q.v.) to eliminate illicit drug trafficking, including extraditing drug traffickers to the United States for trial and imprisonment. During his first year in office he depoliticized U.S. involvement in Central America, cooperated with Soviet First Secretary Mikhail Gorbachev in the region, and supported the UN Security Council's establishment of the UN Observer Group in Central America (q.v.).

In December 1989, he ordered the invasion of Panama in order to arrest General Manuel A. Noriega (q.v.). The fact that Bush's justification for U.S. intervention (q.v.) contained no mention of communist influence and control in Panama appeared to signal the end of the Cold War (q.v.) as a major component of U.S. Latin American policy. In June 1990, President Bush proposed the Enterprise for the Americas Initiative (EAI, q.v.), a hemisphere-wide free trade area. His efforts to organize a UN coalition of states to end Saddam Hussein's occupation of Kuwait were considered a huge success in the 1991 showdown that brought about a quick withdrawal of Iraqi forces from its neighboring state. Later in 1991, he ordered the U.S. Coast Guard and Navy to pick up Haitian refugees (in Caribbean waters) headed for the U.S. and return them to Haiti. In October 1992, President Bush signed the Cuban Democracy Act (the so-called Torricelli Bill, after Representative Robert Torricelli, (D-NJ, its major sponsor). Bush's involvement in the Iran-Contra affair raised questions as to the veracity of his claim that he was not "in the loop" of decision making, and contributed to his loss to Bill Clinton (q.v.) in the 1992 presidential election. *See also* Barco, Virgilio; Contras; Drug Cartels; Central American/Contadora Peace Process; Noriega, Manuel Antonio; Panama, Intervention in by the United States and the OAS, and Elections.

C

CALVO, CARLOS (1822–1906). Argentine diplomat and jurist recognized for his contributions to international legal theory and the doctrine based on his name. Challenging the position of European states that claimed they had a right to intervene on behalf of their nationals when claims arose over civil wars, revolutions, breaches of contract, and the like, Calvo provided the legal means by which Latin American countries could try to reduce or eliminate threats of intervention (q.v.) in their domestic affairs. Calvo enjoyed a long diplomatic career, mostly in Europe, and had an international reputation for his contributions to the legal aspects of conflict resolution arising out of disputes with foreign corporations or persons for compensation for nationalization. *See also* Calvo Doctrine.

CALVO DOCTRINE or CLAUSE. A principle of international law, upheld by most Latin American countries since 1900, that considers intervention (q.v.) a violation of the principle of equality of sovereign nations and declares that no nation has a right to enforce contracts or agreements between its citizens and those of another. In rejecting claims of special treatment, Calvo argued that all disputes had to be settled in the country of origin and that no company could appeal to its government for assistance. While many Latin American countries have used the Calvo Doctrine in contracts with international corporations, it has been widely rejected outside of Latin America. *See also* Calvo, Carlos.

CARDOSO, FERNANDO HENRIQUE (1931-). As president of Brazil (1995-), Cardoso's professional career and ideas about economic development personify the changes that have occurred during the past 40 years in Latin American thinking about the relationship between economic development and the state. Trained as a sociologist, in the 1960s he was a firm believer in neo-Marxist principles favoring socialism and class conflict, dependency theory, and the "center-periphery" structuralist analysis of Raúl Prebisch (q.v.). He taught at the University of São Paulo, where he had studied sociology until the military coup of 1964. Exiled by the new military government, he did not return to Brazil until 1968. His economic and social views were expressed in a major work (co-authored with Enzo Faletto), *Dependency and Development in Latin America*, published in 1979. Upon his return, he opposed the military, became more politically active, and was elected to the Senate in 1986. He helped to organize the Party of Brazilian Social Democracy. In a rapid upward trajectory, he became foreign minister in 1992, Finance minister in 1993, and president in 1994 (he was inaugurated in January 1995).

As a presidential candidate he disavowed his earlier economic views, by now convinced that a modified capitalist model, with emphasis on monetarist economic policies, privatization, and free trade, was the solution to Brazil's economic woes. President Cardoso was the leader in the formation of the Southern Cone Common Market (MERCOSUR, q.v.) in 1991, and he is pursuing its expansion as either an alternative to the North American Free Trade Agreement (NAFTA, q.v.) or a powerful base for bargaining with the United States over terms for entering or associating with NAFTA. One of the most significant outcomes of this political and economic change in Brazil is that Argentina, once its traditional rival, is working more closely with President Cardoso, the regional pace-setter. *See also* Southern Cone Common Market (MERCOSUR).

CARIBBEAN. A subregional group of states that is also referred to as the Caribbean Basin (q.v.). It includes both the island and insular states in and around the Caribbean Sea; the latter include Mexico, the Central American states (except El Salvador), and the northern South American states. A cultural-political division is also made between the Commonwealth Caribbean States (q.v.), the former dependencies or territories of Great Britain, and the Hispanic, or Latin American, the former colonies of Spain. Haiti, an ex-colony of France, is often placed in the latter category. Suriname is an ex-colony of the Netherlands. Another category includes the dependencies of Britain, France, Holland, and the United States. *See also* Circum-Caribbean.

CARIBBEAN AID COUNCIL. An agency of the government of Trinidad and Tobago that gave various forms of economic aid to Caribbean

Common Market (CARICOM, q.v.) members during the oil boom of the 1970s. It was disbanded in 1984.

CARIBBEAN BASIN. A group of island or insular states and dependencies in or around the Caribbean Sea, including those found in the West Indies, Central America (excluding El Salvador), and parts of northern South America. Also referred to as the Circum-Caribbean (q.v.).

CARIBBEAN BASIN INITIATIVE (CBI). Acting upon a proposal of Jamaican Prime Minister Edward Seaga, U.S. President Ronald Reagan announced the CBI at an Organization of American States (OAS) meeting in February 1982. Although not approved by the U.S. Congress for two years, it provided for 12 years of duty-free access for most U.S. imports from designated beneficiaries. At the outset 20 exporting countries and territories stood to benefit from this preferential treatment of certain goods destined for the U.S. market. When originally proposed by President Reagan, the plan was strongly endorsed by Canada, Mexico, and Venezuela, but they became critical when it was clear that its intent was political, to isolate and pressure the pro-Castro Sandinista government of Nicaragua. The CBI got off to a slow start, but several countries—Dominica, the Dominican Republic, and Jamaica—later benefitted greatly from the preferential trade provisions. Since the original 12-year period, the CBI has been renewed and extended, and the United States has favored its continuation even after the approval and implementation of the North American Free Trade Agreement (NAFTA, q.v.).

CARIBBEAN-CANADIAN COOPERATION AGREEMENT (CARIB-CAN). Formed in 1980 to facilitate Caribbean economic cooperation and trade with Canada, particularly the exportation of the former's labor-intensive products. Under the Caribbean Common Market (CARICOM, q.v.) initiative, CARIBCAN later became mainly a one-way free trade and investment conduit.

CARIBBEAN COMMISSION. A bi-regional body that replaced the Anglo-American Caribbean Commission (AACC, q.v.) in 1946 as a four-member group including France and the Netherlands, both with important Caribbean territories. This commission held regular meetings as the West Indian Conference until 1959 when it ceased to exist; in 1961 it transformed itself into the Caribbean Council. This broadened council including representatives of the European dependencies lasted only until 1965 due to conflicts with the West Indies Federation (WIF).

CARIBBEAN COMMUNITY (CC) and CARIBBEAN COMMON MARKET (CARICOM). A customs union established by the Treaty of Chaguaramas signed in Trinidad and Tobago by the prime ministers of Barbados, Guyana, Jamaica, and Trinidad and Tobago in July 1973. After ratification in August 1974, it replaced the Caribbean Free Trade Association (CARIFTA, q.v.), and by then Belize, Dominica, Grenada, St. Lucia, St. Vincent and the Grenadines, and Montserrat— former members of CARIFTA—had become members. Antigua and Barbuda, the Bahamas (only CC), and St. Kitts and Nevis joined later, bringing the total to 13 Commonwealth Caribbean (CWC) members. Permanent observer status was later given to four non-CWC states— the Dominican Republic, Haiti, Suriname, and Venezuela. The Dominican Republic (1995) and Haiti (1996) have since become members of the CC. The headquarters and secretariat are located in Georgetown, Guyana.

The major organ of CARICOM is the Council, which is composed of a government minister appointed by and representing each member government. The Council has the responsibility for developing, maintaining, and operating CARICOM and for settling all disputes that arise among its members. In the late 1980s an increasing dissatisfaction with CARICOM developed because of the emerging consensus that effective regional integration was the key to survival. In July 1989 this resulted in the heads of government calling for the creation of an independent West Indian Commission (WIC) to evaluate and make recommendations for improving CARICOM in general and for achieving economic integration in particular. The WIC presented a progress report (*Towards a Vision of the Future*) in June 1991, and its final report, *Report of the West Indian Commission: Time for Action*, was presented in July 1992. It recommended the creation of three new organs: a CARICOM Assembly, a CARICOM Supreme Court and a most important CARICOM Commission with new authority to oversee the integration process. However, the governments were unwilling to approve a commission with such authority, fearing this would jeopardize their sovereignty. *See also* West Indies Federation (WIF).

CARIBBEAN COUNCIL. *See* Caribbean Commission; Anglo-American Caribbean Commission.

CARIBBEAN DEVELOPMENT BANK (CDB). The CDB was created by an agreement signed by 16 regional and two nonregional states or dependencies in Kingston, Jamaica, in October 1969. It became effective and held its first meeting in January 1970. The 20 regional members (countries and territories) include the Commonwealth Caribbean

(CWC, q.v.) plus three Latin American nations—Colombia, Mexico, and Venezuela—and five nonregional countries: Canada, France, Germany, Italy, and the United Kingdom. The purpose of the bank is to further the economic cooperation, growth, development, and integration of its members, particularly the less developed ones. The authorized capitalization of the bank in 1995 was $401 million with subscribed capital at $448 million. In addition to its various special accounts (special funds resources and special development fund), the other special funds include contributions from Canada, Nigeria, Trinidad and Tobago, and the United States as well as from the Inter-American Development Bank (IADB, q.v.), International Development Association (IDA), the European Community (EC, q.v.), and the Venezuelan Trust Fund (VTF).

The CDB's policy-making body is the Board of Governors, composed of 21 governors who are representatives of the original members plus Colombia, France, Germany, Italy, Mexico, and Venezuela. The board meets annually. The managing organ is the Board of Directors, made up of 17 members, 12 representing the regional members and 5 representing the nonregional ones. Its headquarters are in St. Michael, Barbados.

CARIBBEAN FREE TRADE ASSOCIATION (CARIFTA). Created three years after the collapse of the West Indies Federation (WIF, q.v.) by an agreement signed in Antigua and Barbuda in December 1965, CARIFTA did not become official until May 1968. All the eventual 12 members were in the Commonwealth and included four independent states (Barbados, Guyana, Jamaica, and Trinidad and Tobago), seven British associated states, and one colony. CARIFTA was committed to achieving a free trade area, a minimum level of cooperation, which it later attained. The Caribbean Development Bank (CDB, q.v.) was established in 1969. The major organ of government is the Council of Ministers, composed of a representative from each member, and the headquarters and Secretariat are located in Georgetown, Guyana.

CARIBBEAN GROUP FOR COOPERATION IN ECONOMIC DEVELOPMENT (CGCED). A multinational aid group established by the World Bank (WB, q.v.) in 1977 for the purpose of bringing together a number of state and international financial institutions to mobilize economic assistance for the area. In 1978, the group created the Caribbean Development Facility to assist with the aid process.

CARIBBEAN LEGION. A conglomerate of armed exile groups from Cuba, the Dominican Republic, Honduras, El Salvador, and Nicaragua founded by José Figueres of Costa Rica to oppose directly Caribbean and Central American dictatorships. It was active from 1946 to 1950. The filibustering expeditions contained distinct leadership and sponsorship but lacked the coherent military force such as the group's name implies. The most prominent expeditions targeted Rafael L. Trujillo's (q.v.) dictatorship in the Dominican Republic, but others participated in the Costa Rican civil war in 1948. Figueres used the Caribbean Legion and heavy support from Guatemala to coordinate the revolution in Costa Rica that removed Teodoro Picado in 1948. The shadow armies of the Caribbean Legion ceased to exist in 1950 after the Organization of American States (OAS, q.v.) established a series of "principles and standards" that served to restrict the activities of political exiles in their efforts to terminate dictatorships in the Caribbean.

CARIBBEAN OIL FACILITY. Formed by the Caribbean Community (CC, q.v.) in 1980 to help its members finance their purchases of oil. *See also* San José Accord or Agreement.

CARTAGENA GROUP. As a mechanism for dealing with the debt crisis of the 1980s, the Cartagena Group emerged in June 1984 to represent most of the Latin American debtor governments. At a meeting in Quito, Ecuador, in early 1984, sponsored by the United Nations Economic Commission on Latin America and the Caribbean (ECLAC, q.v.) and the Latin American Economic System (LAES, q.v.), a solution for the debt problem was presented: reduced debt payments and interest rates, a lengthening of maturities, and elimination of trade barriers. As a result of a tepid response by creditors, 11 Latin American governments formed the Cartagena Group, a formal consultative mechanism, and agreed to meet on a regular basis. The Cartagena Group has also met to discuss matters of regional concern and foreign policy issues. Its members are Argentina, Bolivia, Brazil, Chile, Colombia, the Dominican Republic, Ecuador, Mexico, Peru, Uruguay, and Venezuela.

CARTELS, COMMODITY. *See* Drug Cartels; Appendix VII.

CARTER, JIMMY (1924-). U.S. president (1977–1981) who actively pursued a foreign policy based on the protection of human rights (q.v.). He helped to enact relevant legislation in Congress and used human rights as his foreign policy motif, primarily against dictatorial, military, and nonelected governments in Latin America. He favored an OAS Inter-American Peace Force to deal with the Anastasio Somoza regime in Nicaragua, but the effort to unseat Somoza in this way failed. He was successful in negotiating two new Panama Canal (q.v.) treaties, one providing for Panama to assume complete control of the canal by the year 2000 and the other concerning the neutrality of the canal. Years after leaving office, he helped negotiate the peaceful return of President Aristide (q.v.) to Haiti in 1994. President Carter seems to have enjoyed more public respect for his leadership activities out of office than those when he was president in the 1970s. *See also* Central American/Contadora Peace Process; Human Rights; Nicaragua Revolution; Panama Canal Treaties; Somoza Dynasty/Family.

CASTRO, FIDEL (1926-). A Cuban revolutionary leader and master politician who played a major role in overthrowing the corrupt and repressive government of Fulgencio Batista (q.v.) and successfully pitting the United States and the Soviet Union against each other during the Cold War (q.v.). Driven more by antiimperialist nationalism than Marxist socialism, Castro has managed to survive for almost four decades, while more than eight U.S. presidents have tried to engineer his overthrow. Throughout his career as the dominant political figure in Cuba, Castro has struggled to rid his country of foreign control and reduce the poverty and illiteracy so common in Latin America. Cuba's ostracism by the Organization of American States (OAS, q.v.) during the height of the Cold War and Castro's refusal to comply with OAS requirements to rejoin it have served to undermine efforts to bring greater harmony among the members of the inter-American system. While recent secretaries-general of the OAS have called for Cuba's return to the organization, an initiative supported by many Latin American countries, the United States continues to oppose Cuba's return. *See also* Cuba, Collective Sanctions and Suspension by the OAS.

CENTER FOR LATIN AMERICAN MONETARY STUDIES (CLAMS)/CENTRO DE ESTUDIOS MONETARIOS LATINOAMERICANOS (CEMLA). Proposed at a meeting of Central Bank Technicians in Santiago, Chile, in 1949, CLAMS was formally established in September 1952. It is a teaching and research institute for promoting a better understanding of banking, fiscal, and monetary policies in terms of the general economy of the region and improving the qualifications of personnel in central banks and other financial agencies. Advisers and lecturers for the classes and seminars are provided by a number of international lending agencies (e.g., the Inter-American Development Bank [IADB, q.v.], International Monetary Fund [IMF, q.v.], World Bank [q.v.], European central banks, and the Organization of American States [OAS, q.v.]). Funds come from the

United States Agency for International Development (AID), the IADB, and the IMF, as well as from private foundations.

CLAMS's structure consists of an Assembly of all members, which meets bi-annually, and a Governing Board of five members. The Bank of Mexico has a permanent seat on the latter since its headquarters are in Mexico City. There are 65 members, 30 associate members (the central banks of most Commonwealth Caribbean, including the East Caribbean Community, and the Latin American countries), and 35 collaborating members, including the Economic Commission for Latin America and the Caribbean (ECLAC), the IADB, and international and regional financial institutions; a number of nonhemispheric central banks, mainly in Europe, and a few members in Asia also belong.

CENTRAL AMERICAN BANK FOR ECONOMIC INTEGRATION (CABEI)/BANCO CENTROAMERICANO DE INTEGRACIÓN ECONÓMICA (BCIE). Established by an agreement signed by the governments of El Salvador, Guatemala, Honduras, and Nicaragua at a meeting in Nicaragua in December 1960. Costa Rica became its fifth member in 1963. It began operating in 1961 with the principal goal of implementing the economic integration and balanced economic growth of the member countries. CABEI's resources are directed through four financial funds (ordinary, economic integration, housing and social development), and there is also an independent and separate fund (Common Market). In 1985, the bank formed the Fund for the Economic and Social Development of Central America (FONDESCA), a transitional body to allow countries outside the region to participate in CABEI. The structure consists of the Board of Governors, the highest authority, made up of the minister of Economy and the Central Bank president of each member and the Board of Directors, with an elected (by the Board of Governors) member from each country. The bank is headquartered in Tegucigalpa, Honduras.

CENTRAL AMERICAN COMMON MARKET (CACM)/MERCADO COMÚN CENTROAMERICANO (MCC). The creation of the CACM began with the formation of the Central American Economic Integration Program in August 1952, when five states' ministers organized a Committee for Economic Cooperation of the Central American Isthmus. This led to the General Treaty of Central American Economic Integration, signed by El Salvador, Guatemala, Honduras, and Nicaragua in December 1960; Costa Rica joined in 1962. This treaty became effective in June 1961. It incorporated the 1958 Agreement on the Regime for Central American Integration Industries as well as the 1958 Multilateral Treaty of Central American Free Trade and

Economic Integration and the 1959 Central American Agreement on the Equalization of Import Duties and Charges (plus its Protocol). An agreement was signed in 1964 to establish a Central American Monetary Council (CAMC, q.v.). The three bodies established for administering the CACM were: the Meeting of Ministers Responsible for Central American Economic Integration, to direct and coordinate economic integration, made up of the members' ministers of Economy or of External Commerce; the Forum of Vice-Ministers of Economy, to apply and administer the treaty, composed of a delegate and an alternate from each member; and the Permanent Secretariat (SIECA, Secretaría Permanente del Tratado General de Integración Económica Centroamericana), headed by a secretary-general and located in Guatemala City.

In 1971, the Secretariat started developing a new integration model for the region; a draft treaty (to replace the general treaty) for a Central American Economic and Social Community was presented to the member states' presidents in March 1976. This was followed by the signing in December 1984 of a new Convention on Central American and Customs Regulations, which became effective in September 1985 (the new Central American Tariff System went into effect in January 1993). Later that year an agreement was signed with the European Community (EC, q.v.), providing for economic cooperation and EC assistance. Five years later the five presidents of the CACM countries signed a declaration of support for the peace initiatives in El Salvador, Guatemala, and Honduras. They also appealed for revitalization of the CACM, which had been a casualty of the many years of fighting and strife stemming from the Reagan administration's efforts to bring down the Nicaraguan government and Nicaragua's efforts to assist the FMLN in El Salvador. In early 1992, CACM member governments started discussions with the Caribbean Common Market (CARICOM, q.v.) governments about the formation of a Caribbean and Central American free trade zone.

CENTRAL AMERICAN/CONTADORA PEACE PROCESS. Following Ronald Reagan's (q.v.) election as president of the United States, internal violence and international tensions increased in Central America, particularly between Nicaragua and El Salvador and between the Sandinistas in Nicaragua and the United States. Having replaced the Somoza dictatorship in 1979, the Sandinista government proceeded to aid the efforts of leftist guerrillas (Farabundo Martí National Liberation Front—Frente Farabundo Martí de Liberación Nacional) in neighboring El Salvador. Under the Reagan Doctrine (q.v.), Washington provided large amounts of aid and support for the government of El Salvador, claiming that Nicaragua's "communist" government was responsible for the strife. The growing fear of U.S. intervention (q.v.) in Nicaragua prompted the presidents of four countries—Colombia, Mexico, Panama and Venezuela—to meet in order to decide upon a peace initiative to forestall such interference. They met on the Panamanian island of Contadora in January 1983, constituted themselves as the Contadora Group (CG), and initiated diplomatic negotiations among the Central American states in an effort to work out a settlement and prevent outside intervention. Thus began the Contadora Process, the first phase of the Central American Peace Process, one that was completely outside the Organization of American States (OAS, q.v.). A few years later, however, the OAS and the United Nations would become actively involved. Thereafter, Contadora missions visited various Central American countries while their foreign ministers met to decide how to defuse the Central American crisis; in early September foreign ministers from the Contadora Group countries met to draw up their objectives plan. Meanwhile, the October 1983 U.S. intervention in Grenada (q.v.) increased fears of a similar invasion in Nicaragua.

While the CG actively pursued negotiations and drafted numerous peace treaties from 1983 to1985, the United States, although outwardly supporting the process, carried out covert actions against Nicaragua, mining harbors and organizing an exile military force. By 1984, the Contras were openly operating out of neighboring Honduras. Nicaragua brought these interventionary actions before the UN Security Council in 1982 and 1984, but the United States vetoed critical resolutions. In April 1984, Nicaragua brought a case against the United States before the International Court of Justice (ICJ, q.v.), and it ruled in favor of Nicaragua, against the Reagan administration, in June 1986. To further undermine the Sandinista revolution in Nicaragua, the United States imposed an economic embargo in May 1985; yet all the while Washington continued diplomatic relations with the Sandinista government. Although both the United Nations and the OAS General Assemblies passed resolutions in support of the Contadora Process in 1983 and 1984 respectively, and the CG expanded to include the Support Group (Argentina, Brazil, Peru, and Uruguay) in July 1985, the actions of the United States against Nicaragua and its mishandling of the CG's negotiations and draft treaties undermined the process, resulting in an impasse.

In a major effort to revive the Contadora Process, the Rio Group (q.v.) was formed in December 1986 (composed of the eight foreign ministers of the CG and the SG plus the secretaries-general of the OAS and UN), and its visit with the Central American presidents in January 1987 seemed to offer some promise for an end to the conflict. What really revived the peace process was the February 1987 proposal, opposed by the Reagan administration, by Costa Rican President Oscar Arias (q.v.), accompanied by a major commitment to bring about peace at a meeting in Esquipulas, Guatemala, in August. Thus began the second phase, Esquipulas II or the Esquipulas Process, of the Central American Peace Process.

The key issue of compliance with and verification of the peace process, a preoccupation of the United States all along, was resolved when a new CIAV (Comisión Internacional de Apoyo y Verificación / International Commission of Support and Verification) with both OAS and UN participation was approved in August 1989. By this time the Central American presidents had the backing of the new Bush administration in Washington, which was anxious to get the contentious Central American issue off the foreign policy agenda.

Subsequent meetings led to the Central American presidents requesting that UN Secretary-General Javier Pérez de Cuéllar (q.v.) establish the UN Observer Group in Central America (ONUCA, q.v.). Significantly, the approval by the UN Security Council in November 1989, and the deployment of ONUCA in December, marked the *first* instance of a direct UN presence and involvement in peacemaking and peacekeeping in Latin America. With the major duty of assuring peace accord compliance by all parties (states and national sides) and disarming the Contras, ONUCA was commanded by a Spanish general, had as its major enforcement arm a battalion of Venezuelan paratroopers, and drew up to 255 military observers from a dozen countries. Beginning in April 1990 the CIAV-UN oversaw the disarming of the Contras in Honduras and their repatriation to Nicaragua, while the CIAV-OAS concentrated on their safety and protection in the latter country. The process was greatly facilitated by the fact that Violeta Barrios de Chamorro (q.v.) was elected president—and Sandinista President Daniel Ortega (q.v.) was defeated—in the February 1990 Nicaraguan elections. President Ortega had requested in 1989 that the UN secretary-general provide an election observer group, which was established as the UN Observer Group for the Verification of Elections in Nicaragua (ONUVEN, in Spanish).

The joint OAS-UN model for Nicaragua was revised for bringing about a settlement in El Salvador; established at the end of December 1991, it became an exclusive UN one, known as the UN Observer Group in El Salvador (ONUSAL, Organización Naciones Unidas en El Salvador). The same was applied later to government-guerrilla negotiations to end the civil war in Guatemala—both parties preferring the UN as a mediator rather than other international organizations. *See also* International Court of Justice (ICJ); Nicaragua, Insurrection in of Sandinistas and Collective Sanctions by the OAS; Nicaraguan Revolution; Somoza Dynasty/Family.

CENTRAL AMERICAN COURT OF JUSTICE (CACJ). Constant revolts and turmoil in Central America resulted in a Central American Peace Conference in Washington, D.C., in 1907. The five states from the area signed a Treaty of Peace and Friendship and created the court, which was inaugurated in Cartago, Costa Rica, in May 1908. The five-member court dealt with ten cases before its most difficult and final one—the Bryan-Chamorro Canal Treaty between Nicaragua and the United States. The CACJ decided in favor of Costa Rica and El Salvador in 1917, finding that Nicaragua had violated their rights. Nicaragua had refused to appear before the court, arguing that it lacked jurisdiction, and after the ruling denounced the treaty that had created the court and withdrew its judge in protest. The court became defunct in 1918. A follow-up conference in Washington, D.C., in late 1922 and early 1923 negotiated a number of peaceful settlement accords, one creating a new Central American Tribunal that did not receive the necessary ratifications for approval.

CENTRAL AMERICAN DEFENSE COUNCIL (CADC)/CONSEJO DE DEFENSA CENTROAMERICANO (CONDECA). In 1965 the United States sponsored the establishment of this defense and security body, based on an agreement between defense ministers rather than heads of state, mainly to deal with Cuban-inspired insurgency. Its original members were El Salvador, Guatemala, and Honduras; Costa Rica refused any affiliation, and Panama accepted observer status. The progress in military cooperation made under the leadership of the U.S. Southern Command in Panama was set back by the 1969 Soccer War (q.v.) between Honduras and El Salvador. Panama withdrew in 1968, and Honduras followed in 1973. After the overthrow of Somoza by the Sandinistas in 1979, CONDECA ceased to exist as a multilateral defense and security pact. However, a major attempt was made by the Reagan administration in 1983 to revive it for dealing with the Nicaraguan government. Guatemala, Honduras, and El Salvador were solicited to reestablish the body, but the effort failed. *See also* Security, Changing Concepts of; Somoza Dynasty/Family.

CENTRAL AMERICAN INTEGRATION SYSTEM (CAIS). *See* Organization of Central American States (OCAS).

CENTRAL AMERICAN MONETARY COUNCIL (CAMC)/CONSEJO MONETARIO CENTROAMERICANO (CMC). The council resulted from the Agreement for the Establishment of a Central American Monetary Union, signed in February 1964 and put into effect the following month. The agreement was replaced by another, the Central American Monetary Agreement, in October 1974. The council's purpose was to promote by regular consultation the coordination of credit, exchange, and monetary policies that would lead to a Monetary Union. The members are the presidents of the five Central Banks of Costa Rica, El Salvador, Guatemala, Honduras, and Nicaragua. There is an elected executive secretary who administers the Central American Monetary Stabilization Fund (established in 1970) and the Central American Clearing House (established in 1961). The council's Secretariat is located in San José, Costa Rica, while the Clearing House is headquartered in Tegucigalpa, Honduras.

CENTRAL AMERICAN PARLIAMENT (CAP)/PARLAMENTO CENTROAMERICANO (PARLACEN). An advisory body proposed by Guatemala in 1986 at a Central American peace process (q.v.) presidential summit meeting for the purpose of aiding economic and political integration. The Constituent Treaty of the CAP was signed by the five Central American states in 1987 and began functioning in 1991. As of 1995, Costa Rica had not ratified the treaty, due to reservations concerning its political powers. Representation was designed to transcend nationalist rivalries by having each country's 20 deputies directly elected by popular vote. Former presidents and vicepresidents would serve as ex-officio representatives for five years after leaving office. The parliament is located in Esquipulas, Guatemala, and mainly advises the various institutions involved in Central American integration, especially the Central American Common Market (CACM, q.v.). Although it only possesses advisory and recommendatory powers, it is slowly becoming a useful political forum at the subregional level.

CENTRO DE ESTUDIOS MONETARIOS LATINOAMERICANOS (CEMLA). *See* Center for Latin American Monetary Studies (CLAMS).

CENTRO INTERAMERICANO PARA EL DESARROLLO REGIONAL (CINDER). *See* Inter-American Center for Regional Development (IACRD).

CENTRO LATINOAMERICANO DE ADMINISTRACIÓN PARA EL DESARROLLO (CLAD). *See* Latin American Center for Development Administration.

CHACO WAR (1932–1935). A costly war between Bolivia and Paraguay for possession of an area called the Chaco Boreal, a desolate region bordering the two countries. Both nations had laid claim to the territory since gaining their independence in the 1820s. Despite being fought for seemingly worthless territory, the Chaco War turned out to be the bloodiest war in twentieth-century South America. Having lost its route to the sea in the War of the Pacific (q.v.), Bolivia thought it could secure passage to the Atlantic via the Paraguay River, gain control over vast oil resources (a mistaken belief since little known reserves existed in the region), and redeem its national honor, sullied by losses of territory in past wars. Paraguay sought to maintain sovereignty over territory it had settled and restore its national honor, lost in the Paraguayan War in the 1880s.

Although Paraguay's victory enabled it to keep most of the Chaco area, an outcome mediated and ratified by a commission made up of the United States and five Latin American states, the war had important consequences for both countries. Bolivia's "Chaco generation" of veterans organized peasant leagues, labor unions, and new reformist and revolutionary political parties that helped bring about the 1952 Revolution. Paraguay suffered from continual political instability, a succession of military governments, and setbacks in economic development. Both sides agreed to a cease-fire in 1935, but the war did not formally end until 1938.

CHAMORRO, VIOLETA. *See* Barrios de Chamorro, Violeta.

CHARTER ON THE ECONOMIC RIGHTS AND DUTIES OF STATES (CERDS). First proposed by Mexican President Luis Echeverría in 1972 at the third United Nations Conference on Trade and Development (UNCTAD III), and approved with a United Nations General Assembly resolution in 1974. The resolution dealt with fair terms of trade for developing countries, abolition of International Monetary Fund (IMF, q.v.) conditionality rules for new loans, and a new world currency linked to the price of primary materials. The charter stressed Latin American control over its natural resources, the importance of state sovereignty, and the regulation of foreign investment. The main provisions of the charter were soon recognized as the features called for in the New International Economic Order (NIEO, q.v.), an earlier United Nations General Assembly resolution. Even though the proposal carried by a wide margin, efforts to mandate a code of conduct for foreign investment were opposed by the United States and other industrial powers that preferred a voluntary code. The opposition of developed countries to the request for a mandatory code of conduct contributed to the nullification of the charter itself. *See also* Echeverría, Luis; Group of Seventy-Seven (G-77).

CHICAGO BOYS or SCHOOL/*LOS* CHICAGO BOYS. A collection of free-market economists, trained at the University of Chicago and strongly influenced by the monetarist economic policies of Milton Friedman and Arnold Harberger (q.v.), who advised the Pinochet (q.v.) dictatorship on economic reform measures between 1975 and the mid-1980s. Stressing orthodox monetarist policies, these young technocrats challenged the structuralist/import substitution industrialization (q.v.) model of economic growth popular in Latin America since the 1950s and helped to substitute a free market approach with restrictions on the money supply, reduction of the size of the public sector, minimal state intervention (q.v.) in the economy, and the encouragement of foreign investment. These economic policies brought inflation under control and contributed to high rates of economic growth, but at a price: unemployment, the increasing misery of the poorer sectors of society, and the concentration of economic assets in the hands of a few. Through the instruction of Professor Harberger at the University of Chicago and later at the University of California, Los Angeles, the ideas of economic reform first introduced in Chile have spread through the ranks of technically skilled policymakers throughout the region. *See also* Harberger, Arnold; Pinochet Ugarte, Augusto; Prebisch, Raúl.

CHILE. *See* Allende, Salvador; Chicago Boys; Cold War; Pinochet Ugarte, Augusto.

CIRCUM-CARIBBEAN. A group of states and dependencies located in and on the Caribbean Sea. *See also* Caribbean; Caribbean Basin.

CLINTON, WILLIAM J. (1946-). Bill Clinton (as he prefers to be called) defeated George Bush (q.v.) for the presidency of the United States in 1992 by stressing domestic themes such as the state of the economy, and criticizing Bush for devoting too much time to foreign policy. As the first U.S. president to be elected after the Cold War (q.v.), Clinton devoted little time and energy to foreign affairs. During his first term (1993–1997), however, he emphasized the "enlargement" of the world of democracy and free markets, foreign policy themes that largely ignored the prior emphasis on national security. Clinton's relations with Latin America involved mainly four countries—Haiti, Mexico, Colombia, and Cuba—where, with the exception of Mexico, he was forced to respond to crises that many critics claimed contained no danger to vital U.S. interests in the region.

In dealing with Haiti, President Clinton faced the unpleasant task of deciding what to do about thousands of refugees who left in rickety boats in the aftermath of a military coup, and the fate of controversial President Jean-Bertrand Aristide (q.v.) who had fled into exile in the United States. During the 1992 presidential campaign, Clinton criticized President Bush's policy of picking up Haitian refugees at sea and forcibly returning them to the ravages of a harsh dictatorship. However, before Clinton was inaugurated, he reversed himself and announced that he would pursue the same policy then in effect. During his first two years in office he strongly favored the return of overthrown Haitian President Aristide, and played a major role in the 1992–1994 OAS (q.v.) and United Nations economic sanctions (q.v.) against the military government. To bring closure to the Haitian crisis, Clinton requested UN Security Council approval for a multilateral military force, led by the United States, to intervene in Haiti to force the removal of the recalcitrant military regime. A force of 21,000 U.S. troops landed in September 1994 after ex-President Jimmy Carter had negotiated the military leaders' resignation and departure. Shortly thereafter, Aristide returned to Haiti to resume his duties as constitutional president.

In neighboring Mexico, President Clinton's decisions on controversial issues such as trade, financial difficulties, immigration, and drug trafficking, differed little from past Republican administrations. Clinton strongly supported the creation of NAFTA (q.v.) and lobbied hard for its passage in Congress, and displayed positive views of Mexican economic reforms, while remaining quiet on questions of democracy, human rights, and corruption (qq.v.). When the Mexican peso crisis developed in December 1994, the Clinton administration took the initiative and arranged a joint U.S.-IMF credit and loan package of $50 billion to alleviate the financial pain. After evidence of rampant drug-related corruption inside the Mexican government, Clinton faced the tough choice of having to decertify Mexico because of an inadequate commitment to the drug war. Although he opposed the decertification of Mexico, he was in favor of decertifying Colombia. In dealing with Colombia's President Ernesto Samper (q.v.), alleged to have accepted $6 million in campaign funds from the Cali drug cartel (q.v.), Clinton faced fewer obstacles at home in formulating a response than in Mexico.

Clinton's own interests and agenda contributed to his policies toward Cuba. Although a "moderate" on the U.S. trade embargo against Fidel Castro (q.v.), Clinton decided to take a hard-line position in the wake of the crisis provoked in February 1996 when Castro's air force shot down two small civilian planes piloted by Cuban-American members of "Brothers to the Rescue," an exile group in Miami. After the deaths of several Cuban-American pilots in the affair, he approved the Cuban Liberty and Democratic Solidarity Act (also known as the Helms-Burton Act, after Senator Jesse Helms, R-NC, and Representative Dan Burton, R-Ind.), which permitted legal suits by Cuban-Americans against foreign companies engaged in the use of their former property on the island. However, Clinton has bargained successfully for a presidential waiver clause of this most controversial aspect of the legislation, refusing since his reelection in 1996 to implement the part of the law permitting such suits.

In an effort to further improve U.S.-Latin American relations, Bill Clinton has engaged in hemispheric summitry and reversed previous U.S. restraints on the sale of military equipment to governments in the region. For example, he hosted, and was a strong supporter of the Summit of Americas meetings in Miami, Florida in December 1994 and made his first trip to Latin America early in his second term, a visit that enabled him to herald his democracy promotion and trade initiatives. In August 1997, he announced that he was ending ex-President Carter's 1978 ban on sale of advanced U.S. fighter aircraft to Latin America, a move critics claim will divert scarce economic resources from poverty programs and revive tensions between countries where calm had once prevailed. *See also* Aristide, Jean-Bertrand; Bush, George; Cuba, Collective Sanctions and Suspension by the OAS; Cuba, Intervention in by the United States; Cuban Revolution; Drug Cartels; Economic Sanctions; Haiti, Sanctions by the OAS and the UN, Military Intervention by a UN Force; North American Free Trade Agreement (NAFTA); Salinas de Gortari, Carlos; Samper, Ernesto; Summit of the Americas.

COLD WAR. A critical period of world history from 1947 to 1990, marked by intense ideological, political, and economic hostility between the United States and the Soviet Union, that had a major impact on U.S.-Latin American relations and the inter-American system. The Cold War contributed to numerous forms of U.S. intervention (q.v.) in the internal and external affairs of Latin American and Caribbean countries, including the overthrow of Guatemalan President Jacobo Arbenz Guzmán (1954), the Bay of Pigs invasion (1961), the Dominican intervention (1965, q.v.), the Contra (q.v.) war against the Sandinista government of Nicaragua (1981–1989), and the Grenada invasion (q.v.) (1983). Inside Latin America, the Cold War contributed to the perpetuation of several dictatorships, military takeovers, massive human rights (q.v.) violations against opposition forces, and the expanded power of the military, all as a bulwark against communism. Military campaigns against political opposition forces in Argentina, Chile, El Salvador, Guatemala, and Uruguay, led to the formation of death squads, disappearances of purported "enemies" of the government, and the deterioration of democratic principles.

The Cold War served as the catalyst for the political hostility between the United States and Cuba over the pace and direction of the Cuban Revolution (q.v.). The Cuban Missile Crisis of October 1962 (q.v.), a direct result of the Bay of Pigs invasion and the growing struggle between Kennedy and Khrushchev over Cuba, raised the possibility of nuclear war between the super powers, although this was narrowly averted by compromises between Washington and Moscow on the status of Cuba. Paradoxically, the United States continues its "cold war" hostility toward Cuba despite the collapse of the Soviet Union, the termination of huge Soviet subsidies to Castro's government, the end of support for left-wing guerrillas in Central and South America, and the withdrawal of Cuban troops from parts of Africa. The Cold War generated a heightened concern for security among U.S. policymakers in Washington, which in turn led to the commitment of large amounts of economic and military aid to allies in Latin America and the Caribbean beginning in the early 1950s.

The United States spent $13.4 trillion (in 1997 dollars) to wage the Cold War between 1948 and 1991, costs that many analysts consider higher than necessary with negative consequences throughout the world. A small amount of this total was spent to counter the Soviet-Cuban "threat" in the Western Hemisphere, but Latin Americans did not benefit from the Cold War, even though they sometimes supported anticommunist initiatives in exchange for U.S. economic and military largesse. For example, the Soviet-American rivalry exacerbated ideological and political intolerance in the region, often leading to massive human rights (q.v.) violations and hundreds of thousands of civilian deaths, and neglect of serious internal problems such as poverty, environmental degradation, corruption (q.v.), and the weakening of democratic institutions and processes through the support of "friendly" dictators. The Cold War also served to undermine the legitimacy of the Organization of American States (OAS, q.v.) as a mechanism for resolving disputes and advancing the economic and social development of Latin America and the Caribbean. During the Cold War, the United States converted the OAS into an anticommunist alliance against Cuba and the Dominican Republic by emphasizing the primacy of the OAS (an organization over which it had considerable clout) over the United Nations in dealing with regional disputes. The Cold War with its emphasis on anticommunism affected every aspect of inter-American relations, dictating political and security policy, influencing the distribution of economic assistance and multilateral aid programs, and shaping the agenda of inter-American conferences. The Cold War undermined the years of good will and trust between Latin America and the United States that was fostered by "good neighbor" policies from 1925 to 1950.

COLLECTIVE SECURITY. *See* Organization of American States (4a); Regional Security System (RSS); Security, Changing Concepts of.

COLOMBIA. *See* Barco, Virgilio; Betancur, Belisario; Clinton, William J.; Drug Cartels; Gaviria Trujillo, César; Korean War.

COMISIÓN ANDINA DE JURISTAS (CAJ). *See* Andean Commission of Jurists.

COMISIÓN ECONÓMICA PARA AMÉRICA LATINA Y EL CARIBE (CEPAL). *See* Economic Commission for Latin America and the Caribbean (ECLAC); Prebisch, Raúl.

COMISIÓN ESPECIAL DE COORDINACIÓN LATINOAMERICANA (CECLA). *See* Special Committee on Latin American Coordination (SCLAC).

COMISIÓN INTERAMERICANA PARA EL CONTROL DEL ABUSO DE DROGAS (CICAD). *See* Inter-American Drug Abuse Control Commission (IADACC).

COMISIÓN INTERAMERICANA DE PAZ (CIP). *See* Inter-American Peace Committee (IAPC).

COMISIÓN DE PESCA CONTINENTAL PARA AMÉRICA LATINA (COPESCAL). *See* Commission for Inland Fisheries of Latin America (CIFLA).

COMITÉ INTERGUBERNAMENTAL DE LOS PAÍSES COORDINADOR DE LA CUENCA DEL PLATA. *See* Intergovernmental Committee on the River Plate Basin.

COMMISSION FOR INLAND FISHERIES OF LATIN AMERICA (CIFLA)/COMISIÓN DE PESCA CONTINENTAL PARA AMÉRICA LATINA (COPESCAL). Twenty-member body, consisting of governmental authorities from Latin American and Caribbean countries, created to promote the efficient utilization of inland fishery resources in 1976. Its major functions center on aquacultural activities and the formulation of scientific bases for fishery production and regulation.

COMMON MARKETS. *See* Andean Group (AG); Caribbean Community (CC) and Caribbean Common Market (CARICOM); Central American Common Market (CACM); Eastern Caribbean Common Market (ECCM); Southern Cone Common Market (MERCOSUR).

COMMONWEALTH CARIBBEAN LEADERS. A generation of leaders (two in the case of Norman and Michael Manley, father and son respectively, of Jamaica), mostly trained in Britain, who exercised decisive leadership roles in the independence and development of their new countries. They were independent, dynamic, and strong-willed men with socialist, anticapitalist, and anti-imperialist beliefs who were friends of Fidel Castro (q.v.) and supported the Cuban Revolution (q.v.). Each stressed the sovereign right of his country to pursue its own development and foreign policies. These leaders aspired to Third World (q.v.) leadership both globally—they were active in the North-South struggle—and regionally, particularly in the Caribbean. As personal friends they worked together (with the exception of Forbes Burnham of Guyana) on issues of major concern to the Caribbean area. However, their domestic development models resulted in major difficulties with the International Monetary Fund (IMF, q.v.), and their foreign policies during the Cold War (q.v.) produced serious problems with the United States.

The four most important of these leaders of this period were Maurice Bishop of Grenada (q.v.), Forbes Burnham of Guyana, Michael Manley of Jamaica, and Eric Williams of Trinidad and Tobago. Both Burnham and Manley were educated in London: the former at London University, the latter at the London School of Economics. Manley's early career as a journalist and newspaper editor, and later as a trade union organizer, played a key role in his success as a Caribbean politician. Before Guyana became independent in 1966, the British and the United States intervened on behalf of Burnham and his party to assure that communist dentist Cheddi Jagan would not retain power. From 1964 to 1970 Prime Minister Burnham maintained good relations with the two countries, but in 1970 he declared Guyana to be a Cooperative Socialist State. Washington and London were further angered by his blatantly favorable relations with the revolutionary governments in Cuba, Nicaragua, and Grenada (until Bishop was killed in 1983). Burnham's one-party system and foreign policy reversals were the main reasons he encountered hostility from the United States in addition to criticism in Guyana. Burnham died in 1985, and his People's National Congress Party was voted out of power in 1992 during the country's first democratic election in 28 years. After winning the presidency in 1992, Cheddi Jagan proved to be more mellow and less ideological in his efforts to reform the Guyanese economy. He died in Washington, D.C., after suffering a heart attack in 1997. Manley returned to office in 1988 as a moderate but soon resigned for reasons of ill health. He died in Kingston, Jamaica in 1997 after suffering from prostate cancer.

Eric Williams provides the best example of a West Indian scholar-politician, for he was trained as a historian at Oxford University and taught at Howard University in Washington, D.C., before joining the Caribbean Commission (q.v.). He later resigned from the commission and entered politics by founding and leading a political party (the People's National Movement). While prime minister of Trinidad and Tobago from independence (1962) until his death in 1981, he pursued a nonalignment policy and had close relations with Cuba. Williams was also a strong opponent of the Organization of Eastern Caribbean States, (OECS, q.v.) invitation to the Reagan administration to invade Grenada in 1983.

COMMONWEALTH OF NATIONS. An association of the United Kingdom and around 30 states that once were British colonies, reflecting the British legal and political system. Economic and political cooperation and other ties are still maintained although most of the former colonies have become independent. In 1967, "Associated States" formed among those in the Caribbean. Another group is the "Dependencies." A number of the "dependencies" such as Jamaica and Trinidad and Tobago began gaining their independence in the early 1960s. There are now a total of 13 independent Commonwealth Caribbean states (CWC).

CONSEIL INTERGOUVERNEMENTAL DES PAYS EXPORTA-TEURS DE CUIVRE (CIPEC). *See* Intergovernmental Council of Copper Countries (ICCEC).

CONSEJO DE DEFENSA CENTROAMERICANO (CONDECA). *See* Central American Defense Council (CADC).

CONSEJO MONETARIO CENTROAMERICANO (CMC). *See* Central American Monetary Council (CAMC).

CONTADORA GROUP (CG) and CONTADORA PEACE PROCESS. *See* Central American/Contadora Peace Process.

CONTRAS. Counterrevolutionaries or *contra-revolucionarios* made up mostly of Nicaraguan exiles whose primary aim was to overthrow the Sandinistas. The Reagan administration organized and equipped the group, one that operated mostly out of neighboring Honduras, as its major instrument for bringing down that government. The Iran-Contra affair stemmed from revelations in 1986 that the Reagan administration was engaged in the illegal diversion of "profits" from the clandestine sale of arms to Iran in order to maintain support for what President Reagan called "freedom fighters." Although the Contra war failed militarily, it inflicted great pain on Nicaragua, destroying sections of the nation's infrastructure along with over 30,000 deaths before the conflict ended. The Contras became part of the peace process negotiations in 1988 and were finally disarmed and repatriated in 1990. The economic tragedy stimulated much of the domestic discontent in Nicaragua that led to the Sandinista defeat in the February 1990 elections. *See also* Central American/Contadora Peace Process; Nicaraguan Revolution; Reagan Doctrine.

COOPÉRATION ECONOMIQUE ASIE-PACIFIQUE (CEAP). *See* Asia-Pacific Economic Cooperation (APEC).

CORRUPTION. The historic depth of bribery, illegal enrichment, and improper inducements to public officials in the Americas has led to recent concerted efforts by inter-American organizations to deal more forthrightly with the problem of corruption. Although a slippery term that carries multiple definitions and interpretations in public life, there is now a universal sense that flagrant abuse of the public trust in the pursuit of illicit goals or private gain undermines the legitimacy of democratic systems, fosters disrespect for the judicial process, and constitutes the loss of significant sums of money for corporations and governments when contracts are lost due to the nonpayment of bribes. For almost 20 years the United States has been the only country to prohibit its corporations from bribing foreign officials to win contracts. This is now changing with growing international concern about corrupt practices among public officials that have come to light in the wake of scandals that have forced some politicians from office and sent others to jail. Arrogant and ostentatious corruption at the highest level contributed to the removal from office of Brazil's Fernando Collor in 1992, Venezuela's Carlos Andrés Pérez in 1993, and Ecuador's Abdalá Bucarám in 1997. The end of the Cold War (q.v.) and the spread of free-market economics and common markets have made government decisions more transparent, thereby increasing accountability and fostering less tolerance for corrupt practices.

In recent months, the Organization of American States (OAS, q.v.), international lending agencies such as the World Bank (q.v.) and International Monetary Fund (IMF, q.v.), and the 28 democracies in the Organization for Economic Cooperation and Development (OECD) have all taken steps to curb corruption. The OAS now has a convention outlawing cross-border bribery and "illicit enrichment" of public officials in the hemisphere that has been signed by 23 of its 34 participating members, including the United States. The Inter-American Convention Against Corruption, adopted in Caracas, Venezuela, in 1996, is designed to help in the investigation of bribery charges and the expedition of extradition procedures among the member states. The world's first international legal instrument to combat corruption in the hemisphere entered into force on March 7, 1997, after Paraguay and Bolivia ratified the Convention (only two countries need to ratify the agreement for it to become binding on all signatories).

The World Bank, which in 1995 disbursed $19 billion in development loans, has instituted procedural rules that empower it to investigate corruption cases and to blacklist corporations and governments found guilty of large-scale graft. The International Monetary Fund has made "tackling corruption" a top priority, authorizing its managing director to press for anticorruption reforms in borrowing countries. The Inter-American Development Bank (IADB, q.v.) has been a strong backer of the OAS's convention to fight bribery and corruption. In May 1997, the 29-nation Organization for Economic Cooperation and Development agreed to outlaw the bribery of foreign officials by the end of 1998. The OECD anti-bribery pact represents the first global accord making it a crime to engage in bribery to obtain lucrative contracts that have become the focus of intense competition among governments and multinational corporations.

Corruption can exist in all types of governments, and it has not disappeared with the spread of democracy in the Americas and elsewhere. In fact, democratic rule has created new incentives for corruption, as increased political competition often leads to the need for higher and higher levels of campaign contributions. *See also* Batista, Fulgencio; Cuban Revolution; Democracy; Drug Cartels; International Monetary Fund (IMF); Organization of American States (OAS); Pérez, Carlos Andrés.

COUNCIL ON MUTUAL ECONOMIC ASSISTANCE (COMECON). Originally established in 1949, COMECON was designed as a trade arrangement to increase economic activity within the Soviet bloc after Moscow forced its East European satellites to forgo Marshall Plan aid. Soviet clients such as Cuba and Vietnam, among others, became associated with COMECOM later (Cuba joined in 1974), but it collapsed with the Soviet Union in 1990 and ceased to exist in 1991.

CUBA. *See* Batista, Fulgencio; Castro, Fidel; Cold War; Cuba, Collective Sanctions and Suspension by the OAS; Cuba, Intervention by the United States; Cuba, Missile Crisis with the United States; Cuban Revolution.

CUBA, COLLECTIVE SANCTIONS AND SUSPENSION BY THE OAS. The Eighth Meeting of Foreign Ministers met on the basis of the Rio Treaty in Punta del Este, Uruguay, in January 1962 to consider Cuba's changing foreign relations and political activities. The states that favored suspension and sanctions stressed its "transformation" in terms of economic and military dependence on the Soviet Union, human rights (q.v.) violations, and subversion—all contrary to legal and political principles of the Inter-American System (IAS, q.v.). By barely the required two-thirds vote, resolutions were passed excluding Cuba from further participation in the Organization of American States (OAS, q.v.) in general and the Inter-American Defense Board (IADB, q.v.) in particular, thus suspending the sale of arms and military equipment to the island. The Organ of Consultation met again to consider Cuba in 1964, after Cuban arms and a plan for revolution were found in Venezuela in late 1963.

This attempt to export revolution—a violation of the nonintervention (q.v.) principle—was corroborated, and the Ninth Meeting of Foreign Ministers met under the Rio Treaty in Washington, D.C., in July 1964. Additional sanctions—legally binding on only those states that had signed the Rio Treaty—were approved against Cuba: breaking off diplomatic and consular relations, suspending most commercial trade, and ending most sea transportation with the island. Continued Cuban subversion in Latin America prompted another Meeting of Ministers, the 12th, convening in Washington, D.C., during the summer of 1967. The earlier sanctions were reaffirmed and strengthened. An increasing number of Latin American governments—some leftist, e.g., that of Salvador Allende (q.v.) in Chile and those in Ecuador, Peru, and Panama—became part of a movement over the next few years to lift the mandatory sanctions. Mexico, however, has never complied with nor accepted the sanctions as legally binding. The movement was eventually successful at the 16th Meeting of Ministers in San José, Costa Rica, in July 1975, when the "Freedom of Action" resolution was passed. Thereafter, most states reestablished relations with Cuba; the United States, however, remained the principal exception. *See also* Cuba, Intervention in by the United States; Cuban Revolution.

CUBA, INTERVENTION IN BY THE UNITED STATES. The steady deterioration in Cuban-U.S. relations following Fidel Castro's (q.v.) coming to power in January 1959, which included Cuban nationalization of the property of U.S. citizens and companies, a U.S. embargo on its exports to Cuba, and closer ties between Cuba and the Soviet Union resulted in President Dwight Eisenhower approving a plan for a Central Intelligence Agency (CIA)-organized Cuban exile invasion force. Newly elected President John F. Kennedy ordered the invasion to go forward, despite the overwhelming support for Castro inside

Cuba. The Cuban Brigade, created by the CIA and trained in Guatemala, left from Nicaragua in April 1961, headed for imminent disaster for both the members of the Cuban Brigade and the Kennedy administration. The defeat and capture of most members of the brigade at the Bay of Pigs (Bahía de Cochinos) boosted Castro's political legitimacy, pushed Cuba closer to the Soviet Union, and set the stage for the 1962 Missile Crisis between the United States and the Soviet Union. Of the 1,453 brigade members, 114 were killed and more than 1,100 were captured by Castro's superior forces. The brigade prisoners were released in December 1962 in exchange for medical supplies sent by the United States. *See also* Castro, Fidel; Cuba, Missile Crisis with the United States; Cuban Revolution; Cold War.

CUBA, MISSILE CRISIS WITH THE UNITED STATES. A two-week crisis that developed in October 1962 when U.S. spy planes discovered Soviet nuclear missile launching pads under construction in Cuba. President Kennedy announced their discovery in a dramatic television address on October 22, 1962, stating that the situation "constitutes an explicit threat to the peace and security of all the Americas, in flagrant and deliberate defiance of the Rio Pact of 1947, the traditions of this Nation and Hemisphere, . . . [and] the Charter of the United Nations." In response, Kennedy imposed a "strict quarantine on all offensive military equipment to Cuba," demanded the removal of the Soviet missiles, called for an immediate meeting of the OAS Organ of Consultation (q.v., 4a) and an emergency session of the UN Security Council (q.v.). By the time of the Missile Crisis, Cuban participation in the OAS (q.v.) had already been suspended by an Organ of Consultation meeting in Uruguay in January 1962. The OAS Council met the next afternoon, acting provisionally as the Organ of Consultation under the Inter-American Treaty of Reciprocal Assistance (IATRA), or Rio Treaty. After the security threat presentation of the United States, the OAS unanimously passed a resolution calling for the withdrawal from Cuba of all missiles, prevention of the shipment of weapons to Cuba, support for the "quarantine" plan of the United States, and the informing of the UN Security Council of the action taken by the OAS. That evening President Kennedy approved an order on "Interdiction of the Delivery of Offensive Weapons to Cuba," which would go into effect the next afternoon against "prohibited material" and would be enforced by the secretary of defense.

The "offensive quarantine" was applied against incoming ships as announced, and the United States presented its case in the UN. Although the UN approved a plan whereby the UN secretary-general would appoint a verification group to witness the missile withdrawal,

Castro (q.v.) rejected the plan. The result was a successful bilateral withdrawal agreement between the two superpowers, and the U.S. naval "quarantine" ended on November 20. However, the Soviets required an exchange in which the United States pledged not to invade Cuba and to remove secretly comparable missiles from bases in Turkey within six months. The showdown in October 1962 raised international concerns over the possibility of nuclear war and the importance of dealing with the nuclear arms race driven by the Cold War (q.v.). United States policymakers remained convinced of the necessity of getting rid of Fidel Castro through clandestine means, including sabotage and assassination. *See also* Cold War.

CUBAN REVOLUTION. Major event in Cuban history and U.S.-Cuban relations that produced a dramatic effect on U.S.-Latin American relations, the Cold War (q.v.), the Inter-American System (IAS, q.v.), and the effectiveness of inter-American organizations such as the Organization of American States (OAS, q.v.). Led by Fidel Castro (q.v.) and his 26th of July Movement, the Cuban revolution first overthrew the Batista (q.v.) dictatorship on January 1, 1959, and proceeded to initiate radical programs designed to achieve the goals of nationalization and economic independence from the United States, a dream of many Cubans reaching back to the Ten Years' War almost a century earlier. Initially a nationalist revolt against foreign domination and domestic corruption (q.v.), the Cuban Revolution gradually became more radical and adopted a Cuban variant of communist ideology as part of its program for a new Cuba free from the strangling tentacles of U.S. imperialism.

The lasting power of Fidel Castro and the degree of success of the Cuban Revolution is still a subject of intense debate, but many attribute Castro's political longevity to his early alignment of Cuba with the Soviet Union, endorsement of a clever blend of communist and nationalist ideology, a social welfare system that has produced a relatively high quality of life despite the lack of political freedom, decades of counterproductive U.S. hostility toward the revolution, and the good fortune of being able to export the counterrevolution to the United States, only 90 miles away. Since the end of the Cold War in 1990, Castro has struggled to adapt the Cuban political and economic system to declining Soviet subsidies, the need for foreign investment, and greater hostility from the United States (largely the result of the powerful Cuban lobby in key electoral states such as Florida, New Jersey, and New York). Nevertheless, the odds seem to be in Castro's favor that he will celebrate the 40th anniversary of the Cuban Revolution on January 1, 1999, a remarkable feat of survival for any revolutionary leader.

CUSTOMS UNIONS. *See* Andean Pact; Caribbean Community (CC) and Common Market (CARICOM); Central American Common Market (CACM); Southern Cone Common Market (MERCOSUR).

D

DECLARATION OF CARACAS, 1954. Controversial anticommunist resolution that passed at the 10th Inter-American Conference of the Organization of American States (OAS, q.v.), in Caracas, Venezuela, in March 1954. Worried about the communists in the elected government of Jacobo Arbenz Guzmán in Guatemala, U.S. Secretary of State John Foster Dulles managed to overcome Latin American resistance to such a blatant political maneuver by passing the resolution with 17 in favor, one against (Guatemala), and two abstentions (Mexico and Argentina). Three months later Washington engineered the covert overthrow of Arbenz, one of the major events of the Cold War (q.v.) that served to put an end to the Good Neighbor Policy (q.v.) and would later become a model of future CIA covert interventions in the Western Hemisphere. *See also* Cold War; Organization of American States (OAS, 4a).

DECLARATION OF LIMA, 1938. Statement resulting from the Eighth International Conference of American States held in Lima, Peru, creating the mechanism for meetings of consultation of ministers of Foreign Affairs. These intermittent and sporadic meetings were changed to annual meetings of the General Assembly of the Organization of American States (OAS, q.v.) after 1970, in accordance with the 1967 revision of the OAS Charter. *See also* Inter-American Security System (IASS); Regional Security System (RSS); Security, Changing Concepts of; World War II.

DECLARATION OF LIMA, 1954. *See* United Nations, Third Conference on the Law of the Sea (UNCLOS III).

DECLARATION OF PUNTA DEL ESTE, 1962. Product of the Eighth meeting of OAS foreign ministers in Punta del Este, Uruguay, designed to resolve the diverging policies of OAS members toward the Cuban government headed by Fidel Castro (q.v.). While the meeting did result in a general statement sharply refuting the compatibility of Marxism-Leninism with the Inter-American System (q.v.) and specific proposals excluding the Cuban government from participation in the OAS and the sale of arms to Cuba, the Punta del Este Declaration did illustrate the difficulty of achieving some form of collective security among the increasingly dissimilar members of the OAS. *See also* Cold War; Cuba, Collective Sanctions and Suspension by the OAS; Inter-American Security System (IASS); Regional Security System (RSS).

DECLARATION OF SANTIAGO, 1952. *See* United Nations, Third Conference on the Law of the Sea (UNCLOS III).

DECLARATION OF SANTIAGO, 1991. *See* Haiti, Sanctions by the OAS and the UN, Military Intervention by a UN Force.

DECLARATION OF VIÑA DEL MAR. Document signed at the sixth Ibero-American Summit (Chile, November 10–11, 1996), by Fidel Castro Ruz and 20 other Latin American heads of state. The declaration details a major public consensus on democracy and the importance of political change in the hemisphere and identifies the regional framework governing Cuba's attempt at international reinsertion. One of its three parts, "Governability for an Effective and Participatory Democracy," lays out principles and ideals that clash with traditional forms of state socialism and authoritarianism in Cuba. In reaction to economic liberalization ideology, the declaration calls for measures to strengthen small and medium businesses in order to address the problems of the poor in Latin America. The Helms-Burton Act receives harsh criticism: the declaration claims it violates the norms and principles of international law, the United Nations Charter, the World Trade Organization, and the spirit of cooperation and friendship that should govern the international community. Future summits are scheduled for Venezuela (1997), Portugal (1998), and Cuba (1999). *See also* Democracy; World Trade Organization.

DEMOCRACY. Inter-American organizations have always been concerned with the theory and practice of democratic government: a system in which popular sovereignty allows individuals to rule through their elected representatives. Although the meaning and interpretation of democratic rule is not uniform throughout the Americas, principles such as individualism, civil liberties, freedom, and equality have gained in importance, as have procedural principles like competitive and free elections, majority rule, tolerance and acceptance of opposition groups, constitutional protections of individual rights, and limits on the exercise of political power. Yet the ideals of liberal democracy have never been adequately matched with the practice of governing in the region. Because of a history of civil wars, brutal dictatorships, military interventions, human rights violations, and gross economic and social inequalities, forging a democratic system in Latin America has been a slow and tortuous process.

When the OAS Charter was drafted and approved at the Bogotá meeting in 1948, it included among its principles the "effective exercise of representative democracy"; however, it was often subordinated to that of "national sovereignty" and the nonintervention principle (q.v.) (Article 15). At that time, when the majority of Latin American governments were under military control, the prevailing view in the Organization of American States (OAS, q.v.) was that collective action to promote representative democracy would violate the important concept of nonintervention. It was not until 1960 that the OAS acted for the first time as an "antidictator alliance" when it sought to apply collective sanctions to force the removal of Dominican dictator Rafael L.Trujillo (q.v.). It took over 20 years before the OAS began to assign a high priority to and was willing to consider collective measures to promote democracy, and this coincided with the beginning of a transition to democracy in the Americas in the early 1980s, beginning with Ecuador (1979), Peru (1980), Argentina (1983), and Brazil (1984). The emphasis on democracy was made apparent at the 1991 OAS General Assembly meeting in Chile when the Santiago Commitment to Democracy Declaration was approved, giving the secretary-general authority to call a meeting to consider appropriate countermeasures if a democratically elected government was overthrown in the region. The first application was against Haiti's military *junta* in 1991, resulting in OAS approval of economic sanctions. Another example of this new priority was the 1993 creation of the Unit for the Promotion of Democracy (see "Organization of American States," 4b).

Since the late 1960s, the OAS has been regularly concerned with democratic procedures and has been monitoring and observing elections. OAS election observers have been to El Salvador, Haiti, Nicaragua, and Paraguay, among others, to oversee the propriety of democratic norms and procedures. More recently, members of the OAS have realized that economic freedom can have an impact on democratization, but the relationship between the two is tenuous at best. Promoting integral and sustainable development (q.v.) and reducing poverty have also become part of OAS efforts to promote and sustain democracy. Despite these efforts, illicit drug trafficking, corruption (q.v.), and other illegal practices continue to undermine efforts by inter-American organizations to firmly establish democracy in the Americas.

Politicians and political scientists have become enamored with the theory that democracies do not go to war against one another. In his 1994 State of the Union address, President Bill Clinton declared that "democracies don't attack each other," and "are more likely to keep the peace." Whether in fact this observation is true for the Western Hemisphere, there is no doubt that democracy promotion rhetoric has become a major part of discourse among inter-American organizations and political leaders. *See also* Human Rights; Organization of American States (OAS, 4b and c); World Bank.

DEVELOPMENT BANKS. *See* Arab Latin American Bank (ARLA-BANK); Caribbean Development Bank (CDB); Central American Bank for Economic Integration (CABEI); Eastern Caribbean Central Bank (ECCB); Inter-American Development Bank; World Bank.

DOCTRINES. *See* Calvo Doctrine; Drago Doctrine; Estrada Doctrine; Johnson Doctrine; Monroe Doctrine; Reagan Doctrine; Rodríguez Larreta Doctrine; Tobar Doctrine.

DOMINICAN REPUBLIC, COLLECTIVE SANCTIONS BY THE OAS. The attempt of Dominican dictator Rafael L. Trujillo (q.v.) to kill democratic President Rómulo Betancourt (q.v.) of Venezuela in June 1960 prompted the latter to call for a meeting of the Organ of Consultation under the Inter-American Treaty of Reciprocal Assistance (IATRA, q.v.) to consider the former's "intervention" (q.v.). The case was taken up at the sixth Meeting of Foreign Ministers in Costa Rica in August to consider the action to be taken once an Organization of American States (OAS, q.v.) investigating committee had established the complicity of Trujillo. By more than a two-thirds vote the ministers approved diplomatic and economic sanctions to be in effect until the Dominican government ceased constituting "a danger to the peace and security of the hemisphere." What was especially significant about the action was that it was the first time that the OAS had approved and applied collective sanctions. These sanctions were continued and also expanded to trade restrictions in 1961 and were in effect almost 17 months until January 1962, even though Trujillo was assassinated in May 1961. They were also used to bring about a transition to democracy (q.v.); therefore, it also marked the first use of the OAS as an "anti-dictator alliance."

In the turmoil following Trujillo's death, the sanctions were used as an economic weapon, particularly in the U.S. cutoff of the purchase of Dominican sugar, to exact a promise from President Joaquín Balaguer (q.v.) to hold free elections. Elections were subsequently scheduled and held in December 1962, although Balaguer was forced into exile. The president-elect was Juan Bosch (q.v.), a longtime Trujillo opponent who returned from exile. Although he was favored and supported by Washington (his government was a great beneficiary of

President Kennedy's Alliance for Progress [q.v.]), he was overthrown by the military in 1963 after only seven months in office. Subsequent events led to a coup and countercoup, precipitating a civil war and U.S. military intervention (q.v.), followed by OAS involvement by means of the recently established Inter-American Commission on Human Rights (IACHR, q.v.) and especially by its first Inter-American Peace Force (IAPF).

DOMINICAN REPUBLIC, INTERVENTION IN BY THE UNITED STATES AND THE OAS PEACE FORCE. Following the overthrow of Juan Bosch (q.v.) in September 1963, the government changed from a military *junta* to one headed by a civilian nonelected "president" (one recognized by President Lyndon Johnson). In April 1965, a military faction loyal to deposed President Bosch staged a coup and removed the civilian government. This provoked the rest of the armed forces to rally to the cause of the overthrown government, resulting in a civil war. Fearing that the latter would be defeated by the "leftist" pro-Bosch side, the Johnson administration justified sending in U.S. troops, beginning in late April, as preventing a "second Cuba." (There continues to be great debate about both the accuracy and probability of this assessment by the United States.) The U.S. troop buildup in support of the anti-Bosch side soon reached a total of 22,000 and assured the defeat of the "leftist" side. After its troops landed, the United States turned to the Organization of American States (OAS, q.v.) for the first time, in order to obtain its multilateral endorsement of the U.S. unilateral action and to assure OAS involvement and presence in the Dominican Republic. The United States concentrated on the creation of an Inter-American Peace Force (IAPF, q.v.). The tenth meeting of ministers convened upon the basis of the OAS Charter in Washington, D.C., in May, and there was great Latin American criticism of the U.S. action, for it was viewed as a clear violation of the nonintervention principle. After much debate and opposition, a resolution establishing the IAPF was finally passed (with a bare two-thirds majority vote). Its "formation" required the transformation of the U.S. military command and forces in the Dominican Republic. This was done by placing a Brazilian general in command and adding troops from Brazil (the largest number), Honduras, Nicaragua, and Paraguay and three officers and 20 policemen from El Salvador and Costa Rica. The main contributors were states with military governments; most countries with civilian, elected governments refused to participate. At the outset the Latin American component amounted to 14 percent of the force; it later increased to 30 percent after the United States began withdrawing some of its forces. An OAS ad hoc committee finally negotiated an agreement in August between the two sides, providing for "national reconciliation" and forming an interim government to prepare for national elections. The elections were held on June 1, 1966, and ex-President Balaguer was elected; he was inaugurated in August, and the last members of the Peace Force were withdrawn six weeks later. The Inter-American Commission on Human Rights (IACHR, q.v.) was also involved in the civil war. A number of visits were made to the respective zones of the two sides to investigate charges and rumors of the torture and execution of prisoners. The United Nations became involved in this case, due to the unpopularity of the U.S. intervention (q.v.), over strong opposition by Washington. The UN Security Council held many meetings on the topic, permitted both Dominican sides to be represented, and passed a resolution authorizing the secretary-general to send a representative (and military adviser) to the country. *See also* Balaguer, Joaquín; Dominican Republic, Collective Sanctions by the OAS; Intervention and Nonintervention; Johnson Doctrine.

DRAGO DOCTRINE. A principle of international law enunciated in 1902 by Argentine Foreign Minister Luis María Drago that opposes the use of military intervention (q.v.) or occupation in another country for the purpose of collecting a public debt. Although based on the Calvo Doctrine (q.v.), the Drago Doctrine rejected the prevailing view that economic claims gave a nation the legal right to intervene militarily in the internal affairs of another country. The Drago Doctrine was provoked by the 1902 naval blockade imposed on Venezuela by Germany, Great Britain, and Italy after the Venezuelan government had defaulted on bonds issued with nationals of those countries. Drago's diplomatic note received wide support throughout Latin America and at the second Hague Conference (1907), but the United States managed to tone down the anti-interventionist language before the doctrine was adopted. *See* also Calvo Doctrine.

DRUG ABUSE AND TRAFFICKING, OAS AND UN EFFORTS. *See* Drug Cartels; Inter-American Drug Abuse Control Commission (IA-DACC); United Nations, Drug Control.

DRUG CARTELS. Extremely powerful, private illicit drug production and smuggling operations run out of several Latin American, Caribbean, and Asian countries. The most notorious cartels operating in Latin America have been located in Colombia (known for those headquartered in Medellín and Cali), Mexico, Peru, Bolivia, Panama, the Bahamas, and Puerto Rico. Currently, Colombia is the world's largest producer of cocaine, and second largest grower of coca leaf behind

Peru. Because of the high demand for drugs such as cocaine, marijuana, and heroin—and vast profits—the drug cartels have been able to hire private armies, buy local judges and politicians, distort national development programs, and contribute to corruption (q.v.) and human rights (q.v.) abuses. The economic impact of drug production is visible in its providing of employment, foreign exchange, and stabilizing economies beset by declining prices of primary exports. Politically, drug cartels have corrupted politicians, judges, and segments of the police and armed forces. In Bolivia and Peru, coca farmers have formed powerful pressure groups and have been successful in opposing government programs of eradication and interdiction. In February 1997, Mexico's top anti-drug official was jailed on corruption charges after revelations that he had been informing and protecting Mexican drug cartel members.

After the death of Pablo Escobar (known as the godfather of the Medellín cartel) in Colombia in 1993, the Cali cartel, under the direction of drug traffickers Gilberto and Miguel Rodríguez Orejuela, quickly became the world's largest in the refining, smuggling, and distribution of cocaine. The Cali cartel's grip on world control was weakened in 1995 by the arrest of its leaders and the revelation that it contributed to the successful election campaign of President Ernesto Samper. Despite being cleared of charges that Cali drug dealers financed his election to the tune of $6 million in 1996, Samper was pressured to leave office by the United States and leading business and industrial groups in Colombia because of the extent of his narco-corrupted government.

To take collective action against drug trafficking and cartels throughout the hemisphere, the Organization of American States (OAS, q.v.) created the Inter-American Drug Abuse Control Commission (CICAD, q.v.) in the 1980s. Both the OAS and the United Nations have been in favor of reducing supply and demand on a more equal basis, but their authority is severely limited since international cooperation is voluntary. Bilateral efforts to counter the power of drug cartels have often led to the signing of extradition treaties for trying and punishing drug kingpins abroad. The United States and Colombia signed an extradition treaty in 1979, and it was implemented by Colombia on various occasions in the mid-1980s. However, domestic opposition to it led presidential candidate César Gaviria (q.v.) to campaign against it and, once elected, terminate the agreement. Gaviria was elected secretary-general of the OAS in 1994 with strong backing from the United States.

To strengthen the U.S. antinarcotics efforts at home and abroad, the U.S. Congress passed the Anti-Drug Abuse Act of 1986, a law that mandated the annual International Narcotics Control Strategy Report to assess the situation in the drug-producing and trafficking nations around the world, 19 of which were in Latin America and the Caribbean. Panama (1988) and Colombia (1996 and 1997) were "decertified" by the United States for their insufficient efforts in the eradication of illicit drugs. In an unprecedented move in July of 1996, the Clinton administration canceled President Samper's visa in hopes of generating more pressure on the president to resign. By September 1996 President Samper's vice president had resigned, claiming he could no longer be associated with such a drug-corrupted government. Ten years after Congress passed the Anti-Drug Abuse Act controversies still swirl over the nature of the problem; the interconnection between drug cartels and various guerrilla groups; the impact of drug trafficking and U.S. national security; the domestic drug market; and the exact role of the Central Intelligence Agency (CIA) in the drug wars in the Western Hemisphere. The world's volume of trade in illicit drugs is estimated to be close to $150 billion annually. *See* Inter-American Drug Abuse Control Commission (IADACC); United Nations, Drug Control.

E

EARTH SUMMIT, RIO DE JANIERO. *See* Environment; United Nations Conference on the Environment and Development (UNCED); United Nations Environmental Program (UNEP).

EASTERN CARIBBEAN CENTRAL BANK (ECCB). The bank, which replaced the East Caribbean Currency Authority, was established in October 1983, three months after an agreement was signed by the seven governments of Antigua and Barbuda, Dominica, Grenada, Montserrat, St. Kitts and Nevis, St. Lucia, and St. Vincent and the Grenadines. (Anguilla joined in 1987.) Its purpose is to promote economic development, credit, and exchange conditions for balanced growth and development of the economies, promote and maintain monetary stability, and to regulate the availability of credit and money. Headquartered in Basseterre, St. Kitts, its two major governing bodies are the Monetary Council and the Board of Directors; the latter is responsible for policy and general administration.

EASTERN CARIBBEAN COMMON MARKET (ECCM). The smaller islands of the Eastern Caribbean formed the ECCM in 1968, a year after they achieved associated statehood with Britain, for the purpose of functional cooperation. In 1966, the Council of Ministers of the West Indies Associated States (WISA, q.v.) was created as a political decision-making body. In July 1981 the Organization of Eastern Caribbean States (OECS, q.v.) was established, the result of a treaty approved in October 1980 at a meeting of WISA. Both the ECCM and WISA were superseded by the OECS; its purpose is member cooperation and unity, harmonization of foreign policy, and economic development. It has the same membership as the Caribbean Development Bank (CDB, q.v.), with the exception of Anguilla. (The British Virgin Islands became an associate member in 1984.) The organization is headed by a director-general, the primary decision-making body is the Authority of Heads of Government, and the Secretariat is located in Castries, St. Lucia.

ECHEVERRÍA, LUIS. *See* Charter on the Economic Rights and Duties of States (CERDS).

ECONOMIC COMMISSION FOR LATIN AMERICA AND THE CARIBBEAN (ECLAC)/COMISIÓN ECONÓMICA PARA AMÉRICA LATINA Y EL CARIBE (CEPAL). A United Nations regional economic commission founded in 1948 to initiate and coordinate policies for the promotion of economic development in the Latin American region. In 1984, it expanded its title and operations to include the Caribbean states and territories. Its members include the countries and territories of Latin America and the Caribbean. In addition, Canada, France, Italy, the Netherlands, Portugal, Spain, the United Kingdom, and the United States are members and also important aid donors for much of ECLAC's projects in the region.

One of five regional commissions established by the United Nations, ECLAC conducts research and analysis, publishes information, provides technical assistance training courses, and cooperates with national, regional, and international organizations. ECLAC's studies and conferences helped to create the Central American Common Market (CACM, q.v.); the Latin American Free Trade Association (LAFTA, q.v.); and the Inter-American Development Bank (IADB, q.v.). Other recommendations, such as import substitution industrialization (q.v.) as a means of spearheading economic development, have been greeted with little political or economic enthusiasm in the region. Since its inception in the late 1940s, the following prominent Latin American economists have served as ECLAC executive secretaries: Gustavo Martínez Cabañas (Mexico) 1949–1950; Raúl Prebisch (q.v., Argentina) 1950–1963; José Antonio Mayobre (Venezuela) 1963–1967; Carlos Quintana (Mexico) 1967–1972; Enrique Iglesias (Uruguay) 1972–1985; Norberto González (Argentina) 1985–1987; and Gert Rosenthal (Guatemala) since 1987.

ECONOMIC SANCTIONS. Coercive measures administered by governments and international organizations that are designed to change existing policies of the affected state. The appeal of this kind of diplomatic tool is that punitive action can be applied in different dosages to the target state in hopes of changing its political behavior. U.S. policymakers have also found punitive trade embargoes appealing because they can easily appease domestic constituencies as "taking action" and enable public officials to avoid, or postpone, more difficult policy choices. Whether for stopping terrorism, curtailing the drug trade, improving the human rights situation, or promoting democracy, economic sanctions provide a powerful opiate to punish and control other nations without having to invade militarily. Depending on the severity of the situation, policymakers can withdraw special government-granted privileges—foreign aid, loan guarantees, most favored nation (MFN) status—or apply more restrictive measures, such as the freezing of assets, access to important capital markets, or the ending of all trade.

The United States has used economic sanctions against Chile, the Dominican Republic, Colombia, Cuba, Grenada, Guatemala, Haiti, Nicaragua, and Panama to accomplish a variety of policy goals, during the Cold War (q.v.) and after. Since the mid-1980s, the United States has mandated an annual certification ritual where 32 countries are judged according to their aggressiveness in combating narcotics trafficking. Colombia has been the main target of U.S. decertification efforts: for two years in a row (1996 and 1997) it has suffered economic sanctions, including dramatic aid reductions and an automatic "no" vote on any loan requests to the International Monetary Fund (IMF, q.v.), World Bank (q.v.), and other multinational financial institutions.

In the multilateral arena, economic sanctions also exist but must be applied with the consent of the organization's members according to international law. For example, articles 39, 41, and 42 of the United Nations Charter provide a mechanism for the use of economic sanctions. According to Article 19 of the Charter of the Organization of American States (q.v.), "No State may use or encourage the use of coercive measures of an economic or political character in order to force the sovereign will of another State and obtain from it advantages of any kind." However, the OAS can impose collective economic sanctions on member states if approved by the requisite number of voting members—two-thirds. In the case of Cuba during the Cold War, the OAS imposed a trade embargo from 1964 to 1975. More recently, in an effort to promote democracy in the hemisphere, the OAS approved a resolution (Santiago Commitment to Democracy) that requires the OAS secretary-general to call a meeting of the Permanent Council if a democratically elected government is overthrown. The Permanent Council can then decide if economic sanctions are warranted to help restore democracy in the member state. In 1996, the Southern Cone Common Market (MERCOSUR, q.v.) penned a "democracy guaranty clause" that would apply economic sanctions to any country that deviated from established democratic principles.

While punitive trade embargoes are often quite appealing, they rarely achieve their stated objectives. The U.S. economic sanctions against Cuba that have been applied for over 33 years have not toppled the Cuban Revolution (q.v.): Fidel Castro's power and stature on the island are enhanced by the U.S. trade embargo and other punitive measures. Economic sanctions did not bring down the Noriega (q.v.) regime in Panama or the military *junta* in Haiti under René Préval. In both cases, U.S. military force, not the strains of economic restrictions, was required to bring about the desired outcome. Economic sanctions hurt business interests and generate tensions with important and friendly trading partners. If economic sanctions contribute to human rights violations, poor health, and loss of life of innocent citizens or negatively affect the majority of the population, then sanctions can become more immoral than the evil they seek to eliminate. Thus, economic sanctions themselves constitute a human rights violation. When sanctions are imposed either unilaterally or multilaterally they tend to undermine the legitimacy of the state or international organization applying them. Finally, once sanctions are imposed, hostility increases, and the target states become less willing to compromise. U.S.-Colombian cooperation declined after the Clinton administration imposed economic sanctions—a freeze on trade and investment financing, refusal to approve economic assistance, and ban on travel to the United States by Colombian President Ernesto Samper—in 1996 because of strong evidence that its president was implicated in drug-related contributions to his election campaign. Despite the weakness, if not futility, of economic sanctions, the political advantages that stem from the rhetorical stance of such measures will no doubt obviate efforts to eliminate them in the conduct of inter-American relations. From 1993 to 1996, the United States imposed economic sanctions or passed legislation that threatened to do so 60 times against 35 countries, seven of which were in the Latin American or Caribbean region (see Table, p. 82). *See also* Cuba, Collective Sanctions and Suspension by the OAS; Democracy; Dominican Republic, Collective Sanctions by the OAS; Haiti, Sanctions by the OAS and the UN, Military Intervention by a UN Force; Ortega, Daniel; Panama, Intervention by the United States and the OAS, and Elections; Trujillo Molina, Rafael.

BASIS OF U.S. ECONOMIC SANCTIONS, 1993–1996

Country	Drug Trafficking	Environmental Violations	Human and Political Rights Abuses	Nuclear Proliferation	Terrorism
Brazil		X			
Colombia	X				
Cuba	X		X	X	X
Guatemala			X		
Haiti	X		X		
Mexico			X		
Nicaragua			X		X

Source: *New York Times* 20 April 1997

EMBARGO OF CUBA. *See* Cold War; Cuba, Collective Sanctions and Suspension by the OAS; Cuban Revolution.

EMBARGOES OF ORGANIZATION OF PETROLEUM EXPORTING COUNTRIES (OPEC). Although founded in 1960 at the behest of Venezuela to try to raise oil prices, the influence of the Organization of Petroleum Exporting Countries (OPEC) was not experienced until 1973, when its Arab members convinced some of the non-Arab members to impose an oil embargo against Western countries that supported Israel during the fourth Arab-Israeli War in October of 1973. The instigators were mainly the Arab members who sought to punish the United States for its support of Israel. (The Israeli Air Force had used U.S. air bases in Spain [q.v.] for resupply, which was contrary to the U.S.-Spain Base Agreement.) The two Latin American members of OPEC—Venezuela and Ecuador (withdrew in 1992)— enjoyed the benefits of the quadrupling of oil prices in 1974 but saw fewer benefits from the second round of cuts by the OPEC cartel in 1978/79, since many of the Western states were better prepared through conservation and other measures. The Ford administration and the U.S. Congress made no distinction between OPEC members and the countries that had joined the embargo against the West, and it passed punitive legislation in retaliation that did great harm to Venezuela and Ecuador despite the fact that they did not cooperate with the embargo. Non-OPEC members such as Mexico and Great Britain also stimulated production and exploration, which mitigated the economic impact. Whatever the short-term gains by the oil producers, the real losers were Latin American and Third World (q.v.) importers of petroleum that spent most of the decade of the 1980s struggling to extricate themselves from huge foreign debts. *See also* Spain.

ENTERPRISE FOR THE AMERICAS INITIATIVE (EAI). An economic policy initiative announced by President George Bush (q.v.) to a group of administration officials and business community members on June 27, 1990. Bush's new program—what he called "our new initiative"—had three pillars (free trade, investment reform, and debt reduction that was linked to the protection of the environment) and was designed to cover the whole hemisphere, from the Arctic Circle in Canada to Tierra del Fuego in Argentina. His proposal set the stage for the later approval of the North American Free Trade Agreement (NAFTA, q.v.), in 1993. *See also* Bush, George; North American Free Trade Agreement (NAFTA).

ENVIRONMENT. International and inter-American organizations have devoted more attention and funds to the environment in recent years, and there is increasing cooperation among the United Nations Environmental Program (UNEP), the Inter-American Development Bank (IADB) and the Organization of American States (OAS) (q.q.v.) in dealing with environmental matters. The United Nations has been the prime mover in the field since its first conference (on the "Human Environment") in 1972 and establishment later that year of UNEP. In 1994, the IADB reorganized in order to deal more effectively with environmental issues. For example, it created three new regional Environment and Natural Resources Management Divisions within new Regional Operations Departments, a new Environment Division within new Social Sections and Sustainable Development Departments, and its Environment Committee was restructured. Also in 1994, the IADB and the United Nations Development Program (UNDP, q.v.) reactivated the Latin American and Caribbean Commission on Development and Environment. (There also exists a Caribbean Environment Program Network.) In 1995 the OAS began organizing a new Unit on the Environment, which will join the recently created Unit on Democracy and Unit on Trade. *See also* Earth Summit, Rio de Janeiro; Inter-American Development Bank (IADB); Organization of American States (OAS, 4b and c); United Nations Development Program (UNDP); United Nations Environmental Program (UNEP).

ESTRADA DOCTRINE. A recognition (q.v.) policy formulated by Mexican Foreign Minister Genaro Estrada in 1930 in response to the need for legitimacy of governments that come to power through revolutionary means. Given its difficulties in obtaining diplomatic recognition from the United States during its own revolution, Mexico developed a sympathy for the plight of other revolutionary governments. The Estrada Doctrine argued that recognition should be *de facto*, accepting the government in actual control, not based on political considerations inherent in the selective application of *de jure,* or legal, recognition. Despite the enthusiastic reception that the Estrada Doctrine received among Latin Americans, the United States has continued to base its recognition policy on political and national interest considerations. *See also* Recognition and Nonrecognition of States, Governments, and Insurgents; Tobar Doctrine.

EUROPEAN COMMUNITY (EC). Collective name for the international organizations and functional communities that form part of Europe's efforts to achieve economic and political integration. Beginning with only six members—Belgium, France, Italy, Luxembourg, the Netherlands and West Germany—the EC has grown to 16 members from all parts of Europe. Through the Lomé Conventions (q.v.), Caribbean states are linked at the associate level with EC/EU trade and aid activities. *See also* European Union (EU); Institute for European-Latin American Relations (IELAR); Lomé Conventions.

EUROPEAN UNION (EU). A product of the Maastricht Treaty of 1993, the European Union partially supersedes the European Community (EC, q.v.) and is designed to expand the concept of integration to include the establishment of a common foreign and security policy, unified standards of justice, and improved police protection. Members include the earlier 12 EC members plus the recent addition (1995) of Austria, Finland, Norway, and Sweden. Others from Eastern Europe and the Baltic states may join in the near future. Through the Lomé Conventions (q.v.)—aid and trade preferences—Caribbean nations now have preferential access to European markets for their goods, both manufactured and agricultural produce. They also receive marketing assistance, some technology transfer, and have access to a limited amount of EU aid and soft loans. *See also* European Community; Lomé Conventions.

F

FALKLANDS/MALVINAS WAR. War over a disputed island territory in the South Atlantic known as the Falkland Islands by the British and Las Islas Malvinas by the Argentines that lasted for 25 days in 1982. The basis of the war was Argentina's legal and historical claim to title since independence in 1816, when it adhered to the boundaries of Spain's Viceroyalty of Rio de la Plata, which at that time included the islands. Argentina took over administration and occupied them a few years later. However, the British and some other European powers had laid claim much earlier and, in 1833, the British took them over militarily, expelled the Argentines, and has occupied them ever since. Argentina has never given up its claim to title, and in the 1970s the two states entered into regular negotiations about the islands' status, with Argentina confident that a transitional arrangement for their return (and the restoration of Argentine sovereignty) could be reached. However, Argentina's military government (under General Leopoldo Galtieri) ordered an invasion on April 2, 1982, apparently to fan nationalism and turn attention away from a disastrous economic situation. He assumed that a quick victory could be achieved, the British would not respond, and the United States would remain neutral.

At first, the British marines were quickly overcome and the islands occupied by Argentine troops. Both the United Nations Security Council (UNSC) and the OAS (q.v.) Permanent Council met to decide upon a response, the former first and the OAS later. A debate resulted between the protagonists and their supporters about which organization—the global or regional one—was appropriate. Argentina preferred the latter, the Organ of Consultation meeting upon the basis of the Inter-American Treaty of Reciprocal Assistance (IATRA, q.v.), which would mean that the Commonwealth Caribbean States (CWC, q.v.), except one, could not participate since they were not parties to the treaty. Argentina assumed that they would be pro-British, while the Latin American states would be sympathetic to its cause since they accepted its legal claim to the islands and were pro-OAS. Before its NATO ally, Great Britain, formulated its position on the crisis, the United States preferred the OAS meeting on the basis of the OAS Charter, thus including these states. Once Britain's position on the controversy became clear, favoring the United Nations since it was a permanent member of the UNSC, the United States changed its position in favor of the United Nations. The UNSC acted first, passing a resolution calling for Argentine withdrawal, a cessation of hostilities, and a diplomatic solution; later the OAS offered its good offices.

At the outset the Latin American states were critical of and not sympathetic to Argentina because it had resorted to force first, thus violating the principle of nonintervention (q.v.). However, as Secretary of State Alexander Haig neared the end of his unsuccessful shuttle diplomacy to negotiate a settlement, it became clear that Washington was *not* neutral but was siding with its North Atlantic Treaty Organization (NATO, q.v.) ally. Then, the majority of the Latin American states shifted their position, turning against the United States to support Argentina. Thereafter, the European Community (EC, q.v.) imposed sanctions on Argentina as the British armada was en route to the Falklands. The OAS 20th Meeting of Consultation was convened (based on the Rio Treaty) at the request of Argentina, and the majority attending shifted to support Argentina as the British force arrived in the area. In late April, as the battle raged, the OAS meeting passed a pro-Argentine resolution and called on the British to withdraw. After that resolution, the United States imposed sanctions on Argentina and gave military aid to Britain; a late-May OAS resolution requested that the United States halt aid to Britain and criticized it for "abandoning and betraying" the Inter-American System (IAS, q.v.) and condemned Britain's disproportional attacks and the EC sanctions. During May 1982, the British proceeded to overwhelm the poorly trained and unenthusiastic Argentine conscripts, at first winning battles at sea and in the air and later several land battles that lasted until the Argentines surrendered on East Falkland Island on June 14. The costly and humiliating defeat forced Galtieri's government out and set the stage for the transition to democracy (q.v.) with the election of Raúl Alfonsín (q.v.) as president in 1983. The pro-UN/ British and anti-OAS/Argentine stance of the United States seriously eroded U.S.-Latin American relations and undermined the OAS as an effective body for resolving hemispheric disputes. *See also* Alfonsín, Raúl; South Atlantic Treaty Organization (SATO).

FARABUNDO MARTÍ NATIONAL LIBERATION FRONT. *See* Frente Farabundo Martí de Liberación Nacional (FMLN).

FONDO MUNDIAL INTERNACIONAL (FMI). *See* International Monetary Fund (IMF).

FONDS MONÉTAIRE INTERNATIONAL (FMI). *See* International Monetary Fund (IMF).

FORD, GERALD (1913-). *See* Embargoes of Organization of Petroleum Exporting Countries (OPEC).

FOREIGN CORRUPT PRACTICES ACT (FCPA). *See* Corruption; Democracy.

FREEDOM OF ACTION DECLARATION or RESOLUTION. *See* Cold War; Cuba, Collective Sanctions and Suspension by OAS.

FREE TRADE AGREEMENTS. *See* Caribbean Free Trade Association (CARIFTA); Free Trade Area of the Americas (FTAA); North American Free Trade Agreement (NAFTA); Group of Three (G-3).

FREE TRADE AREA OF THE AMERICAS (FTAA)/AREA DE LIBRE COMERCIO DE LAS AMÉRICAS (ALCLA). At the 1994

Summit of the Americas (q.v.) meeting in Miami, Florida in December 1994, the countries of the Western Hemisphere announced their desire to create a hemisphere-wide free trade area in which barriers to trade and investment would be progressively eliminated. The 34 attending nations (Cuba was excluded) did not agree upon a single path to achieve the FTAA, or define it contents, but they did agree to conclude the negotiations by no later than 2005. There was, however, an implicit assumption that the eventual FTAA would go beyond the commitments made at the Uruguay Round to the World Trade Organization (q.v.).

The resurgence of regional and bilateral trade pacts in the Americas is currently driven by five major regional trade agreements and economic integration arrangements—NAFTA, MERCOSUR, CACM, CARICOM, and the Andean Pact (qq.v.)—as well as other preferential trade agreements among OAS (q.v.) member states. These include the Caribbean Basin Initiative (CBI, q.v.), the Group of Three (G-3, q.v.), and the Association of Caribbean States (ACS, q.v.). With the proliferation of various trade agreements—ones resulting in disagreements that often necessitate more negotiations—designed to liberalize and facilitate greater trade has come a confusing array of rules and regulations that have served to hinder trade rather than promote it.

There are currently five alternative paths to the FTAA. The first would include NAFTA (q.v.) as the core of a growing hemispheric free trade. The second path would extend MERCOSUR to create a South American Free Trade Area (SAFTA). Thus, an expanded MERCOSUR would become one of two poles for hemispheric trade based on Brazil's emergence as a major regional power within South America. A third path would involve some sort of MERCOSUR-NAFTA agreement centering on two blocs led by Brazil and the United States. A fourth path consists of bringing together the major regional trading groups to establish the building blocks for the FTAA. This approach, a convergence of regional trade groups, has generated different perspectives on how best to accomplish the FTAA: Brazil is in favor of a period of consolidation but the United States is opposed on the grounds that this will take too much time. The fifth and final approach to a FTAA is to stress hemispheric negotiations built on a system of working groups, an approach similar to that being followed by APEC (q.v.). Whichever path is taken in producing a free trade area for the hemisphere, it is clear that for the process to succeed, it will have to include all 34 countries attending the Miami Summit and ensure equality of participation in all phases of the preparatory and negotiating process. The U.S. embargo against Cuba, which is opposed by most OAS members, will continue to impede the process.

See also, Andean Pact; Association of Caribbean States; Caribbean Basin Initiative; Caribbean Common Market; Central American Common Market; Southern Cone Common Market; North American Free Trade Agreement.

FRENTE FARABUNDO MARTÍ DE LIBERACIÓN NACIONAL (FMLN)/FARABUNDO MARTÍ NATIONAL LIBERATION FRONT. *See* Central American/Contadora Peace Process.

FRENTE SANDINISTA DE LIBERACIÓN NACIONAL (FSLN)/ SANDINISTA NATIONAL LIBERATION FRONT. *See* Central American/Contadora Peace Process; Nicaragua, Insurrection in of Sandinistas and Collective Sanctions by the OAS; Nicaraguan Revolution; Somoza Dynasty/Family.

FUERZA INTERAMERICANA DE PAZ (FIP)/INTER-AMERICAN PEACE FORCE (IAPF). *See* Dominican Republic, Intervention in by the United States, and the OAS Peace Force.

FUJIMORI, ALBERTO (1938-). President of Peru (1990–1995; 1995– 1999) of Japanese origin (*nisei*), known for his economic liberalization, recentralization of government authority, and reduction of political violence. His economic shock program contributed to a drastic reduction in inflation, the reduction of government employees by more than 400,000, and the opening of the economy to foreign investment. During his first term in office, Fujimori was successful in countering political violence with the capture of the principal leaders of the Shining Path/El Sendero Luminoso (q.v.) and Túpac Amaru Revolutionary Movement (TARM). However, in April 1992 Fujimori suspended Congress and the judicial branch in a self-coup (*autogolpe*) designed to help restore government authority over the economy and to carry on the struggle against terrorists; these actions were criticized by the inter-American community and the Organization of American States (OAS, q.v.) as derailing Peru's democracy. With his supporters in Congress, who helped him to write a new constitution providing for a second term, Fujimori became the first Peruvian president to be elected for two successive terms in 1995. This endorsement seemed to vindicate his economic security measures, human rights (q.v.) violations, and authoritarian moves that had undermined the democratic process (q.v.). He has engaged in further constitutional maneuvering that could possibly allow him to run for a third term in the year 2000. In 1997, he orchestrated a spectacular rescue of more than 70 hostages, held by the leftist Túpac Amaru Revolutionary Movement inside the Japanese ambassador's residence for over five months. President Fujimori's autocratic style of combating corruption (q.v.), terrorism, and a faltering economy has generated widespread criticism in Peru, particularly among those who feel that democracy (q.v.) has suffered at the hands of the executive and the military. *See also* Shining Path.

G

GARCÍA, ALAN (1949-). President of Peru (1985–1990) who clashed with several international lending agencies over Peru's ability to pay its international debts. At his inauguration in July 1985 he announced that Peru would set aside no more than 10 percent of its export earnings for debt servicing. He further angered the International Monetary Fund (IMF, q.v.) in 1986 when he declared his intention of setting his own interest rate for servicing the debt.

GAVIRIA TRUJILLO, CÉSAR AUGUSTO (1947-). A journalist and politician, he served as president of Colombia (1990–1994), one of the youngest in this century. As president he worked against narcotics-linked terrorism as well as drug trafficking. Although earlier he had campaigned against the extradition treaty with the United States, which caused considerable tension, his close and active cooperation in dealing with the drug trade as president won him strong support from Washington. He brought about long-overdue constitutional reform and opened up Colombia's political system. Many of his economic policies were progressive and in keeping with the current trend toward free trade and privatization. In 1994, he was elected secretary-general of the Organization of American States (OAS, q.v.) and in that position has exercised dynamic leadership, directing an impressive expanding role for and revitalization of the OAS. *See also* Drug Cartels; Appendix II; Organization of American States (OAS, secretary-general).

GENERAL AGREEMENT ON TARIFFS AND TRADE (GATT). Multilateral trade organization founded by treaty in 1947 to advance the principle of free trade in the aftermath of World War II. It was replaced by the World Trade Organization (WTO, q.v.) on January 1, 1995. With its own Secretariat and complaint procedures, GATT's purpose was to reduce tariffs and nontariff barriers and to help create rules of conduct for world trade. While GATT stressed the importance of two rules—the most favored nation (MFN, q.v.) principle of nondiscrimination and trade reciprocity—it also permitted exceptions such as customs unions (e.g., Southern Cone Common Market [MER-

COSUR, q.v.]) and free trade associations (e.g., North American Free Trade Agreement [NAFTA, q.v.]) or other such regional arrangements. Eight rounds of talks were held between the first GATT round in Geneva in 1947 (23 states participating) and the conclusion of the Uruguay round in 1993 (116 states participating), each designed to push beyond the previous rounds on tariff reductions. The major benefit from GATT for the smaller economies of Latin America and the Caribbean was the opportunity to gain entry to larger markets and to overcome the limitations of having to negotiate bilateral trade agreements. *See also* World Trade Organization (WTO).

GONDRA, MANUEL (1871–1927). Paraguayan statesman, president (1910–1911; 1920–1921), and scholar known for his authorship of a treaty to prevent war among the American states in 1923. While serving in the Paraguayan government, Gondra helped to reorganize Paraguay's army and clarified its legal claim to the disputed Chaco region. *See also* Chaco War; Gondra Treaty.

GONDRA TREATY (1923). Treaty crafted by Manuel Gondra (q.v.) that lays down procedures for dispute settlement between the American republics through an impartial investigation of the facts related to the international controversy. The Gondra Treaty called for the establishment of permanent commissions in Washington, D.C., and Montevideo, Uruguay to administer conflict resolution measures. The provisions of the Gondra Treaty are considered the inspiration of the present-day mechanisms for peacekeeping by the Organization of American States (OAS) (q.v.). By placing emphasis on internal mechanisms for solving international problems, the Gondra Treaty is significant in calling for the Latin American states to settle disputes by themselves.

GOOD NEIGHBOR POLICY OF FRANKLIN D. ROOSEVELT. Major Latin American policy of the United States, associated with Franklin D. Roosevelt (q.v.), based on nonintervention (q.v.), noninterference, and trade reciprocity during the 1930s and 1940s. By renouncing intervention (q.v.) and treating Latin Americans as friends and equals, the Good Neighbor Policy sought to reverse a pattern of U.S. intervention, commercial domination, and military occupation going back to the nineteenth century. During the presidencies of Herbert Hoover (1929–1933) and Franklin D. Roosevelt (1933–1945), it helped to build the Inter-American System (IAS, q.v.), improve U.S.-Latin American relations, restore trade flows in the Western Hemisphere, and create a hemispheric bloc against the Axis powers.

Although mostly judged a foreign policy success, particularly in bringing greater harmony and unity throughout the hemisphere prior to and during World War II (q.v.), the Good Neighbor Policy suffered when the Cold War (q.v.) policies of the United States led to unilateral actions, covert intervention, and the determination to fashion a solid anticommunist bloc among the Latin American states. Others were critical of some U.S. ambassadors who carried the concept of noninterference to the point of ignoring the actions of Caribbean dictators such as Rafael L. Trujillo (q.v.) in the Dominican Republic and Brazil's Getúlio Vargas. *See also* Rodríguez Larreta Doctrine.

GRENADA, INTERVENTION IN BY THE UNITED STATES. Eric Gairy won the 1972 elections for the presidency of Grenada (independence came in 1974), but his oppressive and dictatorial rule provoked a national reaction in which Maurice Bishop, a London-trained lawyer, became the leader of the New Jewel Movement (NJM) opposition in the government. During a visit to the United States in 1979 Gairy was overthrown by the NJM, a revolutionary socialist group. Parliament was quickly dissolved and a People's Revolutionary Government established under the charismatic Bishop, one rejecting the British Westminster model and committed to creating a new Grenada. The Reagan (q.v.) administration became concerned about the open support of the Soviet bloc and the close ties that were established with Cuba, particularly the Cuban training of Grenada's new army along with its providing economic aid and Cuban workers for extending the runway of Greanda's main airport.

A major crisis developed when a split took place in the Central Committee, resulting in the arrest and imprisonment of Bishop and his supporters, their execution in mid-October 1983, and a hard line faction's declaration of martial law. This prompted a meeting of the Organization of Eastern Caribbean States (OECS, q.v.) that voted, on the basis of its 1981 treaty, to request that the United States intervene in order to establish law and order. The United States accepted and sent in an invasion force of 5,300, which was joined by 300-plus militia and policemen from four OECS members (Antigua and Barbuda, Dominica, St. Lucia, and St. Vincent) and two nonmembers (Barbados and Jamaica), on October 25. President Reagan justified the U.S. action as protecting "innocent lives" (including U.S. citizens, mostly students at two medical schools and tourists), ending the "chaos," and restoring "law and order." The action provoked great controversy, especially among the Latin American states, who argued that the Organization of American States (OAS, q.v.), not the OECS, was the appropriate regional body and the United States was not a member of the latter. The United States countered that the OECS was a subregional organization under the OAS. While the OAS did not pass a critical resolution, the UN General Assembly did by 108 to 9, and the United States vetoed this resolution in the Security Council, although it was supported by 11 members, including France. Despite several hundred casualties, mainly Cuban and Grenadian, the U.S. citizens were rescued and order reestablished, U.S. troops were withdrawn by mid-December, and new elections were held in 1984. *See also* Organization of Eastern Caribbean States (OECS).

GROUP OF EIGHT (G-8). *See* Rio Group.

GROUP OF FIFTEEN (G-15)/GROUPE DES QUINZE. A caucus group established in 1989 at the ninth Conference of Heads of State or Government of Nonaligned Countries to assist the South in devising common strategies for dealing with the rest of the world. The G-15's major functions are to promote South-South cooperation, encourage cooperation among interregional economic groups, strengthen multilateral cooperation with industrialized nations, devise common approaches to deal with external debt, improve terms of trade, coordinate efforts to improve the environment (q.v.), and reduce or eliminate distorting agricultural trade subsidies. Members include Argentina, Brazil, Jamaica, Mexico, Peru, Venezuela, and five African, three Asian, and one European country (Yugoslavia).

GROUP OF LATIN AMERICAN AND CARIBBEAN SUGAR EXPORTING COUNTRIES (GLACSEC)/GRUPO DE PAÍSES LATINOAMERICANOS Y EL CARIBE PARA LA EXPORTACIÓN DE AZÚCAR (GEPLACEA). Founded in 1974 as a forum of consultation on the sale and production of sugar, GLACSEC's major activities include the improvement of the production and exportation of sugar. Members include 23 Latin American and Caribbean countries that account for about 45 percent of world sugar exports and 66 percent of world sugar cane production.

GROUP OF RIO. *See* Rio Group.

GROUP OF SEVENTY-SEVEN (G-77). A caucus group of 128 (original membership consisted of 77) Third World (q.v.) countries formed in 1964 to offer a more united front against the developed states at the United Nations Conference on Trade and Development (UNCTAD) conferences and other multilateral negotiations. The G-77 led the campaign in the 1970s to create a New International Economic Order (NIEO, q.v.) that would stress centrally planned policies on a global scale with more emphasis on distributive justice than market forces. Through resolutions presented at UNCTAD meetings and elsewhere, the G-77 pushed for guaranteed prices for markets and commodities, heavy regulation of multinational corporations, and modification of International Monetary Fund (IMF, q.v.) and World Bank (q.v.) voting rules to benefit its membership. *See also* New International Economic Order (NIEO).

GROUP OF THREE (G-3)/GROUPE DES TROIS/GRUPO DE LOS TRES. During the fifth meeting of the Cartagena Group's (q.v.) foreign ministers in Mexico in 1989, three made a commitment to found the Group of Three in order gradually to remove trade barriers between themselves and to stimulate cooperation with Central America and the Caribbean. The formal agreement establishing the G-3— covering rules of origin, market access, trade in services, intellectual property, and government services—was signed by Colombia, Mexico, and Venezuela in 1994 and went into effect in early 1995. While commerce between Colombia and Venezuela is still governed by the Andean Group (AG, q.v.), trade barriers between the three countries are to be completely eliminated within ten years. *See also* Cartagena Group.

GROUPE DES QUINZE. *See* Group of Fifteen (G-15).

GROUPE DES TROIS. *See* Group of Three (G-3).

GRUPO ANDINO (GA). *See* Andean Group.

GRUPO DE PAÍSES LATINOAMERICANOS Y EL CARIBE PARA LA EXPORTACIÓN DE AZÚCAR (GEPLACEA). *See* Group of Latin American and Caribbean Sugar Exporting Countries (GLACSEC).

GRUPO DE LOS TRES. *See* Group of Three (G-3).

GUATEMALA, INTERVENTION IN BY THE UNITED STATES AND OAS DEBATE. The Eisenhower administration believed that the Guatemalan government of Jacobo Arbenz (1950–1954) was "communist infiltrated" and this in turn led to the sponsorship of a resolution at the 1954 10th Inter-American Conference (Caracas, Venezuela) that would lay the basis for joint action if a Latin American government came under communist control. The meeting produced the Declaration of Caracas (q.v.), establishing a multilateral justification for future intervention (q.v.) in Guatemala. The arrival of an arms shipment to Guatemala from Eastern Europe shortly after the conference prompted Washington to sign mutual defense pacts with, and airlift arms to, neighboring Honduras and Nicaragua. In June 1954, an armed band of insurgents led by an exiled Guatemalan army officer (Carlos Castillo Armas) and equipped indirectly by the United States, entered the country from Honduras. Guatemala appealed to both the UN Security Council and the OAS Inter-American Peace Committee, charging its two neighbors with aggression. (At the time Guatemala had ratified neither the Rio Treaty [q.v.] nor the OAS Charter.)

The view that prevailed in the United Nations debate (the Soviet Union backed Guatemala) was that the Organization of American States (OAS, q.v.) had priority in settling a dispute (under UN Charter articles 33 and 52). The OAS Peace Committee met and decided to send a subcommittee to Guatemala to investigate, but Guatemala would not permit it to enter until it had exhausted its second appeal to the UN. When that appeal was denied, Guatemala agreed to the subcommittee's entry. The OAS approved and set a date for the Fifth Meeting of Consultation, but before that date and the arrival of the subcommittee, the Arbenz government was overthrown and replaced by the leader of the counterrevolutionaries, Col. Castillo Armas. Several years later, a Guatemalan military president permitted the training in his country of the CIA-backed Cuban Brigade for the U.S.-sponsored Bay of Pigs invasion of Cuba in 1961.

Since that time, a progression of mainly nonelected, oppressive military leaders has continued, accompanied by a persistent opposing leftist guerrilla movement, one dealt with harshly by the military. As a part of the Central American Peace Process, representatives of the government and the Guatemalan National Revolutionary Unity (URNG) guerrillas first began meeting to consider a settlement in March 1990 in Norway. Limited progress was made until the United Nations stepped in as mediator in January 1994, conducting a series of talks between the government and rebels that would eventually culminate in an ambitious peace accord signed in December 1996, effectively ending the protracted war that started in 1954.

The 1991 Santiago Resolution on Representative Democracy provided a basis for OAS action against President Jorge Serrano Elías when he staged an "auto-coup" by dissolving the Congress, dismissing judges, and suspending the constitution in May 1993. The Permanent Council authorized the visit of a fact-finding mission under Secretary-General João Baena Soares (q.v.), which met with and issued a warning to Serrano and the armed forces. Serrano soon resigned and left the country, the Congress selected ex-Attorney General for Human Rights Ramiro de León Carpio as president, and the Guatemalan Constitution was restored. *See also* Central American/Contadora

Peace Process; Cold War; Democracy; Human Rights; Intervention and Nonintervention.

GUEVARA, ERNESTO "CHE" (1928–1967). An Argentine physician and Marxist revolutionary who personally tried to carry out revolutions in Latin America, unsuccessfully in Guatemala in 1953, successfully in Cuba six years later, but unsuccessfully in Bolivia in 1967. After the CIA-backed overthrow of Jacobo Arbenz in Guatemala in 1954, Guevara claimed he adopted communist ideology. The following year he met the two Castro brothers in Mexico City and became a member of Fidel Castro's (q.v.) original group of revolutionaries who landed in Cuba from Mexico on the yacht *Granma* in December 1956. He was committed to fomenting revolutions against capitalist, dictatorial, and imperialist governments and states, and he wrote a how-to book, *Guerrilla Warfare*, published in 1960, based upon the overthrow of the dictator Batista (q.v.). As Castro's leading adviser, he was a major organizer and planner for institutionalizing the Cuban Revolution (q.v.). In his positions as head of the National Agrarian Reform Institute and National Bank of Cuba and minister of Industry, he stressed wide state control and ownership along with economic planning. He believed that Cuba could transform its political culture to conform to the new political system he envisioned creating a "new socialist man" who responded to "moral incentives," not "material" ones. Guevara later resigned from the government and left Cuba to launch a revolution in Bolivia where he was captured and killed in 1967. He was buried in a secret grave in southern Bolivia, along with six of his revolutionary comrades, until his remains were unearthed and identified in 1997. *See also* Bolivian Revolution; Cuban Revolution.

GULF WAR. Brief war (1990–1991) carried out by a U.S.-led Gulf coalition against Iraqi forces that had invaded and annexed Kuwait. With United Nations Security Council approval to use force against Iraqi leader Saddam Hussein's troops, the United States, and some token forces from other UN members (including troopships and a small force from Argentina), destroyed the Iraqi air force in a matter of hours, and within three days the Iraqis surrendered. President Carlos S. Menem's offer of military assistance seemed to rest on his Syrian ancestry and desire to improve relations with the United States and its European trading partners. Iraq intermittently refused to cooperate with UN ceasefire and inspection teams until 1993, when it formally agreed to comply with the ceasefire resolutions and accepted weapons inspections.

GUYANA. *See* Caribbean Community (CC); Cold War; Commonwealth Caribbean Leaders.

H

HAITI, SANCTIONS BY THE OAS AND THE UN, MILITARY INTERVENTION BY A UN FORCE. Haiti was the first American colony after the United States to gain its independence, in 1804 as the result of a successful slave revolt against French troops. Thereafter, the country was divided and united, plagued by turmoil and oppression, and ruled by tyrants and presidents in manipulated elections. There were 38 presidents until François Duvalier was "elected" in 1957. The Duvalier regime, father and son (Jean-Claude), lasted until 1986, when the son was forced to leave the country. While his departure set the stage for a transition to democracy (q.v.), there was a four-year interregnum during which a new constitution was written and approved, an aborted and manipulated election was held, and various military men ruled harshly until a provisional government was formed in early 1990. It was not until December 1990 that Haiti's first free and honest elections were held, resulting in the election of Father Jean-Bertrand Aristide (q.v.) as president. After almost eight months in office, he was overthrown by the military in September 1991. Thereafter, the Organization of American States (OAS, q.v.) and the United Nations (and the U.S.) spent three years applying various economic sanctions in an unsuccessful effort to force out the military and return Aristide to office, thus "restoring a democratically elected" government. The situation finally required military intervention (q.v.), in September 1994, and President Aristide was returned and "restored" in mid-October.

The basis for OAS sanctions to return Aristide (who was inaugurated in February 1991) was laid at the annual OAS General Assembly meeting in Santiago, Chile, in June 1991, with the approval of a resolution (no. 1080) that became known as the Santiago Commitment to Democracy. It stated that if a coup removed a democratically elected government, the secretary-general was to call a meeting of the Permanent Council within ten days for the purpose of deciding what action to take. When Aristide was overthrown in late September, the Santiago Resolution was invoked, and the Council began meeting as the Ad Hoc Meeting of Ministers of Foreign Affairs. At an October 8 session the ministers voted to impose economic sanctions on the military government as a means of forcing it out and to create a civilian mission for restoring democracy (to be called OAS-DEMOC). With the sanctions in effect in late November there were continuing negotiations throughout 1992 with the military government and visits to Haiti by OAS-DEMOC, the Inter-American Commission on Human Rights (IACHR, q.v.), and the secretary-general, but all failed to work out a settlement. In December, the OAS turned to the UN, which then imposed economic sanctions and an oil embargo in June 1993. These measures resulted in the signing of the Governors Island accord, a phased plan for the future return of Aristide. However, the military reneged on the plan, and the UN renewed and expanded its economic sanctions in the fall of 1993 and summer of 1994.

In July, the UN Security Council approved the use of force against the Haitian military and the creation of a UN peacekeeping body to police the country during the national elections in 1995 and the inauguration of the new president in February 1995. On September 17, two days before the U.S. military force of 21,000 landed, a mission headed by former President Jimmy Carter (q.v.) negotiated the resignation of the military government. Over the next several months, Aristide was finally returned (October), most U.S. troops were withdrawn (December), and a UN force of 6,000 consisting of 2,400 from the United States and the rest from Bangladesh and India was left in charge of maintaining order. Local and national elections were held in 1995, and the new president (René Préval) was inaugurated in February 1996. A reduced UN force remained in Haiti until the fall of 1997. A number of other states together contributed several hundred police, including a large Canadian contingent, which remained to train a new Haitian police force. *See also* Aristide, Jean-Bertrand; Clinton, William J.; Intervention and Nonintervention.

HARBERGER, ARNOLD. Former University of Chicago economics professor, now at the University of California at Los Angeles, who has been instrumental in training three generations of economists from Latin America in anti-statist and free-market economic policies. Many of Harberger's former students are now government ministers, central bank governors, and top businessmen who have pushed policy goals such as fiscal discipline, low inflation, stable currency, freer trade, and expanded foreign investment. Harberger's influence was felt first in Chile under the Pinochet (q.v.) dictatorship, when some of his students advised the government to radically revamp economic policies to respond to market incentives. Now referred to as "Los Chicago Boys," these young Ph.D. technocrats have put their stamp on government economic policies throughout the region, from El Salvador to Argentina. Widely criticized for aiding Pinochet's dictatorship, Harberger (referred to affectionately as "Alito" by his former students in Latin America) was denied the vice presidency of the American Economic Association in the late 1970s. Now in his seventies, Harberger continues to instruct young Latin American graduate students in the virtues of the free market and evils of statist economic policies among the governments in the region that are desperately trying to democratize and grow economically. *See also* Chicago Boys; Pinochet Ugarte, Augusto.

HELMS-BURTON ACT. *See* North American Free Trade Agreement (NAFTA); Clinton, William J.; Cuban Revolution.

HUMAN RIGHTS. The commitment to the promotion and protection of human rights by the American states has steadily evolved over the past six decades (beginning in the 1930s and continuing into the 1990s) from the passing of resolutions declaring human rights to be important and their protection desirable goals, to binding legal obligations (with enforcement mechanisms) that apply to all members of the Organization of American States (OAS, q.v.). The OAS Charter, certain treaties, legal institutions, and inter-American practice have reflected this evolution in which the earlier principle of nonintervention (q.v.) was the all-important duty of every state, one that transcended even commitments to human rights and democracy (q.v.). This priority has changed, beginning with national and international efforts in the late 1970s and culminating in the 1991 Santiago Declaration and the 1993 Managua Protocol of Amendment to the OAS Charter (q.v.). This change in inter-American priorities is the result of a relatively new consensus developed to support the transition to democracy at the expense of the nonintervention (q.v.) principle, and the resultant human rights progress reflected in the increasingly active Inter-American Commission on Human Rights (IACHR, q.v.), in operation since 1960, and the Inter-American Court of Human Rights (IACt, q.v.), functioning since 1978.

The initial major American commitment to human rights was made near the end of World War II (q.v.) in a resolution adopted on the "International Protection of the Essential Rights of Man" at the Inter-American Conference on Problems of War and Peace (Mexico City, 1945). The Inter-American Juridical Committee (IAJC, q.v.), functioning since 1942, was requested to prepare a draft. This was approved at the Ninth International Conference of American States (Bogotá, Colombia, 1948), which also drafted and approved the OAS Charter as well as the American Declaration of Rights and Duties of Man.

Approved as a declaration but not as a convention, and despite the failure to create an Inter-American Court of Human Rights, it marked a major step in the process of human rights being transformed from a morally to a legally binding commitment. Human rights were included in the OAS Charter (Article 5) among the 12 "Principles" reaffirmed by the American states. In late 1959, eight years after the charter went into effect, the Inter-American Commission on Human Rights was established. A decade later, at the 1969 Inter-American Special Conference on Human Rights (San José, Costa Rica), the American Convention on Human Rights (Pact of San José) was approved, which both incorporated the 1948 American Declaration on the Rights and Duties of Man and created the Inter-American Court of Human Rights. The convention went into effect in 1978, and the court was established in San José, Costa Rica, and began functioning the next year. *See also* Haiti, Sanctions by the OAS and the UN, Military Intervention by a UN Force.

I

IMPORT SUBSTITUTION INDUSTRIALIZATION (ISI) or IMPORT SUBSTITUTION. An economic development strategy based on protective tariffs on industrial imports in order to benefit domestic manufacturers. Championed by Latin American economists and technocrats, ISI was supposed to allow industrialization while minimizing the dependence on foreign investments. It flourished as a strategy of economic development in the 1930s, but it proved expensive by expanding foreign debt and imports without a corresponding penetration of lucrative export markets. By the early 1970s, ISI was recognized as a failure as economic conditions worsened, and policymakers found it necessary again to rely on traditional exports of primary products (bananas, coffee, oil, sugar, etc.) and foreign capital to help cover the costs of economic growth. In seeking a way out of the ISI dilemma, Latin American countries began to form common markets to trade with each other rather than the United States and Europe. When these failed to expand production and reduce dependency, Latin American governments turned to privatization (selling off state enterprises to private investors), market-oriented allocation of goods and services, and enlarged common markets. Chile led the way in the 1970s by combining the military authoritarianism of the Pinochet (q.v.) dictatorship with the ideas of free-market economists, trained by Milton Friedman and Arnold Harberger (q.v.) at the University of Chicago, to implement a "shock treatment" by shifting the burdens of economic stabilization to the poor and eliminating most social welfare programs. *See also* Andean Group; Chicago Boys; Economic Commission for Latin America and the Caribbean (ECLAC); Harberger, Arnold; Prebisch, Raúl.

INSTITUTE FOR EUROPEAN-LATIN AMERICAN RELATIONS (IELAR)/INSTITUTO DE RELACIONES EUROPEO-LATINO-AMERICANAS (IRELA). Founded in 1984 by the Commission of the European Communities, IELAR is located in Madrid and directed by the German Latin Americanist Wolf Grabendorff. With growing interest in Latin America and the Caribbean by the European Community (EC, q.v.) and the European Union (EU, q.v.), IELAR functions as a think tank, collecting and analyzing information on European-Latin American issues, organizing conferences and colloquia, and publishing documents on a broad range of subjects. Designed to promote links with Latin America, IELAR is the only biregional institute for European-Latin American cooperation.

As a result of its strong ties to the European Union, IELAR has been granted observer status at the main fora for European-Latin American dialogue: the ministerial meetings between the Rio Group (q.v.) and the EU; the conferences of the San José process between the foreign ministers of the EU and Central America; and the inter-parliamentary conferences between the European and Latin American Parliaments. During its first ten years of existence IELAR published more than 225 publications, over half of which were issued in more than one language. The creation and success of IELAR symbolize the important role that European states play in the economic and political life of Latin America and the Caribbean, particularly in their efforts to pursue economic interests multilaterally through their regional economic organizations, rather than bilaterally like the United States. *See also* European Community (EC); European Union (EU); Lomé Conventions.

INSTITUTE FOR LATIN AMERICAN INTEGRATION (INTAL)/INSTITUTO DE INTEGRACIÓN LATINOAMERICANO (ALADI). Affiliated institution of the Inter-American Development Bank (IADB, q.v.) designed to study the regional integration process, conduct research associated with the integration process, organize training courses and seminars on various aspects of economic integration, and provide advisory services to the IADB and other public and private institutions. Founded in 1964 as a permanent department of the bank, it became an independent entity in 1991. *See also* Inter-American Development Bank (IADB).

INSTITUTO DE INTEGRACIÓN LATINOAMERICANO (ALADI). *See* Institute for Latin American Integration (INTAL).

INSTITUTO DE RELACIONES EUROPEO-LATINOAMERICANAS (IRELA). *See* Institute for European-Latin American Relations (IELAR).

INSTITUTO INTERAMERICANO DE CRIANÇA (IIC). *See* Inter-American Children's Institute (IACI).

INSTITUTO INTERAMERICANO DEL NIÑO (IIN). *See* Inter-American Children's Institute (IACI).

INTER-AMERICAN CENTER FOR REGIONAL DEVELOPMENT (IACRD)/CENTRO INTERAMERICANO PARA EL DESARROLLO REGIONAL (CINDER). The creation of the Venezuelan government and the Organization of American States (OAS, q.v.), IACRD is designed to promote development through courses on project planning, formulation, evaluation, and execution. The IACRD conducts seminars and research on regional development and offers technical assistance to the member states of the OAS.

INTER-AMERICAN CHILDREN'S INSTITUTE (IACI)/INSTITUTO INTERAMERICANO DEL NIÑO (IIN)/INSTITUTO INTERAMERICANO DA CRIANÇA (IIC). A specialized agency of the Organization of American States (OAS, q.v.) located in Montevideo, Uruguay. Founded in 1927 as an organization for the protection of children, it did not become part of the OAS until 1949. The IACI's humanitarian focus aims to stimulate and promote an awareness of all problems related to children, adolescents, motherhood, and the family in the Americas. As a center for social action, the IACI carries out programs in the fields of education, health, social legislation, social service, and statistics on the condition of children and the family. Each member country of the OAS participates in the IACI, except Cuba, which has been a nonparticipating member of the OAS since 1962.

INTER-AMERICAN COMMISSION ON HUMAN RIGHTS (IACHR). Increasing turmoil in the Caribbean in the late 1950s—mainly attributable to exile group activity against Batista (q.v.) in Cuba and Trujillo (q.v.) in the Dominican Republic—prompted the fifth Meeting of Consultation of the OAS (Santiago, Chile, 1959) to consider the problem. After agreeing that the lack of democracy and massive human rights (q.v.) violations were at the heart of these tensions, the meeting approved the creation of the Inter-American Commission on Human Rights. The IACHR became effective in 1960.

Although it possessed limited authority, the seven-member commission began looking into the human rights situation in a number of countries. For example, it investigated the treatment of prisoners during the 1965 civil war in the Dominican Republic (q.v.). The IACHR cannot visit a country for an investigation without that government's consent, and each commission member is elected in his/her own individual capacity, not as a representative of his/her own government, but as a representative of the OAS (q.v.). The 1967 Protocol of Buenos Aires brought about amendments to the OAS Charter (effective in 1970) that elevated the organizational status of the IACHR to that of a formal charter organ, giving it new institutional and constitutional legitimacy. Later it was granted the authority to receive individual petitions and to hold outside hearings when a violator state refused to grant entry. *See also* Caribbean Legion; Nicaragua, Insurrection in of Sandinistas and Collective Sanctions by the OAS; Organization of American States (OAS, 1 and 4b).

INTER-AMERICAN COURT OF HUMAN RIGHTS (IACHR). Created by the 1969 American Convention on Human Rights, the Court began functioning in 1979 at its seat in Costa Rica, the same site as the short-lived Central American Court of Justice (q.v.). There are seven judges from states that are parties to the convention (although the United States is not a party, Costa Rica permitted one U.S. naturalized citizen who is a distinguished international human rights scholar, Thomas Buergenthal, to take its seat). The court has the authority to issue advisory opinions, which it has done in increasing numbers; they may be requested by the IACHR (q.v.) and by convention or non-convention parties. Its major authority is to decide contentious cases, which may be brought to the court only by the IACHR or a state party to the convention. At the time of a state's ratification of the convention, it may indicate that it accepts the convention as legally binding and the compulsory jurisdiction of the court in contentious cases. When a sufficient number of states party to the convention had accepted the court's compulsory jurisdiction, the court began exercising it for the first time in 1988. *See also* International Court of Justice (ICJ), *Nicaragua v. United States of America.*

INTER-AMERICAN DEFENSE BOARD (IADB)/LA JUNTA INTER-AMERICANA DE DEFENSA. *See* Organization of American States (OAS, 4a).

INTER-AMERICAN DEVELOPMENT BANK (IADB). The oldest (1959) and largest of the regional multilateral development banks that focus on economic and social development in Latin America and the Caribbean. After suggestions offered by the Economic Commission for Latin America (q.v.) and its executive secretary Raúl Prebisch (q.v.), an agreement creating the IADB was drawn up by a special committee of the Organization of American States (OAS, q.v.). Headquartered in Washington, D.C., the IADB (sometimes the IDB acronym is used) currently has a membership of 46 nations, including the United States, Canada, Japan, Israel, and 16 European nations. It also has offices in 25 Latin American member countries and a European office in Paris. During 1993, the IADB approved 93 loans amounting to slightly more than $6 billion, the majority of which were for physical and social infrastructure such as energy, transportation and communications, the environment (q.v.) and public health, education, science and technology, and urban development.

The bank's guaranteed loan fund is financed by member contributions, especially those of the United States, and by the sale of bank bonds. Loans are made to governments or government-guaranteed entities. To provide loans to private enterprises, the IADB sponsored the formation of the Inter-American Investment Corporation in 1989, which is composed of most members. Voting strength in the IADB is based on the size of a member's contributions; the U.S. holds 35 percent of votes on the Board of Executive Directors, proportional to its contribution to the Bank's capital. The Inter-American Development Bank served as a model of regional lending and financing for the Asian and African Development Banks. The current president of the IADB is Enrique V. Iglesias of Uruguay.

INTER-AMERICAN DRUG ABUSE CONTROL COMMISSION (IA-DACC)/COMISIÓN INTERAMERICANA PARA EL CONTROL DEL ABUSO DE DROGAS (CICAD). While the efforts of the United Nations in the field of narcotics control and its Commission on Narcotic Drugs date back to 1946, those of the Organization of American States (OAS, q.v.) are of more recent origin, dating to a 1987 conference in Rio de Janeiro, Brazil, that approved the Inter-American Program of Action Against the Illicit Use and Production of Narcotic Drugs and Psychotropic Substances and Traffic Therein. The OAS then established CICAD to develop and administer the goals of a drug control program, and it began functioning in 1987. The commission has 29 members (Cuba and a few of the very small Commonwealth Caribbean states are not members) and holds two regular sessions per year. It also works closely with the Pan American Health Organization (PAHO, q.v.) and the United Nations. Its staff is located at the OAS General Secretariat in Washington, D.C. *See also* Drug Cartels; United Nations, Drug Control.

INTER-AMERICAN JURIDICAL COMMITTEE (IAJC). As a legal advisory body, the IAJC replaced the Inter-American Neutrality Committee during World War II (q.v.) and was under the Inter-American Council of Jurists in the original Organization of American States (OAS, q.v.) Charter. The 1967 Protocol of Buenos Aires amendments abolished the latter and elevated the Juridical Committee to the principal advisory body on legal matters and the promotion of the development and codification of international law. There are currently 11 jurists on the IAJC, and it is headquartered in Rio de Janeiro, Brazil. Each summer since 1974 it has offered a course on International Law. *See also* Organization of American States (OAS, 3).

INTER-AMERICAN NUCLEAR ENERGY COMMISSION (IANEC). Founded in 1959 as a part of the Organization of American States (OAS, q.v.), IANEC helps to coordinate and develop nuclear energy research among the member states. It also organizes conferences, awards fellowships, and provides financial assistance to nuclear energy research institutions in the hemisphere. *See also* Agency for the Prohibition of Nuclear Weapons in Latin America and the Caribbean; Treaty of Tlatelolco.

INTER-AMERICAN PEACE COMMITTEE (IAPC)/COMISIÓN INTERAMERICANA DE PAZ (CIP). *See* Organization of American States (OAS, 4a).

INTER-AMERICAN REGIONAL ORGANIZATION OF WORKERS/ORGANIZACIÓN REGIONAL INTERAMERICANA DE TRABAJADORES (ORIT). Founded in Mexico City in 1951, ORIT superseded the 1948 noncommunist Inter-American Federation of Labor and was the American affiliate of the 1949 International Confederation of Free Trade Unions founded in London. The confederation cooperates and works with the International Labor Organization, a specialized agency of the United Nations. Its main purpose was to organize and bring together noncommunist labor unions in Latin America. It runs a labor college in Mexico to train labor leaders. ORIT was associated with and received, particularly during the tense labor union competition with communist-affiliated or infiltrated unions in the 1950s and 1960s, considerable financial assistance and support from organized labor in the United States, and the American Federation of Labor-Congress of Industrial Organizations (AFL-CIO).

INTER-AMERICAN SECURITY SYSTEM (IASS). The foundation for the current security system in the Western Hemisphere was laid during World War II (q.v.), and it evolved further during the Cold War (q.v.). From the beginning, the United States was the prime mover of such a system and dominated its structure and philosophy. Some scholars argue that there have actually been two security systems: one called the Inter-American Military System (IAMS) created, maintained, and run by the United States during World War II and continued at varying levels with shifting priorities since the 1940s; and a second, an ineffective, multilateral one that was a part of the Organization of American States (OAS, q.v.). The latter system's military bodies were kept deliberately weak because the Latin American states feared U.S. control of them, and the United States did not want to be restricted, preferring its own system, which was directed by its Southern Command in the Panama Canal Zone.

The principal military body formed during World War II was the Inter-American Defense Board (IADB, q.v.), established at the 1942 Third Meeting of Ministers of Foreign Affairs (Rio de Janeiro). It was assumed that after the war the IADB would became an integral, permanent part of the OAS structure. But at the Ninth International Conference (Bogotá, 1948), which drafted the OAS Charter, it was kept as a special, independent OAS agency with offices some distance from the OAS seat. Since then it has been mainly an advisory body outside the formal OAS structure, and the formation of the anticipated permanent Inter-American Peace Force (IAPF) has never materialized. All OAS member states are represented on the IADB by officers from their respective military services. The first, last, and only IAPF was established during the Dominican civil war (q.v.), after the U.S. military intervention (q.v.), and was due to a special set of controversial circumstances. Although proposed since then, e.g., by the Carter administration for Nicaragua in 1979, its reestablishment has always been turned down. In 1962 the board established the Inter-American Defense College at Ft. Lesley McNair in Washington, D.C., an educational institution that offers a nine-month program to a quota of high-ranking officers from each member state. The 1970 Protocol of Buenos Aires amendments replaced the earlier Inter-American Peace Committee (q.v.) with the provisional Inter-American Committee on Peaceful Settlement. The latter, along with the Advisory Defense Committee—formed in 1948 but never activated—are waiting for the ratification of the 1993 Protocol of Washington amendments to be made permanent and activated. *See also* Organization of American States (OAS, 4a); World War II.

INTER-AMERICAN SYSTEM (IAS). The IAS is the composite of the accumulated legal principles, political practices and policies, administrative arrangements, and organizations that have developed and been approved by the American states in order to achieve common objectives. One of the most important legal principles, *the* most important for a long time, was that of nonintervention (q.v.). The Organization of American States (OAS, q.v.) is the major multilateral organization through which this system operates. There is an increasing number of component organizations whose goals are primarily economic development and/or regional integration: development banks such as the Caribbean Development Bank (CDB) and Inter-American Development Bank (IADB) (qq.v.); and common markets such as the Central American Common Market (CACM) and the Southern Cone Common Market (MERCOSUR) (q.q.v.). Those that are pursuing mainly political goals include the Rio Group and Cartagena Group (qq.v.). *See also* Regional Security System (RSS).

INTER-AMERICAN TREATY OF RECIPROCAL ASSISTANCE (IATRA) or RIO TREATY. This was the first of three treaties that were to serve as the basis for the postwar American regional system (one coordinated with the UN global system) and it was approved at a special 1947 conference, the Inter-American Conference for the Maintenance of Continental Peace and Security in Rio de Janeiro, Brazil. The other two treaties—the American Treaty on Pacific Settlement and the OAS Charter (q.v.)—were approved at the 1948 Ninth International Conference of American states in Bogotá, Colombia. The former never obtained enough ratifications to go into effect.

IATRA was a collective security treaty that went into effect in 1948 and became important during the Cold War (q.v.), especially for concerted action against Cuba. The two most important articles, one as the basis for action and the other for the measures to be taken, were Articles 6 and 8. The former provided that if any American state's territorial "integrity," "sovereignty or political independence" was "affected by an aggression which is not an armed attack or by any extra-territorial or intra-continental conflict, or by any other . . . situation that might endanger the peace . . ." the Organ of Consultation was to meet at once "in order to agree on the measures . . . [to] be taken for the common defense and for the maintenance of the peace and security of the Continent." Article 8 provided for a range of "measures" of increasing severity, from "recalling chiefs of diplomatic missions" and "breaking" diplomatic and consular relations, to the "use of armed force." These measures required a two-thirds majority (14 votes) and were then "binding" on all IATRA parties "with the sole exception that no State shall be required to use armed force without its consent" (Article 20).

From 1973 to 1975, there was an unsuccessful effort, led by the military government of Peru, with strong support from Ecuador and Panama, to amend both IATRA and the OAS Charter, mainly the former as a "child of the cold war." For this effort the OAS created a Special Commission to Study and Propose Measures for Strengthening the Inter-American System (SCSPMSIAS). Though directed against the United States, with resolutions passed on "collective economic security for development" and "integral development," there were not enough votes to approve formal amendments. However, the work of the UN's Special Committee on the Question of Defining Aggression resulted in an amendment to IATRA when the UN General Assembly adopted the Committee's list of "offenses" constituting aggression in late 1974. The OAS parties to IATRA subsequently incorporated the list into Article 9. *See also* Intervention and Nonintervention; Organization of American States (OAS, 1 and 4a); Security, Changing Concepts of.

INTER-AMERICAN TROPICAL TUNA COMMISSION (IATTC). Founded in 1949 in Washington, D.C., by Costa Rica and the United States, the IATTC investigates the biology and population dynamics of tropical tunas (primarily in the eastern Pacific Ocean) to ascertain the effects of fishing and other factors on tuna stocks. The IATTC promotes appropriate conservation measures to maintain sustainable catches as well as efforts to prevent the needless killing of dolphins in tuna nets. Members include Costa Rica, France, Japan, Nicaragua, Panama, the United States, and Vanuatu. Mexico (1978), Canada (1984), and Ecuador (1968) withdrew from the IATTC after joining earlier, due in large part to disagreements over conservation measures adopted by the commission.

INTERGOVERNMENTAL COMMITTEE ON THE RIVER PLATE BASIN/COMITÉ INTERGUBERNAMENTAL DE LOS PAÍSES COORDINADOR DE LA CUENCA DEL PLATA. International organization composed of members from Argentina, Brazil, Paraguay, and Uruguay to study the development of the principal rivers in the River Plate Basin with emphasis on navigation and the environment.

INTERGOVERNMENTAL COUNCIL OF COPPER EXPORTING COUNTRIES (ICCEC)/CONSEIL INTERGOUVERNEMENTAL DES PAYS EXPORTATEURS DE CUIVRE (CIPEC). International organization founded in 1967 as a commodities group designed to coordinate research and information policies among its four permanent members: Chile, Peru, Zaire, and Zambia. *See also* Appendix VII.

INTERNATIONAL BANK FOR RECONSTRUCTION AND DEVELOPMENT (IBRD). *See* World Bank.

INTERNATIONAL COFFEE AGREEMENT. *See* Appendix VII.

INTERNATIONAL COURT OF JUSTICE (ICJ). The ICJ succeeded the Permanent Court of International Justice of the League of Nations and began functioning in 1946 as the "principal judicial organ" of the UN. This 15-member body has two categories of seats: permanent—China, Britain, France, the Soviet Union, and the United States—and nonpermanent, the other ten members. Terms on the bench are nine years for a permanent seat judge and two years for a nonpermanent seat judge. Each judge's vote is equal. Before the court was constituted, an agreement (often called a "gentleman's agreement") had been reached that there would be two judges from Latin America. (At that time there were 20 Latin American states among the 51 members of the UN.) The Latin American states would rotate the two seats among themselves. With an increasing number of Commonwealth Caribbean states (CWC, q.v.) gaining their independence and joining the UN, especially in the 1970s, the Latin American and CWC states decided that one judge should come from the latter. This decision was carried out in the 1980s. During the Cold War (q.v.) the United States led successful efforts to prevent a Cuban judge from being elected to the ICJ; however, it was unsuccessful in preventing a Nicaraguan judge from being elected in the late 1980s. *See also* International Court of Justice (ICJ), *Nicaragua v. United States of America.*

INTERNATIONAL COURT OF JUSTICE (ICJ), *NICARAGUA V. UNITED STATES OF AMERICA.* Nicaragua brought a case before the ICJ in April 1984, charging the United States with "training, supplying and directing military and paramilitary actions against . . . [Nicaragua]" in order to "overthrow or destabilize the Government of Nicaragua." Nicaragua asked the ICJ to rule that the United States had violated international law (q.v.) and requested that it pay reparations for the damages. (A few days before Nicaragua filed its petition, the United States had vetoed a critical Nicaraguan resolution in the UN Security Council). Just prior to and in anticipation of Nicaragua's filing its case before the court in 1984, the United States announced its denial of ICJ (q.v.) jurisdiction for two years for "Central American disputes arising out of or related to events in Central America." The United States argued that the ICJ lacked jurisdiction since Nicaragua had never accepted jurisdiction (in the transfer from the League of Nation's court to that of the UN), and the ICJ was not "institutionally designed" to deal with such a regional conflict. In May, the ICJ rejected the U.S. request for dismissal, holding that it had jurisdiction, and issued "provisional measures," calling on the United States to halt its blockading or mining of Nicaragua ports and to respect Nicaragua's "sovereignty" and "political independence."

Nevertheless, the United States ignored these interim measures. In November, the ICJ ruled formally on its having jurisdiction to consider the case. The United States then announced its withdrawal from the case. The ICJ handed down its major decision (on the merits) in June 1986, which included 16 different points, each voted on separately. Most of the votes of the 15-member court—including those of two judges from Latin America—broke down at least 12 to three, others 14 to one, the one being the vote of the U.S. judge, in favor of Nicaragua. The ICJ rejected the U.S. collective self-defense argument on behalf of the Salvadoran government against the FMLN (Frente Farabundo Martí de Liberación Nacional, q.v.) and accepted Nicaragua's claims of intervention (q.v.) and violation of international law and ruled that the United States had a duty to pay damages. The United States refused to accept the ruling and later failed to appear when the ICJ met to determine the amount of reparations to be paid. *See also* Central American/Contadora Peace Process.

INTERNATIONAL LAW (IL). The body of customs, practices, agreements, and treaties that form a legal order that provides a common framework for international relations among sovereign states. International law is important because it provides institutions, concepts and principles, and procedures by which states maintain diplomatic relations, carry on trade and commerce, and resolve inter-state disputes. For example, the concept of sovereignty, and its important corollary, nonintervention (q.v.), helps to promote friendly relations and places restraints on hostile actions. In the development of the Inter-American System (IAS, q.v.), the weaker Latin American states stressed sovereignty and its corollary in an effort to curtail the power and blatant interventions (q.v.) in their internal affairs by the United States that stretched back to the 19th century. These interventions were justified by the United States in several ways. First, by a series of corollaries to the Monroe Doctrine (q.v.), beginning with the Mexican-American War (q.v.) in the 1840s, that had become part of U.S. Latin American policy since the middle of the nineteenth century. The various corollaries to the Monroe Doctrine were also buttressed by the ideas of "Manifest Destiny" and the "White Man's Burden." Second, U.S. interventions were justified in terms of maintaining stability, promoting economic development, exporting democracy (q.v.) and protecting human rights (q.v.), fighting communism, and combating narcotics trafficking.

During the Cold War (q.v.), relations between the United States and Latin America suffered because of the lack of U.S. respect for and reliance on international law. Washington policymakers often acted to meet the needs of national security as they saw them, rather than concern themselves with a scrupulous regard for international legal principles. During the 1980s, covert actions and military interventions in Central America and the Caribbean were widely condemned as violations of international law. The invasion of Grenada (q.v.) and military measures against Sandinista Nicaragua (including the creation and support of the Contras [q.v.]), which the International Court of Justice (ICJ, q.v.) found to be illegal, provide several examples of how the Cold War damaged inter-American relations and respect for international law. Attempts to apply U.S. law extraterritorially in the case of the Helms-Burton Act have also been widely condemned as a violation of international law by inter-American and international organizations. In dealing with human rights, the United States, while insisting on monitoring the human rights obligations of other states, has resisted adhering to international covenants and conventions, and international scrutiny of human rights conditions at home.

In opposing U.S. intervention, there was a Latin American effort to develop a regional legal approach, in effect an American international law that made the nonintervention principle much more absolute, thus greatly narrowing the grounds for permissible intervention. Even though a regional school did not receive wide acceptance, this preoccupation and legalistic approach, from a U.S. perspective, did result in the nonintervention principle being made the cornerstone (*la piedra angular*) of the Inter-American System and the most important principle in the 1948 OAS Charter. In traditional international law, the "subjects" were sovereign states, while the "objects" were individuals or persons; international law applied only to the former while the latter were bound only by the laws of their own state. With the passing of time, however, particularly since World War II (q.v.) and due to the efforts of the United Nations, other international organizations, and a number of governments, individuals have become the subjects of international law in certain areas. One is human rights, where individuals have certain rights under international law (e.g., freedom from torture) that the national laws and practices of their state/government must respect. However, the Inter-American Commission on Human Rights (IACHR, q.v.) reflects traditional IL because it cannot enter a state to conduct an investigation without that state's formal consent. *See also* Álvarez, Alejandro; Calvo Doctrine; Drago Doctrine; Intervention and Nonintervention; Monroe Doctrine.

INTERNATIONAL MONETARY FUND (IMF)/FONDO MUNDIAL INTERNACIONAL (FMI)/FONDS MONÉTAIRE INTERNATIONAL (FMI). A specialized lending agency associated with, but not under the authority of, the United Nations, created by the Bretton Woods Conference in 1944 to promote international monetary and financial cooperation. The major objectives of the IMF are: promoting market economies, high growth rates, and free trade and correcting balance of payments problems and currency exchange rate instability. Economic decisions are made upon the basis of a weighted system of voting in which there is a direct correlation between the amount of capital each state subscribes, its assigned quota (the major source of IMF funds), and its total number of votes. As a result, five industrialized nations—France, Germany, Japan, the United Kingdom and the United States—have more than 40 percent of the votes, half of which belong to the United States. In contrast, the five Central American countries combined possess less than one half of one percent of the weighted voting power.

The IMF provides financial support for its members, mainly short-term, and there are conditions for the support (called "conditionality") that have often put certain Latin American and Caribbean countries at odds with the fund. Under the Articles of Agreement, a member country is obligated to comply with the terms of a stand-by arrangement, which requires the recipient of financial support to pursue a prescribed austerity program (one usually requiring inflation reduction, currency devaluation, and the end of subsidies on exports and public services), or the disbursement of funds will be held up. Because of the severe debt crisis that hit Latin American countries like Brazil, Mexico, Argentina, and Chile in the 1980s, dependency on IMF loans became critical for making the required interest and loan payments and avoiding national bankruptcy. Recent structural adjustment programs (q.v., a Structural Adjustment Facility, SAF, was created in 1986)—designed to improve a country's foreign investment climate and to achieve financial stability—have created great resentment and hostility on the part of the governments required to implement the austerity measures.

In some cases, the implemented measures have contributed to social and political unrest: in fact, at times anti-IMF riots have resulted. In early 1997, Haiti's efforts to comply with IMF austerity measures (cut public spending, collect unpaid taxes, privatize state-run enterprises, and reduce the size of the government bureaucracy) in order to get foreign loans led to serious antigovernment protests and strikes. A strike was called by the Anti-International Monetary Fund Committee after security guards fired on a mob that attacked a food warehouse, killing one man. The protesters blamed the economic pain of high inflation and unemployment on the Préval government's efforts to comply with IMF lending guidelines and public policy constraints.

Since the debt crisis, most of the states in the region have been moving slowly and with varying degrees of enthusiasm away from the closed, highly regulated economic systems of the 1950s and 1960s toward open, market-oriented economies. As of 1996, the IMF had loan agreements with 12 Latin American and Caribbean governments: Argentina, Bolivia, Costa Rica, El Salvador, Guyana, Honduras, Mexico, Nicaragua, Panama, Peru, Uruguay, and Venezuela. In addition to these 12 states, the other regional members of the IMF include Antigua and Barbuda, the Bahamas, Barbados, Belize, Brazil, Canada, Chile, Colombia, Dominica, the Dominican Republic, Ecuador, Grenada, Guatemala, Haiti, Jamaica, Paraguay, St. Kitts and Nevis, St. Lucia, St. Vincent and the Grenadines, Suriname, Trinidad and Tobago, and the United States. The IMF is offering to link "good governance" with its lending policies. Using Argentina as the first of what could become a model for other developing countries, the offer would make an IMF line of credit dependent on evidence of government policies aimed at spending on health and education, improving the tax system and court practices, strengthening private property rights, and opening government ledgers to the public. The proposed agreement is the outgrowth of studies that show that sound economic policies and good governing practices produce significantly higher levels of real income growth.

The IMF is governed and managed by an annual Board of Governors (one from each member) meeting, an Executive Board (composed of 24 who handle the day-to-day business), and a managing director selected by the Executive Board. The current managing director of the fund is Michel Camdessus, a Frenchman, now serving his third five-year term. A consistent practice of the fund, reflecting an early understanding among its members, is that its managing director is a European, while that of the World Bank is a U.S. citizen. *See also* Import Substitution Industrialization (ISI); Structural Adjustment Programs (SAPs); World Bank.

INTERNATIONAL ORGANIZATION OF BANANA EXPORTERS (IOBE). *See* Appendix VII.

INTERNATIONAL SEABED AUTHORITY (ISA). *See* United Nations, Third Conference on the Law of the Sea (UNCLOS III); Tuna War.

INTERNATIONAL TIN AGREEMENT. *See* Appendix VII.

INTERVENTION and NONINTERVENTION. The theme of intervention has been a constant in U.S.-Latin American relations and until recently was the most frequently heard complaint of the Latin American and Caribbean states. Concerns over it reach back to the early years after independence, but intervention gained in importance after the U.S. Civil War. It was clearly the most important element of hemispheric politics between 1895 and the 1930s. Latin American complaints about foreign involvement in their internal affairs were well-founded. First, they feared for almost 100 years after gaining independence that their former mother countries would try to regain control or forcibly collect payment of debts. Second, they feared U.S. intervention after the Mexican-American War (q.v.) and the constant referral to the Monroe Doctrine (q.v.) as a means of maintaining its hegemony and protecting its economic and security interests. In response, the smaller and weaker Latin American and Caribbean states stressed international law and the role of international organizations to counterbalance the international power of the United States. The doctrines of Calvo and Drago (qq.v.) were deliberate efforts to reinforce sovereign rights and nonintervention duties among unequal states.

Turning to the League of Nations (q.v.) was another channel of response to intervention, as was the effort to construct an American regional school of international law, one that placed particular stress on nonintervention. In the 1920s, it became clear to the United States that the development of an effective regional system depended upon its abandonment of interference and acceptance of the principle of nonintervention. As part of the Good Neighbor Policy (q.v.) in the 1930s, Washington accepted the nonintervention provisions of several treaties, which in turn resulted in a high level of inter-American cooperation during World War II (q.v.).

When the OAS Charter was drafted and approved in Bogotá, Colombia, in 1948, the all-important principle of nonintervention—the cornerstone of the regional system, from the Latin American perspective—was incorporated into Article 15. The U.S. reversions to intervention, contrary to the OAS Charter, during the Cold War (q.v.) regularly provoked Latin American (and later Commonwealth Caribbean) opposition, impairing U.S.-Latin American and CWC relations, and undermined the legitimacy of the Organization of American States (OAS). This fierce opposition led these states to turn to the United Nations as a counterpoise to the United States and reinforced the developing North-South axis and Third World (q.v.) unity. With the end of the Cold War, the continuing U.S. embargo against Cuba (q.v.), including its strengthening by the 1992 Cuban Democracy Act and the 1995 Helms-Burton Act, it can be argued, is a form of U.S. intervention in Cuba. *See also* Calvo Doctrine; Cold War; Cuba, Intervention in by the United States; Dominican Republic, Intervention in by the United States and the OAS Peace Force; Drago Doctrine; Grenada, Intervention in by the United States; Nicaraguan Revolution;

International Law; Panama, Intervention in by the United States, and Elections; Organization of American States (OAS, 1).

INTERNATIONAL WHEAT COUNCIL (IWC). *See* Appendix VII.

J

JAGAN, CHEDDI (1918–1997). *See* Commonwealth Caribbean Leaders.

JOHNSON, LYNDON B. (1908–1973). *See* Dominican Republic, Intervention in by the United States, and the OAS Peace Force; Johnson Doctrine.

JOHNSON DOCTRINE, of LYNDON B. JOHNSON. A central feature of U.S. Latin American policy after the U.S. intervention in the Dominican Republic (q.v.) in April 1965 that proclaimed that intervention (q.v.) was acceptable to defeat communism in the hemisphere. In what became known as a "no second Cubas" policy, President Lyndon B. Johnson pledged that "the American nations cannot, must not, and will not permit the establishment of another Communist government in the Western Hemisphere." Thus, on the basis of the 1965 Dominican intervention, this change in U.S. policy toward communism in the hemisphere was soon characterized as a doctrine in the president's name.

Latin America held a much lower priority in Johnson's administration than during the short tenure of the Kennedy administration. The Alliance for Progress (q.v.) became a greater political instrument in Johnson's hands as he developed more interest in maintaining the status quo and a greater tolerance for military-authoritarian regimes in that process. The main features of his doctrine were its complete unwillingness to risk another communist government in the hemisphere and belief in U.S. military intervention as an acceptable and ready means—illustrated by U.S. intervention during the 1965 civil war in the Dominican Republic—to maintain hegemony in the Caribbean. The quick success of U.S. military intervention in defeating a few communist forces in the Dominican Republic in 1965 led, according to some historians and political scientists, to the rapid U.S. troop build-up in Vietnam over the following year. *See also* Cold War; Dominican Republic, Intervention in by the United States and the OAS Peace Force; Intervention and Nonintervention.

K

KENNEDY, JOHN F. (1917–1963). *See* Alliance for Progress; Cuba, Intervention in by the United States; Cuba, Missile Crisis with the United States.

KOREAN WAR. During this three-year war, 1950–1953, in which the United Nations Security Council approved a multilateral force to aid South Korea in stemming aggression from North Korea (only one Latin American country, Colombia, sent troops), the Cold War (q.v.) was being institutionalized, and the world role of the United States and its relations with Latin America were being transformed. Despite the fact that the OAS (q.v.) Charter became effective in 1951, the United States was more interested in opposing communist threats in Europe and Asia than assisting Latin America with its pressing economic problems. In so doing it failed to honor its World War II (q.v.) promises to repay Latin America economically for its important support and assistance during the war. This attitude toward Latin America was evident in the United States' opposition to the creation of the Inter-American Development Bank (IADB, q.v.), a United Nations Economic Commission for Latin America (ECLA) proposal, until 1959. It was not until the perception of a communist threat in Guatemala in 1954 that the United States finally turned to Latin America, with no interest in economic development policies or democratization (q.v.). In using the Central Intelligence Agency to covertly remove democratically elected Jacobo Arbenz, the United States signaled the end of the Good Neighbor Policy (q.v.) and its lack of interest in the nonintervention (q.v.) provisions of the OAS Charter when national security interests are an issue. *See also* Cold War; Declaration of Caracas; Guatemala, Intervention in by the United States and OAS Debate.

KUBITSCHEK, JUSCELINO. *See* Alliance for Progress; Operation Pan America.

L

LA JUNTA INTERAMERICANA DE DEFENSA. *See* Inter-American Defense Board (IADB).

LARRETTA DOCTRINE. *See* Rodríguez Larretta Doctrine.

LATIN AMERICAN ASSOCIATION OF DEVELOPMENT FINANCE INSTITUTIONS (LAADFI)/ASOCIACIÓN LATINOAM-

ERICANA DE INSTITUCIONES FINANCIERAS DE DESAR-
ROLLO (ALIDE). LAADFI promotes cooperation among 125
regional development financing bodies in 25 countries in the region.
Nineteen collaborating banks and financial institutions also participate in LAADFI's activities.

LATIN AMERICAN CENTER FOR DEVELOPMENT ADMINIS-
TRATION/CENTRO LATINOAMERICANO DE ADMINISTRA-
CIÓN PARA EL DESARROLLO (CLAD). Multinational organization composed of government representatives from 24 Latin
American and Caribbean countries and Spain that works to enact state
reform in member countries. CLAD works on political-administrative
decentralization and social sector organization while promoting the
exchange of information, research, and seminars on state reform and
public management.

LATIN AMERICAN COMMON MARKETS. *See* Andean Group (AG);
Caribbean Community (CC); Central American Common Market
(CACM); Eastern Caribbean Common Market (ECCM); Southern
Cone Common Market (MERCOSUR).

LATIN AMERICAN CONSENSUS. *See* Special Latin American Coordinating Committee (SLACC).

LATIN AMERICAN ECONOMIC SYSTEM (LAES)/SISTEMA ECO-
NÓMICO LATINOAMERICANO (SELA). Multinational economic
integration organization, consisting of 27 Latin American and Caribbean countries, designed to promote the principles of equality, sovereignty and independence of states, solidarity, nonintervention (q.v.),
and respect for differences in political, economic, and social systems.
To better promote economic and social development, LAES provides
a permanent system of consultation and coordination for the adoption
of common positions and strategies. Cuba is a member of LAES,
while the United States is not. *See also* Embargoes of Organization
of Petroleum Exporting Countries (OPEC).

LATIN AMERICAN ENERGY ORGANIZATION (LAEO)/ORGANI-
ZACIÓN LATINOAMERICANA DE ENERGÍA (OLADE). Multilateral organization whose major purpose is to promote energy cooperation and integration among its 26 members. LAEO was created
by the Lima Agreement, signed in November 1973 and effective in
December 1974. Its Permanent Secretariat, headquartered in Quito,
Ecuador, began functioning in 1975. The first Extraordinary Meeting
of Ministers was held in July 1979, producing the Pronouncement of

San José (Costa Rica) that provided a political framework for regional cooperation on energy matters. (The Meeting of Ministers of Energy convenes annually and forms the policy-making body of the organization.) At its 1981 meeting, the ministers directed the Permanent Secretariat to develop a Latin American Energy Cooperation Program (LAECP). Many of LAEO's activities have received support from the European Community (EC), Inter-American Development Bank (IADB), Organization of Petroleum Exporting Countries (OPEC), and the World Bank (WB) (q.q.v.). LAEO's 26 members include all of the Latin American countries, Canada, Haiti, Suriname, and among the Commonwealth Caribbean countries, Barbados, Grenada, Guyana, Jamaica, and Trinidad and Tobago.

LATIN AMERICAN FREE TRADE ASSOCIATION (LAFTA)/ASOCIACIÓN LATINOAMERICANA DE LIBRE COMERCIO (ALALC). Established by the Treaty of Montevideo in 1960, LAFTA's purpose was to create a free trade area for Latin America within a period of 12 years. For a period of 20 years, LAFTA struggled to achieve its goals but eventually failed due to an overly ambitious timetable, inability to accommodate different levels of economic development among its member states, and the twin forces of foreign debt and protectionism. LAFTA's perceived inequities contributed to the 1969 ratification of the Andean Pact (q.v.) to allow the member states (Bolivia, Chile, Colombia, Ecuador, Peru, and later, Venezuela) to pursue their own agendas independently of LAFTA. LAFTA was replaced with the Latin American Integration Association (LAIA, q.v.) in 1980, initiating a renewed effort at regional economic integration, but it has languished with the numerous free trade proposals that have emerged in the 1990s.

LATIN AMERICAN INTEGRATION ASSOCIATION (LAIA)/ASOCIACIÓN LATINOAMERICANA DE INTEGRACIÓN (ALADI). Multinational economic integration association established in 1980 by the Montevideo Treaty to replace the Latin American Free Trade Association (LAFTA, q.v.). It includes members (divided into three categories according to level of development) from Argentina, Bolivia, Brazil, Chile, Colombia, Ecuador, Mexico, Paraguay, Peru, Uruguay, and Venezuela. The treaty was fully ratified in March 1982. LAIA's major activities include the promotion and regulation of reciprocal trade, economic cooperation, market expansion through preferential tariffs, and technical assistance. Unlike LAFTA, LAIA has no definite timetable for creation of a full common market. Latin American states with observer status include Costa Rica, Cuba, the

Dominican Republic, El Salvador, Guatemala, Honduras, Nicaragua, and Panama.

An important feature of LAIA is its allowance for "outward" projection, linkages or agreements with Latin American nonmember countries or integration organizations and with other developing countries or economic groups outside the Americas. International organizations with observer status in LAIA include the United Nations Economic Commission for Latin America and the Caribbean (ECLAC), United Nations Development Program (UNDP), European Union (EU), Inter-American Development Bank (IADB), and the Organization of American States (OAS) (q.q.v.). In June 1994, the first Interpretative Protocol to the Montevideo Treaty was signed, allowing member states to establish preferential trade agreements with developed nations, and waiving on a temporary basis the most favored nation (MFN, q.v.) clause. *See also* Most Favored Nation (MFN).

LATIN AMERICAN PARLIAMENT/PARLAMENTO LATINOAMERICANO. Founded in 1965 as a permanent democratic institution, the parliament's basis for representation was designed to assure that all the major political movements or trends in each country's legislature were represented proportionately. Although its institutional basis was clarified and strengthened by a 1987 treaty, the resolutions of the parliament are only recommendations to the member governments and political parties. The main purpose of the parliament was to support economic development and integration and facilitate political coordination. There are 19 state members, and its headquarters is in Caracas, Venezuela.

LAW OF THE SEA. *See* United Nations, Third Conference on the Law of the Sea (UNCLOS III).

LEAGUE OF NATIONS. The world's first permanent (sitting in peacetime) international security organization inspired by President Woodrow Wilson in the aftermath of World War I (q.v.). Although the league never included all the Great Powers (the United States never joined since the Senate failed to ratify the covenant of the league), and could not claim to have created even the minimum conditions for collective security, nine Latin American countries (Bolivia, Brazil, Cuba, Guatemala, Haiti, Honduras, Nicaragua, Panama, and Peru) became charter members in 1919, and several others joined during the 1920s.

The Latin American members aligned themselves with the league in hopes of counterbalancing the growing economic and political power of the United States and the economic dominance of Britain in the Western Hemisphere. Fearing the possibility of future direct foreign intervention (q.v.) in hemispheric affairs, and not having forgotten European attempts throughout the nineteenth century, Latin America hoped the League would afford a legal means for countering U.S. policies such as Roosevelt's Big Stick (q.v.), various corollaries attached to the Monroe Doctrine (q.v.), and British economic designs in the Caribbean. The Latin American nations that joined the league were attracted by the principles of nonintervention (q.v.) (Article X) and the peaceful settlement of disputes but were disappointed in Article XXI, which described the Monroe Doctrine as a "regional understanding" instead of a unilateral declaration of policy by the United States. Nevertheless, the league turned out to be the wrong vehicle for challenging the United States and Europe, since the United States failed to become a member and efforts to mediate a peaceful solution to international conflicts such as the Chaco War (q.v.) and the Leticia dispute failed. By 1938, most of the Latin American and Caribbean members had dropped out of the league and turned to bilateral strategies for dealing with the United States. *See also* World War I.

LLERAS CAMARGO, ALBERTO (1906–1990). A former president of Colombia (1945–1946; 1958–1962), he was director of the Pan American Union (1947–1948) before becoming the first secretary-general of the Organization of American States (OAS, q.v.), 1948–1954. He became frustrated with his limited powers and the criticisms of his constrained initiatives and announced his resignation at the 10th Inter-American Conference (Caracas, 1954), declaring emphatically in his so-called "Caracas statement" that: "The Organization is neither good nor bad; it can do nothing else than what the governments which are members . . . want it to be." *See also* Pan American Union; Appendix II.

LOMÉ CONVENTIONS. Three aid and preferential trade agreements first signed in 1975 between the European Community (EC, q.v.), and later the European Union (EU, q.v.), and 49 African, Caribbean, and Pacific Countries Group of States (ACP, q.v.) to promote export earnings by the Third World (q.v.). The original agreement applied only to 12 Commonwealth Caribbean Countries (CWC, q.v.) but was later extended to include the Dominican Republic, Haiti, and Suriname. The original convention was revised and redrafted three times between 1979 and 1989, expanding the number of ACP countries from 49 to 69, allowing for preferential access to EC/EU markets for both manufactured and agricultural (especially sugar) goods, as well as marketing assistance and some technology transfer. In the latest accord (Lomé IV), the agreement was extended for another ten years,

1990–2000. *See also* African, Caribbean, and Pacific Countries Group of States (ACP); Commonwealth Caribbean Countries (CWC).

M

MCCOMIE, VALERIE T. (1920-). The first assistant secretary-general of the Organization of American States (OAS, q.v.) from the Commonwealth Caribbean. Prior to this Barbadian's election, the position was occupied by a Central American. *See also* Organization of American States (OAS, 3); Appendix II.

MANGER, WILLIAM (1899–1994). Known as "Mr. Pan American Union" because of his long career with the organization, Manger began working at the Pan American Union (q.v.) in 1919 and in 1948 became the first assistant secretary-general of the Organization of American States (OAS, q.v.). He later resigned from the position, believing that it should not be held by a citizen of the United States but one from Latin America. *See* Pan American Union (PAU); Appendix II.

MANLEY, MICHAEL of JAMAICA. *See* Commonwealth Caribbean Leaders.

MANLEY, NORMAN of JAMAICA. *See* Commonwealth Caribbean Leaders.

MENEM, CARLOS S. of ARGENTINA. *See* Alfonsín, Raúl; Gulf War.

MERCADO COMÚN CENTROAMERICANO (MCC). *See* Central American Common Market (CACM).

MERCADO COMÚN DEL SUR (MERCOSUR). *See* Southern Cone Common Market.

MEXICAN-AMERICAN WAR. A humiliating, one-sided war between 1846 and 1848 that grew out of the U.S. annexation of Texas in 1845 and President James Polk's expansionist desires in the western half of the United States. When Mexico refused to accept the Rio Grande River as the boundary between the two countries or to sell California and part of New Mexico, President Polk sent U.S. forces into the disputed territories in a clear provocation of the recalcitrant Mexicans. A few days after the clash in May 1846, the U.S. Congress declared war. Mexico was no match for the United States, since the country was deeply divided politically and strife-torn and its army had little training and was poorly equipped, while the U.S. forces had excellent leadership, training, and equipment. U.S. forces had little trouble capturing Vera Cruz and Mexico City and then forcing Mexico to sign the onerous Treaty of Guadalupe-Hidalgo in February 1848. Mexico was forced to cede to the United States four present-day states and parts of three others. As a result of the war with the United States, Mexico lost 55 percent of its territory, in return for which it received an indemnity of only $15 million. The humiliating defeat left Mexico embittered with its northern neighbor. Polk's imperialistic muscle-flexing confirmed the dogma of Manifest Destiny and established the Polk Corollary to the Monroe Doctrine (q.v.), in effect restricting the transfer of territory from one foreign country to another in the Americas. By putting limits on the exercise of Latin American sovereignty, President Polk's interpretation was a precursor to the Big Stick (q.v.) Policy of the United States fifty years later. The trauma of the Mexican-U.S. War of the 1840s is still very much alive in Mexico where the event is known as the American Intervention. *See also* Monroe Doctrine; Big Stick Policy.

MEXICAN REVOLUTION. Contemporary Mexico is the product of a violent revolution that lasted from 1910 to 1920. It was not as radical as many other twentieth-century revolutions, but it was the first to topple its traditional oligarchy made up of landowners, the Church, and the military—and remove foreign control over its economy. The causes of the Mexican Revolution are numerous but the most important are foreign economic penetration, distortions in land ownership, class struggle, local autonomy, and the lack of opportunity for upward mobility. The revolutionary forces that were unleashed by these developments directed their vengeance on the aging regime of Porfirio Díaz, a friend of foreign investors and the traditional oligarchy, who ignored the extreme poverty of the masses and ruled with an iron hand. Led by liberal Francisco Madero and others, the battle cry of "effective suffrage, non-reelection, and redistribution of land" helped to mobilize sufficient segments of the opposition to defeat the dictator. Madero then took over as president of Mexico, but his emphasis on political reform, however, led to his assassination in 1913. Civil war and years of instability and strife followed with a process of musical chairs occurring among a series of civilian and military leaders, most of whom were later assassinated. Unlike other Latin American revolutions, Mexico's insurgency lacked both a dominant leader and a unifying political party or movement. With the absence of a charismatic figure such as Fidel Castro (q.v.), the Mexican Revolution followed a more gradual and moderate course after 1920.

A new constitution was approved in 1917, one that set forth the revolution's main goals: land distribution and labor unions to benefit peasants and workers, and confiscation and nationalization of the wealth of the Church, landlords, and foreign businesses. Certain provisions of the constitution were implemented while others were not, due to the agenda and commitment of different presidents as well as the opposition of the affected interest groups. For the first few decades of the revolution, Mexico tried to avoid a direct confrontation with the United States over the more controversial aspects of the 1917 Constitution.

In order to bring about stability and implement the revolution's social goals, a new political party—National Revolutionary Party, PRN—was formed in 1928, one of the postinsurrectionary innovations designed to bring Mexico's regional political chiefs and the plethora of small political parties under a single umbrella. The name of the dominant party was changed to Instititutional Revolutionary Party (PRI) in the 1940s, by then an established political force that monopolized continuing control of the presidency, the cabinet and bureaucracy, and of the two-house legislature (until July 1997 when the PRI lost control of the Chamber of Deputies). With this governing arrangement, each president and the head of the PRI hand-picked the new president; elections became pro-forma, and the government and party (by now one) and the election process became increasingly corrupt and riddled with fraud. It was an arrangement, according to one critic of Mexican politics, in which "the President leads; the legislature accepts; [and] the bureaucracy implements." In the name of revolutionary change, the PRI and the revolutionary family skillfully deflected challenges to their political power and protected much of the status quo. In exchange for the stability provided by the Mexican system during the Cold War, Washington found no need to invoke the Monroe Doctrine (q.v.) to deal with communist threats, or question the undemocratic character of Mexican politics. For a long time there was a debate in Mexico about whether the government was still pursuing the original goals of the revolution. As the PRI aged, an increasing number of critics and opposition parties argued that the revolution was "dead" or that the goals/ideals had been "betrayed." The insurrection in southern Mexico in 1994, led by a group calling itself the Zapatista National Liberation Front, and the revelations of crime and corruption during the presidency of Carlos Salinas de Gortari (q.v.) that would contribute to his self-imposed exile in Ireland, seemed to remove all doubt about the health of the revolution.

There has been an important anti-foreign, mainly anti-U.S. dimension to the Mexican Revolution. This attitude stems from the legacy of the Mexican-American War (q.v.), U.S. ownership and exploitation of Mexico's oil and mining resources during the Díaz era, and U.S. military interventions against Veracruz in 1914 and General Pershing's "punitive expeditions" across the Mexican border in 1916. Ending foreign control was an important part of the 1917 Constitution, implemented during the 1930s with the nationalization of the assets of foreign oil companies. As a result, Mexico has placed great emphasis upon international law (q.v.), particularly the principles of sovereignty and nonintervention (q.v.). The 1930 Estrada Doctrine (q.v.) was formulated by a Mexican diplomat to remove all political considerations from the process of granting or withholding diplomatic recognition. This anti-foreign legacy required that Mexican presidents criticize, or not appear too cooperative with, the United States. However, the enthusiastic support of the North American Free Trade Agreement (NAFTA, q.v.) by President Salinas represented a major departure from this tradition. Throughout the twentieth century, Mexico has provided strong support for other Latin American revolutions, particularly those in Bolivia, Cuba, and Nicaragua. *See also* Bolivian Revolution; Cuban Revolution; Estrada Doctrine; International Law; Intervention and Nonintervention; Nicaraguan Revolution.

MEXICO. *See* Clinton, William J.; Mexican-American War; North American Free Trade Agreement (NAFTA); Organization of American States (OAS).

MONROE DOCTRINE. A fundamental component of U.S.-Latin American policy that rejects European expansion in the Western Hemisphere, establishes a sphere of influence under U.S. control, and, until the end of the Cold War (q.v.), frequently served as a justification for U.S. intervention (q.v.). Monroe's message to Congress in 1823 was a unilateral pronouncement with no legal basis, since it was never ratified by the Congress of the United States. Monroeism—a combination of U.S. paternalism, interventionism, and domination of the Western Hemisphere—contributed to Latin America's legal and political efforts to curb the imperialist tendencies of the United States throughout most of the twentieth century. Many of Latin America's nationalistic responses to U.S. policies can be attributed to the U.S. utilization and interpretation of the Monroe Doctrine after the U.S. Civil War. Often seen as anachronistic by the Latin American states, the Monroe Doctrine is still mentioned, mostly by conservative U.S. policymakers who argue that it has relevance for U.S. relations with Latin America, no matter what the historical record reveals. *See also* Big Stick Policy; Intervention and Nonintervention; Roosevelt, Theodore.

MORA, JOSÉ A. (1897–1975). A career diplomat from Uruguay, Mora served as the third secretary-general of the Organization of American States (OAS, q.v.) and wrote about his tenure in office in *From Panama to Punta del Este* (1968). *See also* Organization of American States (OAS, Organs . . . General).

MOST FAVORED NATION (MFN). An illusive term used by most trading partners to imply that trade will be carried out with reciprocity. Under the terms of the General Agreement on Tariffs and Trade (GATT, q.v.), MFN is somewhat of a misnomer since most trading partners have this arrangement. In most cases, MFN status between trading partners means that no unique discrimination is allowed rather than the existence of special trading privileges. As a diplomatic tool, MFN status is sometimes used by the U.S. Congress as a way to get its views across in the conduct of foreign relations. After the president of the United States has judged whether a country's progress on human rights (q.v.) justifies renewal, Congress has the authority to pass a resolution overturning the authority. However, MFN is often no more than a symbolic debate over international trade issues since large states such as China know that trade as an American interest is much more important than other issues such as human rights, democratization, or nonproliferation. As of 1997, Cuba is the only Latin American country out of seven worldwide that the United States has decided deserves loss of most favored nation status. *See also* General Agreement on Tariffs and Trade (GATT).

MOVIMIENTO REVOLUCIONARIO TÚPAC AMARU (MRTA). *See* Fujimori, Alberto.

MUTUAL ASSISTANCE OF THE LATIN AMERICAN GOVERNMENT OIL COMPANIES/ASISTENCIA RECÍPROCA PETROLERA ESTATAL LATINOAMERICANA (ARPEL). Organization of state enterprises founded in 1965 to promote technical and economic development, Latin American integration, interchange of technical assistance and information, and meetings and lectures concerning the petroleum industry. Members include state oil enterprises in Argentina, Bolivia, Brazil, Canada, Chile, Colombia, Costa Rica, Cuba, Ecuador, Jamaica, Mexico, Nicaragua, Paraguay, Peru, Suriname, Trinidad and Tobago, Uruguay, and Venezuela.

N

NEW INTERNATIONAL ECONOMIC ORDER (NIEO). In 1974 at the sixth Special Session of the United Nations, the Third World (q.v.)

states were successful in adopting the Declaration on the Establishment of a New International Economic Order. This Declaration was the culmination of a decade-long movement of increasing cooperation and influence of developing countries and the embodiment of a shift on economic issues from an East-West to a North-South axis. The major steps in this movement included the formation in 1964 of the Special Committee on Latin American Coordination (SCLAC, q.v.) and the Group of Seventy-Seven (G-77, q.v.) in preparation for the first meeting of the United Nations Conference on Trade and Development (UNCTAD) in Geneva in 1964 (UNCTAD later became a permanent organ of the General Assembly); the subsequent meetings of UNCTAD every four years; and the third United Nations Conference on the Law of the Sea (UNCLOS III, q.v.), which held its first session in New York in 1973. The second meeting was held in Caracas in 1974, and the other sessions continued until December 1982, when the final convention was ready to consider.

The NIEO Declaration called for replacing the present international economic system, which these less developed states maintained was dominated by the Western, developed capitalist states, with one that would benefit and contribute to the growth and modernization of the developing states. These states used UNCLOS III as a means of bringing about NIEO. Later that year, the same group of states assured the adoption of a General Assembly resolution creating the Charter on the Economic Rights and Duties of States (CERDS, q.v.). Of related concern and a high priority for these states, and their view of multinational corporations, was their strong advocacy of a compulsory code of conduct (one enforced by the UN) applied to restrain the domestic involvement of such companies. The more powerful developed states opposed such a code but instead favored one that was voluntary.

NICARAGUA, INSURRECTION IN OF SANDINISTAS AND COLLECTIVE SANCTIONS BY THE OAS. The Frente Sandinista de Liberación Nacional (Sandinista National Liberation Front—FSLN) began opposing the Somoza (q.v.) family in the 1960s and escalated their guerrilla attacks until they were leading a popular insurrection against Somoza's National Guard by 1978. Major battles were fought between the two sides, and arms were coming in for the FSLN, mainly from Cuba but also from Panama and Venezuela, transhipped to Costa Rica via Panama. "Neutral" Costa Rica permitted this, due to its long history of problems with the Somozas. The United States supported and supplied Somoza in the conflict until he refused to accept mediation. President Jimmy Carter (q.v.) actively pursued a mediation effort in an attempt to work out a reconciliation between Somoza and the FSLN. The effort was made by the Tri-Partite International Commission of Friendly Cooperation and Conciliation, headed by the United States and the ambassadors of the Dominican Republic and Guatemala. When Somoza rejected the final mediation plan in December 1978, Washington cut off aid and arms and turned against him.

While the ill-fated mediation effort was underway, the Organization of American States (OAS, q.v.) became increasingly involved. The 17th Meeting of Consultation convened in September 1978, and the United States proposed that the Inter-American Commission on Human Rights (IACHR, q.v.) visit Nicaragua to investigate the charges of human rights violations by the National Guard. The commission visited Nicaragua, investigated, and submitted a very critical report. The OAS also investigated Nicaraguan violations of Costa Rica's border and created an Ad Hoc Commission of Observers to monitor the area. In October the ministers at the 17th meeting censured Nicaragua for its attacks on Costa Rican civilians. On account of the escalating scope and scale of military operations in Nicaragua in 1979, the Carter administration began to work through the OAS to resolve the conflict. At an emergency session of the 17th meeting, Secretary of State Cyrus Vance made a proposal based on the 1965 Dominican Republic model (q.v.): establishing a "government of national reconciliation" and providing an OAS force for the "maintenance of the peace." His proposal had few supporters and was quickly dropped. Instead, the meeting passed a resolution in late June, which blamed the Somoza regime's human rights violations as the cause of the conflict and called for its "immediate and definitive replacement" along with the installation of a democratic (q.v.) government and the holding of free elections. This resolution was unprecedented, for it was the *first* time that the OAS had called for the "replacement" of a head of state. Thereafter, more and more OAS members broke relations with Nicaragua and began recognizing the Sandinista provisional government in Costa Rica. In July 1979, the National Guard surrendered, Somoza fled the country, and the provisional government took over. The Carter administration soon recognized the new government and promised economic assistance. *See also* Somoza Dynasty/Family.

NICARAGUAN REVOLUTION. Major revolt against the Somoza Dynasty (q.v.) that culminated in the July 1979 removal of Anastasio Somoza Debayle and the notorious National Guard by a broad coalition of revolutionary forces including the Frente Sandinista de Liberación Nacional (FSLN, Sandinista National Liberation Front). By the time the Sandinista-led rebel coalition took power, the war to remove

Somoza had killed 50,000 (almost two percent of the population), and the country was faced with an estimated $1.5 billion in property losses and huge foreign debt inherited from the previous government. Although the United States wanted Somoza out of power, it was anti-Sandinista in its Nicaragua policy but in the end could not prevent them from winning power, a situation that mirrored the U.S. response to the Cuban Revolution (q.v.) some 20 years earlier. By 1979, numerous Latin American governments and the Organization of American States (OAS, q.v.) had openly sided with the opposition gaining momentum against Somoza. Sandinista opposition to U.S. mediation efforts prior to the demise of Somoza increased, first when Washington tried to engineer a new government without Sandinista participation and second when it tried to use the OAS to back a peacekeeping force, a thinly disguised proposal to intervene against the Sandinistas.

Once in power, the Sandinista government drew its inspiration from the anti-imperialist stance of an earlier generation of Nicaraguans who opposed U.S. intervention (q.v.) in Nicaragua. Despite the fact that several of the members of the collective leadership of the Sandinistas were Marxists or Marxist-oriented, the Nicaraguan revolution did not mimic the Cuban revolution under Fidel Castro (q.v.). Government policies aimed for a redistribution of wealth and income along socialist lines, but the regime was hardly totalitarian in its political and economic orientation.

Nevertheless, the government's close ties with Cuba and the Soviet Union generated the necessary policy motivation to mount a counterrevolution against the revolutionary leadership. First under President Carter and then with a vengeance during the Reagan (q.v.) administration, the United States began a counterrevolution designed to destabilize and remove the Sandinistas from power. The centerpiece of this effort was a Contra (q.v.) army of former National Guard officers and soldiers and political allies of the former dictator financed through clandestine appeals to foreign governments and wealthy private individuals during the Reagan administration. When the Iran-Contra scandal broke in 1986 and the Central American Peace Accords were signed the following year, the ability of the Contras to sustain themselves ended.

Despite over $400 million in direct U.S. aid to the Contras by 1990, the Sandinistas struggled on to sustain their revolutionary programs. By subjecting themselves to democratic elections in 1990, the Sandinistas hoped to move forward with the rebuilding of Nicaragua without having to devote large sums to the anti-Contra effort. With Daniel Ortega (q.v.) running on the FSLN ticket and Violeta Barrios de Chamorro (q.v.) on a coalition ticket called UNO in the February 1990 elections, the Sandinista revolution came to a halt as the Chamorro ticket won and replaced the Sandinista leadership for what would become a long and difficult six-year term of office. Daniel Ortega tried to camouflage his revolutionary past in campaigning for another go at the presidency in 1996 but was defeated handily by archconservative José Arnoldo Alemán, former Mayor of Managua. *See also* Ortega, Daniel; Somoza Dynasty/Family.

NONALIGNED MOVEMENT (NAM). A basically Third World (q.v.) movement founded in 1955 at the Bandung Conference to address mutual themes and concerns such as anticolonialism, neutrality toward the Cold War (q.v.), and opposition to racism. By raising economic and social issues to the agenda of international organizations, members of the nonaligned movement were able to vent their grievances against the superpowers entangled in the web of the Cold War. NAM's chronic lack of unity and deeply divergent interests, differing levels of development, and conflicting political ideologies weakened its ability to serve as a united front for Third World issues and interests. The end of the Cold War served to undermine the original purpose of NAM, and by the 1990s it appeared to be drifting on a sea of irrelevance and economic animosities. While many Western nations viewed Fidel Castro (q.v.) as a puppet of the Soviets, he was elected chairman (1979–1983) of the Nonaligned Movement and held a summit meeting in Havana in 1979. *See also* Cold War; Third World.

NONINTERVENTION, PRINCIPLE OF. *See* Intervention and Nonintervention.

NORIEGA, MANUEL ANTONIO (1936-). A Panamanian military leader who, as chief of the National Guard from 1983 to 1989, played a key role in U.S. Central American policy during the Reagan and Bush (qq.v.) administrations. After graduating from the Peruvian Military Academy, which enabled him to become a National Guard officer, Noriega attended the U.S. School of the Americas in Panama. Despite his ruthless and antidemocratic methods of governing Panama after the death of fellow officer Omar Torrijos in 1981, Noriega provided critical intelligence to the United States, Cuba, and Israel and also served as a source of drug smuggling and money laundering for the Medellín drug cartel. While a paid informant for the United States, he helped ship arms from Cuba to the Sandinista rebels in Nicaragua and later joined the United States in funneling arms to the Contras (q.v.) during the Reagan (q.v.) administration. After annulling the 1989 presidential elections in Panama—an act condemned by the Organization of American States (OAS, q.v.)—and being indicted for drug smuggling in the United States, General Noriega's removal was engineered by the United States.

Despite OAS negotiations, trade sanctions by the United States, and two failed coup attempts Noriega remained in power. Reacting to domestic pressure in the United States and the deteriorating situation in Panama, President Bush decided to intervene militarily on December 20, 1989, to try to capture the Panamanian troublemaker. Reaction to the invasion by the Latin American and Caribbean countries was quick and negative: two days after the invasion the OAS passed a resolution condemning the military intervention and calling for the withdrawal of American troops. The United Nations followed with a similar resolution with corresponding results. In the OAS resolution, 20 nations voted in favor, seven abstained, and the United States cast the sole negative vote. After almost two weeks in hiding, Noriega gave himself up to U.S. agents and was quickly taken to Miami for trial on a variety of narcotics charges. After being sentenced to 40 years in prison, General Noriega now resides in a federal prison in Miami, Florida, but his removal has had virtually no impact on the reduction of money laundering and drug trafficking through the isthmus. Noriega's assistance with various kinds of intelligence—he had face-to-face meetings with then-Vice President Bush and CIA Director William Casey—made him a valuable asset during the turbulent 1980s. Until the Iran-Contra scandal erupted in 1986–1987, revealing Noriega's role, the United States was willing to overlook his gunrunning, money laundering, and drug smuggling in the isthmus. It was because of Noriega's close association with Colombia's Medellín drug cartel (q.v.) that President Bush ordered the U.S. military invasion to arrest him, at a cost of 24 American lives, over 1,000 Panamanian deaths, and a cost of over a million dollars. *See also* Bush, George; Panama, Intervention in by the U.S. and the OAS, and Elections; Panama Canal.

NORTH AMERICAN FREE TRADE AGREEMENT (NAFTA). Comprehensive free trade agreement between Canada, Mexico, and the United States signed in October 1992, ratified in November 1993, and entered into force on January 1, 1994. The main provisions of NAFTA include the almost total removal of trade and investment restrictions over a 15-year period. Trade disputes are to be settled in the first instance by intergovernmental consultation; if the dispute is not resolved within 30 to 40 days, any government may call a meeting of the Free Trade Commission to settle the issue. If the Commission fails to settle the dispute, a panel of experts in the relevant field is appointed to adjudicate matters. In 1993, as a result of protectionist opposition in the United States and Canada, two "side agreements" established commissions with formal powers to provide safeguards for workers' rights and environmental protection. With representatives from each country, a review panel of experts has the power to impose fines and trade sanctions, but only with regard to the United States and Mexico, since Canada opted to enforce compliance with NAFTA by means of its own legal system. Prior to the ratification of NAFTA, the Rio Group (q.v.) called for it as a first step toward a hemisphere-wide trade agreement. Negotiations for the admission of Chile to the Agreement were to begin in 1995, but congressional opposition in the United States put a halt to the inclusion of a fourth member. In a strange twist of events, shipments of illicit drugs into the United States from Mexico have increased due to NAFTA's tariff and regulatory reductions.

In March 1996, Canada requested consultations (the first step in determining whether to issue a challenge under NAFTA's dispute settlement process) with the United States to explain U.S. plans to implement the Cuban Liberty and Democratic Solidarity (Libertad) Act (also known as the Helms-Burton Act). Canada considers the legislation an improper extraterritorial extension of U.S. jurisdiction that violates principles of international law when settling claims for expropriated property. In June 1996, spearheaded by Mexico and Canada, the Organization of American States (OAS, q.v.) adopted a resolution (the United States was the lone dissenter) sharply criticizing laws that obstruct international trade and investment such as Helms-Burton. Members of the European Union (q.v.) have also criticized the Helms-Burton Act for its extraterritorial reach and have brought the matter before the World Trade Organization (WTO, q.v.). The Clinton administration has been unsuccessful in persuading other Latin American countries to join in the Helms-Burton crusade against Cuba; at a meeting of the Rio Group in August 1996, Clinton envoy Madeleine Albright tried in vain to twist arms in favor of U.S. Cuban policy. Opposition to NAFTA in the United States, and the declining interest in pushing toward a hemispheric free trade area, have been the major forces in expanding other economic integration efforts such as the Southern Cone Common Market (MERCOSUR, q.v.), common markets in Latin America and the Caribbean, and greater trade with members of the European Union. *See also* Clinton, William J.

NORTH ATLANTIC TREATY ORGANIZATION (NATO). Despite its historic commitment to avoiding entangling alliances in peacetime, the United States agreed to form a security alliance with its Western European allies in 1948–1949. Its major purpose was to serve as a collective military deterrent to the Soviet Union. Twelve nations— Canada and the United States and ten European—signed the treaty in

April 1949; three other European states joined in the early 1950s. When the Cold War (q.v.) ended in 1990, NATO foreign ministers agreed that a unified Germany could be included in the organization. General Alexander Haig served as NATO commander during the 1970s (1974–1979), but his experience was of little benefit in preventing the Falklands/Malvinas War (q.v.) between a North Atlantic Treaty member (Britain) and a member (Argentina) of the Organization of American States (q.v.). During this war in 1982 the United States maintained that the UN, not the Organization of American States, had jurisdiction over the belligerents. The United States aided and sided with its NATO ally, which embittered Argentina and undermined the importance of the OAS in resolving hemispheric disputes. The NATO treaty allows for a unified command structure with hundreds of thousands of armed men and women, which is not permitted within the Charter of the Organization of American States. *See also* Falklands/Malvinas War; South Atlantic Treaty Organization (SATO).

O

OPERATION PAN AMERICA. A precursor program for the economic and social development of Latin America proposed by Brazilian President Juscelino Kubitschek in 1958. President Kubitschek argued in a letter to President Eisenhower that Latin America's underdevelopment problems would have to be solved before the region could effectively resist leftist subversion and serve the interests of the United States in the Cold War (q.v.). Kubitschek proposed a 20-year development program with $40 billion in economic assistance to meet the developmental needs of Latin America. Despite continuing promises from the Eisenhower administration, it was not until the 1959 triumph of Fidel Castro (q.v.) that a sense of urgency to go forth with a new economic program in the region swept Washington. President Kubitschek's proposal eventually became part of the Alliance for Progress (q.v.) in 1961. *See also* Alliance for Progress.

ORFILA, ALEJANDRO (1925-). An Argentine diplomat and secretary-general of the Organization of American States (OAS, q.v.) (1975–1980; 1980–1984). Before becoming the fifth OAS secretary-general, he was Argentina's ambassador to the United States. Orfila's first term as OAS secretary-general was the most notable, as he presided over the signing of the treaties between Panama and the United States in 1977 that granted Panama full sovereignty over the Panama Canal (q.v.) in 1999. *See also* Organization of American States (OAS, Organs . . . General), Panama Canal.

ORGANISMO PARA LA PROSCRIPCIÓN DE LAS ARMAS NUCLEARES EN AMÉRICA LATINA Y EL CARIBE (OPANAL). *See* Agency for the Prohibition of Nuclear Weapons in Latin America and the Caribbean (APNWLA); Treaty of Tlatelolco.

ORGANIZACIÓN DE ESTADOS AMERICANOS (OEA). *See* Organization of American States (OAS).

ORGANIZACIÓN DE ESTADOS CENTROAMERICANOS (ODECA). *See* Organization of Central American States (OCAS).

ORGANIZACIÓN DEL TRATATO DEL ATLÁNTICO SUR (OTAS). *See* South Atlantic Treaty Organization (SATO).

ORGANIZACIÓN LATINOAMERICANA DE ENERGÍA (OLADE). *See* Latin American Energy Organization (LAEO).

ORGANIZACIÓN NACIONES UNIDAS EN CENTROAMERICA (ONUCA)/UN OBSERVER GROUP IN CENTRAL AMERICA. *See* Central American/Contadora Peace Process.

ORGANIZACIÓN NACIONES UNIDAS EN EL SALVADOR (ONU-SAL)/UN OBSERVER GROUP IN EL SALVADOR. *See* Central American/Contadora Peace Process.

ORGANIZACIÓN REGIONAL INTERAMERICANA DE TRABAJADORES (ORIT). *See* Inter-American Regional Organization of Workers.

ORGANIZATION OF AMERICAN STATES (OAS)/ORGANIZACIÓN DE ESTADOS AMERICANOS (OEA). This is the oldest regional organization in the Western Hemisphere and the general descendent of the Pan American Movement (PAM, q.v.), going back to the Panama Conference that Simón Bolívar organized in 1826. It is the particular descendent of the first International Conference of American States held in Washington, D.C., from 1889 to 1890. The OAS is the culmination of a series of PAM and inter-American (i.e., between the Latin American states and the United States) conferences, agreements, and practices. (See Appendix I for a list of conferences.) It is also the principal diplomatic channel of the Inter-American System (IAS, q.v.). In keeping with the decision of a 1910 conference designating the Pan American Union (PAU, q.v.) as the Permanent Secretariat in Washington, D.C., the OAS is headquartered in the U.S. capital.

1. Charter of the OAS (COAS) and Amendments. It was drawn up and approved at the Ninth International Conference of American States held in Bogotá, Colombia, in 1948, and went into effect in 1951. The COAS is coordinated with the United Nations Charter in terms of peaceful settlement of disputes and enforcement action by means of the latter's Chapter VIII on "Regional Arrangements." The original COAS stated its "essential purposes" in Chapter I, Article 4, as the following:

a) To strengthen the peace and security of the continent;
b) To prevent possible causes of difficulties and to ensure the pacific settlement of disputes;
c) To provide for common action on the part of those States in the event of aggression;
d) To seek the solution of political, juridical and economic problems . . .; and
e) To promote, by cooperative action, their economic, social, and cultural development.

Chapter II, Article 5, provided the governing "principles" of

a) International law . . .;
b) . . .Respect for the personality, sovereignty and independence of States, and the faithful fulfillment of obligations derived from treaties . . .;
d) The solidarity of the American States and the high aims which are sought . . . require [their] political organization on the basis of the effective exercise of representative democracy;
e) The American States condemn war of aggression: victory does not give rights;
f) An act of aggression against one American State is an act of aggression against all [of them].

Although Chapter III on the Fundamental Rights and Duties of States declared that there were both equal rights and duties, the duty of nonintervention (q.v.) was stressed as the most important, for three articles (15, 16, and 17) were devoted to it. Article 15 makes this crucial statement:

No State or group of States has the right to intervene, directly or indirectly, for any reason whatever, in the internal or external affairs of any other State. The foregoing principle prohibits not only armed force but also any other form of interference or attempted threat against the personality of the State or against its political, economic and cultural elements.

The 1948 COAS has been formally amended four times: first, by the 1967 Protocol of Buenos Aires; second, by the 1985 Protocol of

Cartagena de Indias; third, by the 1993 Protocol of Managua; and fourth, by the 1992 Protocol of Washington. The Protocol of Buenos Aires was approved at the third Special Inter-American Conference held in February 1967, and the amendments went into effect in February 1970. The impetus for the amendments was the Latin American states' desire to strengthen the economic and social provisions, their priority, and weaken the political and security provisions, the U.S. priority. They were also concerned about an increasing number of small ex-British Caribbean Commonwealth states becoming members. What resulted was a great expansion of the economic and social duties and roles of the OAS. This was evidenced by the increased status and actions of its two councils, the Inter-American Economic and Social Council (IAECOSOC) and the Inter-American Council for Education, Science, and Culture (IACESC). The "Council" became the Permanent Council, and some of its powers were given to an annual General Assembly meeting, which replaced the former and defunct (since 1954) quadrennial Inter-American Conference. The Permanent Council was also elevated and given authority to act provisionally as the Organ of Consultation, the Meeting of Consultation of Ministers of Foreign Affairs. The General Secretariat was assigned more duties and given more power. (See 3 below.) Article 9 prevented a non member from joining if it were involved in an ongoing territorial dispute with a member, thus precluding the admission of two Commonwealth Caribbean states—Belize (in dispute with Guatemala) and Guyana (in dispute with Venezuela). (See 2 below.) The Inter-American Commission on Human Rights (IACHR, q.v.) was also upgraded.

The second set of amendments, the Protocol of Cartagena de Indias, was approved at the 14th Special Session of the General Assembly held in that Colombian city in 1985 and went into effect in November 1988. These amendments were prompted by certain interventions: Argentina's 1982 attack on the British Falkland Islands and the resultant Falklands/Malvinas (q.v.) or South Atlantic War (q.v.); the U.S. 1983 invasion of Grenada (q.v.); and the U.S. involvement in Nicaragua in 1983–1985 during the Central American/Contadora Peace Process (q.v.). There was also concern about democratization, and the concept of integral development was added. The amendments reaffirmed the nonintervention principle, strengthened the political role of the secretary-general in peaceful settlement, and eliminated Article 9 as a qualification for membership. While the Protocol of Washington, approved at a 1992 special General Assembly, has not yet received the necessary ratifications, it includes new provisions to strengthen representative democracy and to protect human rights (q.v.), and the elimination of extreme poverty is set as a new OAS goal. One article provides for the suspension of an OAS member if its democratically elected government is overthrown.

The third set of amendments, the Protocol of Managua, approved by the 1993 General Assembly held in Nicaragua and became effective in January 1996, emphasized and strengthened the role of the OAS in economic development and regional integration. A new Inter-American Council for Integral Development (IACID) has replaced the two former councils—Economic and Social and Education, Science, and Culture.

Finally, the Protocol of Washington amendments were approved at the 17th Special General Assembly session in 1992, and they became effective in September 1997 with Venezuela's ratification. Their main import is to strengthen further OAS collective action in support of democracy by suspending a member of its "democratically constituted government has been overthrown by force." Such action requires a two-thirds vote of the 35 members. Mexico opposed the "punitive character" of the amendment.

2. **Membership.** The original number of OAS members was 21—20 Latin American countries (including Haiti) and the United States. Cuba's *government* was suspended from participating in the OAS in 1962, but not the Cuban *state,* since no provisions exist in the charter for expelling a member state. In the late 1960s, some British territories began gaining their independence and applied for membership, mainly to meet the requirement of OAS membership in order to join and obtain loans from the Inter-American Development Bank (IADB, q.v.). Exceptions to the rule were made for Canada, Belize, and Guyana: Canada did not join the OAS until 1990, and the other two until 1991 (until the 1985 OAS amendments that eliminated Article 9's exclusion of them were approved, Belize and Guyana were denied OAS membership). Trinidad and Tobago and Barbados joined in 1967 and were the first in a series of newly independent Commonwealth Caribbean States (CWC, q.v.) to apply for membership, reaching a total of 12 in 1991. Suriname, a former Dutch colony, joined in 1977. The OAS had 35 members by 1991, a total that has not changed since.

Starting in 1971, the OAS approved a category of permanent observers, which in 1996 had grown to 40 states (including the European Community), both developed and developing, from around the world.

3. **Organs and Structure.** The present structure (see Appendix V) is the result of the three protocols of amendment to the COAS summarized in the previous section and is composed of the following organs and bodies: the General Assembly (GA); the Permanent Council (PC) and the Inter-American Council for Inte-

gral Development (IACID); the Organ of Consultation, the Meeting of Consultation of Ministers of Foreign Affairs (MMFA); specialized organizations and other entities; and the General Secretariat (GS). Three other bodies that are also linked to both the GA and the Secretariat are the Inter-American Commission on Human Rights (IACHR, q.v.), Inter-American Court of Human Rights (IACtHR) in San José, Costa Rica, and the Inter-American Juridical Committee (IAJC) (q.q.v.) in Rio de Janeiro, Brazil. All OAS members (except Cuba) are represented in the GA, the councils and the Organ of Consultation, and the specialized organizations and other entities on a voluntary basis while the commission, court, and juridical committee have limited, representative membership. Equality of voting prevails in all OAS organs and bodies, for there is no system of weighted voting or veto among members as exists in certain specialized agencies or organs of the United Nations.

The GA is the plenary body and holds an annual session; these meetings are held in different OAS member countries. It also holds special sessions. The PC meets regularly, at least twice monthly, at OAS headquarters in Washington, D.C., and serves as the executive organ; it has the authority to meet as the provisional Organ of Consultation if there is an emergency situation. This organ, the Meeting of Consultation of Ministers of Foreign Affairs, which has the responsibility of dealing with threats to the peace and other emergencies, often meets in the locale of the crisis. (See 4a and b below.)

The OAS structure also includes two categories of commissions, institutes, and organizations, the specialized organizations and other entities. The former includes the following six groups: the Pan American Institute of Geography and History (PAIGH) in Mexico City; the Inter-American Indian Institute (IAII) in Mexico City; the Inter-American Institute of Agriculture (IAICA) in San José, Costa Rica; the Pan American Health Organization (PAHO, q.v.) in Washington, D.C.; the Inter-American Children's Institute (IACI, q.v.) in Montevideo, Uruguay; and the Inter-American Commission of Women (IACW) in Washington, D.C. The latter category includes three bodies (all headquartered in Washington, D.C.): the Inter-American Nuclear Energy Commission (IANEC, q.v.); the Inter-American Drug Abuse Control Commission (IADACC, q.v.); and the Inter-American Telecommunications Commission (IATC).

The General Secretariat is located in Washington, D.C. (mainly in the 1910 Pan American Union building), and is headed by the secretary-general (SG, q.v.) and the assistant secretary-general (ASG) who serve for five years. (See Appendix

II for names and terms of office of past holders of these positions.) There has developed over the years a general practice and understanding about the nationality, subregion, and former office of the SG and ASG. The practice has required the SG to be a Latin American from a South American country and usually a former president (Alejandro Orfila [q.v.] from Argentina and João Clemente Baena Soares [q.v.] from Brazil were diplomats and ambassadors). Concerning the ASG, while the first two were U.S. citizens (William Manger [q.v.] and William Sanders), all others have been Latin American ministers or diplomats from Central American countries. With the admission of an increasing number of Commonwealth Caribbean states, the practice changed to that of selecting the ASG from one of these countries. The amendments to the COAS and certain GA resolutions have strengthened the initiative and powers of the SG, particularly in the areas of conflict resolution, the promotion of democracy (q.v.), and economic development. Two relatively new units indicating important OAS priorities were created by the GA in 1993: the Unit for the Promotion of Democracy and the Trade Unit—the Special Committee on Trade (SCT), which replaced the Special Committee for Consultation and Negotiation (SCCN, q.v.).

The General Secretariat is composed of a number of permanent or special secretariats to the General Assembly, the Meeting of Consultation, and the Permanent Council, as well as for the Inter-American Commission on Human Rights (IACHR) and for some of the specialized organizations and other entities. There is an Executive Secretariat for the new Council for Integral Development. For internal organization, there is a Secretariat for Legal Affairs and a Secretariat for Management.

When the Organization of American States was established, the funds for the general, regular budget were assigned on the basis of a quota system in terms of a state's general ability to pay. The United States agreed to a quota of 66 percent with Argentina, Brazil, and Mexico in descending order providing together about 20 percent. In the late 1960s and early 1970s, expanding OAS activities steadily required additional funds; at the same time, some members were in arrears, including the United States. At the 1976 OAS General Assembly the United States made a case for the reduction of its quota to 49 percent, which would be reduced from 66 by one percent per year until the 49 percent level was reached. This proposal was not approved. The nonpayment of quotas by the United States and other states resulted in a financial crisis and near bankruptcy for the OAS in the 1980s. In 1990, the OAS General Assembly approved a U.S. reduced quota of 59 percent, after which the United States began paying its new share plus part of its arrearage. Thereafter, the OAS set a total assessment level of $69 million for the two-year budget period 1994 and 1995. The 1995 general budget, from both quota and voluntary contributions, was $111 million. The financial situation of the OAS has been improving since 1990, but it is still a problem that limits the organization's activities, particularly efforts to expand its role in promoting democracy (q.v.) and regional integration/trade.

4. **Roles and Functions.**
   a. Collective security, conflict resolution, peaceful settlement, and peacekeeping/making. The primary basis for action when there is a security threat to a member or members of the OAS is the 1947 Inter-American Treaty of Reciprocal Assistance (IATRA or Rio Treaty, q.v.). The Meeting of Consultation of Ministers of Foreign Affairs (MMFA) can be convoked upon the basis of Article 6: "If the inviolability or the territory or the sovereignty or political independence of any American State should be affected by an aggression which is not an armed attack or by an extra-continental or intra-continental conflict, or by any other fact or situation that might endanger the peace of America." (Article 9 lists the acts that may be characterized as "aggression.") Article 8 provides the range of "measures" to be taken: from the "recall of chiefs of diplomatic missions; breaking of diplomatic relations; . . . partial or complete interruption of economic relations [to the] . . . use of armed force." Various sanctions, which required a two-thirds majority (14 votes), were applied against the Dominican Republic (1960, q.v.) and Cuba (1962, 1964 and 1967, q.v.) and the first and only Inter-American Peace Force (IAPF, q.v.) was created in 1965 and sent to the Dominican Republic after its civil war and U.S. military intervention (q.v.).

   When the OAS is meeting on the basis of the Rio Treaty, only those members that are parties to the latter may participate. After Cuba was suspended in 1962, it abrogated the treaty. Trinidad and Tobago is the only Commonwealth Caribbean State that is a party, ratifying it in 1967. Canada is not a party. The last meeting of the OAS upon the basis of the Rio Treaty, which was called by Argentina, was to consider Argentina's invasion of the Falklands/Malvinas (q.v.) and the resultant South Atlantic War (q.v.). Certain bodies that deal with defense and peace and the peaceful settlement of disputes are important subgroups of the OAS. The Inter-

American Defense Board (IADB), created in 1942 and made a part of the OAS budget in 1948, has had a close liaison relationship with the OAS. One of the controversial aspects of the IADB is the Inter-American Defense College, a dependency created in 1962. Efforts to deal with the IADB and the Inter-American Defense College, located at Ft. Lesley McNair in Washington, D.C., have presented a number of difficult problems, particularly when budget-conscious bureaucrats target the IADB or college for severe budget cuts. The Advisory Defense Committee, established in 1948, has never met nor been activated. The present Inter-American Committee on Peaceful Settlement, under the Permanent Council and replacing the Inter-American Peace Committee via the 1970 Protocol of Buenos Aires, is provisional and is also waiting for the Protocol of Washington to be ratified.

Another basis for convoking the Organ of Consultation provided in the original COAS under Article 39 (now Article 60) was to "consider problems of an urgent nature and of common interest to the American States." Sanctions require a two-thirds vote (when there were 21 members of the OAS this meant 14; today this means 23 with 34 voting members). Since the 21st MMFA, the OAS Permanent Council has dealt with crises as an Ad Hoc MMFA; for example, the coup in Haiti (q.v.) in 1991, President Fujimori's dissolution of the National Congress in Peru in 1992, and the *auto-golpe* (self-coup) in Guatemala (q.v.) in 1993.

b. Promotion of democracy and protection of human rights. The OAS has assigned an increasingly higher priority to democracy and human rights, which are interrelated, until they have become of primary concern to the organization. The Inter-American Commission on Human Rights (IACHR) has become much more active and important after its status was raised, and it was made a permanent organ by the 1967 Protocol of Buenos Aires. It was further strengthened by the American Convention on Human Rights (Pact of San José), which was approved by the Inter-American Specialized Conference on Human Rights in Costa Rica in 1969. This convention also provided for the creation of an Inter-American Court of Human Rights (IACtHR); it was established (in Costa Rica) in 1978 after the convention was ratified.

The high priority assigned to promoting democracy was evidenced at the 1991 OAS General Assembly in Santiago, Chile, when the "Santiago Commitment to Democracy" was adopted, followed by the approval of an implementing resolution (no. 1080) on "Representative Democracy." If a democratically elected government was overthrown, this resolution required the OAS secretary-general, to call a meeting of the Permanent Council within ten days to consider the action to be taken. The first action taken by the OAS upon the basis of the Santiago Commitment was against the military government in Haiti in 1991. The second was against Peru in 1992 and the third against Guatemala in 1993. In 1993 the OAS also created a new permanent body, the Unit for the Promotion of Democracy. Additionally, for a number of years the OAS has been regularly monitoring and observing elections in member countries.

c. Economic development and integration and trade. The long-standing Latin American interest—and later that of the Commonwealth Caribbean—in economic development and regional integration (q.v.), prompted by the Economic Commission for Latin America and the Caribbean (ECLAC, q.v.), reinforced by the Alliance for Progress (AP, q.v.), and manifested in the 1967 Protocol of Buenos Aires, has been greatly strengthened and stimulated by a number of developments in the 1990s (see Table, p. 142). These include U.S. President George Bush's Enterprise for the Americas Initiative (EAI, q.v.) proposal in June 1990; the approval of the North American Free Trade Agreement (NAFTA, q.v.) in 1993 and becoming effective in early 1994; the Summit of the Americas meeting in the United States in late 1994; and a new OAS secretary-general, César Gaviria Trujillo (q.v.), in 1995. Also in the 1990s, the members of the OAS became increasingly aware of the interrelationship of democracy and economic development while focusing upon integral development. For example, the 1993 OAS GA approved the "Declaration of Managua for the Promotion of Democracy and Development." The importance of trade was indicated by the GA's creation of the Trade Unit at the same meeting, and the Protocol of Managua established a new single council, the Council for Integral Development, which came into being when the protocol was ratified in January 1996.

The energetic new OAS secretary-general, César Gaviria Trujillo, has taken over and incorporated certain agenda items and resolutions from the Summit of the Americas, particularly those dealing with regional integration and trade, along with the economic democracy/human rights nexus, for the purpose of creating a new mission for reviving the OAS. The recent modifications of the OAS indicate a more active role in the multilateral issues facing its member states in the 21st century. Aspirations for solving hemispheric problems multilaterally will always involve political struggles between isolationism and internationalism, as evidenced by the growing disinterest in international organizations in the United States and the large sums of money owed these organizations by the U.S. government and others. The OAS will celebrate the 50th anniversary of the signing of its Charter in 1998.

ORGANIZATION OF CENTRAL AMERICAN STATES (OCAS)/OR-GANIZACIÓN DE ESTADOS CENTROAMERICANOS (ODECA). In an attempt to reestablish Central American unity, five states— Costa Rica, Guatemala, Honduras, Nicaragua, and El Salvador— signed a charter founding OCAS in October 1951 in El Salvador. (It went into effect in January 1952.) OCAS began operating in 1955 for the purpose of strengthening the ties between the five states, furthering the peaceful settlement of disputes, and promoting developments in the cultural, economic, and social fields. A new charter, signed in Panama (invited to join) in December 1962 became effective in March 1965. Its three major organs were the Meeting of Heads of State (the "supreme organ"), the Conference of Ministers of Foreign Affairs (the "principal organ" and decision-making body, operating on the basis of the rule of unanimity), and the Executive Council (the "permanent organ"). In addition, there was a Legislative Council (made up of three legislators from each member's legislature), Court of Justice (made up of each member's Supreme Court chief justice), Economic Council, Cultural and Educational Council, and Defense Council. There was also a Central American Bureau, headed by a secretary-general, which constituted the Secretariat located in El Salvador. In the 1970s, the activities and programs of OCAS were suspended due to civil unrest; however, it was revived in 1991 by means of a protocol and a new treaty (General Treaty for Central American Economic Integration), which created the Central American Integration System (CAIS—Sistema de Integración Centroamericano, SICA); the CAIS began functioning in early 1993 and reestablished the former Economic Council. Honduras, which had withdrawn from OCAS in 1970, rejoined the CAIS as an active member. The Secretariat is in Guatemala City and is referred to as the Secretaría Permanente del Tratado General de Integración Económica Centroamericana (SIECA).

ORGANIZATION OF EASTERN CARIBBEAN STATES (OECS). A seven-member subregional organization founded in 1981 by Antigua and Barbuda, Dominica, Grenada, Montserrat, St. Kitts and Nevis, St. Lucia, and St. Vincent and the Grenadines to promote economic integration, security, and political stability in the Eastern Caribbean. The treaty creating the OECS was signed in October 1980 at the 25th

OAS MEMBERSHIP IN REGIONAL TRADE AGREEMENTS

Trade Agreement	Member Countries	Effective Date
Andean Group/Pact (AG)	Bolivia, Chile, Colombia, Ecuador, Peru, Venezuela	1969
Association of Caribbean States (ACS)	All CARICOM members plus Colombia, Costa Rica, Cuba, the Dominican Republic, Guatemala, Guyana, Haiti, Honduras, Nicaragua, Panama, Suriname, Mexico, Venezuela	1995
Caribbean Basin Initiative (CBI)	All CARICOM members plus Costa Rica, the Dominican Republic, El Salvador, Guatemala, Haiti, Honduras, Nicaragua (after 1990), Panama	1991
Caribbean Common Market (CARICOM)	Antigua & Barbuda, the Bahamas, Barbados, Belize, Dominica, Grenada, Guyana, Jamaica, St. Kitts & Nevis, St. Lucia, St. Vincent & the Grenadines, Suriname, Trinidad & Tobago	1973
Central American Common Market (CACM)	Costa Rica, El Salvador, Guatemala, Honduras, Nicaragua	1961
Central American Integration System (CAIS)	Same as Central American Common Market	1993
Free Trade Area of the Americas (FTAA)	Hemisphere-wide free trade area now under negotiation	2005
Group of Three (G-3)	Colombia, Mexico, Venezuela	1995
Latin American Economic System (LAES)	All OAS member states except Antigua and Barbuda, the Bahamas, Belize, Canada, Dominica, the Dominican Republic, St. Lucia, St. Vincent & the Grenadines, St. Kitts & Nevis, United States	1974
Latin American Integration Association (LAIA)	Argentina, Bolivia, Brazil, Chile, Colombia, Ecuador, Mexico, Paraguay, Peru, Uruguay, Venezuela	1980
North American Free Trade Agreement (NAFTA)	Canada, Mexico, United States	1994
Southern Cone Common Market (MERCOSUR)	Argentina, Brazil, Paraguay, Uruguay plus two associate members, Bolivia and Chile	1994

Meeting of the West Indies Associated States (WISA, q.v.) Council of Ministers and entered into force in July 1981. The OECS replaced WISA, a political decision-making body founded in 1961 and the Eastern Caribbean Common Market (ECCM, q.v.), established in 1968 as an associate institution of the Caribbean Community (CC, q.v.). The OECS's major goals are to promote cooperation and unity, sovereignty and harmonization of foreign policy objectives, and economic integration. Article 8 of its treaty provides for mutual security. It was on the basis of this article that the OECS members met in 1983, after the death of Maurice Bishop (q.v.) of Grenada, and requested U.S. intervention (q.v.) in Grenada. Four OECS states joined the United States, Barbados, and Jamaica in the invasion.

The principal decision-making organ of the OECS is the Authority of Heads of Government, which meets at least two times per year. Substantive work is carried out by four committees—Foreign Affairs, Defense and Security, Economic Affairs, and Legal Affairs. The organization is headed by a director-general, the chief executive officer, responsible to the authority, who oversees the functioning of the General-Secretariat (located in St. Lucia) and the Economic Affairs Secretariat (located in Antigua and Barbuda). Several agencies were established in the 1980s to deal with illicit drug trafficking, investment promotion, and export development. *See also* Grenada, Intervention in by the United States; Reagan, Ronald; Reagan Doctrine; West Indies Associated States (WISA).

ORGANIZATION OF PETROLEUM EXPORTING COUNTRIES (OPEC). Multinational petroleum producing cartel founded in 1960 by Iran, Iraq, Kuwait, Saudi Arabia, and Venezuela to raise oil prices in a concerted manner. By 1975 OPEC had increased its membership to 13, with Ecuador joining Venezuela as the second South American member of the organization. OPEC's influence was felt in two embargoes (q.v.) against Western states, one in 1973 and the other in 1978–79. By the time of the second embargo, Western states were less affected, due to conservation and increased production by non-OPEC producers such as Mexico, Norway, and Britain. With world oil prices flat since 1989 and severe divisions within its membership due to the Iran-Iraq War and the Gulf War, OPEC has suffered from the inherent weakness of all commodity cartels. The high cost of participating in OPEC ($2 million per year) contributed to Ecuador's decision to drop out in 1992. *See also* Embargoes of Organization of Petroleum Exporting Countries (OPEC); Appendix VII.

ORTEGA, DANIEL (1945-). Revolutionary leader and president (1984–1990) who headed the Sandinista government in Nicaragua during its 11-year confrontation with the Reagan and Bush (qq.v.) administrations before being defeated by Violeta Barrios de Chamorro (q.v.) in his 1990 reelection bid. His early education took place at private church schools (he studied briefly for the priesthood), and he attended law school at the University of Central America before being recruited into Sandinista guerrilla ranks in 1963. He was tortured and served time in prison from the late 1960s to the mid-1970s, and he was part of the guerrilla leadership that directed the final military operations against Somoza's (q.v.) National Guard in 1979. Ortega then became a leading member and representative of the governing junta. He was its nominee for president in the 1984 election and won by a landslide. As president, he was pragmatic and focused on economic planning and obtaining foreign assistance; his good personal relationship with Soviet First Secretary Mikhail Gorbachev assured Soviet economic and military aid after a U.S. embargo was declared. After his reelection defeat, Ortega kept his seat on the Sandinista National Directorate and title "Commander of the Revolution" and remains a figure of considerable political influence inside Nicaragua. He decided to run for president on a "moderate" FSLN (Frente Sandinista de Liberación Nacional, Sandinista National Liberation Front, q.v.) ticket in 1996 but was soundly defeated again, this time by José Arnoldo Alemán, the conservative former mayor of Managua.

P

PACIFIC WAR. *See* War of the Pacific.

PACTO ANDINO. *See* Andean Group.

PANAMA CANAL. President Theodore Roosevelt (q.v.) is given—and claimed—credit for the U.S. gaining control over Panama (Colombia's northern province at the time) in 1903 from a bankrupt French company and completing the construction of the canal, which opened in 1914. When an uprising took place in Panama (the role of the United States in it is debated), Roosevelt gave orders that prevented the latter's troops from reaching the area to put down the revolt. This assured its success and the declaration of Panama's independence, which Washington at once recognized. In 1903 the Hay-Bunau-Varilla Treaty was signed, giving the United States control "in perpetuity" over a ten-mile wide strip of land as "if it were the sovereign of the territory." The United States agreed to pay Panama a lump sum of $10 million and $250,000 per year (this annual payment was steadily increased over the years and was almost $2 million in 1955). With the passing of time the canal became a bone of contention between the two countries as nationalistic Panamanians objected to their second class status and the privileges of U.S. citizens, the many U.S. military bases that made up the Southern Command, and inadequate compensation by the United States. Tension mounted over "flag incidents," in which Panamanians replaced the U.S. banner with their own, resulting in riots in the late 1950s that escalated into major confrontations and battles involving U.S. police and army personnel, resulting in mounting casualties on both sides. The 1964 riots cost 24 lives and resulted in hundreds of injuries and great property damage. Panama responded by breaking relations with the United States and appealing to both the Organization of American States (OAS, q.v.) and the United Nations, charging the United States with "aggression." The OAS Permanent Council was convoked, acting provisionally as the Organ of Consultation, to investigate the situation.

Finally, the two countries agreed, the United States reluctantly, to negotiate new treaties governing the canal and their military relations. The on-again and off-again negotiations caused mounting tension in Panama, leading to an unprecedented meeting of the UN Security Council in Panama City in March 1973. The U.S. veto of a resolution to "guarantee full respect for Panama's effective sovereignty over all of its territory" provoked further controversy. Negotiations continued, and the United States reported at the 1975 OAS General Assembly meeting that "significant advances" had been made. However, it was President Jimmy Carter (q.v.) who was firmly in support of new treaties, for he believed that they would serve the U.S. national interest by improving U.S.-Panamanian relations in particular and U.S.-Latin American relations in general. His administration actively pursued negotiations, ones that were unpopular in conservative Republican circles (Governor Ronald Reagan [q.v.] of California was a leading critic). The process of negotiation was facilitated on the Panamanian side by populist "President" Omar Torrijos—as a National Guard colonel he had staged a coup in October 1968, removing an elected president, and took over—because he kept a lid on Panamanian nationalism during the difficult period of negotiations.

The negotiations finally culminated in two new treaties, which were signed by Carter and Torrijos on September 7, 1977, at an elaborate ceremony attended by most Latin American heads of state at the OAS headquarters. They were the Panama Canal Treaty (operation and defense of the canal) and the Treaty Concerning the Permanent Neutrality and Operation of the Panama Canal (international status). The former provides that Panama will take over complete management and operation of the canal when the treaty expires on December 31, 1999. The latter treaty states that each country has a right to defend the security and neutrality of the canal. The U.S. Senate required the stipulation that the U.S. could use force to reopen or restore the canal's operation and that in time of war U.S. warships could go "to the head of the line" in order to cross through. After a long debate in the U.S. Senate in 1978, the two treaties were approved by a close vote (a two-thirds majority was required) of 68–32. Ratifications were exchanged in June. Thereafter, the OAS formally endorsed the treaty.

PANAMA, INTERVENTION IN BY THE UNITED STATES AND THE OAS, and ELECTIONS. The Reagan (q.v.) administration decided in mid-1987 that Noriega's act of removing an elected president, human rights (q.v.) violations in suppressing dissent, and drug trafficking and money laundering made his removal from office and departure from Panama a necessity. To that end, Washington suspended economic and military aid, imposed economic sanctions, and then shortly thereafter indicted Noriega on drug charges in a Florida court in February 1988. Efforts to remove him became complicated, due to the presidential elections in the United States and the botched effort to have Panama's president remove Noriega. This fiasco was followed by secret negotiations to work out an arrangement for his resignation and departure. Noriega finally refused to go along, and the United States applied an economic embargo and froze bank assets. The United States then explored a "covert" option, but it was not promising. With the U.S. election over and George Bush (q.v.) in the White House, the issue of Noriega was placed on hold until the May 1989 elections in Panama. The attacks on the opposition candidates and Noriega's cancellation of the elections when his chosen slate appeared to be losing provoked a crisis and provided another basis for action against him. This time the Organization of American States (OAS, q.v.) became involved, and the United States decided to work through it.

The OAS convened the 21st Meeting of Consultation in mid-May in order to deal with the election crisis. After condemning Noriega's human rights and electoral "abuses," the foreign ministers established a three-member mediation team (the foreign ministers of Ecuador, Guatemala, and Trinidad and Tobago) to meet with him to work out a transitional government, to be followed by the holding of national elections. For three months the mediators negotiated with Noriega, making five major visits and extending the deadline for the establishment of the provisional government. In July, the deadline was extended to September 1. However, it became clear that the mediation effort was hopeless, for Noriega refused to agree to any terms unless all U.S. sanctions were ended. The OAS abandoned its effort. When the United States expanded its sanctions, the hostility of members of the Panamanian Defense Force (PDF) toward U.S. military personnel and their dependents in Panama steadily increased. One shooting death and increasing threats set the stage for the U.S. invasion in December.

President Bush initiated "Operation Just Cause" and ordered U.S. troops into Panama on December 20. He presented the justification for his action that morning: he referred to the ongoing crisis with Panama the past two years and stated that the "goals" of the United States "have been to safeguard the lives of Americans, to defend democracy in Panama, to combat drug trafficking and to protect the integrity of the Panama Canal (q.v.) Treaty." He also stated that the United States had attempted to resolve the crisis "through diplomacy and negotiations," which had been "rejected" by Noriega. He also referred to Noriega's threats to U.S. citizens and stressed his "obligation" to protect them. Interestingly, neither the Monroe Doctrine (q.v.) nor communism played a part in Washington's justification for Operation Just Cause. Then Bush announced that the United States recognized the coalition that had won the annulled election headed by Guillermo Endara as the government of Panama after the United States had administered Endara's oath of office and that it was lifting the economic sanctions. In the ensuing days, 22,500 U.S. combatants were flown in to supplement the 13,000 troops stationed there as a part of the Southern Command, and battles were fought to defeat the PDF and search for Noriega, who had gone into hiding before seeking asylum in the papal nunciature.

Although the invasion was popular in the United States, both the OAS and the United Nations passed resolutions against it. Despite reservations about the legality of the operation, most Panamanians seemed to support the U.S. invasion. The OAS Permanent Council adopted a critical resolution deploring the action, calling for the cessation of hostilities and demanding a U.S. withdrawal. A similar resolution was passed by the UN General Assembly, while one was vetoed by the United States (joined by Great Britain and France) in the UN Security Council. Noriega was finally located, later surrendered to U.S. authorities in early January 1990, and was arrested and sent to Florida to stand trial on drug charges. This marked the first time a foreign head of state was kidnapped and brought to trial under another nation's law. The U.S. intervention achieved its primary objective, the capture of General Noriega, but it cost the Unites States $163 million in military operations expenditures, 23 American lives and over 350 casualties, and the enmity of its Latin American neighbors and others around the world. The planning and conduct of the invasion of Panama served as a prelude to the Gulf War two years later.

See also Bush, George; Intervention and Nonintervention; Noriega, Manuel Antonio.

PAN AMERICAN HEALTH ORGANIZATION (PAHO). Founded in 1902 as the Pan American Sanitary Bureau, PAHO is both an OAS specialized organization and a regional arm of the World Health Organization (WHO, q.v.) designed to coordinate regional efforts to improve health by maintaining close relations with national health oganizations and WHO. *See also* World Health Organization (WHO).

PAN AMERICAN UNION (PAU). The PAU was the Secretariat of the Union of American Republics, approved in 1910 at the Fourth Conference (Mexico City), which replaced the earlier International Union of American States and its Commercial Bureau. The headquarters building at the corner of Constitution Avenue and 17th Street NW, Washington, D.C., was dedicated and inaugurated in April 1910. The Pan American Union building is now the headquarters of the Organization of American States (OAS, q.v.), including the seat of the Permanent Council and Hall of the Americas. Although the OAS Charter, drafted and approved at the 1948 Ninth Conference (Bogotá), did not become effective until 1951, the name "Organization of American States" did not replace that of "Pan American Union" on the building until the early 1970s.

PARAGUAYAN WAR. *See* War of the Triple Alliance.

PARLAMENTO CENTROAMERICANO (PARLACEN). *See* Central American Parliament (CAP).

PARLAMENTO LATINOAMERICANO. *See* Latin American Parliament.

PÉREZ, CARLOS ANDRÉS (1926-). President of Venezuela (1974– 1979; 1988–1993) best known for his petroleum nationalization policies, Third World (q.v.) leadership activities, and efforts to counter U.S. Central American policy through the Contadora peace process (q.v.). While one of Venezuela's most charismatic and popular politicians during his first term in office, Pérez faced two unsuccessful coup attempts in 1992 and corruption (q.v.) charges that led to his impeachment in 1993 and conviction on embezzlement charges in 1996. During his first term Pérez spent freely and nationalized liberally but had to confront economic readjustment demands stemming from high inflation, heavy government subsidies, and the continued low price of oil during his troublesome second term.

PÉREZ DE CUÉLLAR, JAVIER (1920-). Peruvian statesman and first Latin American secretary-general of the United Nations. Although initially a compromise candidate, he was popular enough to be re-elected and held the post from 1982 to 1992. His emphasis on diplomatic activism helped pave the way for a more involved role for the UN in international mediation and peacekeeping efforts. He was less successful (some say as a result of his Peruvian background) in utilizing the good offices of the UN to resolve the Argentine/British dispute that led to the Falklands/Malvinas War (q.v.) than in brokering an end to the Iran-Iraq War and mediating the civil war in El Salvador. *See also* Central American/Contadora Peace Process; Organization of American States (OAS).

PERMANENT OBSERVERS OF OAS. *See* Organization of American States (OAS); Appendix IV.

PERÓN, JUAN D. (1895–1974). President of Argentina (1946–1955; 1973–1974) and military figure who admired European fascism and ran a populist regime through an eclectic mix of ideologies designed to mobilize the working classes in his favor. During his first presidential term he welcomed Nazis who fled Germany after World War II (q.v.). Stressing Argentine nationalism, Perón opposed both British and U.S. involvement in Latin American affairs. Peronist Youth members, along with other Latin American university students including Fidel Castro (q.v.) of Cuba, were sent to Bogotá, Colombia, in 1948 to demonstrate against the inter-American meetings that would create the Organization of American States (OAS, q.v.). After nearly two decades in exile in Spain, Perón managed to return to power through a surrogate, but he lacked the legitimacy he once had and died in office in 1973. After Perón's death, his third wife, Isabel, ruled briefly before being overthrown by the military in 1976. This period of harsh military rule included what Argentine's call the Dirty War (1976–1981), in which thousands were killed or disappeared as the military sought to hunt down the leftist enemies of the regime. *See also* Democracy; Human Rights; World War II.

PINOCHET UGARTE, AUGUSTO (1915-). Army officer, head of state, and president (1973–1989) known for his major role in the coup that toppled Salvador Allende (q.v.) in 1973 and led to 16 years of harsh authoritarian rule in what had once been a highly democratic Chile. Under his dictatorship, nearly 2,000 opponents of the regime were killed, and another 1,000 disappeared in a scheme to "save" Chile from communism. Pinochet's economic policies were driven by young technocrats and foreign economic advisers called the "Chicago

Boys" (q.v.), who pushed free-market economic policies, foreign loans, and denationalization of major sectors of the economy, a reversal of Allende's socialist economic solutions to Chile's development problems. After being repudiated in a plebiscite in 1988, Pinochet decided not to run for president the following year but managed to retain the post of army commander-in-chief following the return to democratic rule with the election of Patricio Aylwin in 1990. By expanding the powers of the Chilean military over civilian politics—retaining the post of commander-in-chief of the military, obstructing judicial efforts to prosecute military officers convicted of human rights (q.v.) abuses, and appointing eight senators sympathetic to retaining the military's political guardian role—General Pinochet symbolizes the fragile aspects of democracy building in Latin America. Pinochet's relatively successful economic policies, and the return to democracy, enhanced Chile's reputation as a regional model of development in the 1990s and a prime candidate for inclusion in an expanded North American Free Trade Agreement (NAFTA, q.v.). In 1996, Chile joined the Southern Cone Common Market (MERCOSUR, q.v.) as its prospects for NAFTA membership appeared to fade. *See also* Allende, Salvador; Chicago Boys; Cold War; Harberger, Arnold; North American Free Trade Agreement (NAFTA); Southern Cone Common Market (MERCOSUR).

PLAZA LASSO, GALO (1906–1987). Served as ambassador to the United States and president of Ecuador (1948–1952) before being elected the fourth OAS secretary-general. *See also* Organization of American States (OAS); Appendix II.

PREBISCH, RAÚL (1901–1986). Argentine economist and one of the key intellectual leaders of the structuralist school seeking to achieve economic growth and modernization in Latin America. As executive secretary of the Economic Commission for Latin America (ECLA, q.v.) from 1950 to 1963, Prebisch advocated Keynesian and neo-Keynesian policies of government stimulation and basic institutional changes designed to spur economic development. In the history of Latin American economic development, Prebisch argued, developed nations ("the center") impeded the economic and social progress of underdeveloped countries ("the periphery") by deeming the latter mere suppliers of raw materials rather than industrialized participants in the international economy. Although his theories often changed as the world economy evolved, Prebisch's views are still controversial in view of the continuing dilemmas of economic development faced by the Latin American countries at the dawn of the 21st century. Prebisch died in 1986 while director-general of the Latin American

Institute for Economic and Social Planning. *See also* Economic Commission on Latin America and the Caribbean (ECLAC); Chicago Boys; Import Substitution Industrialization (ISI).

PREFERENTIAL TRADE AGREEMENTS. *See* Caribbean Basin Initiative (CBI); Caribbean-Canadian Cooperation Agreement (CARIBCAN); Caribbean Common Market (CARICOM).

PROTOCOLS OF AMENDMENT TO THE OAS CHARTER of Buenos Aires (1967), Cartagena de Indias (1985), Washington (1992), and Managua (1993). *See* Organization of American States (OAS, 1).

R

REAGAN DOCTRINE. A controversial foreign policy emanating from U.S. President Ronald Reagan's (q.v.) State of the Union address in 1985 calling for aid to all anticommunist insurgents, people he referred to as "freedom fighters" and the moral equivalent of those who fought in the American War of Independence. There continues to be considerable disagreement about what the doctrine actually was in both theory and practice and what actions, both covert and overt, were justified and if they were compatible or incompatible with international law (IL, q.v.). In general, it appeared that a distinction was made between authoritarian, conservative military governments on the one hand and totalitarian, leftist (communist) governments on the other. The former were assisted by the United States, because they could be influenced and pressured to change (to hold elections), while the latter were not, because they resisted such "conversion." Another apparent feature was the supplying of aid to indigenous resistance groups, which was justified as combatting totalitarian regimes.

The Reagan Doctrine was foreshadowed in the 1983 intervention in Grenada (q.v.) and applied in Central America to bring down the Sandinista government of Nicaragua. The doctrine relied on both *covert* (mining Nicaragua's harbors and organizing the Contras [q.v.]) and *overt* (supplying the Contras in neighboring Honduras and providing billions of dollars of military and economic aid to El Salvador) means of achieving U.S. foreign policy objectives. The Reagan administration tried to justify its intervention (q.v.) as the collective self-defense provided for under the OAS Charter and the Rio Treaty: it argued that the Nicaraguan government was aiding the Farabundo Martí Front for National Liberation in its armed struggle to overthrow the government in El Salvador. However, the International Court of Justice (ICJ) in *Nicaragua v. The United States of America* (q.v.)

ruled against that rationale. The U.S. Congress later cut off all funds to the Contras. Therefore, the Reagan Doctrine was partially repudiated, even though President Reagan continued to maintain that he was a Contra too and would support them to the bitter end if necessary.

REAGAN, RONALD (1911-). While President of the United States (1981–1989) he developed a Latin American policy in which he placed the Caribbean and Central America in the context of the East-West struggle, continued the trade embargo against Cuba, ordered the 1983 invasion of Grenada (q.v.), and developed and applied the Reagan Doctrine (q.v.) against Nicaragua, which also undermined the Central American/Contadora peace process (q.v.). Reagan also laid the basis for U.S. intervention (q.v.) against drugtraffickers, since they seemingly posed a security threat to the United States beginning in the 1980s. *See also* Intervention and Nonintervention; Noriega, Manuel Antonio; Panama, Intervention in by the United States and the OAS, and Elections; Recognition and Nonrecognition of States, Governments, and Insurgents.

RECOGNITION AND NONRECOGNITION OF STATES, GOVERN-MENTS, AND INSURGENTS. Recognition and nonrecognition have always been diplomatic tools used by policymakers (particularly U.S.) to express pleasure with, or disapproval of a new state's status or policies, a changed political situation (including the status of a new government), or insurgents trying to overthrow an old and discredited government. It is the right under international law of a sovereign state to recognize or to refuse to recognize a newly independent state or a state's new government. It is a political decision with economic and legal effects, for recognition is the basis for exchanging diplomats, trading, borrowing money, and protecting one's citizens. Some examples of nonrecognition of a state's independence are the U.S. refusal to recognize that of Haiti (1804) and the Dominican Republic (1844) until after its own Civil War (1861–1865). Illustrating the nonrecognition of new governments, Mexico never recognized the government of General Francisco Franco (1939–1975), and the United States regularly refused to recognize military governments that overthrew civilian, elected ones. The United States did not recognized the revolutionary government of Fidel Castro (q.v.) but President Eisenhower soon broke relations. At times certain Latin American leaders proposed as a means of favoring democratically elected leaders a policy of collective nonrecognition applied toward a military junta that removed such a government. President Betancourt of Venezuela (q.v.) advocated such a policy, and a Mexican proposal, the Tobar Doctrine (q.v.), was well known for its efforts to establish a policy of joint intervention (q.v.) to put an end to revolutions and refuse recognition to *de facto* governments that were established by revolutions (or *coups d'etat*) against constitutional regimes.

Another form of recognition important in international law is that of a state of *belligerency*. When an outside state grants it to antigovernment insurgents fighting to overthrow the existing government, the insurgents acquire international personality, and the armed struggle ceases being a domestic, internal matter. Outside states may now openly aid the insurgents by selling them arms and loaning them money. Until the formal recognition of belligerency, such assistance would be considered intervention in a state's internal affairs. A good example of this is the popular Sandinista-led insurrection against General Anastasio Somoza (q.v.) of Nicaragua in the late 1970s. The Andean Group (AG, q.v.) recognized the existence of a state of belligerency in Nicaragua in June 1979, shortly before Somoza's National Guard was defeated. However, well before this formal action two Andean Group members—Colombia and Venezuela, as well as other neighboring states (Cuba, Costa Rica, Mexico, and Panama)—had been covertly aiding the Sandinistas due to the great unpopularity of the dictator Somoza and the wide public support given the insurrection. *See* Nicaragua, Insurrection in of Sandinistas and Collective Sanctions by the OAS; Tobar Doctrine.

REGIONAL SECURITY SYSTEM (RSS). Even though the Organization of Eastern Caribbean States (OECS, q.v.) had been created in 1981 and its treaty dealt with security matters (Article 8 gave the Defense and Security Committee "responsibility for coordinating the efforts . . . [of members] for collective defense and the preservation of peace and security against external aggression"), it was not until October 1982 that the RSS was formed. It was accomplished by a memorandum of understanding signed in Dominica by Antigua and Barbuda, Barbados, Dominica, St. Lucia, and St. Vincent and the Grenadines. The RSS became operational in February 1983 at a meeting in St. Lucia that negotiated the formal arrangements. Both St. Kitts and Nevis and Grenada joined after the U.S. invasion of Grenada (q.v.). What prompted the establishment of the RSS were certain security problems in the eastern Caribbean, including mercenary plots and acts, a coup (in Grenada in 1979) and coup attempts, and an insurrection. Units from the RSS participated in the peacekeeping force that maintained internal security in Grenada following the 1983 U.S. invasion. Proposals and efforts to expand the RSS have been made by various members, but they have been unsuccessful. Foreign aid is provided to the RSS by Great Britain, Canada, and the United States.

The main policy-making organ of the RSS is the Council of Ministers, which is made up of the members' defense ministers. A regional security coordinator heads a Central Liaison Office that exercises operational command. The coordinator has regular contact with both the British and U.S. military via the area's British high commissioner (UKHCEC) and the U.S. Military Liaison Office in the Eastern Caribbean (USMLOEC). RSS headquarters are in Barbados.

REVOLUTIONS. *See* Bolivian Revolution; Cuban Revolution; Mexican Revolution; Nicaraguan Revolution.

RIO GROUP (RG). The basis for this group was laid when the four-member Contadora Support Group (SG)—Argentina, Brazil, Peru, and Uruguay—joined the original four-member Contadora Group of Colombia, Mexico, Panama, and Venezuela in 1985. In 1986 the two groups merged into the Rio Group after a conference in Rio de Janeiro, forming the Group of Eight. While its first goal was the revival of the Contadora peace process (q.v.), which was then transformed into the Esquipulas process, its next goal became the consolidation of the democratic (q.v.) process on a much broader scope, reflecting the group's more South American character. The group soon evolved into a forum for intra-Latin American presidential diplomacy, where the members did not favor institutionalization (originally they had envisioned the forum as a Latin American G-77 [q.v.]). The Rio Group considered and became involved in a number of crises, and its size steadily increased. The group did not take sides in the upheavals (aborted elections and the U.S. intervention and arrest of Noriega [q.v.] in Panama [q.v.], but it did suspend Panama as a member (it was permitted to rejoin in 1993).

Beginning in 1990, the membership steadily increased, making the number eight obsolete: Bolivia, Chile, Ecuador, and Paraguay joined. Now it was the Group of Twelve, and by 1995 it had become the Group of Fourteen. Since then it has been moving toward almost total Latin American membership, with the growing membership of the Commonwealth Caribbean states. The group's broadening scope was made clear at a 1990 meeting in Caracas, when strengthening the Organization of American States (OAS, q.v.) was added as a goal. The group shifted its focus to economic issues and at the same time strongly endorsed the 1991 Declaration of Santiago on Representative Democracy (q.v.) and the OAS action against the military regime that had removed Haiti's President Aristide (q.v.). The group's broadening role was also indicated at a late 1992 meeting in Buenos Aires, Argentina, where it proclaimed itself an "international interlocutor."

One of the concerns of many members was that the Rio Group did not receive Washington's recognition as a legitimate political group (the United States ignored it until 1993), perhaps due to disagreements over Cuba. Since the 1992 U.S. Cuban Democracy Act, the Rio Group has simultaneously condemned the U.S. embargo and advocated a democratic transition in Cuba. In 1993, however, President Clinton recognized the Rio Group when he sent a message to its Presidential Summit (Santiago, Chile), asking for its support of the North American Free Trade Agreement (NAFTA, q.v.). As opposed to U.S.-Latin American relations, those between the Rio Group and the European Union (EU, q.v.) have been close and regular. For example, there is an annual EU-RG meeting in New York when the UN General Assembly begins its fall session. *See also* Association of Southeast Asian Nations (ASEAN); Central American/Contadora Peace Process; Clinton, William J.; Institute for European-Latin American Relations (IELAR); North American Free Trade Agreement (NAFTA).

RIO TREATY. *See* Inter-American Treaty of Reciprocal Assistance (IATRA); Security, Changing Concepts of.

RODRÍGUEZ LARRETA DOCTRINE. A proposal by Uruguayan Foreign Minister Eduardo Rodríguez Larreta in 1945–1946 to use collective intervention (q.v.) to oppose dictators and promote democracy and human rights (q.q.v.) in Latin America. Although implicitly directed against Argentina because of its fascist-inclined leaders, the plan had broad implications for the principles governing inter-American relations. Arguing that the inter-American commitment to democracy and human rights should transcend the principle of nonintervention (q.v.), Rodríguez Larreta wanted the nations of the hemisphere to take collective multilateral action to restore full democracy once its principles had been violated. The doctrine was fully endorsed by the United States and supported (with some reservations) by six Latin American governments, but the remainder of the Latin American states rejected the plan, arguing that no modification of the principle of nonintervention was permissible, even if it served to insulate dictatorships and human rights violators. Efforts to link democracy promotion and human rights protection with collective intervention have been resuscitated now that the Cold War (q.v.) has ended, and the Organization of American States (OAS, q.v.) has taken a firm stand against nondemocratic forms of rule. *See also* Declaration of Santiago, 1991; Intervention and Nonintervention; Organization of American States (OAS); Southern Cone Common Market (MERCOSUR); Appendix VI, OAS Charter (Article 22).

ROOSEVELT, FRANKLIN D. (1882–1945). President of the United States (1933–1945) who presided over a period of harmonious relations between the United States and Latin America using his Good Neighbor Policy (q.v.) of cooperation, nonintervention (q.v.), and mutual respect. Much of Roosevelt's Good Neighbor Policy was driven by what he confronted at home (the Great Depression) and abroad (the coming of World War II [q.v.]). Roosevelt needed improved diplomatic relations in order to expand trade with Latin America and keep the Nazis out the Western Hemisphere. In addition, he hoped to form some means of collective security among the American states. While Roosevelt endorsed the principle of nonintervention in the internal affairs of the United States' neighbors to the south, entered into collective security (q.v.) arrangements, lowered trade barriers, and ended U.S. military occupation of Haiti, critics failed to see this as the basis of a new approach to Latin America, considering it simply a more benign form of U.S. imperialism and domination, particularly in the tendency to ignore the abuses of dictators such as Somoza (q.v.) and Trujillo (q.v.) as long as they remained strong supporters of the United States. *See also* Good Neighbor Policy; Security, Changing Concepts of; World War II.

ROOSEVELT, THEODORE (1858–1919). Politician, statesman, and president (1901–1909) who had a significant impact on U.S. policy toward Latin America. He played a key role in separating Panama from Colombia, securing a favorable treaty with Panama (rather than Nicaragua) to complete the construction of the Panama Canal (q.v.), and expanding U.S. power in the Caribbean with the Roosevelt Corollary to the Monroe Doctrine (q.v.) in 1904. As an ardent advocate of a U.S. imperial role in Latin America, Roosevelt initiated controversial policies that were harshly criticized by many Latin Americans and North Americans alike. Despite his Big Stick (q.v.) diplomacy in Latin America, however, Roosevelt intervened less than President Woodrow Wilson (1913–1921). The Roosevelt Corollary defended the Monroe Doctrine and expanded its policing role in the Caribbean and Central America, at the same time keeping predatory European governments out of the U.S. sphere of influence. *See also* Big Stick Policy; Monroe Doctrine; Panama Canal; Spanish-American War.

S

SALINAS DE GORTARI, CARLOS (1948–). After earning an economics degree in his native Mexico, Salinas went to Harvard and earned three (two M.A.s and a Ph.D.) graduate degrees, mainly in political economy. On his return to Mexico, he began working his way up in the dominant party (Institutional Revolutionary Party, Partido Revolucionario Institucional [PRI]), dealing mostly with financial matters. He then joined the administration of Miguel de la Madrid, taking responsibility for economic and social policy and later for budgeting and planning. Once elected president (1988–1994), Salinas pursued an aggressive policy of economic liberalization and political modernization. He attempted to downsize the role of the government in the economy and stressed privatization of banking and many other state-owned enterprises. He proposed creating a regional free trade bloc with Canada and the United States, which resulted in the formation of NAFTA in 1995. He also strongly supported the Central American Peace Process (q.v.): Mexico was one of the four original 1983 Contadora members. Unfortunately for Salinas and the Mexican people, his policies were not always successful, and serious internal political and economic problems developed in 1994: a revolutionary peasant uprising in Chiapas, the assassination of the PRI presidential nominee, in which his brother was implicated, and the sudden collapse of the Mexican peso. He was at one time considered for the position of the first head of the new World Trade Organization (WTO, q.v.) but was not successful in this pursuit. After his six-year term as president, Salinas left Mexico humiliated and under a cloud of suspicion in the shooting death of Luis Donaldo Colosio, a close friend, and the assassination of a prominent PRI politician in 1994. He has consistently denied any role in these activities but has chosen to live in exile in Dublin, Ireland, since 1995.

His legacy of corruption and economic crisis led to the growth of a major organized opposition to the ruling party, Institutional Revolutionary Party, PRI; the first real electoral challenge came in the July 1997 midterm elections in which for the first time in 68 years, the PRI lost control of the 500-seat Chamber of Deputies, as well as the mayorality of Mexico City—won by the leader of the leftist Democratic Revolutionary Party. *See also* Clinton, William J.; Drug Cartels; North American Free Trade Agreement (NAFTA).

SAMPER, ERNESTO. *See* Clinton, William J.; Drug Cartels.

SANDINISTA NATIONAL LIBERATION FRONT. *See* Frente Sandinista de Liberación Nacional (FSLN).

SAN JOSÉ ACCORD or AGREEMENT. This 1978 agreement, also called the Joint Oil Facility, between Mexico and Venezuela, two oil exporters, was an arrangement to provide oil at concessionary prices to the oil dependent and importing states in the Caribbean and Central America. Trinidad and Tobago is the only Caribbean state that has oil to export.

SECURITY, CHANGING CONCEPTS OF. Following World War II (q.v.), the meaning and nature of hemispheric security was defined and explained in terms of the Cold War (q.v.) with the so-called realist "Cold War paradigm"and involved the military as a primary force for opposing communism. During this era, "collective security" (q.v.) became the theme. The use of military force to maintain it usually occurred after civilian means (e.g., economic sanctions, q.v.) had been unsuccessful. The means for achieving security included both collective-multilateral and unilateral efforts, the former approved by a regional organization as "collective action" (the Organization of American States [OAS, q.v.]) and the latter by a state acting alone, sometimes resorting to intervention (q.v.), contrary to inter-American agreements and the nonintervention principle enshrined in the OAS Charter (e.g., the United States). The Cold War (q.v.) provided a rationale for the United States to act alone and in violation of the OAS Charter, particularly the ban on intervention. In pursuit of its own view of the communist threat and its security interests, it was successful in converting the OAS into an "anticommunist alliance," particularly in dealing with Castro's Cuba (q.v.).

The 1947 Rio Treaty (q.v.) provided the first basis and rationale for collective action in Article 6 and collective means in Article 8. The 1948 OAS Charter's Chapter V on "Collective Security" provided a similar basis. These two major treaties were used as the basis for the future conversion of the OAS into an "anticommunist alliance." The United States played an important role outside the OAS in terms of military security via the Inter-American Military System (IAMS), continued from World War II (q.v.), and the Central American Defense Council (CADC, q.v.), formed in the early 1960s. The Alliance for Progress (q.v.), announced by President Kennedy a month before the 1961 Bay of Pigs disaster, which became an OAS program in 1962, emphasized economic development and reform as a means of dealing with communist influence and also included a new nonmilitary role for members of the armed forces—engaging in civic action that included building schools and roads among other activities. The U.S. (and Latin American) military was also trained to deal with guerrillas and engage in counterinsurgency, a new mission for the United States for which it was ill prepared. Nevertheless, the U.S. intervened in the Dominican Republic in 1965 under the Johnson Doctrine (q.v.).

The U.S. preoccupation with security led the Latin American states, fixed on economic development, to propose amendments to the OAS Charter. The resultant 1967 Protocol of Buenos Aires amendments (q.v.), effective in 1970, increased the economic commitments and strengthened the economic role of the OAS and weakened its political-security functions. In the early 1970s, another amendment movement arose, focusing on the Rio Treaty. The Latin American states initiating this effort, mainly Peru, viewed the Rio Treaty as a "child of the Cold War," and they objected to the U.S. view of security and use of the treaty. Although this movement was unsuccessful (it was referred to as SCSPMSIAS, the Special Commission to Study and Propose Measures for Strengthening the Inter-American System), it did approve a new concept—"collective economic security for development." SCSPMSIAS also initiated the termination of the OAS's role as an anticommunist alliance: in 1975 the OAS approved the Freedom of Action (San José) Resolution, which released members from the OAS resolutions imposing sanctions on Cuba. Thereafter, most Latin American and Caribbean states normalized their relations with Cuba. In the early 1980s, the United States justified its 1983 intervention in Grenada (q.v.) and continuing intervention in Nicaragua (q.v.) on Cold War grounds with the Reagan doctrine (q.v.). The U.S. invasion of Panama (q.v.) in late 1989, however, used a new rationale—the elimination of drug trafficking—reflecting a new view of hemispheric security.

With the collapse of the Soviet Union and the end of the Cold War in 1989, a new approach to security was called for, along with new rationales for collective action and unilateral intervention. In the words of OAS Secretary-General César Gaviria, "The Great Paradox is that the welcome disappearance of communism as a basic threat has created a conceptual crisis in strategic thinking." There have been several efforts to work out a new security concept, and the number of activities that involve a security dimension has steadily increased, including drug trafficking, migration, democracy and human rights (qq.v.), economic development, and the environment (q.v.). The 1991 OAS Declaration of Santiago emphasized democracy and human rights and was applied to Haiti after the September coup. The 1992 Caribbean formation of the Regional Security System (RSS, q.v.) enabled many of its small state members to deal more effectively with drug trafficking and migration. The OAS has been working on a new operational security concept, and the emerging reformulation is called "regional cooperative security" or "cooperation for hemispheric security." Greatly influenced by the work of the UN Observer Group in El Salvador (ONUSAL, q.v.), the Committee on Hemispheric Security is evaluating the implementation of certain security measures that were approved at a 1995 Regional Conference on Confidence- and Security-Building Measures in Santiago, Chile. The Advisory Defense Committee became actively involved in working out the proper security measures once it became official when the 1992 Protocol of Washington amendments were approved and went into effect in September 1997. *See also* Cold War; Inter-American Treaty of Reciprocal Assistance (IATRA); Intervention and Nonintervention; Regional Security System (RSS).

EL SENDERO LUMINOSO (SL). *See* Shining Path.

SHINING PATH/EL SENDERO LUMINOSO (SL). Popular name for the Revolutionary Communist Party of Peru, founded by dissident Maoist philosophy professor Abimael Guzmán and dedicated to the complete destruction of existing political and economic institutions and the creation of a new communal and socialist society. Known for its violent attacks against the Peruvian state, the SL moved from intimidation of the countryside in the 1960s to urban terrorism by the mid-1980s. Efforts by Peruvian governments to subdue the SL and capture its leadership led to massive human rights (q.v.) violations by the military and government secret service organizations. In 1993, President Alberto Fujimori (q.v.) suspended constitutional rights and closed Parliament in an effort to mount a more vigorous attack on the SL. After the arrest of Guzmán in late 1993, the SL remained a weakened force in Peruvian society but still managed to commit random acts of violence and terrorism despite government efforts to put an end to its guerrillas. Once believed to number 8,000, it is down to less than 800, and a dispirited and divided leadership further undermine its ability to threaten the Peruvian state. *See also* Fujimori, Alberto; Human Rights.

SISTEMA DE INTEGRACIÓN CENTROAMERICANO (SICA). *See* Latin American Economic System (LAES).

SISTEMA ECONÓMICO LATINOAMERICANO (SELA). *See* Latin American Economic System (LAES).

SOCCER WAR, OF HONDURAS AND EL SALVADOR. In July 1969, hostilities broke out between these two Central American Common Market (CACM, q.v.) members, and CACM progress came to a halt. Stopping the conflict was a great challenge for the Organization of American States (OAS, q.v.). Although called the Soccer War because of nationalist riots after three soccer matches, particularly ones in Honduras directed against Salvadoran immigrants, the real cause was Salvadorans migrating—about 300,000 leaving their densely populated country—and settling in neighboring Honduras. Pressure had been building up over land and jobs for years, and it came to a boil over soccer, resulting in Hondurans attacking Salvadorans and their property.

The OAS first became involved in early summer, when El Salvador appealed to the Commission on Human Rights, charging Honduras with "genocide." The commission sent a subcommittee to investigate, and Honduras requested a meeting of the Organ of Consultation under the Rio Treaty (q.v.), which was done with the Permanent Council acting provisionally the day after Salvadoran troops moved into Honduras. The council appointed a special committee to investigate. The ensuing 13th Meeting of Consultation adopted resolutions calling for the suspension of hostilities and the withdrawal of troops, the creation of a vigilance system, guarantees to protect the human rights of nonnationals, and an end to mass media propaganda. For a time, El Salvador refused to withdraw its troops, pending human rights (q.v.) guarantees for its nationals in Honduras. As a result, the foreign ministers came close to branding El Salvador an aggressor and applying sanctions. Finally, El Salvador agreed to withdraw, making an agreement possible. Later that year a special Inter-American Conference on Human Rights met in Costa Rica and adopted the American Convention on Human Rights, the Declaration of San José. *See also* Central American Defense Council (CADC); Organization of American States (OAS, 4b).

SOMOZA DYNASTY/FAMILY. The patriarch of the family was Anastasio Somoza (1896–1956), whom the United States made commander of the National Guard during its final occupation (1927–1933) of Nicaragua. A year after the United States withdrew, its president had completed peace negotiations with Augusto César Sandino, a guerrilla leader and popular hero throughout Latin America, but Somoza had him killed. The Sandinistas would later take their name after him in forming the Sandinista Front for National Liberation (Frente Sandinista de Liberación Nacional, FSLN, q.v.), which led the insurrection that overthrew his son, Anastasio Somoza Debayle ("Tachito") in 1979. The elder Somoza used the National Guard as his base of power, had himself "elected" president on several occasions, and ruled the country as a rich dictator until he was assassinated in 1956. His elder son, Luis (1922–1967), a liberal member of the congress, took over and was elected president. During this period his younger brother, Anastasio Jr., commanded the National Guard and opposed his modernization and liberalization policies. When Luis died in 1967, Anastasio Jr. took over and ruled as dictator until his National Guard was defeated in July 1979 by FSLN-led forces. After arriving in Miami, Florida, disagreements with the new government in Managua contributed to Somoza being denied exile in the United States. He soon fled to Paraguay, where he was protected by the dictator General Alfredo Stroessner until he was assassinated by Argentine leftists in 1980.

All three, father and sons, had studied in the United States (Luis at several universities, and Anastasio Jr. graduated from West Point), were fluent in English (including the vernacular of U.S. politicians), and pro-United States. The Somozas were amenable to assisting the United States in its efforts to overthrow Arbenz in Guatemala in 1954 and allowed CIA-trained Cuban exiles to leave from Nicaragua for their campaign to overthrow Fidel Castro (q.v.) at the Bay of Pigs in 1961. For more than four decades Washington maintained close, friendly relations with Nicaragua under the Somozas. The last Somoza, Anastasio Jr., left Nicaragua a bitter man, critical of the ingratitude of the United States for forcing his departure after years of support for the United States and its Cold War (q.v.) policies. He called President Carter "Fidel Carter" and told U.S. representatives in Managua before leaving that "I helped them [Washington policymakers] for thirty years to fight communism. I'd like the American people to pay back the help we gave in the Cold War. The U.S. can't afford to lose a good partner. I am transitory but the reds are not." *See also* Nicaragua, Insurrection in of Sandinistas and Collective Sanctions by the OAS; Nicaraguan Revolution; Ortega, Daniel.

SOUTH ATLANTIC TREATY ORGANIZATION (SATO)/ORGANI-ZACIÓN DEL TRATATO DEL ATLÁNTICO SUR (OTAS). With growing concern over Soviet naval influence in the Caribbean (both in Cuba and in the Caribbean region as a whole) in the early 1970s, the United States proposed the creation of a multilateral counterforce to the Soviet presence. Fearing a threat to U.S. trade routes to and in the South Atlantic, General Alexander Haig, then Commander of the North Atlantic Treaty Organization (NATO, q.v.) (officially, SHAPE, Supreme Headquarters of Allied Powers in Europe), proposed in 1976 the creation of SATO as an adjunct to NATO and a naval alliance to counter the Soviets. In General Haig's plan, the force would be composed of the naval forces of the Southern Cone states—Argentina, Brazil, Chile, and Uruguay—and the navy of the Republic of South Africa.

The SATO plan was welcomed at first, facilitated by the fact that these South American states were all under military rule and Argentina's long-held view of itself as the naval defender of the South Atlantic. Brazil, however, as a result of its historical rivalry with Argentina, was unwilling to accept Argentine dominance. Moreover, Brazil was expanding its economic ties with other former Portuguese colonies (e.g., Angola in southwest Africa) and would not associate itself with South Africa. Brazil's reticence was also tied to U.S. pressure stemming from President Carter's human rights policy (q.v.) in Latin America. Chile also found it difficult to consider joining SATO with Argentina in view of its on-going Beagle Channel Islands dispute (q.v.), which brought the two countries to the brink of war in 1978. However, in 1981, while the Vatican was mediating the Beagle Channel Islands controversy, a Chilean admiral offered limited support for a SATO proposal that would exclude Argentina and consist of the navies of Chile, Brazil, Great Britain, and South Africa. This modification, of course, was unacceptable to Argentina. The 1982 South Atlantic War (q.v.) further divided these states and exacerbated relations with the United States, as well as greatly dimishing Argentina as a naval power. In the end, the idea for a multilateral South Atlantic naval force failed with each of its prospective member states, including the United States, preferring to go it alone. *See also* Beagle Channel Islands Dispute; North Atlantic Treaty Organization (NATO).

SOUTH ATLANTIC WAR. *See* Falklands/Malvinas War.

SOUTHERN CONE COMMON MARKET (MERCOSUR). The largest trade bloc in Latin America, originally established by Argentina and Brazil (1990) but later joined by Uruguay and Paraguay (1991). Chile (1996) and Bolivia (1997) joined MERCOSUR as associate members, while other South American countries are contemplating membership. Subregional integration groups and other countries are also interested in dealing with MERCOSUR to expand trade and investment. Based on the Treaty of Asunción, MERCOSUR aims to eliminate tariffs among its partners, coordinate macroeconomic policies, establish a common external tariff for third parties outside of MERCOSUR, create a body to solve trade disputes, establish the Council of the Common Market (an organ of highest decision-making authority), and create the Common Market Group to handle technical aspects of the negotiation process. Since 1991, MERCOSUR has been successful in promoting more competition, investments, and a broader market.

With a combined population of 210 million, MERCOSUR members have a combined Gross Domestic Product (GDP) of close to $1 trillion and total trade of $175 billion. MERCOSUR accounts for 60 percent of Latin America's GDP and 40 percent of all trade. With MERCOSUR now a potentially powerful counterpoint to the North American Free Trade Agreement (NAFTA, q.v.) and with increasing trade ties to Europe and Asia, the United States may find itself in the position of having to negotiate with the five members in this bloc. At its meeting in June 1996 in Argentina, MERCOSUR members (including Bolivia) signed a "democracy guaranty clause" that would suspend commercial benefits to any country that deviated from democratic (q.v.) principles. The genesis of the democratic protection provision was the important role MERCOSUR played in thwarting the attempted military coup in Paraguay in April 1996. MERCOSUR marks the end of the traditional rivalry between Argentina and Brazil that was reinforced by the Cold War (q.v.), where the latter was pro-United States until changes were initiated during the Carter administration. As one of the two trading blocs that dominate the Americas, MERCOSUR (led by Brazil) has clashed with NAFTA members over the pace and direction for opening up national markets. MERCOSUR would like the Free Trade Area of the Americas (FTAA, q.v.) to start in 2005 (the timetable agreed upon at the Miami Summit in 1994), while NAFTA (led by the United States) wants the FTAA to start in the year 2000. MERCOSUR has recently influenced the learning of the respective languages—Spanish and Portuguese—of Argentina and Brazil. In Brazil, for example, Spanish is now challenging English as the most popular second language. Portuguese is now obligatory for Argentine diplomats as the demand for French and Italian fades in response to the need for linguistic skills in commercial transactions, attributable to the recent creation of the Southern Cone Common Market. *See also* Cardoso, Fernando Henrique; Free Trade Area of the Americas (FTAA).

SPAIN. As a colonial power for over 300 years (400 years in the case of Cuba), Spain's presence in the Americas has deep roots, and the Spanish legacy continues to influence the social, economic, and political life of the region. The loss of its colonies during the first two decades of the nineteenth century, and the U.S. fear that the European Holy Alliance powers would help it regain control of the New World, was a key factor leading to the Monroe Doctrine (q.v.) in 1823. By the end of the century, the final defeat of Spain by the United States in the Spanish-American War (q.v.) assured the end of Spain's presence in Latin America. Nevertheless, Spain retained ties to the Americas that were difficult to erase, and throughout the twentieth century, especially in the interwar period, important economic, trade, and cultural relations between it and Latin America were cultivated. Relations improved during the dictatorship of General Francisco Franco, particularly after he won the Spanish Civil War (1936–1939) and established absolute control. Franco made a point of trying to increase commercial relations by stressing the mutual cultural and religious heritage, what he called *Hispanidad,* between Spain and Latin America. As a result of his pro-Axis and fascist stance during World War II (q.v.), he was excluded from the United Nations, but he lobbied the Latin American states to support Spain's admission and was successful in gaining membership in 1955.

Franco and his regime were admired by Latin American dictators, Juan D. Perón of Argentina (q.v.) and Rafael L. Trujillo (q.v.) of the Dominican Republic, among others. He was a shrewd and cunning politician; in one critical decision he negotiated a 1953 mutual defense pact with the United States, which brought Spain $225 million in economic aid in exchange for granting the United States military bases for guarding the North Atlantic Treaty Organization's (NATO, q.v.) southern flank. At the same time, despite his virulent anticommunist/Soviet position, he maintained close relations with and aided Fidel Castro's (q.v.) government in Cuba. Franco stood firm against U.S. pressure to cut his ties with the island, but this did not prevent Spain and the United States from regularly renewing their economic and military base agreements.

At times Franco and other Spanish leaders have attempted to play an intermediary role between the United States and Latin America. This was particularly evident during the term of socialist prime minister Felipe González (1982–1996) who was often critical of U.S. policy, particularly in Central America. The European Community (EC, q.v.), through its Institute for European-Latin American Relations (IRLAR, q.v.) located in Madrid, strongly supported the Central American/Contadora Peace Process (q.v.) and criticized U.S. policy for its lack of regard for Central American sovereignty. Spain was actively involved in the UN Observer Group in Central America (ONUCA), where a Spanish general commanded the group, and Spanish soldiers and policemen complemented the multilateral force, a role welcomed by President Daniel Ortega (q.v.) of Nicaragua. Spain is now much more active in inter-American relations, especially those involving dispute resolution and the democratization process. It is currently the largest foreign investor in Cuba and a staunch opponent of the Helms-Burton Act.

SPANISH-AMERICAN WAR. Originally the United States opposed Cuban independence in the early part of the nineteenth century on the grounds that a free and independent Cuba might foment a slave revolt or that a European power might decide to use it as a base of operations against the United States, but by the end of the century it reversed this position. After three years of struggle to end Spanish colonialism in Cuba, the United States found itself being inexorably drawn into the conflict with Spain. The Hearst media empire used the conflict in Cuba to sell more newspapers, and imperialist elements within the Republican Party clamored for the United States to intervene in the Cuban war for independence from Spain after 400 years of colonial possession. The immediate pretext for U.S. intervention (q.v.) in the war was the sinking of the *U.S.S. Maine* in Havana harbor in 1898; President McKinley was opposed to war with Spain but was unable to forestall the building sentiment for military action inside Congress and among the American public. Congress declared war two months after the sinking of the *Maine,* but the first battle was fought in the Philippines in May, resulting in the destruction of the Spanish fleet. U.S. troops (among them Theodore Roosevelt [q.v.] and his soon-to-be-famous Rough Riders) landed in Cuba in June and helped defeat the poorly equipped Spanish. The Spanish navy in the Caribbean was destroyed in July, and Spain surrendered in August. With the Treaty of Paris (signed in December), Spain lost its presence in Latin America, and the United States acquired Guam, Puerto Rico, and the Philippines.

The U.S. military occupation of Cuba began in January 1899, and it assumed the right of supervising national elections. A new 1901 Cuban Constitution incorporated the Platt Amendment (approved by the U.S. Congress as a rider to an army appropriation bill), which gave the United States the right to intervene to assure Cuban independence and to maintain law and order. Thereafter, the United States leased Guantánamo Bay, where it established a major naval base. Cuba became independent in 1902, but U.S. troops were repeatedly required to quell revolts on the island. Under the Platt Amendment, U.S. troops returned to rule Cuba between 1906 and 1909 and for shorter periods until the Platt Amendment was abrogated in 1936. The Spanish-American War (known as the Cuban-Spanish-American War in Cuba) ended the Spanish empire in the Americas and helped to transform the United States into a hegemonic power in the Western Hemisphere. Theodore Roosevelt used his war experience to gain the presidency and influence his Latin American policy. *See also* Big Stick Policy; Intervention and Nonintervention; Monroe Doctrine; Roosevelt, Theodore.

SPECIAL COMMITTEE ON LATIN AMERICAN COORDINATION (SCLAC)/COMISIÓN ESPECIAL DE COORDINACIÓN LATIN-OAMERICANA (CECLA). An exclusively Latin American consultative body, SCLAC was established at an Inter-American Economic and Social Council (IAECOSOC) conference in São Paulo, Brazil, in late 1963. Its goal was to present a unified Latin American position at the first United Nations Conference on Trade and Development (UNCTAD, q.v.) meeting in Geneva in 1964. The first SCLAC meeting was held in Argentina in 1964, and it laid the basis for Latin America's future commercial policies with the developed countries.

STANDBY ARRANGEMENT. *See* International Monetary Fund (IMF).

STRUCTURAL ADJUSTMENT PROGRAMS (SAPs). Lending programs, usually in the form of loans by the World Bank and the International Monetary Fund (IMF, q.q.v.), designed to help stabilize a country going through a period of neoliberal economic reform. The acceptance of these loans requires that certain macroeconomic policies, determined by the lender, are followed to assist with the structural adjustment of its economy. *See also* International Monetary Fund (IMF); World Bank.

SUMMIT OF THE AMERICAS/CUMBRE DE LAS AMÉRICAS. An important hemispheric meeting in Miami, Florida in late 1994 composed of 34 democratically elected heads of state. President Bill Clinton (q.v.) called for the meeting and presided over its deliberations that eventually culminated in the creation of a new agenda for the members of the Organization of American States (OAS, q.v.). Cuba was not invited to the historic meeting, which led to some criticism of its exclusion and the negative impact of the U.S. trade embargo (q.v.) against Castro's Cuba. During the December meeting a "Declaration of Principles" was approved that included 23 initiatives and 100 action items that were placed in four major categories: democracy, trade, poverty, and sustainable development. A 28-page "Plan of Action" was drawn up to implement the "principles," and the OAS was assigned specific duties in a number of areas: democracy, human rights, corruption, drug trafficking, terrorism, and security. Among these areas of responsibility, the promotion of trade and the strengthening of democracy were designated as of highest priority. The OAS was also given the task of facilitating and overseeing the process of regional integration and free trade, which was eventually to lead to the establishment of the Free Trade Area of the Americas (FTAA) by the year 2005. The principal agencies of the OAS carrying out this assignment are the Special Committee on Trade and the 1995 Unit on Trade (see Organization of American States, 4c). The OAS's other major assigned responsibility—promoting democracy—was to be carried out by its Unit for Democracy (see Organization of American States, 4b). At the end of the Miami Summit, Canada, Mexico, and the United States invited Chile to join NAFTA (q.v.), an invitation that was stalled by conservative members of the U.S. Congress until 1997. The next Summit of the Americas is scheduled for Santiago, Chile, in 1998. *See also* Clinton, William J.

SUSTAINABLE DEVELOPMENT. A relatively new approach to economic development in Latin America and the Caribbean that recognizes the importance of balancing the practices common to industrialization and modernization with the use of appropriate technologies and moderation of patterns of consumption and rate of exploitation of a country's resource base. A sustainable approach to economic development employs strategies that include a recognition of the importance of conserving nonrenewable resources (e.g., petroleum), replenishing renewable resources (e.g., clean air and water), and appreciating the limits of industrial growth. Inter-American organizations and the United Nations have held conferences on the importance of the relationship between the environment (q.v.) and development, emphasizing forest protection, maritime cleanup, habitat protection, and biological diversity. *See also* Amazon Pact; Environment; Inter-American Development Bank (IADB); United Nations Conference on the Environment and Development (UNCED); United Nations Environment Program (UNEP); United Nations, Third Conference on the Law of the Sea (UNCLOS III).

T

THIRD WORLD. This category developed in the late 1940s includes a large number of states that were not really committed to either the West (led by the United States) or the East (led by the Soviet Union) in the Cold War (q.v.). Instead, these states preferred to be neutral or nonaligned, and most of them shared the common characteristics of being debtors, poor and underdeveloped, and located in Africa, Asia, and Latin America. More of the African and Asian states were neutral and nonaligned. Some observers, using World Bank (q.v.) figures, have referred to a "Fourth World" group, the poorer members of the Third World, often considered to include Haiti, Honduras, Guyana, and El Salvador. In contrast, the First World included the United States and its allies, while the Second World was comprised of the Soviet Union and its communist associates.

With the emergence of the Cold War and the resultant East-West axis, the major struggle involved the First and Second worlds. Later, as the number of states in the Third World category developed a sense of unity, particularly on economic issues, and began operating as a bloc, a North-South axis emerged. With the passing of time and on certain issues, the North-South axis transcended the East-West axis. The Third World's developing unity and bloc voting in the United Nations (e.g., the Group of Seventy-Seven [q.v.]) resulted in the establishment of the United Nations Conference on Trade and Development (UNCTAD, q.v.) in 1964, which continues to meet every four years in a Third World capital. This was followed by the UN General

Assembly's approval of two resolutions in 1970. One called for the establishment of a New International Economic Order (NIEO, q.v.), and the other approved the Charter on the Economic Rights and Duties of States (CERDS, q.v.). The Third World states worked as a bloc to serve their interests during the Third UN Conference on the Law of the Sea (UNCLOS III, q.v.), 1974–1982, which was conducted on a North-South axis. Several of the Latin American and Caribbean states were very active at this conference. *See also* Cold War; Group of 77 (G-77); New International Economic Order (NIEO); Nonaligned Movement (NAM); United Nations, Third Conference on the Law of the Sea (UNCLOS III).

TOBAR DOCTRINE. Arguing that a formula was needed to put an end to revolutions in the Americas, Ecuadorian diplomat Carlos R. Tobar proposed a theory of recognition in 1907 in which there should be a policy of joint intervention (q.v.) to put an end to internal strife and the American nations should "refuse recognition to *de facto* governments that had been established by revolutions against the constitutional regime." At a Central American Peace Conference in Washington in 1907, Tobar's proposal was adopted. U.S. President Woodrow Wilson incorporated the Tobar Doctrine into his own theory of recognition, thus abandoning the Jeffersonian principle of recognizing any government that had "the expression of popular will," regardless of its origin or character. Until the Good Neighbor Policy (q.v.), the Tobar Doctrine and Wilsonian recognition theory were both the objects of much distrust and hatred by the American republics. In 1930, Mexican Foreign Minister Genaro Estrada challenged the Tobar Doctrine by arguing that when a new government has political control of the state, it should be automatically recognized (q.v.). Since the 1930s the Tobar Doctrine has increasingly given way to the recognition theory contained in the Estrada Doctrine (q.v.). *See also* Estrada Doctrine; Good Neighbor Policy; Recognition and Nonrecognition of States, Governments, and Insurgents.

TORRIJOS, OMAR. *See* Panama, Intervention in by the United States and the OAS, and Elections.

TREATY FOR AMAZON COOPERATION. *See* Amazon Pact.

TREATY OF TLATELOLCO. An agreement signed by 14 states in 1967 (in effect in 1968) declaring the Latin American region a "nuclear weapons-free zone." As of mid-1994, all of the Latin American states, except Cuba, have ratified the treaty and appropriate protocols, and all declared members of the nuclear "club" have agreed to honor the zone defined in the treaty. Rivals Argentina and Brazil, under military rule until the early 1980s, refused to become parties for many years, each waiting for the other to go first. Argentina finally ratified it in January 1994, followed by Brazil in May. Chile became a party to the treaty at the same time as Argentina. Although it contains no sanctions against those states that violate the treaty, it is considered a beneficial complement to the Nuclear Nonproliferation Treaty signed in 1968. *See also* Agency for the Prohibition of Nuclear Weapons in Latin America and the Caribbean (APNWLA).

TRUJILLO MOLINA, RAFAEL L. (1891–1961). Military leader and politician well-known for his long and brutal dictatorship in the small Caribbean nation of the Dominican Republic. Trujillo was a graduate of the military academy established by the United States during its occupation of the country from 1916 to 1924. When the United States withdrew after supervising national elections, he was the commander of the Dominican National Police (later National Armed Forces). He used this position to manipulate his 1930 election as president and consolidated power by eliminating all opposition groups and converting the Dominican Republic into a family-run fiefdom that would last until his assassination in May 1961. As a means of changing his international image after he ordered the massacre of Haitians (around 20,000 were killed) in 1937, he invited thousands of refugees (Jews from Germany and Republican exiles from Spain's civil war) to the Dominican Republic, even though he was an admirer of both Francisco Franco and Adolf Hitler. During the Cold War (q.v.) he was a loyal supporter of the United States until it and other Organization of American States (OAS, q.v.) member states imposed economic sanctions on the Dominican Republic for the unsuccessful 1960 effort to kill a leading critic, democratic President Rómulo Betancourt (q.v.) of Venezuela. This event marked the first time the OAS would be used as an example of a "antidictator alliance". *See also* Balaguer, Joaquín; Betancourt, Rómulo; Caribbean Legion; Intervention and Nonintervention.

TUNA WAR. The basis for this crisis was laid when Chile, Ecuador, and Peru claimed a 200-mile zone to protect tuna, via the 1952 Santiago Declaration resulting in a dispute that had to be resolved at the Third United Nations Conference on the Law of the Sea (UNCLOS III, q.v.). The United States particularly objected to the claim, arguing in terms of traditional international law that the area beyond the three-mile territorial sea was the high seas and open to all. The enforcement of these states' claimed right to regulate tuna fishing resulted in the

Tuna War when Ecuador and Peru seized and fined U.S. private fishing boats in the 1950s and 1960s.

The United States felt so strongly it refused to accept their claims, thus giving them legitimacy, that it reimbursed the fishing boat captains for the fines. The conflict was temporarily solved in July of 1963 when the civilian government of Ecuador was overthrown by a military coup and quickly recognized (q.v.) by the Kennedy administration, contrary to officially stated policy. Washington's recognition policy in this case involved a "secret agreement" in which the U.S. tuna fleet was allowed to fish in the disputed area with impunity. *See also* United Nations, Third Conference on the Law of the Sea (UN-CLOS III).

TÚPAC AMARU REVOLUTIONARY MOVEMENT. *See* Movimiento Revolucionario Túpac Amaru (MRTA).

U

UNION OF BANANA EXPORTING COUNTRIES (UBEC)/UNIÓN DE PAÍSES EXPORTADORAS DE BANANO (UPEB). Seven-member commodity organization founded in 1974 as an intergovernmental agency to assist in the production/cultivation and marketing of bananas, securing the best prices for the producer countries, the collection of statistics, and compilation of bibliographies on the subject. Members include Colombia, Costa Rica, Guatemala, Honduras, Nicaragua, Panama, and Venezuela.

UNIÓN DE PAÍSES EXPORTADORAS DE BANANO (UPEB). *See* Union of Banana Exporting Countries (UBEC).

UNITED NATIONS CONFERENCE ON THE ENVIRONMENT AND DEVELOPMENT (UNCED). Second of the major international conferences on the environment (q.v.) held in Rio de Janeiro in 1992 and popularly known as the "Earth Summit" and "Eco 92." With 30,000 delegates from over 178 nations, the conference produced a controversial 800-page action plan entitled "Agenda 21," which emphasized programs for achieving sustainable development (q.v.) on a global scale through the twenty-first century. Two controversial conventions were signed at the conference—the UN Framework Convention on Climate Change and the Convention on Biologic Diversity—and a third nonbinding agreement on protecting forests. Guidelines for human behavior toward the environment contained in the Rio Declaration on Environment and Development were also issued. Critics of the international conference felt that population, poverty, and development issues received too little attention, while others praised the meeting for bringing a degree of saliency to the consequences of not taking concerted action on environmental issues. The Bush administration refused to sign the Convention on Biologic Diversity, but the Clinton administration ratified it in 1993. *See also* Environment; United Nations Development Program (UNDP); United Nations Environment Program (UNEP).

UNITED NATIONS DEVELOPMENT PROGRAM (UNDP). Founded in 1965 to provide a single administrative apparatus for United Nations aid and development projects. Most of the assistance is nonmonetary, i.e., the provision of the services of experts, consultancies, equipment, and fellowships for advanced study abroad. Its policy-making body is the Council (which meets annually), composed of representatives of 48 countries (27 from developing and 21 from developed countries). There are four regional bureaus, all administered by the Secretariat in New York City (one of which deals with Latin America and the Caribbean), and there are 24 UNDP offices in the region, seven in the Caribbean, including Cuba, one in Mexico, and one in each Central American and South American state. However, with most development aid being channeled either bilaterally or through the International Monetary Fund (IMF) and the World Bank (q.q.v.) in the 1990s the UNDP's role in development assistance has remained minimal. *See also* Environment; United Nations Environmental Program (UNEP).

UNITED NATIONS, DRUG CONTROL. United Nations drug control efforts started in 1946 when it took over the League of Nations's (q.v.) functions in the field and formed the Commission on Narcotic Drugs (one of the six functional commissions of the Economic and Social Council). In 1961, the International Narcotics Control Board was established, and two decades later the UN created a Division of Narcotic Drugs and the UN Fund for Drug Abuse Control. Several conventions and protocols have been adopted under UN auspices: the 1961 Convention on Psychotropic Substances (amended by the 1972 Protocol) integrated most of the earlier treaties, and the 1971 Convention on Psychotropic Substances extended and modernized drug control. After a 1984 General Assembly Declaration on the Control of Drug Trafficking and Drug Abuse, the Commission on Narcotic Drugs was asked to prepare a new and broader convention draft. This resulted in the 1988 UN Convention against Illicit Traffic in Narcotic Drugs and Psychotropic Substances, which entered into force in 1990. The regional members of the UN that ratified at that time were: the

Bahamas, Bolivia, Chile, Mexico, Nicaragua, Paraguay, and the United States. *See also* Drug Cartels; Inter-American Drug Abuse Control Commission (IADACC).

UNITED NATIONS ENVIRONMENT PROGRAM (UNEP). The program was established in 1972 by the UN General Assembly as recommended at that year's UN Conference on the Human Environment (Stockholm, Sweden). Its legislative body is the Governing Council, composed of 58 governmental representatives. Later, an Environment Co-ordination Board was created under the Administrative Committee for Coordination. In 1977, the functions of the former were taken over by the latter, and in 1979, a Committee of Designated Officials for Global Environmental Matters was appointed to deal with the transferred functions. In 1991, the Global Environment Facility, which is managed jointly by the United Nations Development Program (UNDP, q.v.), the UNEP, and the World Bank (q.v.), began operating.

Five global environmental conventions have been negotiated and adopted under UNEP's auspices. Two of them were drafted and signed by over 150 states at the UN Conference on the Environment and Development (UNCED, q.v.) in Rio de Janeiro, Brazil, in June 1992. Another convention was held in Uruguay in late 1992. An International Environmental Technology Center was opened in Japan in 1995. There are currently six regional offices, including two in the Western Hemisphere (New York and Mexico City). *See also* Earth Summit; Environment; Sustainable Development; United Nations Development Program (UNDP).

UNITED NATIONS OBSERVER GROUP IN CENTRAL AMERICA/ ORGANIZACIÓN NACIONES UNIDAS EN CENTROAMERICA (ONUCA). *See* Central American/Contadora Peace Process.

UNITED NATIONS OBSERVER GROUP IN EL SALVADOR/OR-GANIZACIÓN NACIONES UNIDAS EN EL SALVADOR (ONU-SAL). *See* Central American/Contadora Peace Process.

UNITED NATIONS, SPECIAL UNITED NATIONS FUND FOR ECONOMIC DEVELOPMENT (SUNFED). Established in 1959 to provide a new avenue for development aid, SUNFED merged with the Expanded Program of Technical Assistance (EPTA) in 1965 to form the United Nations Development Program (UNDP, q.v.).

UNITED NATIONS, THIRD CONFERENCE ON THE LAW OF THE SEA (UNCLOS III). A series of conferences was held between 1958 and 1994 to settle differences among participants divided roughly between a North (developed and industrialized) and South (developing) economic and political axis. The third conference was very different from the first two (in 1958 and in 1960), both in the number of participants and the length of the deliberations. While the earlier two conferences had over 80 participants and lasted only a few weeks, the third consisted of over 150 participants and went on for nine years. To deal with the North, the South used bloc caucusing and bargaining to press for a compromise agreement in which the territorial sea would extend to 12 miles and an Exclusive Economic Zone to 188 miles (200 miles total). In an effort to revise the code of maritime law, UNCLOS III established an International Seabed Authority (ISA) with the power to oversee a mining company ("the Enterprise") that would guarantee Third World (q.v.) countries access to all available nonmilitary mining technology.

The controversial nature of this arrangement contributed to the slow pace of ratification of the new code between 1982 and 1993. Among the Caribbean and Latin American states active in UNCLOS III were the Bahamas, Brazil, Chile, Jamaica, Mexico, Peru, Trinidad and Tobago, and Venezuela. The convention had the necessary 60 ratifications to go into effect in November 1994, but the United States was not one of them. Since the mid-1980s, there had been negotiations between the developed states (especially the United States) and the developing ones concerning the former's objections to ISA. Once an Implementation Agreement was reached in 1994, President Clinton sent the 1982 convention and the 1994 agreement to the U.S. Senate for its approval. While waiting for Senate approval, however, the United States did take part in the inaugural session of the ISA at its headquarters in Kingston, Jamaica, in November 1994. The law of the sea is one area in which the Latin American states have had a major impact—positive and negative—on multilateral diplomacy dealing with energy and the environment (q.v.), often in opposition to the wishes of the United States. *See also* Environment; Sustainable Development; Tuna War; United Nations Environment Program (UNEP).

UNITED NATIONS, WORLD HEALTH ORGANIZATION (WHO). *See* Pan American Health Organization (PAHO); World Health Organization (WHO).

UNITED NATIONS, WORLD TRADE ORGANIZATION (WTO). *See* General Agreement on Tariff and Trade (GATT); World Trade Organization (WTO).

UNITED STATES-LATIN AMERICAN RELATIONS. *See* Alliance for Progress; Big Stick Policy; Cold War; Democracy; Good Neighbor Policy; Intervention and Nonintervention; Monroe Doctrine; Recognition and Nonrecognition of States, Governments, and Insurgents; Tuna War; World War I; World War II.

URUGUAY. *See* Mora, José A.; Rodríguez Larreta Doctrine; Appendix III.

V

VENEZUELA. *See* Betancourt, Rómulo; Central American/Contadora Peace Process; Pérez, Carlos Andrés.

W

WAR OF THE PACIFIC (1879–1884). Major war between Bolivia, Chile, and Peru over control of a desert region rich in guano and nitrates that was formally ended with two U.S.-mediated peace treaties in 1883 and 1884. Chile gained the most, the treaties allowing it to keep all the territory it seized in battle, and Bolivia lost its only outlet to the sea. While some concessions have been made to Bolivia over the years, and the Organization of American States (OAS, q.v.) has often been used to address its long-standing claim, tensions still remain between Chile and Bolivia after more than a hundred years.

WAR OF THE TRIPLE ALLIANCE (1865–1870). Extremely destructive war between Paraguay and Argentina, Brazil, and Uruguay. In one of the bloodiest and cruelest wars in Latin American history, Paraguay lost nearly half of its population of 400,000 and close to 80 percent of its male population. The major cause of the war (sometimes referred to as the Paraguayan War) was the desire of Paraguayan dictator Francisco Solano López to make Paraguay a great power in the Plate River region. Historic rivalries among Brazil, Argentina, and Paraguay, along with the unsettled boundaries of Paraguay, also contributed to the conflict. The war did not end until 1870, when López was killed. The peace settlement required Paraguay to give up 50,000 square miles of land to Brazil and Argentina, pay heavy reparations, and allow allied forces under Brazilian command to remain in Paraguay until 1876. After the war, Paraguay suffered from a destroyed economy, political chaos and periods of rule by petty dictators and ruthless *caudillos*, and the growth of bitter nationalist and irredentist feelings that would eventually give rise to another conflict with Bolivia over the Chaco territory. Despite the death and destruction, some Paraguayans still consider López a national hero for his courage in defending his country's interests against powerful neighboring states. *See also* Chaco War.

WARS. *See* Chaco War; Falklands/Malvinas War; Gulf War; Korean War; Soccer War; Tuna War; War of the Pacific, War of the Triple Alliance; World War I; World War II.

WEST INDIES ASSOCIATED STATES (WISA). A trade group that was absorbed along with the Eastern Caribbean Common Market (ECCM, q.v.) by the Organization of Eastern Caribbean States (OECS, q.v.) in 1981.

WILLIAMS, ERIC. *See* Caribbean Commonwealth Leaders.

WORLD BANK. Founded at the Bretton Woods conference in 1944 as a global lending agency, the World Bank functions as an international public corporation as well as a specialized agency under the United Nations. Its original design was to aid in the recovery of the industrial nations from World War II (q.v.), but its major lending is now in Third World (q.v.) countries. Under its Articles of Agreement (Section 10, Political activity prohibited), the "political character" of a member was not to be a factor in decision making, for only "economic considerations" were to be relevant and "weighed impartially." In practice, however, the political nature of certain regimes became a factor, and democratization and human rights (qq.v.) considerations became increasingly important in the 1970s. In fact, some governments—of Sweden, Norway, and Denmark, as well as the United States—required its representative to apply human rights and political criteria to the credit and loan approval process.

In the aftermath of the Cold War (q.v.), the World Bank has been more active in reducing poverty by increasing lending for primary health and education rather than large-scale projects such as dams and roads in poor countries. To alleviate the damage done by the international debt crisis of the 1980s and the negative impact of International Monetary Fund (IMF, q.v.) requirements for loans, the World Bank has begun to address the problem of structural adjustment programs (q.v.) and their social consequences in Latin America, the Caribbean, and elsewhere. Eradicating corruption (q.v.) is another goal of the World Bank, which basically argues that investors will not enter regions where corrupt political and economic practices erode confidence in financial transactions. All of the countries in the Americas are members of the World Bank except Cuba, which withdrew in 1960. The current president of the World Bank is James D. Wolfensohn, a U.S. citizen. *See also* Corruption; International Monetary Fund (IMF); Structural Adjustment Programs (SAPs); World Bank Group.

WORLD BANK GROUP. This group includes the World Bank (q.v.) and its two affiliates, the International Development Association (IDA) and the International Finance Corporation (IFC). Membership in the World Bank is a requirement for membership in the IDA and in the IFC, and a country must be a member of the IMF before joining the World Bank. The IDA was established in 1960 for the purpose of providing aid to the poorest developing countries to help them raise their standards of living. The terms of assistance are much more flexible for these countries. In 1993, there were 150 members of the IDA. The IFC was established in 1956 for the purpose of promoting private enterprise in developing countries. With 154 members in 1993, it is legally and financially independent of other entities in the group. The World Bank Group first provided aid to Latin American countries in the late 1940s. It granted a development loan to Chile in 1948; an IFC investment in Brazil in 1957; and an IDA credit to Honduras in 1961. *See also* International Monetary Fund (IMF); World Bank.

WORLD HEALTH ORGANIZATION (WHO). A specialized agency of the United Nations that provides advisory services and direct assistance, research, and educational programs worldwide to eradicate or control epidemic diseases such as small pox, measles, polio, and tuberculosis. Founded in 1946 and headquartered in Geneva, Switzerland, it is one of the most successful of international organizations, particularly with its program of immunization of children against certain diseases. However, in other areas such as the AIDS epidemic and female circumcision, WHO has been less effective in many Third World (q.v.) countries. Its broad range of activities and large staff serve to explain its hefty annual budget of $1 billion. Major policy making is conducted through an annual meeting composed of representatives from the member states, but is also attended by representatives of intergovernmental organizations. All members of the OAS (q.v.) are participating members of WHO. *See also* Pan American Health Organization (PAHO).

WORLD TRADE ORGANIZATION (WTO). The world's most important international organization for regulating world trade that superseded GATT (q.v.) on January 1, 1995, following the successful Uruguay round of trade discussions. With headquarters in Geneva,

Switzerland, the WTO members include the original members of GATT as of the date of entry into force of the WTO Agreement. The purpose of the WTO is to serve as the principal international organization concerned with the reduction of trade barriers and enhancement of international trade relations. By providing a set of rules (based on a body of case law built up by the contracting parties) and a negotiating forum, the WTO enables countries to further liberalize world trade by working together to reduce trade barriers. Members from the Western Hemisphere include Antigua and Barbuda, Argentina, Barbados, Belize, Bolivia, Brazil, Canada, Chile, Colombia, Costa Rica, Cuba, Dominica, the Dominican Republic, El Salvador, Guatemala, Guyana, Haiti, Jamaica, Mexico, Nicaragua, Paraguay, Peru, St. Lucia, St. Vincent and the Grenadines, Suriname, Trinidad and Tobago, the United States, Uruguay, and Venezuela. Pending final decisions as to their future commercial policy, the Bahamas, Grenada, and St. Kitts and Nevis may eventually become members.

As a negotiating forum, the WTO functions as an international body to settle trade disputes that arise among members. Under the WTO system, a complaint is referred to a panel of experts who then debate and render a ruling on the matter in contention. The WTO adjudication process can take months and requires that a nation that ultimately loses change its trade practices or offer compensation to the damaged nations. Members that refuse to comply can be targeted for trade retaliation in the form of higher tariffs or other obstacles to their exports. The United States is the biggest user of the organization's dispute-settling process. During the first two years of existence, the WTO has ruled on 59 unfair trade cases, 22 of which were submitted by the United States. In 1996, the United States complained (backed by some Latin American countries) to the WTO that the workings of the European Union (EU, q.v.) banana market regime discriminated against U.S. interests, particularly the Chiquita Brands banana exporter. The Caribbean banana producers are allowed preferential access to the European markets under terms set forth in the Lomé Conventions (q.v.) for ACP (q.v) countries, even though their fruit is more expensive to produce than that of their Latin American competitors. To receive this preferential treatment, the Caribbean banana producers need the continuation of a waiver from WTO rules, one that applied to former colonies and expires in September 1998.

As of late 1996, the WTO was about to consider an EU complaint against the Helms-Burton Act, a U.S. law that allows lawsuits to be filed against companies doing business in Cuba and using property expropriated from U.S. citizens during the early stages of the Cuban Revolution. Europeans fear that the United States will try to claim national security as a rationale for the law if the WTO does eventually rule in favor of the EU claim. Despite some political opposition to the power of the WTO among conservatives in the United States, the country has lost only one case brought against it, a complaint by Venezuela and Brazil. Nevertheless, WTO proceedings are conducted in secrecy, and only a fraction of documents are made public, thus eliminating any mechanism for public participation and accountability. Renato Ruggiero is the director-general of the World Trade Organization. *See also* European Union (EU); General Agreement on Tariffs and Trade (GATT); North American Free Trade Agreement (NAFTA); Lomé Conventions.

WORLD WAR I. Major international conflict that presented the Latin American states with a number of difficult choices concerning how to handle both allies and adversaries. Despite the need for German investment and capital, distrust of Great Britain, and heightened sensitivities to recent U.S. expansion and domination, most of the Latin American nations followed the lead of the U.S. government. Brazil, Cuba, Costa Rica, Guatemala, Haiti, Honduras, Nicaragua, and Panama declared war on Germany. Five states broke off diplomatic relations with Germany—Bolivia, the Dominican Republic, Ecuador, Peru, and Uruguay. Argentina, Chile, and Mexico, with substantial ties to Germany, disputes with the United States, and animosity toward Great Britain, remained fully neutral in the conflict. Mexico, for example, resisted the temptation to support the Germans, despite many disputes with the United States and the lingering resentment over the loss of territory in the Mexican-American War (1846–1848, q.v.). The world war increased Latin American economic and financial reliance on the United States, refocusing trade northward, but also brought considerable prestige in international diplomacy due to the former's involvement with the League of Nations (q.v.) and the International Court of Justice (ICJ, q.v.). All the nations of Latin America ultimately became league members, although some later withdrew, and the aftermath of the war evoked a new confidence in confronting the United States on matters of mutual concern, including trade, defense, military occupation, and intervention (q.v.).

WORLD WAR II. Major international conflict that produced a greater sense of inter-American solidarity (with the exception of Argentina), although it took some time before the Latin American nations would commit themselves to the Allied cause. Before 1940, Latin Americans were more interested in President Roosevelt's Good Neighbor Policy (q.v.) than efforts to combat the developing hostilities in Europe and Asia. However, after the German invasion of Poland in 1939 and the fall of France in 1940, the Latin American nations were prepared to join in the anti-Axis war effort. In 1939, the Declaration of Panama produced the first collective effort to confront the Axis powers, proclaiming a safety belt of 300 to 1,000 miles around the Western Hemisphere. It was agreed that Latin American armies would not be raised to the status of a fighting ally and act only to meet an attack until the U.S. forces could intervene. This arrangement led to agreements to place U.S. military missions in all the countries except Bolivia, a factor in how the United States would conduct its Cold War (q.v.) policies in Latin America after the war. Ultimately, all the Latin American nations would declare war on the Axis powers; the lone holdout was Argentina (until March 27, 1945), which remained reluctant due to a pro-fascist military, large German and Italian immigrant population, and traditional resistance to Washington's dominance over hemispheric affairs.

With the exceptions of Chile (copper), Bolivia (tin), and Venezuela (oil), few of the Latin American countries benefited from the war because of the unimportance of coffee, sugar, and tropical fruits in the conflict. Mexico and Brazil received financial assistance from the United States to build steel mills, but these funds turned out to be highly inefficient means of pushing industrialization programs. In an effort to develop closer ties with the United States, President Getulio Vargas brought Brazil into the war on the side of the Allied powers in 1942 and in 1944 sent a division of 25,000 troops to fight in Italy against the Axis powers. Mexico contributed a squadron of airplanes that fought against Japan toward the end of the war. After the war, the Brazilian army, led by veterans of the Italian campaign, deposed Vargas two months before the December 1945 elections. Significantly, Allied wartime propaganda against tyranny and dictatorships led to growing demands for democratic (q.v.) reforms inside Latin America. By the war's end, diplomatic efforts to strengthen inter-American security had succeeded in paving the way for eventual Latin American participation and membership in the United Nations. Soviet-Latin American relations also improved toward the end of the war with most governments recognizing the USSR for the first time, a development that would allow the Soviet Union to expand its diplomatic, political, and military presence in the region from the 1960s until the 1980s. When the Latin Americans realized that there would be no Marshall Plan to help postwar economic restoration efforts in their part of the world, anti-American nationalism began to grow.

Appendix I

Post-World War II Inter-American Conferences

International Conferences of American States

(Note: While the initial conference, designated as "first," was held in Washington, D.C., 1889–1890, all the subsequent ones were held in Latin America. The official title was changed to "Inter-American Conference" for the 10th. The 11th, although scheduled for Quito, Ecuador, was never held. There were a number of "Special Conferences" until the OAS General Assembly began meeting on an annual basis in 1971.)

9th: Bogotá, Colombia, 1948

Inter-American Conferences

10th: Caracas, Venezuela, 1954

Special Conferences

Inter-American Conference for the Maintenance of Continental Peace and Security: Rio de Janeiro, Brazil, 1947
First Meeting of American Presidents: Panama City, Panama, 1956
First Special Inter-American Conference: Washington, D.C., 1964
Second Special Inter-American Conference: Rio de Janeiro, Brazil, 1965
Third Special Inter-American Conference: Buenos Aires, Argentina, 1967
Second Meeting of American Presidents: Punta del Este, Uruguay, 1967

Meetings of Consultation of Ministers of Foreign Affairs

(Note: The first two were held in Latin America after World War II began in Europe and before the United States declared war.)

Third: Rio de Janeiro, Brazil, 1942
Fourth: Washington, D.C., 1951
Fifth: Santiago, Chile, 1959
Sixth: San José, Costa Rica, 1960
Seventh: San José, Costa Rica, 1960
Eighth: Punta del Este, Uruguay, 1962
Ninth: Washington, D.C., 1964
10th: Washington, D.C., 1965–1966
11th: Washington, D.C.; Buenos Aires, Argentina; Punta del Este, Uruguay, 1967
12th: Washington, D.C., 1967
13th: Washington, D.C., 1969
14th: Washington, D.C., 1971
15th: Quito, Ecuador, 1974
16th: San José, Costa Rica, 1975
17th: Washington, D.C., 1978
18th: Washington, D.C., 1979
19th: Washington, D.C., 1981
20th: Washington, D.C., 1982
21st: Washington, D.C., 1989–1990
Ad hoc meeting: Washington, D.C., 1992
22nd: Washington, D.C.. 1993

Meetings of the OAS General Assembly

Regular

First: San José, Costa Rica, 1971
Second: Washington, D.C., 1972
Third: Washington, D.C., 1973
Fourth: Atlanta, Georgia, USA, 1974
Fifth: Washington, D.C., 1975
Sixth: Santiago, Chile, 1976
Seventh: St. Georges, Grenada, 1977
Eighth: Washington, D.C., 1978
Ninth: La Paz, Bolivia, 1979
10th: Washington, D.C., 1980
11th: Saint Lucia, 1981
12th: Washington, D.C., 1982
13th: Washington, D.C., 1983
14th: Brasilia, Brazil, 1984

Special

First: Washington, D.C., 1970
Second: Washington, D.C., 1970
Third: Washington, D.C., 1971
Fourth: Washington, D.C., 1977
Fifth: Washington, D.C., 1977
Sixth: Washington, D.C., 1978
Seventh: Washington, D.C., 1979
Eighth: Washington, D.C., 1982
Ninth: Washington, D.C., 1982
10th: Washington, D.C.,1984
11th: Washington, D.C., 1984
12th: Washington, D.C., 1984
13th: Washington, D.C., 1985
14th: Cartagena, Colombia, 1985

15th: Cartagena, Colombia, 1985
16th: Guatemala City, Guatemala, 1986
17th: Washington, D.C., 1987
18th: San Salvador, El Salvador, 1988
19th: Washington, D.C., 1989
20th: Asunción, Paraguay, 1990
21st: Santiago, Chile, 1991
22nd: Nassau, Bahamas, 1992
23rd: Managua, Nicaragua, 1993
24th: Belém, Brazil, 1994
25th: Port-au-Prince, Haiti, 1995
26th: Panama City, Panama, 1996
27th: Lima, Peru, 1997
28th: Caracas, Venezuela, 1998

15th: Washington, D.C., 1991
16th: Washington, D.C., 1992

17th: Washington, D.C., 1992
18th: Washington, D.C., 1993

19th: Managua, Nicaragua, 1993
20th: Mexico City, Mexico, 1994
21st: Washington, D.C., 1994

Appendix II

OAS Secretaries-General and Assistant Secretaries-General

Alberto Lleras Camargo and	Colombia	1948–1954
William Manger	United States	1948–1957
Carlos Dávila and	Chile	1954–1955
William Manger		
José A. Mora and	Uruguay	1956–1968
William Sanders	United States	1957–1968
Galo Plaza and	Ecuador	1968–1975
M. Rafael Urquía	El Salvador	1968–1975
Alejandro Orfila and	Argentina	1975–1984
José Luis Zeleya C. and	Guatemala	1975–1980
Valerie T. McComie	Barbados	1980–1990
João Clemente Baena Soares and	Brazil	1984–1994
Valerie T. McComie and		
Christopher R. Thomas	Trinidad and Tobago	1990–1995
César Gaviría Trujillo and	Colombia	1994–1999
Christopher R. Thomas		1995–

Appendix III

Member States of the OAS

Signatory Countries	Date of Deposit of Instrument of Ratification
Antigua and Barbuda	December 1981
Argentina	April 1956
Bahamas, Commonwealth of	March 1982
Barbados	November 1967
Belize	January 1991
Bolivia	October 1950
Brazil	March 1950
Canada	January 1990
Chile	June 1953
Colombia	December 1951
Costa Rica	November 1948
Cuba	July 1952
Dominica, Commonwealth of	May 1979
Dominican Republic	April 1949
Ecuador	December 1950
El Salvador	September 1950
Grenada	May 1975
Guatemala	April 1955
Guyana	January 1991
Haiti	March 1951
Honduras	February 1950
Jamaica	August 1969
Mexico	November 1948
Nicaragua	July 1950
Panama	March 1951
Paraguay	May 1950
Peru	February 1954
St. Kitts and Nevis	March 1984
Saint Lucia	May 1979
Saint Vincent and the Grenadines	December 1981

Suriname	June 1977
Trinidad and Tobago	March 1967
United States of America	June 1951
Uruguay	September 1955
Venezuela	December 1951

Appendix IV

Permanent Observers of the OAS

Country or Regional Group	Date Status was Granted
Algeria	1987
Angola	1991
Austria	1978
Belgium	1972
Bosnia and Herzegovina	1996
Croatia	1995
Cyprus	1985
Czech Republic	1995
Egypt	1977
Equatorial Guinea	1987
European Union	1989
Finland	1988
France	1972
Germany	1972
Ghana	1996
Greece	1979
Holy See (Vatican)	1978
Hungary	1990
India	1991
Israel	1972
Italy	1972
Japan	1973
Kazakhstan	1996
Korea, Republic of	1981
Latvia	1996
Lebanon	1995
Morocco	1981
Netherlands	1972
Pakistan	1988
Poland	1991
Portugal	1975

Romania	1990
Russian Federation	1992
Saudi Arabia	1980
Spain	1972
Sri Lanka	1996
Sweden	1996
Switzerland	1978
Tunisia	1990
Ukraine	1994
United Kingdom	1995

Appendix V

Structural Charts of the OAS

ORGANIZATION OF AMERICAN STATES

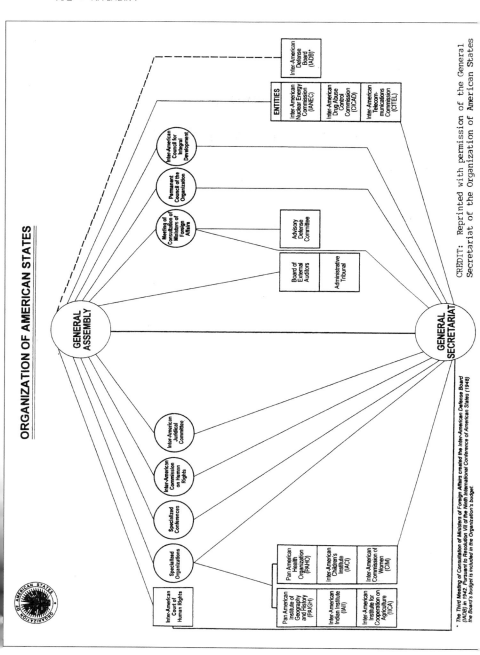

CREDIT: Reprinted with permission of the General Secretariat of the Organization of American States

* The Third Meeting of Consultation of Ministers of Foreign Affairs created the Inter-American Defense Board (IADB) in 1942. Pursuant to Resolution VII of the Ninth International Conference of American States (1948) the Board's budget is included in the Organization's budget.

GENERAL SECRETARIAT — ORGANIZATION OF AMERICAN STATES

CREDIT: Reprinted with permission of the General
Secretariat of the Organization of American States

SECRETARY GENERAL

Cabinet

ASSISTANT SECRETARY GENERAL
(Office of the Assistant Secretary General)

Secretariat to the General Assembly,
the Meeting of Consultation,
the Permanent Council,
and Conferences

Permanent Secretariat
of the Inter-American Commission
of Women

Inter-American Children's Institute

Offices of the General Secretariat
in the Member States

Art Museum of the Americas

Columbus Memorial Library

Trade Unit

Unit for
Promotion of Democracy

Secretariat of the Inter-American
Commission on Human Rights

Secretariat of the Inter-American
Drug Abuse Control Commission

Secretariat of the Inter-American
Telecommunications Commission

Department of Fellowships

Inspector General

Public Information

Protocol

SECRETARIAT FOR LEGAL AFFAIRS

Office of the
Under-Secretary

Secretariat of the
Administrative
Tribunal

Secretariat of the
Inter-American
Juridical
Committee

Department of
Development
and
Codification of
International
Law

Department
of
General
Legal
Services

SECRETARIAT FOR MANAGEMENT

Department
of
Management
Systems and
Information

Department
of
Human
Resources

Department
of
Program-
Budget

Department
of
Financial
Services

Department
of
Material
Resources

EXECUTIVE SECRETARIAT FOR INTEGRAL DEVELOPMENT

Department
of Economic
and
Social
Affairs

Department of
Regional
Development
and
Environment

Department
of
Educational
Affairs

Department of
Scientific and
Technological
Affairs

Department
of
Cultural
Affairs

Appendix VI

CHARTER OF THE ORGANIZATION OF AMERICAN STATES

As amended by the Protocol of Buenos Aires in 1967,
by the Protocol of Cartagena de Indias in 1985
and by the Protocol of Managua in 1993

GENERAL SECRETARIAT
ORGANIZATION OF AMERICAN STATES
WASHINGTON, D.C.

Charter of the Organization of American States

As amended by the Protocol of Amendment to the Charter of the Organization of American States "Protocol of Buenos Aires," signed on February 27, 1967, at the Third Special Inter-American Conference,

by the Protocol of Amendment to the Charter of the Organization of American States "Protocol of Cartagena de Indias," approved on December 5, 1985, at the Fourteenth Special Session of the General Assembly, and by the Protocol of Amendment to the Charter of the Organization of American States "Protocol of Managua," adopted on June 10, 1993, at the Nineteenth Special Session of the General Assembly.

GENERAL SECRETARIAT
ORGANIZATION OF AMERICAN STATES
WASHINGTON, D.C., 1996

Contents

Charter of the Organization of American States*

IN THE NAME OF THEIR PEOPLES, THE STATES REPRESENTED
AT THE NINTH INTERNATIONAL CONFERENCE OF AMERICAN
STATES,

Convinced that the historic mission of America is to offer to man a
land of liberty and a favorable environment for the development of his
personality and the realization of his just aspirations;

Conscious that that mission has already inspired numerous agreements, whose essential value lies in the desire of the American peoples
to live together in peace and, through their mutual understanding and
respect for the sovereignty of each one, to provide for the betterment of
all, in independence, in equality and under law;

Convinced that representative democracy is an indispensable condition for the stability, peace and development of the region;

Confident that the true significance of American solidarity and good
neighborliness can only mean the consolidation on this continent, within
the framework of democratic institutions, of a system of individual liberty and social justice based on respect for the essential rights of man;

Persuaded that their welfare and their contribution to the progress and
the civilization of the world will increasingly require intensive continental cooperation;

Resolved to persevere in the noble undertaking that humanity has
conferred upon the United Nations, whose principles and purposes they
solemnly reaffirm;

Convinced that juridical organization is a necessary condition for security and peace founded on moral order and on justice; and

In accordance with Resolution IX of the Inter-American Conference
on Problems of War and Peace, held in Mexico City,

---

*Signed in Bogotá in 1948 and amended by the Protocol of Buenos Aires in 1967, by the
Protocol of Cartagena de Indias in 1985, and by the Protocol of Managua in 1993. In
force as of January 29, 1996.

**HAVE AGREED
upon the following**

Charter of the Organization of American States

PART ONE

**Chapter I
NATURE AND PURPOSES**

Article 1

The American States establish by this Charter the international organization that they have developed to achieve an order of peace and justice, to promote their solidarity, to strengthen their collaboration, and to defend their sovereignty, their territorial integrity, and their independence. Within the United Nations, the Organization of American States is a regional agency.

The Organization of American States has no powers other than those expressly conferred upon it by this Charter, none of whose provisions authorizes it to intervene in matters that are within the internal jurisdiction of the Member States.

Article 2

The Organization of American States, in order to put into practice the principles on which it is founded and to fulfill its regional obligations under the Charter of the United Nations, proclaims the following essential purposes:

a) To strengthen the peace and security of the continent;

b) To promote and consolidate representative democracy, with due respect for the principle of nonintervention;

c) To prevent possible causes of difficulties and to ensure the pacific settlement of disputes that may arise among the Member States;

d) To provide for common action on the part of those States in the event of aggression;

e) To seek the solution of political, juridical, and economic problems that may arise among them;

f) To promote, by cooperative action, their economic, social, and cultural development; and

g) To achieve an effective limitation of conventional weapons that will make it possible to devote the largest amount of resources to the economic and social development of the Member States.

Chapter II
PRINCIPLES

Article 3

The American States reaffirm the following principles:

a) International law is the standard of conduct of States in their reciprocal relations;

b) International order consists essentially of respect for the personality, sovereignty, and independence of States, and the faithful fulfillment of obligations derived from treaties and other sources of international law;

c) Good faith shall govern the relations between States;

d) The solidarity of the American States and the high aims which are sought through it require the political organization of those States on the basis of the effective exercise of representative democracy;

e) Every State has the right to choose, without external interference, its political, economic, and social system and to organize itself in the way best suited to it, and has the duty to abstain from intervening in the affairs of another State. Subject to the foregoing, the American States shall cooperate fully among themselves, independently of the nature of their political, economic, and social systems;

f) The American States condemn war of aggression: victory does not give rights;

g) An act of aggression against one American State is an act of aggression against all the other American States;

h) Controversies of an international character arising between two or more American States shall be settled by peaceful procedures;

i) Social justice and social security are bases of lasting peace;

j) Economic cooperation is essential to the common welfare and prosperity of the peoples of the continent;

k) The American States proclaim the fundamental rights of the individual without distinction as to race, nationality, creed, or sex;

l) The spiritual unity of the continent is based on respect for the cultural values of the American countries and requires their close cooperation for the high purposes of civilization;

m) The education of peoples should be directed toward justice, freedom, and peace.

Chapter III
MEMBERS

Article 4

All American States that ratify the present Charter are Members of the Organization.

Article 5

Any new political entity that arises from the union of several Member States and that, as such, ratifies the present Charter, shall become a Member of the Organization. The entry of the new political entity into the Organization shall result in the loss of membership of each one of the States which constitute it.

Article 6

Any other independent American State that desires to become a Member of the Organization should so indicate by means of a note addressed to the Secretary General, in which it declares that it is willing to sign and ratify the Charter of the Organization and to accept all the obligations inherent in membership, especially those relating to collective security expressly set forth in Articles 27 and 28 of the Charter.

Article 7

The General Assembly, upon the recommendation of the Permanent Council of the Organization, shall determine whether it is appropriate that the Secretary General be authorized to permit the applicant State to sign the Charter and to accept the deposit of the corresponding instrument of ratification. Both the recommendation of the Permanent Council and the decision of the General Assembly shall require the affirmative vote of two thirds of the Member States.

Article 8

membership in the Organization shall be confined to independent States of the Hemisphere that were Members of the United Nations as of December 10, 1985, and the nonautonomous territories mentioned in document OEA/Ser. P, AG/doc.1939/85, of November 5, 1985, when they become independent.

Chapter IV
FUNDAMENTAL RIGHTS AND DUTIES OF STATES

Article 9

States are juridically equal, enjoy equal rights and equal capacity to exercise these rights, and have equal duties. The rights of each State depend not upon its power to ensure the exercise thereof, but upon the mere fact of its existence as a person under international law.

Article 10

Every American State has the duty to respect the rights enjoyed by every other State in accordance with international law.

Article 11

The fundamental rights of States may not be impaired in any manner whatsoever.

Article 12

The political existence of the State is independent of recognition by other States. Even before being recognized, the State has the right to defend its integrity and independence, to provide for its preservation and prosperity, and consequently to organize itself as it sees fit, to legislate concerning its interests, to administer its services, and to determine the jurisdiction and competence of its courts. The exercise of these rights is limited only by the exercise of the rights of other States in accordance with international law.

Article 13

Recognition implies that the State granting it accepts the personality of the new State, with all the rights and duties that international law prescribes for the two States.

Article 14

The right of each State to protect itself and to live its own life does not authorize it to commit unjust acts against another State.

Article 15

The jurisdiction of States within the limits of their national territory is exercised equally over all the inhabitants, whether nationals or aliens.

Article 16

Each State has the right to develop its cultural, political, and economic life freely and naturally. In this free development, the State shall respect the rights of the individual and the principles of universal morality.

Article 17

Respect for and the faithful observance of treaties constitute standards for the development of peaceful relations among States. International treaties and agreements should be public.

Article 18

No State or group of States has the right to intervene, directly or indirectly, for any reason whatever, in the internal or external affairs of any other State. The foregoing principle prohibits not only armed force but also any other form of interference or attempted threat against the personality of the State or against its political, economic, and cultural elements.

Article 19

No State may use or encourage the use of coercive measures of an economic or political character in order to force the sovereign will of another State and obtain from it advantages of any kind.

Article 20

The territory of a State is inviolable; it may not be the object, even temporarily, of military occupation or of other measures of force taken by another State, directly or indirectly, on any grounds whatever. No territorial acquisitions or special advantages obtained either by force or by other means of coercion shall be recognized.

Article 21

The American States bind themselves in their international relations not to have recourse to the use of force, except in the case of self-defense in accordance with existing treaties or in fulfillment thereof.

Article 22

Measures adopted for the maintenance of peace and security in accordance with existing treaties do not constitute a violation of the principles set forth in Articles 18 and 20.

Chapter V
PACIFIC SETTLEMENT OF DISPUTES

Article 23

International disputes between Member States shall be submitted to the peaceful procedures set forth in this Charter.

This provision shall not be interpreted as an impairment of the rights and obligations of the Member States under Articles 34 and 35 of the Charter of the United Nations.

Article 24

The following are peaceful procedures: direct negotiation, good offices, mediation, investigation and conciliation, judicial settlement, arbitration, and those which the parties to the dispute may especially agree upon at any time.

Article 25

In the event that a dispute arises between two or more American States which, in the opinion of one of them, cannot be settled through the usual diplomatic channels, the parties shall agree on some other peaceful procedure that will enable them to reach a solution.

Article 26

A special treaty will establish adequate means for the settlement of disputes and will determine pertinent procedures for each peaceful means such that no dispute between American States may remain without definitive settlement within a reasonable period of time.

Chapter VI
COLLECTIVE SECURITY

Article 27

Every act of aggression by a State against the territorial integrity or the inviolability of the territory or against the sovereignty or political independence of an American State shall be considered an act of aggression against the other American States.

Article 28

If the inviolability or the integrity of the territory or the sovereignty or political independence of any American State should be affected by an armed attack or by an act of aggression that is not an armed attack, or by an extracontinental conflict, or by a conflict between two or more American States, or by any other fact or situation that might endanger the peace of America, the American States, in furtherance of the principles of continental solidarity or collective self-defense, shall apply the measures and procedures established in the special treaties on the subject.

Chapter VII
INTEGRAL DEVELOPMENT

Article 29

The Member States, inspired by the principles of inter-American solidarity and cooperation, pledge themselves to a united effort to ensure international social justice in their relations and integral development for their peoples, as conditions essential to peace and security. Integral development encompasses the economic, social, educational, cultural, scientific, and technological fields through which the goals that each country sets for accomplishing it should be achieved.

Article 30

Inter-American cooperation for integral development is the common and joint responsibility of the Member States, within the framework of the democratic principles and the institutions of the inter-American system. It should include the economic, social, educational, cultural, scientific, and technological fields, support the achievement of national objectives of the Member States, and respect the priorities established by each country in its development plans, without political ties or conditions.

Article 31

Inter-American cooperation for integral development should be continuous and preferably channeled through multilateral organizations, without prejudice to bilateral cooperation between Member States.

The Member States shall contribute to inter-American cooperation for integral development in accordance with their resources and capabilities and in conformity with their laws.

Article 32

Development is a primary responsibility of each country and should constitute an integral and continuous process for the establishment of a more just economic and social order that will make possible and contribute to the fulfillment of the individual.

Article 33

The Member States agree that equality of opportunity, equitable distribution of wealth and income, and the full participation of their peoples in decisions relating to their own development are, among others, basic objectives of integral development. To achieve them, they likewise agree to devote their utmost efforts to accomplishing the following basic goals:

a) Substantial and self-sustained increase of per capita national product;

b) Equitable distribution of national income;

c) Adequate and equitable systems of taxation;

d) Modernization of rural life and reforms leading to equitable and efficient land-tenure systems, increased agricultural productivity, expanded use of land, diversification of production and improved processing and marketing systems for agricultural products; and the strengthening and expansion of the means to attain these ends;

e) Accelerated and diversified industrialization, especially of capital and intermediate goods;

f) Stability of domestic price levels, compatible with sustained economic development and the attainment of social justice;

g) Fair wages, employment opportunities, and acceptable working conditions for all;

h) Rapid eradication of illiteracy and expansion of educational opportunities for all;

i) Protection of man's potential through the extension and application of modern medical science;

j) Proper nutrition, especially through the acceleration of national efforts to increase the production and availability of food;

k) Adequate housing for all sectors of the population;

l) Urban conditions that offer the opportunity for a healthful, productive, and full life;

m) Promotion of private initiative and investment in harmony with action in the public sector; and

n) Expansion and diversification of exports.

Article 34

The Member States should refrain from practicing policies and adopting actions or measures that have serious adverse effects on the development of other Member States.

Article 35

Transnational enterprises and foreign private investment shall be subject to the legislation of the host countries and to the jurisdiction of their competent courts and to the international treaties and agreements to which said countries are parties, and should conform to the development policies of the recipient countries.

Article 36

The Member States agree to join together in seeking a solution to urgent or critical problems that may arise whenever the economic development or stability of any Member State is seriously affected by conditions that cannot be remedied through the efforts of that State.

Article 37

The Member States shall extend among themselves the benefits of science and technology by encouraging the exchange and utilization of scientific and technical knowledge in accordance with existing treaties and national laws.

Article 38

The Member States, recognizing the close interdependence between foreign trade and economic and social development, should make individual and united efforts to bring about the following:

a) Favorable conditions of access to world markets for the products of the developing countries of the region, particularly through the reduction or elimination, by importing countries, of tariff and non-tariff barriers that affect the exports of the Member States of the Organization, except when such barriers are applied in order to diversify the economic structure, to speed up the development of the less-developed Member States, and intensify their process of economic integration, or when they are related to national security or to the needs of economic balance;

b) Continuity in their economic and social development by means of:

    i.   Improved conditions for trade in basic commodities through international agreements, where appropriate; orderly marketing procedures that avoid the disruption of markets, and other measures designed to promote the expansion of markets and to obtain dependable incomes for producers, adequate and dependable supplies for consumers, and stable prices that are both remunerative to producers and fair to consumers;

ii. Improved international financial cooperation and the adoption of other means for lessening the adverse impact of sharp fluctuations in export earnings experienced by the countries exporting basic commodities;

iii. Diversification of exports and expansion of export opportunities for manufactured and semimanufactured products from the developing countries; and

iv. Conditions conducive to increasing the real export earnings of the Member States, particularly the developing countries of the region, and to increasing their participation in international trade.

Article 39

The Member States reaffirm the principle that when the more developed countries grant concessions in international trade agreements that lower or eliminate tariffs or other barriers to foreign trade so that they benefit the less-developed countries, they should not expect reciprocal concessions from those countries that are incompatible with their economic development, financial, and trade needs.

Article 40

The Member States, in order to accelerate their economic development, regional integration, and the expansion and improvement of the conditions of their commerce, shall promote improvement and coordination of transportation and communication in the developing countries and among the Member States.

Article 41

The Member States recognize that integration of the developing countries of the Hemisphere is one of the objectives of the inter-American system and, therefore, shall orient their efforts and take the necessary measures to accelerate the integration process, with a view to establishing a Latin American common market in the shortest possible time.

Article 42

In order to strengthen and accelerate integration in all its aspects, the Member States agree to give adequate priority to the preparation and carrying out of multinational projects and to their financing, as well as to encourage economic and financial institutions of the inter-American system to continue giving their broadest support to regional integration institutions and programs.

Article 43

The Member States agree that technical and financial cooperation that seeks to promote regional economic integration should be based on the principle of harmonious, balanced, and efficient development, with particular attention to the relatively less-developed countries, so that it may be a decisive factor that will enable them to promote, with their own efforts, the improved development of their infrastructure programs, new lines of production, and export diversification.

Article 44

The Member States, convinced that man can only achieve the full realization of his aspirations within a just social order, along with economic development and true peace, agree to dedicate every effort to the application of the following principles and mechanisms:

a) All human beings, without distinction as to race, sex, nationality, creed, or social condition, have a right to material well-being and to their spiritual development, under circumstances of liberty, dignity, equality of opportunity, and economic security;

b) Work is a right and a social duty, it gives dignity to the one who performs it, and it should be performed under conditions, including a system of fair wages, that ensure life, health, and a decent standard of living for the worker and his family, both during his working years and in his old age, or when any circumstance deprives him of the possibility of working;

c) Employers and workers, both rural and urban, have the right to associate themselves freely for the defense and promotion of their interests, including the right to collective bargaining and the workers' right to strike, and recognition of the juridical personality of associations and the protection of their freedom and independence, all in accordance with applicable laws;

d) Fair and efficient systems and procedures for consultation and collaboration among the sectors of production, with due regard for safeguarding the interests of the entire society;

e) The operation of systems of public administration, banking and credit, enterprise, and distribution and sales, in such a way, in harmony with the private sector, as to meet the requirements and interests of the community;

f) The incorporation and increasing participation of the marginal sectors of the population, in both rural and urban areas, in the economic, social, civic, cultural, and political life of the nation, in order to achieve the full integration of the national community, acceleration of the process of social mobility, and the consolidation of the democratic system. The encouragement of all efforts of popular promotion and cooperation that have as their purpose the development and progress of the community;

g) Recognition of the importance of the contribution of organizations such as labor unions, cooperatives, and cultural, professional, business, neighborhood, and community associations to the life of the society and to the development process;

h) Development of an efficient social security policy; and

i) Adequate provision for all persons to have due legal aid in order to secure their rights.

Article 45

The Member States recognize that, in order to facilitate the process of Latin American regional integration, it is necessary to harmonize the social legislation of the developing countries, especially in the labor and social security fields, so that the rights of the workers shall be equally protected, and they agree to make the greatest efforts possible to achieve this goal.

Article 46

The Member States will give primary importance within their development plans to the encouragement of education, science, technology, and culture, oriented toward the overall improvement of the individual, and as a foundation for democracy, social justice, and progress.

Article 47

The Member States will cooperate with one another to meet their educational needs, to promote scientific research, and to encourage technological progress for their integral development. They will consider themselves individually and jointly bound to preserve and enrich the cultural heritage of the American peoples.

Article 48

The Member States will exert the greatest efforts, in accordance with their constitutional processes, to ensure the effective exercise of the right to education, on the following bases:

a) Elementary education, compulsory for children of school age, shall also be offered to all others who can benefit from it. When provided by the State it shall be without charge;

b) Middle-level education shall be extended progressively to as much of the population as possible, with a view to social improvement. It shall be diversified in such a way that it meets the development needs of each country without prejudice to providing a general education; and

c) Higher education shall be available to all, provided that, in order to maintain its high level, the corresponding regulatory or academic standards are met.

Article 49

The Member States will give special attention to the eradication of illiteracy, will strengthen adult and vocational education systems, and will ensure that the benefits of culture will be available to the entire population. They will promote the use of all information media to fulfill these aims.

Article 50

The Member States will develop science and technology through educational, research, and technological development activities and information and dissemination programs. They will stimulate activities in the field of technology for the purpose of adapting it to the needs of their integral development. They will organize their cooperation in these fields efficiently and will substantially increase exchange of knowledge, in accordance with national objectives and laws and with treaties in force.

Article 51

The Member States, with due respect for the individuality of each of them, agree to promote cultural exchange as an effective means of consolidating inter-American understanding; and they recognize that regional integration programs should be strengthened by close ties in the fields of education, science, and culture.

PART TWO

Chapter VIII
THE ORGANS

Article 52

The Organization of American States accomplishes its purposes by means of: .

a) The General Assembly;

b) The Meeting of Consultation of Ministers of Foreign Affairs;

c) The Councils;

d) The Inter-American Juridical Committee;

e) The Inter-American Commission on Human Rights;

f) The General Secretariat;

g) The Specialized Conferences; and

h) The Specialized Organizations.

There may be established, in addition to those provided for in the Charter and in accordance with the provisions thereof, such subsidiary organs, agencies, and other entities as are considered necessary.

Chapter IX
THE GENERAL ASSEMBLY

Article 53

The General Assembly is the supreme organ of the Organization of American States. It has as its principal powers, in addition to such others as are assigned to it by the Charter, the following:

a) To decide the general action and policy of the Organization, determine the structure and functions of its organs, and consider any matter relating to friendly relations among the American States;

b) To establish measures for coordinating the activities of the organs, agencies, and entities of the Organization among themselves, and such activities with those of the other institutions of the inter-American system;

c) To strengthen and coordinate cooperation with the United Nations and its specialized agencies;

d) To promote collaboration, especially in the economic, social, and cultural fields, with other international organizations whose purposes are similar to those of the Organization of American States;

e) To approve the program-budget of the Organization and determine the quotas of the Member States;

f) To consider the reports of the Meeting of Consultation of Ministers of Foreign Affairs and the observations and recommendations presented by the Permanent Council with regard to the reports that should be presented by the other organs and entities, in accordance with the provisions of Article 90.f, as well as the reports of any organ which may be required by the General Assembly itself;

g) To adopt general standards to govern the operations of the General Secretariat; and

h) To adopt its own rules of procedure and, by a two-thirds vote, its agenda.

The General Assembly shall exercise its powers in accordance with the provisions of the Charter and of other inter-American treaties.

Article 54

The General Assembly shall establish the bases for fixing the quota that each Government is to contribute to the maintenance of the Organization, taking into account the ability to pay of the respective countries and their determination to contribute in an equitable manner. Decisions on budgetary matters require the approval of two thirds of the Member States.

Article 55

All Member States have the right to be represented in the General Assembly. Each State has the right to one vote.

Article 56

The General Assembly shall convene annually during the period determined by the rules of procedure and at a place selected in accordance with the principle of rotation. At each regular session the date and place of the next regular session shall be determined, in accordance with the rules of procedure.

If for any reason the General Assembly cannot be held at the place chosen, it shall meet at the General Secretariat, unless one of the Member States should make a timely offer of a site in its territory, in which case the Permanent Council of the Organization may agree that the General Assembly will meet in that place.

Article 57

In special circumstances and with the approval of two thirds of the Member States, the Permanent Council shall convoke a special session of the General Assembly.

Article 58

Decisions of the General Assembly shall be adopted by the affirmative vote of an absolute majority of the Member States, except in those cases that require a two-thirds vote as provided in the Charter or as may be provided by the General Assembly in its rules of procedure.

Article 59

There shall be a Preparatory Committee of the General Assembly, composed of representatives of all the Member States, which shall:

a) Prepare the draft agenda of each session of the General Assembly;

b) Review the proposed program-budget and the draft resolution on quotas, and present to the General Assembly a report thereon containing the recommendations it considers appropriate; and

c) Carry out such other functions as the General Assembly may assign to it.

The draft agenda and the report shall, in due course, be transmitted to the Governments of the Member States.

Chapter X
THE MEETING OF CONSULTATION OF MINISTERS OF FOREIGN AFFAIRS

Article 60

The Meeting of Consultation of Ministers of Foreign Affairs shall be held in order to consider problems of an urgent nature and of common interest to the American States, and to serve as the Organ of Consultation.

Article 61

Any Member State may request that a Meeting of Consultation be called. The request shall be addressed to the Permanent Council of the

Organization, which shall decide by an absolute majority whether a meeting should be held.

Article 62

The agenda and regulations of the Meeting of Consultation shall be prepared by the Permanent Council of the Organization and submitted to the Member States for consideration.

Article 63

If, for exceptional reasons, a Minister of Foreign Affairs is unable to attend the meeting, he shall be represented by a special delegate.

Article 64

In case of an armed attack on the territory of an American State or within the region of security delimited by the treaty in force, the Chairman of the Permanent Council shall without delay call a meeting of the Council to decide on the convocation of the Meeting of Consultation, without prejudice to the provisions of the Inter-American Treaty of Reciprocal Assistance with regard to the States Parties to that instrument.

Article 65

An Advisory Defense Committee shall be established to advise the Organ of Consultation on problems of military cooperation that may arise in connection with the application of existing special treaties on collective security.

Article 66

The Advisory Defense Committee shall be composed of the highest military authorities of the American States participating in the Meeting of Consultation. Under exceptional circumstances the Governments may appoint substitutes. Each State shall be entitled to one vote.

Article 67

The Advisory Defense Committee shall be convoked under the same conditions as the Organ of Consultation, when the latter deals with matters relating to defense against aggression.

Article 68

The Committee shall also meet when the General Assembly or the Meeting of Consultation or the Governments, by a two-thirds majority of the Member States, assign to it technical studies or reports on specific subjects.

Chapter XI
THE COUNCILS OF THE ORGANIZATION
Common Provisions

Article 69

The Permanent Council of the Organization and the Inter-American Council for Integral Development are directly responsible to the General Assembly, and each has the authority granted to it in the Charter and other inter-American instruments, as well as the functions assigned to it by the General Assembly and the Meeting of Consultation of Ministers of Foreign Affairs.

Article 70

All Member States have the right to be represented on each of the Councils. Each State has the right to one vote.

Article 71

The Councils may, within the limits of the Charter and other inter-American instruments, make recommendations on matters within their authority.

Article 72

The Councils, on matters within their respective competence, may present to the General Assembly studies and proposals, drafts of international instruments, and proposals on the holding of specialized conferences, on the creation, modification, or elimination of specialized organizations and other inter-American agencies, as well as on the coordination of their activities. The Councils may also present studies, proposals, and drafts of international instruments to the Specialized Conferences.

Article 73

Each Council may, in urgent cases, convoke Specialized Conferences on matters within its competence, after consulting with the Member

States and without having to resort to the procedure provided for in Article 121.

Article 74

The Councils, to the extent of their ability, and with the cooperation of the General Secretariat, shall render to the Governments such specialized services as the latter may request.

Article 75

Each Council has the authority to require the other Councils, as well as the subsidiary organs and agencies responsible to them, to provide it with information and advisory services on matters within their respective spheres of competence. The Councils may also request the same services from the other agencies of the inter-American system.

Article 76

With the prior approval of the General Assembly, the Councils may establish the subsidiary organs and the agencies that they consider advisable for the better performance of their duties. When the General Assembly is not in session, the aforesaid organs or agencies may be established provisionally by the corresponding Council. In constituting the membership of these bodies, the Councils, insofar as possible, shall follow the criteria of rotation and equitable geographic representation.

Article 77

The Councils may hold meetings in any Member State, when they find it advisable and with the prior consent of the Government concerned.

Article 78

Each Council shall prepare its own statutes and submit them to the General Assembly for approval. It shall approve its own rules of procedure and those of its subsidiary organs, agencies, and committees.

Chapter XII
THE PERMANENT COUNCIL OF THE ORGANIZATION

Article 79

The Permanent Council of the Organization is composed of one representative of each Member State, especially appointed by the respective

Government, with the rank of ambassador. Each Government may accredit an acting representative, as well as such alternates and advisers as it considers necessary.

Article 80

The office of Chairman of the Permanent Council shall be held by each of the representatives, in turn, following the alphabetic order in Spanish of the names of their respective countries. The office of Vice Chairman shall be filled in the same way, following reverse alphabetic order.

The Chairman and the Vice Chairman shall hold office for a term of not more than six months, which shall be determined by the statutes.

Article 81

Within the limits of the Charter and of inter-American treaties and agreements, the Permanent Council takes cognizance of any matter referred to it by the General Assembly or the Meeting of Consultation of Ministers of Foreign Affairs.

Article 82

The Permanent Council shall serve provisionally as the Organ of Consultation in conformity with the provisions of the special treaty on the subject.

Article 83

The Permanent Council shall keep vigilance over the maintenance of friendly relations among the Member States, and for that purpose shall effectively assist them in the peaceful settlement of their disputes, in accordance with the following provisions.

Article 84

In accordance with the provisions of this Charter, any party to a dispute in which none of the peaceful procedures provided for in the Charter is under way may resort to the Permanent Council to obtain its good offices. The Council, following the provisions of the preceding article, shall assist the parties and recommend the procedures it considers suitable for peaceful settlement of the dispute.

Article 85

In the exercise of its functions and with the consent of the parties to the dispute, the Permanent Council may establish ad hoc committees.

The ad hoc committees shall have the membership and the mandate that the Permanent Council agrees upon in each individual case, with the consent of the parties to the dispute.

Article 86

The Permanent Council may also, by such means as it deems advisable, investigate the facts in the dispute, and may do so in the territory of any of the parties, with the consent of the Government concerned.

Article 87

If the procedure for peaceful settlement of disputes recommended by the Permanent Council or suggested by the pertinent ad hoc committee under the terms of its mandate is not accepted by one of the parties, or one of the parties declares that the procedure has not settled the dispute, the Permanent Council shall so inform the General Assembly, without prejudice to its taking steps to secure agreement between the parties or to restore relations between them.

Article 88

The Permanent Council, in the exercise of these functions, shall take its decisions by an affirmative vote of two thirds of its Members, excluding the parties to the dispute, except for such decisions as the rules of procedure provide shall be adopted by a simple majority.

Article 89

In performing their functions with respect to the peaceful settlement of disputes, the Permanent Council and the respective ad hoc committee shall observe the provisions of the Charter and the principles and standards of international law, as well as take into account the existence of treaties in force between the parties.

Article 90

The Permanent Council shall also:

a) Carry out those decisions of the General Assembly or of the Meeting of Consultation of Ministers of Foreign Affairs the implementation of which has not been assigned to any other body;

b) Watch over the observance of the standards governing the operation of the General Secretariat and, when the General Assembly is not in session, adopt provisions of a regulatory nature that enable the General Secretariat to carry out its administrative functions;

c) Act as the Preparatory Committee of the General Assembly, in accordance with the terms of Article 59 of the Charter, unless the General Assembly should decide otherwise;

d) Prepare, at the request of the Member States and with the cooperation of the appropriate organs of the Organization, draft agreements to promote and facilitate cooperation between the Organization of American States and the United Nations or between the Organization and other American agencies of recognized international standing. These draft agreements shall be submitted to the General Assembly for approval;

e) Submit recommendations to the General Assembly with regard to the functioning of the Organization and the coordination of its subsidiary organs, agencies, and committees;

f) Consider the reports of the other Councils, of the Inter-American Juridical Committee, of the Inter-American Commission on Human Rights, of the General Secretariat, of specialized agencies and conferences, and of other bodies and agencies, and present to the General Assembly any observations and recommendations it deems necessary; and

g) Perform the other functions assigned to it in the Charter.

Article 91

The Permanent Council and the General Secretariat shall have the same seat.

Chapter XIII
THE INTER-AMERICAN COUNCIL FOR INTEGRAL DEVELOPMENT

Article 92

The Inter-American Council for Integral Development is composed of one principal representative, of ministerial or equivalent rank, for each Member State, especially appointed by the respective Government.

In keeping with the provisions of the Charter, the Inter-American Council for Integral Development may establish the subsidiary bodies and the agencies that it considers advisable for the better performance of its duties.

Article 93

The purpose of the Inter-American Council for Integral Development is to promote cooperation among the American States for the purpose of achieving integral development and, in particular, helping to eliminate extreme poverty, in accordance with the standards of the Charter, especially those set forth in Chapter VII with respect to the economic, social, educational, cultural, scientific, and technological fields.

Article 94

In order to achieve its various goals, especially in the specific area of technical cooperation, the Inter-American Council for Integral Development shall:

a) Formulate and recommend to the General Assembly a strategic plan which sets forth policies, programs, and courses of action in matters of cooperation for integral development, within the framework of the general policy and priorities defined by the General Assembly.

b) Formulate guidelines for the preparation of the program-budget for technical cooperation and for the other activities of the Council.

c) Promote, coordinate, and assign responsibility for the execution of development programs and projects to the subsidiary bodies and relevant organizations, on the basis of the priorities identified by the Member States, in areas such as:

1) Economic and social development, including trade, tourism, integration and the environment;

2) Improvement and extension of education to cover all levels, promotion of scientific and technological research, through technical cooperation, and support for cultural activities; and

3) Strengthening of the civic conscience of the American peoples, as one of the bases for the effective exercise of democracy and for the observance of the rights and duties of man.

These ends shall be furthered by sectoral participation mechanisms and other subsidiary bodies and organizations established by the Charter and by other General Assembly provisions.

d) Establish cooperative relations with the corresponding bodies of the United Nations and with other national and international agencies, especially with regard to coordination of inter-American technical cooperation programs.

e) Periodically evaluate cooperation activities for integral development, in terms of their performance in the implementation of policies, programs, and projects, in terms of their impact, effectiveness, efficiency, and use of resources, and in terms of the quality, inter alia, of the technical cooperation services provided; and report to the General Assembly.

Article 95

The Inter-American Council for Integral Development shall hold at least one meeting each year at the ministerial or equivalent level. It shall also have the right to convene meetings at the same level for the specialized or sectorial topics it considers relevant, within its province or sphere of competence. It shall also meet when convoked by the General Assembly or the Meeting of Consultation of Foreign Ministers, or on its own initiative, or for the cases envisaged in Article 36 of the Charter.

Article 96

The Inter-American Council for Integral Development shall have the nonpermanent specialized committees which it decides to establish and which are required for the proper performance of its functions. Those committees shall operate and shall be composed as stipulated in the Statutes of the Council.

Article 97

The execution and, if appropriate, the coordination, of approved projects shall be entrusted to the Executive Secretariat for Integral Development, which shall report on the results of that execution to the Council.

Chapter XIV
THE INTER-AMERICAN JURIDICAL COMMITTEE

Article 98

The purpose of the Inter-American Juridical Committee is to serve the Organization as an advisory body on juridical matters; to promote the progressive development and the codification of international law; and to study juridical problems related to the integration of the developing countries of the Hemisphere and, insofar as may appear desirable, the possibility of attaining uniformity in their legislation.

Article 99

The Inter-American Juridical Committee shall undertake the studies and preparatory work assigned to it by the General Assembly, the Meeting of Consultation of Ministers of Foreign Affairs, or the Councils of the Organization. It may also, on its own initiative, undertake such studies and preparatory work as it considers advisable, and suggest the holding of specialized juridical conferences.

Article 100

The Inter-American Juridical Committee shall be composed of eleven jurists, nationals of Member States, elected by the General Assembly for a period of four years from panels of three candidates presented by Member States. In the election, a system shall be used that takes into account partial replacement of membership and, insofar as possible, equitable geographic representation. No two Members of the Committee may be nationals of the same State.

Vacancies that occur for reasons other than normal expiration of the terms of office of the Members of the Committee shall be filled by the Permanent Council of the Organization in accordance with the criteria set forth in the preceding paragraph.

Article 101

The Inter-American Juridical Committee represents all of the Member States of the Organization, and has the broadest possible technical autonomy.

Article 102

The Inter-American Juridical Committee shall establish cooperative relations with universities, institutes, and other teaching centers, as well as with national and international committees and entities devoted to study, research, teaching, or dissemination of information on juridical matters of international interest.

Article 103

The Inter-American Juridical Committee shall draft its statutes, which shall be submitted to the General Assembly for approval.

The Committee shall adopt its own rules of procedure.

Article 104

The seat of the Inter-American Juridical Committee shall be the city of Rio de Janeiro, but in special cases the Committee may meet at any other place that may be designated, after consultation with the Member State concerned.

Chapter XV
THE INTER-AMERICAN COMMISSION ON HUMAN RIGHTS

Article 105

There shall be an Inter-American Commission on Human Rights, whose principal function shall be to promote the observance and protection of human rights and to serve as a consultative organ of the Organization in these matters.

An inter-American convention on human rights shall determine the structure, competence, and procedure of this Commission, as well as those of other organs responsible for these matters.

Chapter XVI
THE GENERAL SECRETARIAT

Article 106

The General Secretariat is the central and permanent organ of the Organization of American States. It shall perform the functions assigned to it in the Charter, in other inter-American treaties and agreements, and by the General Assembly, and shall carry out the duties entrusted to it by the General Assembly, the Meeting of Consultation of Ministers of Foreign Affairs, or the Councils.

Article 107

The Secretary General of the Organization shall be elected by the General Assembly for a five-year term and may not be reelected more than once or succeeded by a person of the same nationality. In the event that the office of Secretary General becomes vacant, the Assistant Secretary General shall assume his duties until the General Assembly shall elect a new Secretary General for a full term.

Article 108

The Secretary General shall direct the General Secretariat, be the legal representative thereof, and, notwithstanding the provisions of Article 90.b, be responsible to the General Assembly for the proper fulfillment of the obligations and functions of the General Secretariat.

Article 109

The Secretary General, or his representative, may participate with voice but without vote in all meetings of the Organization.

The Secretary General may bring to the attention of the General Assembly or the Permanent Council any matter which in his opinion might threaten the peace and security of the Hemisphere or the development of the Member States.

The authority to which the preceding paragraph refers shall be exercised in accordance with the present Charter.

Article 110

The General Secretariat shall promote economic, social, juridical, educational, scientific, and cultural relations among all the Member States of the Organization, in keeping with the actions and policies decided upon by the General Assembly and with the pertinent decisions of the Councils.

Article 111

The General Secretariat shall also perform the following functions:

a) Transmit *ex officio* to the Member States notice of the convocation of the General Assembly, the Meeting of Consultation of Ministers of Foreign Affairs, the Inter-American Council for Integral Development, and the Specialized Conferences;

b) Advise the other organs, when appropriate, in the preparation of agenda and rules of procedure;

c) Prepare the proposed program-budget of the Organization on the basis of programs adopted by the Councils, agencies, and entities whose expenses should be included in the program-budget and, after consultation with the Councils or their permanent committees, submit it to the Preparatory Committee of the General Assembly and then to the Assembly itself;

d) Provide, on a permanent basis, adequate secretariat services for the General Assembly and the other organs, and carry out their directives and assignments. To the extent of its ability, provide services for the other meetings of the Organization;

e) Serve as custodian of the documents and archives of the inter-American Conferences, the General Assembly, the Meetings of Consultation of Ministers of Foreign Affairs, the Councils, and the Specialized Conferences;

f) Serve as depository of inter-American treaties and agreements, as well as of the instruments of ratification thereof;

g) Submit to the General Assembly at each regular session an annual report on the activities of the Organization and its financial condition; and

h) Establish relations of cooperation, in accordance with decisions reached by the General Assembly or the Councils, with the Specialized Organizations as well as other national and international organizations.

Article 112

The Secretary General shall:

a) Establish such offices of the General Secretariat as are necessary to accomplish its purposes; and

b) Determine the number of officers and employees of the General Secretariat, appoint them, regulate their powers and duties, and fix their remuneration.

The Secretary General shall exercise this authority in accordance with such general standards and budgetary provisions as may be established by the General Assembly.

Article 113

The Assistant Secretary General shall be elected by the General Assembly for a five-year term and may not be reelected more than once or succeeded by a person of the same nationality. In the event that the office of Assistant Secretary General becomes vacant, the Permanent Council shall elect a substitute to hold that office until the General Assembly shall elect a new Assistant Secretary General for a full term.

Article 114

The Assistant Secretary General shall be the Secretary of the Permanent Council. He shall serve as advisory officer to the Secretary General and shall act as his delegate in all matters that the Secretary General may entrust to him. During the temporary absence or disability of the Secretary General, the Assistant Secretary General shall perform his functions.

The Secretary General and the Assistant Secretary General shall be of different nationalities.

Article 115

The General Assembly, by a two-thirds vote of the Member States, may remove the Secretary General or the Assistant Secretary General, or both, whenever the proper functioning of the Organization so demands.

Article 116

The Secretary General shall appoint, with the approval of the Inter-American Council for Integral Development, an Executive Secretary for Integral Development.

Article 117

In the performance of their duties, the Secretary General and the personnel of the Secretariat shall not seek or receive instructions from any Government or from any authority outside the Organization, and shall refrain from any action that may be incompatible with their position as international officers responsible only to the Organization.

Article 118

The Member States pledge themselves to respect the exclusively international character of the responsibilities of the Secretary General and the personnel of the General Secretariat, and not to seek to influence them in the discharge of their duties.

Article 119

In selecting the personnel of the General Secretariat, first consideration shall be given to efficiency, competence, and integrity; but at the same time, in the recruitment of personnel of all ranks, importance shall be given to the necessity of obtaining as wide a geographic representation as possible.

Article 120

The seat of the General Secretariat is the city of Washington, D.C.

Chapter XVII
THE SPECIALIZED CONFERENCES

Article 121

The Specialized Conferences are intergovernmental meetings to deal with special technical matters or to develop specific aspects of inter-American cooperation. They shall be held when either the General Assembly or the Meeting of Consultation of Ministers of Foreign Affairs so decides, on its own initiative or at the request of one of the Councils or Specialized Organizations.

Article 122

The agenda and rules of procedure of the Specialized Conferences shall be prepared by the Councils or Specialized Organizations concerned and shall be submitted to the Governments of the Member States for consideration.

Chapter XVIII
THE SPECIALIZED ORGANIZATIONS

Article 123

For the purposes of the present Charter, Inter-American Specialized Organizations are the intergovernmental organizations established by multilateral agreements and having specific functions with respect to technical matters of common interest to the American States.

Article 124

The General Secretariat shall maintain a register of the organizations that fulfill the conditions set forth in the foregoing Article, as determined by the General Assembly after a report from the Council concerned.

Article 125

The Specialized Organizations shall enjoy the fullest technical autonomy, but they shall take into account the recommendations of the General Assembly and of the Councils, in accordance with the provisions of the Charter.

Article 126

The Specialized Organizations shall transmit to the General Assembly annual reports on the progress of their work and on their annual budgets and expenses.

Article 127

Relations that should exist between the Specialized Organizations and the Organization shall be defined by means of agreements concluded between each organization and the Secretary General, with the authorization of the General Assembly.

Article 128

The Specialized Organizations shall establish cooperative relations with world agencies of the same character in order to coordinate their activities. In concluding agreements with international agencies of a worldwide character, the Inter-American Specialized Organizations shall preserve their identity and their status as integral parts of the Organization of American States, even when they perform regional functions of international agencies.

Article 129

In determining the location of the Specialized Organizations consideration shall be given to the interest of all of the Member States and to the desirability of selecting the seats of these organizations on the basis of a geographic representation as equitable as possible.

PART THREE

Chapter XIX
THE UNITED NATIONS

Article 130

None of the provisions of this Charter shall be construed as impairing the rights and obligations of the Member States under the Charter of the United Nations.

Chapter XX
MISCELLANEOUS PROVISIONS

Article 131

Attendance at meetings of the permanent organs of the Organization of American States or at the conferences and meetings provided for in the Charter, or held under the auspices of the Organization, shall be in accordance with the multilateral character of the aforesaid organs, conferences, and meetings and shall not depend on the bilateral relations between the Government of any Member State and the Government of the host country.

Article 132

The Organization of American States shall enjoy in the territory of each Member such legal capacity, privileges, and immunities as are necessary for the exercise of its functions and the accomplishment of its purposes.

Article 133

The representatives of the Member States on the organs of the Organization, the personnel of their delegations, as well as the Secretary General and the Assistant Secretary General shall enjoy the privileges and immunities corresponding to their positions and necessary for the independent performance of their duties.

Article 134

The juridical status of the Specialized Organizations and the privileges and immunities that should be granted to them and to their personnel, as well as to the officials of the General Secretariat, shall be determined in a multilateral agreement. The foregoing shall not preclude, when it is considered necessary, the concluding of bilateral agreements.

Article 135

Correspondence of the Organization of American States, including printed matter and parcels, bearing the frank thereof, shall be carried free of charge in the mails of the Member States.

Article 136

The Organization of American States does not allow any restriction based on race, creed, or sex, with respect to eligibility to participate in the activities of the Organization and to hold positions therein.

Article 137

Within the provisions of this Charter, the competent organs shall endeavor to obtain greater collaboration from countries not Members of the Organization in the area of cooperation for development.

Chapter XXI
RATIFICATION AND ENTRY INTO FORCE

Article 138

The present Charter shall remain open for signature by the American States and shall be ratified in accordance with their respective constitutional procedures. The original instrument, the Spanish, English, Portuguese, and French texts of which are equally authentic, shall be deposited with the General Secretariat, which shall transmit certified copies thereof to the Governments for purposes of ratification. The instruments of ratification shall be deposited with the General Secretariat, which shall notify the signatory States of such deposit.

Article 139

The present Charter shall enter into force among the ratifying States when two thirds of the signatory States have deposited their ratifications.

It shall enter into force with respect to the remaining States in the order in which they deposit their ratifications.

Article 140

The present Charter shall be registered with the Secretariat of the United Nations through the General Secretariat.

Article 141

Amendments to the present Charter may be adopted only at a General Assembly convened for that purpose. Amendments shall enter into force in accordance with the terms and the procedure set forth in Article 139.

Article 142

The present Charter shall remain in force indefinitely, but may be denounced by any Member State upon written notification to the General Secretariat, which shall communicate to all the others each notice of denunciation received. After two years from the date on which the General Secretariat receives a notice of denunciation, the present Charter shall cease to be in force with respect to the denouncing State, which shall cease to belong to the Organization after it has fulfilled the obligations arising from the present Charter.

Chapter XXII
TRANSITORY PROVISIONS

Article 143

The Inter-American Committee on the Alliance for Progress shall act as the permanent executive committee of the Inter-American Economic and Social Council as long as the Alliance is in operation.

Article 144

Until the inter-American convention on human rights, referred to in Chapter XV, enters into force, the present Inter-American Commission on Human Rights shall keep vigilance over the observance of human rights.

Article 145

The Permanent Council shall not make any recommendation nor shall the General Assembly take any decision with respect to a request for admission on the part of a political entity whose territory became subject, in whole or in part, prior to December 18, 1964, the date set by the First Special Inter-American Conference, to litigation or claim between an extracontinental country and one or more Member States of the Organization, until the dispute has been ended by some peaceful procedure. This article shall remain in effect until December 10, 1990.

Appendix VII

Membership in International Commodity Organizations

(Note: Each organization includes the year it was established, the location of its headquarters, the total number of its members, and the names of regional members.)

BANANAS: Union of Banana Exporting Countries (UBEC)/Unión de Países Exportadores de Banano (UPEB)—1974; Panama City, Panama; Nine members: Colombia, Costa Rica, the Dominican Republic, Ecuador, Guatemala, Honduras, Nicaragua, Panama, and Venezuela. Windward Islands Banana Growers' Association (WINBAN)—1958; Castries, St. Lucia; Four members: Dominica, Grenada, St. Lucia, and St. Vincent and the Grenadines. The Lomé Accord provides for banana exports to the European Community (EC) especially by Belize, Dominica, Grenada, Jamaica, and St. Lucia.

BAUXITE: International Bauxite Association (IBA)—1974; Kingston, Jamaica; 10 members: Guyana, Jamaica, and Suriname.

COCOA: International Cocoa Organization (ICCO)/Organización Internacional del Cacao (OIC)—1973; London, England; 18 exporting members: Ecuador, Grenada, Guatemala, Haiti, Jamaica, Mexico, Trinidad and Tobago, and Venezuela.

COFFEE: International Coffee Organization (ICO)/Organización Internacional del Café (OIC)—1963; London, England; 51 exporting members: Bolivia, Brazil, Colombia, Costa Rica, Cuba, the Dominican Republic, Ecuador, El Salvador, Guatemala, Haiti, Honduras, Jamaica, Mexico, Nicaragua, Panama, Paraguay, Peru, Trinidad and Tobago, and Venezuela.

COTTON: International Cotton Advisory Committee (ICAC)/Comité Consultivo Internacional del Algodón (CCIA)—1939; Washington, D.C.; 47 members: Argentina, Brazil, Colombia, Guatemala, Honduras, Mexico, Nicaragua, Paraguay, Peru, and the United States.

COPPER: Intergovernmental Council of Copper Exporting Countries

(CICEC)/Conseil Intergouvernemental des Pays Exportateurs de Cuivre (CIPEC)—1976; Paris, France; Four members: Chile and Peru.

IRON ORE: Association of Iron Ore Exporting Countries (AIOEC)/ Association des Pays Exportateurs de Fer (APEF)—1975; Geneva, Switzerland; 9 members: Peru and Venezuela.

LEAD AND ZINC: International Lead and Zinc Study Group—1960; London, England; 32 members: Canada, Brazil, and Peru.

OIL: Organization of Petroleum Exporting Countries (OPEC)—1960; Vienna, Austria; 13 members: Venezuela.

SUGAR: Group of Latin American and Caribbean Sugar Exporting Countries (GLACSEC)/Grupo de Países Latinoamericanos y el Caribe para la Exportación de Azúcar (GEPLACEA)—1974; Mexico City, Mexico; 21 members: Argentina, Barbados, Bolivia, Brazil, Colombia, Costa Rica, Cuba, the Dominican Republic, Ecuador, El Salvador, Guatemala, Guyana, Haiti, Honduras, Jamaica, Mexico, Nicaragua, Panama, Peru, Trinidad and Tobago, and Venezuela. International Sugar Organization (ISO)/Organización Internacional del Azúcar (OIS)—1968; London, England; 35 exporting members: Argentina, Barbados, Belize, Bolivia, Brazil, Colombia, Costa Rica, Cuba, the Dominican Republic, Ecuador, El Salvador, Guatemala, Guyana, Honduras, Jamaica, Mexico, Nicaragua, Panama, Peru, and Uruguay.

WHEAT: International Wheat Council (IWC)/Consejo Internacional del Trigo (CIT)—1949; London, England; 47 members: Argentina, Barbados, Bolivia, Canada, Cuba, Ecuador, Panama and the United States.

Appendix VIII

Membership and Participation in Organs, Agencies, Commissions, Conferences, and Programs of the United Nations

Principal Organs

1. **General Assembly (GA)**. All Latin American and Caribbean states are members of the United Nations (UN), which in 1996 had a total of 185 members. Canada, the United States, and the following 20 Latin American states were among the original 51 members of the UN: Argentina, Bolivia, Brazil, Chile, Colombia, Costa Rica, Cuba, the Dominican Republic, Ecuador, El Salvador, Guatemala, Haiti, Honduras, Mexico, Nicaragua, Panama, Paraguay, Peru, Uruguay, and Venezuela.

2. **Economic and Social Council (ECOSOC)**. The original council had 18 members, which included four from Latin America but none from Canada. In 1966, the size was increased to 27, which included five from Latin America and again, none from Canada. In 1973, the size was increased to 54; ten seats were assigned to Latin America and the Caribbean, and one to Canada. The United States has always had a seat in ECOSOC. The council has five regional commissions. The Economic Commission for Latin America and the Caribbean (ECLAC) includes all these states as members, and is headquartered in Santiago, Chile.

3. **International Court of Justice (ICJ)**. The 15-member ICJ has always included two members from Latin America and the Caribbean. The two seats are rotated among these states. A Canadian served as a member for two terms, 1946–1958. The United States has a permanent seat, along with the other members of the Big Five—China, Great Britain, France, the Soviet Union, and the United States—in the Security Council.

4. **Security Council (SC)**. The original SC had six nonpermanent seats in addition to the permanent seats of the Big Five. In 1965, the number of nonpermanent seats was increased to 10. From the start, two

seats have been occupied by Latin American and Caribbean states. While Cuba was in the SC two times—1949–1950 and 1955–1956—before Castro came to power in 1959, it did not return until 1990–1991. Canada was in the SC a number of times, often during the Cold War to balance a seat held by a Soviet Bloc state. The SC held a session once in Latin America: in Panama City in 1964 to consider the battle over the Panama Canal between Panama and the United States.

5. **Trusteeship Council (TC)**. Starting with 11 Trust Territories to administer, by 1977 only one remained before the TC—that of the United States, the Trust Territory of the Pacific Islands. The decreasing membership of the TC, from a high of 22, was in keeping with the requirement that there be parity between those states administering a trust and those not doing so. For the period 1957 through 1962 in particular, one or two Latin American and Caribbean states were elected to three-year terms to maintain the parity.

6. **Secretariat and Secretary-General (S-G)**. While the latter is in charge of the former, recent secretaries-general—e.g., Javier Pérez de Cuéllar from Peru (1982–1991) and Boutros Boutros-Ghali of Egypt (1992–1997)—like the second, Dag Hammarskjold of Sweden (1953–1961), have been very active in peacemaking and peacekeeping. S-G Pérez played an important role in the Central American Peace Process, especially in El Salvador and ONUSAL. He was the first Latin American to be elected S-G and the first insider, for he was a UN under secretary-general at the time. Earlier, he had served as Peru's Permanent Representative to the UN.

Specialized Agencies

(Note: Only a few of the 16 agencies that report to and whose activities are coordinated by ECOSOC are included.)

1. **Food and Agriculture Organization (FAO)**: 1945; Rome, Italy (its first headquarters was in Quebec, Canada); 160 members, including all Latin American and Caribbean states, Canada, and the United States. The Regional Office for Latin America is in Santiago, Chile.

2. **General Agreement on Tariffs and Trade (GATT)**: 1948; Geneva, Switzerland; 111 members, including all Latin American states (a few of the Commonwealth Caribbean states are not members), Canada, and the United States. There have been nine completed "rounds" of multilateral trade negotiations, most of them in Geneva. The only one in Asia was the eighth, the Tokyo "round," which began in 1980. The ninth round, the Uruguay round, the only one held in Latin America,

began in Punta del Este, Uruguay, in September 1986 and ended in 1996.

3. and 4. **International Bank for Reconstruction and Development (IBRD/World Bank/BANK) and International Monetary Fund (IMF/FUND)**: 1946; Washington, D.C.; 178 members, including all states in the region except Cuba. The BANK and FUND work closely together, and all member states must be members of both. Each member has a number of votes based upon the amount of capital it subscribes to each organization. These votes are cast in approving or rejecting credits and loans and for electing the executive directors. The voting percentages of the IMF for 1994 were: Canada, 2.91 percent; Brazil, 1.47 percent; Venezuela, 1.33 percent; Mexico, 1.19 percent; Argentina, 1.05 percent; and the United States, 17.81 percent. The IMF divided Latin America and the Caribbean into two groups, each having its own elected executive director. In 1994, the following group of states elected a Mexican as director (and Venezuelan as alternate): Costa Rica, El Salvador, Guatemala, Honduras, Mexico, Nicaragua, Spain, and Venezuela. The other group with a Canadian director (alternate from Ireland) included: Antigua and Barbuda, the Bahamas, Barbados, Belize, Canada, Dominica, Grenada, Ireland, Jamaica, St. Kitts and Nevis, St. Lucia, and St. Vincent and the Grenadines.

5. **International Civil Aviation Organization (IACO)**: 1947; Montreal, Quebec, Canada; 180 members, including all regional states. There is a Regional Office for North America, Central America, and the Caribbean in Mexico City, Mexico, and a Regional Office for South America in Lima, Peru.

6. **International Labor Organization (ILO)/Organisation Internationale du Travail (OIT)**: 1946; Geneva, Switzerland; 167 members, including all states in the region. In 1977, the United States withdrew but returned in 1980. There is a branch office in Washington, D.C., and a Regional Office for the Americas in Lima, Peru.

7. **United Nations Educational, Scientific, and Cultural Organization (UNESCO)**: 1946; Paris, France; 177 members, including all states in the region except the United States, which withdrew in 1984. There are four regional offices "in" or "for" Latin America and the Caribbean: the Regional Centre for Higher Education in Caracas, Venezuela; Regional Office for Culture in Havana, Cuba; Regional Office for Education in Santiago, Chile; and Regional Office for Science and Technology in Montevideo, Uruguay.

8. **World Health Organization (WHO)**: 1948; Geneva, Switzerland; 182 members, including all states in the region. Its Regional Office for the Americas is the Pan American Sanitary Bureau, which is the Secretariat for the Pan American Health Organization (PAHO)/Organización Panamericana de la Salud (OPS).

Commissions, Conferences, and Programs

1. **Conference on Trade and Development (UNCTAD)**: 1964; Geneva, Switzerland; 180 members, including all states in the region. Its formation was initiated by the developing states as a counterpoise to GATT and a bargaining forum for gaining economic concessions from the developed states. Following the UN General Assembly's 1974 resolution calling for the creation of a New International Economic Order (NIEO), UNCTAD meetings served as a principal means for the developing states to bring about NIEO. UNCTAD was approved as a permanent organ of the General Assembly and meets every three or four years.

Since UNCTAD I in Geneva in 1964, subsequent meetings have been as follows: II in New Delhi, India (1968); III in Santiago, Chile (1972); IV in Nairobi, Kenya (1976); V in Manila, the Philippines (1979); VI in Belgrade, Yugoslavia (1983); VII in Geneva, Switzerland (1987); and VIII in Cartagena, Colombia (1992). UNCTAD membership is divided into four groups with two, A and C, for the developing states; Group C is for Latin America. In preparation for UNCTAD I, the developing states formed a caucus, known as the Group of Seventy-Seven (G-77), which was the number of African, Asian, and Latin American developing states at the time. These states continued this practice before meetings of UNCTAD, as well as the UN General Assembly and the Third UN Conference on the Law of the Sea (UNCLOS III). Even though the original G-77 steadily increased in size to 128 in the 1980s, the G-77 designation has continued to be used.

2. **Development Program (UNDP)/Programa de las Naciones Unidas para el Desarrollo (PNUD)**: 1965; New York City, United States; 175 members, including all states in the region. Many UNDP-financed projects provide aid to developing countries in producing and exporting agricultural and mineral commodities (see Appendix VII). Most of the export commodity projects are implemented for the UNDP by UNCTAD and the World Bank. There are four regional bureaus at the Secretariat in New York City and one in Latin America and the Caribbean. There are 24 field offices in Latin America and the Caribbean: the Commonwealth Caribbean has four of them—in Barbados, Guyana, Jamaica, and Trinidad and Tobago.

3. **Economic Commission for Latin America and the Caribbean (ECLAC)/Comisión Económica para América Latina y el Caribe (CEPAL)**: 1948; Santiago, Chile; 41 members, including all states in the region plus France, Italy, the Netherlands, Portugal, Spain, and the United Kingdom. There are seven branch offices: Washington, D.C.; Mexico City, Mexico; Port-of-Spain, Trinidad and Tobago; Bogotá, Colombia; Brasilia, Brazil; Montevideo, Uruguay; and Buenos Aires, Argentina.

4. **Environmental Program (UNEP)**: 1972; Nairobi, Kenya. There are two regional offices in the region, one for Latin America and the Caribbean in Mexico City, Mexico, and one for North America in New York City, the United States. The UNEP was instrumental in drafting two conventions—the Convention on Climate Change and the Convention on Biological Diversity—that were signed by over 150 states at the UN Conference on Environment and Development ("Earth Summit"), held in Rio de Janeiro, Brazil, in 1992. Later that year the parties to the 1989 Basel Convention on the Control of Transboundary Movements of Hazardous Wastes and Their Disposal met in Montevideo, Uruguay.

5. **High Commissioner for Refugees (UNHCR)**. Created in 1951 to replace the International Refugee Organization (IRO), 1947–1952, with headquarters in Geneva, Switzerland. Two treaties are especially relevant to the High Commissioner's providing international protection: the 1951 Convention Relating to the Status of Refugees and its 1967 Protocol. By 1993, 112 states were parties to the former and the latter, including most states in the region, except the Bahamas, Barbados, Cuba, Grenada, and Trinidad and Tobago. In 1989, the UNHCR held an International Conference on Central American Refugees and in 1991 initiated projects for refugees in El Salvador and Nicaragua. There are five regional bureaus in Geneva, one in the Americas.

6. **New International Economic Order (NIEO)**. At the sixth Special Session of the UN General Assembly, called in 1974 by the developing states to deal with development and trade problems, the G-77 states declared the need to establish a NIEO. This would replace the existing system, one these states believed was dominated by the capitalist, former colonial, and Western developed states. In late 1974, a General Assembly resolution was passed, providing for the Economic Charter of the Rights and Duties of States (CERDS). CERDS made explicit the main components of NIEO.

7. **Third UN Conference on the Law of the Sea (UNCLOS III)**. This conference was called to resolve conflicting claims—many of them between developed and developing states—about fishing, continental shelf, straits, and territorial sea. UNCLOS III began in 1974, with the first session in Caracas, Venezuela, and ended in 1982 in New York City, the United States. There were 150-some participants, including all states in the region. The bargaining and negotiations were mainly on a North/developed states-South/developing states axis. There were many bargaining groups; besides the G-77, there was the Latin American Group (LAG), which had 28 members. Four states voted against the 1982 Convention on the Law of the Sea, including the United States and Venezuela; 17 developed states abstained, including Canada. The developing states, including all in Latin America and the Caribbean (except Venezuela) voted for it. The convention received the necessary rectifications in late 1993 and became effective in 1994.

Appendix IX

Inter-American Organizations: Headquarters Locations and Electronic Addresses

African, Caribbean, and Pacific Group of States (ACP)/Groupes Des Etats d'Afrique, des Caribes et du Pacifique (GEACP)

Address: 451, ave. Georges Henri, B-1200 Brussels, Belgium
Phone: 2 7339600
FAX: 2 7355573

Agency for the Prohibition of Nuclear Weapons in Latin America and the Caribbean/Organismo para la Proscripción de las Armas Nucleares en la América Latina y el Caribe (OPANAL)

Address: Temístocles 78, Col. Polanco, CP 11569, México, DF, Mexico
Phone: 280-4923
FAX: 280-2965

Andean Commission of Jurists (ACJ)/Comisión Andina de Juristas (CAJ)

Address: Los Sauces 285, San Isidro 27, Peru
Phone: 14 407907
FAX: 14 426468

Andean Development Corporation (ADC)/Corporación Andina de Fomento (CAF)

Address: Edificio Torre Central, Apartado de Correos 5086, Avenida Luis Roche con la., Transversal, Piso 5 al 10, Caracas, Venezuela
Phone: 285 55 55
FAX: 00582-284-2880; 0582-284-2553
Telex: 27418 CAFCS VC; 23508 CAF VE

Andean Group (AG) or Andean Pact (AP)/Grupo Andino (GA) or Pacto Andino (PA)

Address: Avenida Paseo de la República 3895, Lima 27; Casilla 181177, Lima 18, Peru
Phone: (51) 14 414212
FAX: (51) 14 420911
Telex: 20104

Arab Latin American Bank (ARLABANK)/Banque Arabe Latinoamécaine/Banco Arab Latinoamericano

Address: Juan de Arona 830, P.O. Box 10070, San Isidro, Lima 100, Peru
Phone: (51) 14 413150
FAX: (51) 14 414277

Asia-Pacific Economic Cooperation (APEC)/Coopération Economique Asie-Pacifique (CEAP)

Address: 438 Alexandra Rd., Alexandra Point Bldg, 19th Floor, Singapore 0511, Singapore
Phone: (65) 276 1880
FAX: (65) 276 1775

Association of Southeast Asian Nations (ASEAN)/Association des Nations l'Asie du Sud-Est (ANASE)/Asociación de Naciones del Asia Sudoriental (ANAS)

Address: Jalan Sisingamangaraja 70A, Kebayoran Baru, PO Box 2072, Jakarta 12110, Indonesia
Phone: (61 21) 71 22 72; 71 19 88
FAX: (61 21) 739 82 34
Telex: 47213-47214 ASEAN JKT

Caribbean Common Market (CARICOM)

Address: Bank of Guyana Building, P.O. Box 10827, Georgetown, Guyana
Phone: 02-69281-9
FAX: 592-2-56194
Telex: 2263 CARISEC GY

Caribbean Development Bank (CDB)

Address: P.O. Box 408 Wildey, St. Michael, Barbados, West Indies
Phone: 809-431-1600
FAX: 809-426-7269
Telex: WB 2287

Center for Latin American Monetary Studies/Centro de Estudios Monetarios Latinoamericanos (CEMLA)/Centre d'études monétaires latino-américaines (CEMLA)

Address: Durango Num. 54, Delegación Cuauhtémoc, México D.F. 06700, México
Phone: 533-03-00 to 09
FAX: 514-65-54
Telex: 01771229 CEMLME

Central American Bank for Economic Integration (CABEI)/Banco Centroamericano de Integración Económica (BCIE)

Address: Apartado Postal 772, Tegucigalpa, D.C., Honduras, C.A.
Phone: 37-2230 to 39
FAX: 504-37-1206; 504-37-3904

Commission for Inland Fisheries of Latin America (CIFLA)/ Comisión de Pesca Continental para América Latina (COPESCAL)

Address: Food and Agriculture Organization of the UN, Fisheries Dept., Via delle Ierme di Caracalla, 1-00100 Rome, Italy
FAX: 6 6799563
Telex: 611127

Eastern Caribbean Central Bank (ECCB)

Address: P.O. Box 89, Basseterre, St. Kitts, St. Kitts and Nevis
Phone: (809-465) 2537/8/9
FAX: (809-465) 1051
Telex: 6828 ECCB SKB KC

Economic Commission for Latin America and the Caribbean (ECLAC)/Comisión Económica para América Latina y el Caribe (CEPAL)

Address: Edif. Naciones Unidas, Avda Dag Hammarskjold, Casilla 179D, Santiago, Chile
Phone: 2 2102000
FAX: 2 080252

Branch Offices of ECLAC:

1. Washington, D.C.

    Address: 1825 "K" Street, N.W., Suite 1120, Washington, D.C. 20006

Phone: (202) 955-5613; (202) 955-5614
FAX: (202) 296-0826
Telex: (023) 440034
E-Mail: ECLAC@tmn.com
World Wide Web: http://www.eclacwash.org

2. Mexico City

   Address: Presidente Masaryk 29, 11570 México D.F.,
   Apartado Postal 6-718, 06600 México D.F.
   Phone: 250-1231; 250-1256
   FAX: 52-5-5311151
   Telex: (022) 1771055 ECLAME

3. Caribbean

   Address: P.O. Box 1113, 2 Frederick Street, Room 300, Port-
   of-Spain, Trinidad and Tobago
   Phone: 62-35595; 62-35428
   FAX: 1-809-6238485
   Telex: 44394

4. Bogotá

   Address: Carrera 16 No. 94-A-62, Apartado Aéreo 75471,
   Botogá, Colombia
   Phone: 218-9834; 236-6884
   FAX: 57-1-2140110
   Telex: (035) 433 16 UNCO

5. Brasilia

   Address: SBS Edificio BNDES-17 Andar, Caixa Postal 04-
   0251, 7000 Brasilia, D.F., Brasil
   Phone: 321-7540; 321-3222
   FAX: 55 61 2259339
   Telex: (038) 611697 ECLA BR

6. Montevideo

   Address: Juncal 1305, Oficina 1002, Casilla de Correo 1207,
   Montevideo, Uruguay
   Phone: 961776; 961580
   FAX: 598-2-921610
   Telex: (032) 26355 CEPAL AR

7. Buenos Aires

Address: Corrientes 2554, Piso 5, Casilla de Correo 4191,
1000 Buenos Aires, Argentina
Phone: 48-3991; 48-9313
FAX: 54-1-3127867
Telex: (033) 22382 CEPAL AR

Group of Fifteen (G-15)/Groupe des Quinze

Address: Technical Support Facility, Ch du Champ d'Ancier 17, Case
postale 326, Ch-1211, Genève 19, Switzerland
Phone: (41 22) 798 42 10
FAX: (41 22) 798 38 49
Telex: 41 53 33 GPQ2 CH

Group of Latin American and Caribbean Sugar Exporting Countries (GLACSEC)/Grupo de Paises de Latinoamericano y el Caribe para la Exportación de Azúcar (GEPLACEA)

Address: Ejército Nacional 373, 1st floor, 11520 México, DF, Mexico
Phone: 250 75 66
FAX: 250 7591
Telex: 01771042

Institute for European-Latin American Relations (IELAR)/ Instituto de Relaciones Europeo—Latinoamericanas (IRELA)

Address: Pedro de Valdivia 10, E-28006 Madrid, Apdo. 2600,
Madrid, Spain
Phone: 34 (1) 561-70-00; 34 (1) 564-50-90
FAX: 34 (1) 562-64 99; 34 (1) 564-49-83
World Wide Web: http:/www.irela.org

Institute for Latin American Integration (INTAL)/Associación Latinoamericana de Integración (ALADI)

Address: Esmeralda 130, Piso 18, Casilla de Correos 39, Sucursal 1,
1035 Buenos Aires, Argentina
Phone: 1 3942265, 1 3942096
FAX: 1 3942293
Telex: 21520 AR BIDBA

Inter-American Center for Regional Development (IACRD)/Centro Interamericano para el Desarrollo Regional (CINDER)

Address: Calle 69, Número 15 D-32, Apartado Postal 1304,
Maracaibo, Venezuela

Phone: 61 516953
FAX: 61 523504
Telex: 61101

Inter-American Children's Institute (IACI)/Instituto Interamericano del Niño (IIN)/Instituto Interamericano da Criança (IIC)

Address: Casilla de Correos 16212, Avenida 8 de Octubre 2904, Montevideo, Uruguay
Phone: (598 2) 47-21-50
FAX: (598 2) 47-32-42
E-mail: piinfa@chasque.apc.org

Inter-American Development Bank (IADB)

Address:1300 New York Ave. NW, Washington, D.C. 20577
Phone: 202-623-1397
FAX: 202-623-1403

Inter-American Institute of Human Rights/Institut Interaméicain des Droits de l'Homme / Instituto Interamericano de Derechos Humanos (IIDH)

Address: Barrio Los Yoses, Apartado Postal 10081-1000, San José, Costa Rica
Phone: (506) 34 04 05; 34 04 04
FAX: (506) 34 09 55
Telex: 22 33 CORTE CR

Inter-American Nuclear Energy Commission (IANEC)

Address: Secretary-General of the OAS, 17th St. & Constitution Ave NW, Washington, D.C. 20006
Phone: 202–458–3368
FAX: 202–458–3167

Inter-American Regional Organization of Workers/Organización Regional Interamericana de Trabajadores (ORIT)

Address: Edif. De la CTM, Vallarta No. 8, 3rd Floor, 06470 México, D.F., Mexico
Phone: (5) 5667024
FAX: (5) 5927329
Telex: 1771699

Inter-American Tropical Tuna Commission (IATTC)

Address: Scripps Institution of Oceanography, 8604 La Jolla Shores
Drive, La Jolla, CA 92037-1508
Phone: 619-546-7100
FAX: 619-546-7133

**Intergovernmental Committee on the River Plate Basin/Comité
Intergubernamental de los Países Coordinador de la Cuenca del
Plata**

Address: Paraguay 755, Segundo Piso, 1057 Buenos Aires, Argentina

**Intergovernmental Council of Copper Exporting Countries
(ICCEC)/Conseil Intergouvernemental des Pays Exportateurs de
Cuivre (CIPEC)**

Address: 39 rue de la Bienfaisance, 75008 Paris, France
Phone: (1) 42-25-00-24
FAX: (1) 42-89-89-11
Telex: 649077

**International Monetary Fund (IMF)/ Fondo Mundial Internacional
(FMI)/Fonds Monétaire International (FMI)**

Address: 700 Nineteenth St. NW, Washington, D.C. 20431
Phone: (202) 623-7000
FAX: (202) 623-4661; 623-7491; 623-4662
World Wide Web: http://dsbb.imf.org

**Latin American Association of Development Finance Institutions
(LAADFI)/Asociación Latinoamericana de Instituciones
Financieras de Desarrollo (ALIDE)**

Address: Apdo Postal 3988, Paseo de la República 3211, Lima 100,
Peru
Phone: 422400
FAX: 428105
Telex: 21037

**Latin American Center for Development Administration (LACDA)/
Centro Latinoamericano de Administración para el Desarrollo
(CLAD)**

Address: Calle Herrera Toro, Qta. CLAD, Sector Los Naranjos, Las
Mercedes, Apartado Postal 4181, Caracas 1010-A, Venezuela
Phone: 2 924064

FAX: 2 918427
Telex: 29076 CLAD VC

Latin American Economic System (LAES)/Sistema Económico Latinoamericano (SELA)

Address: Avenida Francisco de Miranda, Torre Europa, Piso 4,
Chacaito, Apartado de Correos 17035, Caracas 1010-A, Venezuela
Phone: 2 9055111
FAX: 2 9516953
Telex: 23294

Latin American Energy Organization (LAEO)/Organización Latinoamericana de Energía (OLADE)/Organisation Latino-Américaine d'Energie (OLAE)

Address: Ave. Occidental, Sector San Carolos, Casilla Postal 17-11-6413, CCI, Quito, Ecuador
Phone: 539-2-538280; 539-2-538785
FAX: 539-2-539684
Telex: 2728 OLADE ED

Latin American Export Bank (LAEB)/Banco Latinoamericano de Exportaciones (BLADEX)

Address: Calle 50 and Aquilino De La Guardia, Panama City,
Republic of Panama
Phone: (507) 636766
FAX: (507) 69-63-63
Telex: 2240 TRT; 2356 INTEL

Latin American Integration Association (LAIA)/Asociación Latinoamericana de Integración (ALADI)

Address: Calle Cebollati 1461, Casilla de Correo 577, 10001
Montevideo, Uruguay
Phone: 2 401121; 2 495915
FAX: 2 490649

Latin American Parliament/Parlamento Latinoamericano

Address: 28 de Julio; Of. 201, Miraflores, Lima, Peru
Phone: 460977
FAX: 460977

Mutual Assistance of the Latin American Government Oil Companies/Asistencia Recíproca Petrolera Estatal Latinoamericana (ARPEL)

Address: Javier de Viana 2345, Casilla de Correo 1006, 112
Montevideo, Uruguay
Phone: 406993
FAX: 237023
Telex: 22560

Nonaligned Movement (NAM)

Address: c/o Ministry of Foreign Affairs, Jalan Taman Pejambon 6,
Jakarta PUSAT, Indonesia

Organization of American States (OAS)/Organización de los Estados Americanos (OEA)/Organisation des Etats Américains (OEA)

Address: General Secretariat, 17th St. and Constitution Avenue NW,
Washington, D.C., 20006
Phone: 458-3000
FAX: (202) 458-3967
Email: Info@oas.org (Dept. of Public Information)
World Wide Web: http://www.oas.org
Cable: OAS WASHDC

Organization of Central American States (OCAS)/Organización de Estados Centroamericanos (ODECA)

Address: 81 Avenida Norte 520, Colonia Escalón, San Salvador, El
Salvador, C.A.
Phone: 23-2533
Telex: 6248 OECAS LC

Organization of Eastern Caribbean States (OECS)

Address: OECS Central Secretariat, P.O. Box 179, The Morne,
Castries, St. Lucia
Phone: (809) 45 22537/8
FAX: (809) 45 31628

Organization of Petroleum Exporting Countries (OPEC)

Address: Obere Donaustrasse 93, A-1020, Vienna, Austria
Phone: 43 (1) 21 11 20; 43 (1) 26 43 20

Organization of Solidarity of the Peoples of Africa, Asia, and Latin America (OSPAAAL)/Organización de Solidaridad de los Pueblos de Africa, Asia, y América Latina

Address: Apdo 4224, Havana 10400, Cuba
Phone: 30-5520
Telex: 512259

Pan American Health Organization (PAHO)

Address: 525 23rd St. NW, Washington, D.C. 20037
Phone: 202-861-3200
FAX: 202-223-5971
Telex: 248338

Southern Cone Common Market (MERCOSUR)

Address: Rincon 575 P 12, 11000 Montevideo, Uruguay
Phone: 598 2 964590
FAX: 598 2 964590

Union of Banana Exporting Countries (UBEC)/Unión de Países Exportadoras de Banano (UPED)

Address: Apdo 4273, Bank of America, Piso 7, Panama City
Phone: 636266
FAX: 64355
Telex: 2468

World Bank (International Bank for Reconstruction and Development)

Address: 1818 H Street NW, Washington, D.C. 20433
Phone: 202-477-1234
FAX: 202-477-6391
Telex: MCI 64145 WORLD BANK
World Wide Web: http://www.worldbank.org

World Health Organization (WHO)/Organización Mundial de la Salud (OMS)/Organisation Mondiale de la Santé (OMS)

Address: CH-1211 Genève 27, Switzerland
Phone: (41-22) 791-21-11; 791-32-23
FAX: 791-07-46
Telex: 278281 OMS

World Trade Organization (WTO)/Organización Mundial de Comercio (OMC)/Organisation Mondiale du Commerce (OMC)

Address: Rue de Lausanne 154, CH-1211 Genève 21, Switzerland
Phone: (41-22) 739 51 11
FAX: (41-22) 731 42 06
Telex: 412324 OMC/WTO CH

Bibliography

This bibliography is organized into a detailed taxonomy covering international organizations, inter-American organizations (both regional and subregional), and related historical and political events. It is designed to provide the reader with the necessary tools needed for further research and analysis of the growing literature on inter-American organizations and the complex global context in which they operate. Four goals were paramount in the preparation of this part of the book. The bibliography lists the most recent and relevant books (many of which are standard and classic studies or works), monographs, book chapters, official documents (of governments and international organizations), and professional journal articles on inter-American organizations. This includes coverage of the major changes and historical trends that have affected these organizations, also treated at some length in the book's Introduction. Second, because of the often controversial character of international organizations and the conflicting interpretations of the history of U.S. involvement in Latin America and the Caribbean, publications representing various points of view are given when possible. Third, while most of the publications cited here are in English, an effort was made to include leading works in other languages, particularly since inter-American organizations must often work in a multilingual environment. As a result, the reader will find numerous bibliographic citations in Spanish and a few in French, German, and Portuguese. Finally, the bibliography was planned to be as user-friendly as possible. For example, the bibliographic taxonomy is organized by types of international organizations, individual countries, and functional activities, with citations alphabetized within each category or subcategory. Appendix IX includes a list of over 50 inter-American organizations and their headquarters and electronic addresses. For those who have access to the Internet, detailed instructions for tracking down sources located on the World Wide Web (WWW) are provided in the last section of this introduction. The following is a brief discussion of the key works, organized by the major categories included in the bibliography, and their importance to the study of inter-American organizations.

General Topics on International Organizations and Law

This section (part I) of the bibliography contains the most representative books in English and Spanish on international organizations, international law and inter-American and international relations. The principal focus is on intergovernmental organizations (IGOs) and corresponding subjects of importance for understanding how these organizations function within a global and regional system. The leading book on classifying and defining international organizations is *International Organizations* (2nd ed., 1992) by Clive Archer. Other important books are Werner J. Feld and Robert S. Jordan with Leon Hurwitz, *International Organizations: A Comparative Approach* (3rd ed., 1994); and Harold K. Jacobson, *Networks of Interdependence: International Organizations and the Global Political System* (2nd ed., 1984). The same universal-regional division can be applied to the study of international law, for there is also a regional approach, or school, in Latin America called American International Law, based mainly on the work of Chilean judge Alejandro Álvarez. The key volume on this subject is H. B. Jacobini, *A Study of the Philosophy of International Law as Seen in Works of Latin American Writers* (1952). Two recent books of importance to international law and organizations include C. F. Amerasinghe, *Principles of the Institutional Law of International Organizations* (1996) and Robert J. Beck, Anthony Clark Arend, and Robert D. Vander Lugt, *International Rules: Approaches from International Law and International Relations* (1996).

Inter-American and International Relations

The literature on inter-American organizations and inter-American relations continues to grow but is increasingly focused on the place of Latin America and the Caribbean within the international system. The leading work on this subject among U.S. scholars is G. Pope Atkins, *Latin America in the International Political System* (3rd ed., 1995). In this study, Atkins treats the Latin American region as a subsystem operating within the larger international system. Peter Calvert, a British scholar, makes an important contribution with *The International Politics of Latin America* (1994). The broader dimension of inter-American relations is examined in a volume edited by Abraham F. Lowenthal and Gregory F. Treverton, *Latin America in a New World* (1994). Latin American scholars have also developed an interest in their own international relations and provide interesting interpretations that often contrast with those of their North American and European counterparts. The leading works by Latin American scholars are: Demetrio Boersner, *Relaciones Internacionales de América Latina: Breve Historia* (1990);

Heraldo Muñoz and Joseph S. Tulchin, eds. *Latin American Nations in World Politics* (2nd ed., 1996); and Luciano Tomassini, *Relaciones Internacionales de la América Latina* (1981).

Three recent works focus on different aspects of U.S.-Latin American relations, including the actual process of U.S. decision making toward Latin America. David W. Dent edited *U.S.-Latin American Policymaking: A Reference Handbook* (1995), a well-organized volume with an extensive bibliography on each of the institutions involved in the policy making process. Two other recent works are Michael J. Kryzanek, *U.S.-Latin American Relations* (3rd. ed., 1996) and John D. Martz, ed., *United States Policy in Latin America: A Decade of Crisis and Challenge* (2nd ed., 1995).

There are fewer books that examine the role of the Caribbean in international affairs, but a few important books by scholars in or from the Caribbean who have tackled this subject include Jacqueline A. Braveboy-Wagner, *The Caribbean in World Affairs: The Foreign Policies of the English-Speaking States* (1989) and Jorge Heine and Leslie F. Manigot, eds., *The Caribbean and World Politics: Cross-Currents and Cleavages* (1988). A leading work by a U.S. scholar is Lester D. Langley, *The United States and the Caribbean in the Twentieth Century* (4th ed., 1989).

Regional Organizations

Regional organizations are the subject of part II of the bibliography, but the major focus is almost entirely on the Organization of American States (OAS). The ten sections that comprise this vast section, and the corresponding bibliography, should leave the reader with no doubt as to the importance of the OAS as the major political actor in the Inter-American System. However, the publication pattern on the OAS is a spotty one, reflecting its changing role in the Americas over the past 50 years. After its founding, it exercised an important role in the 1950s and 1960s, and the outpouring of literature on the OAS mirrored that role; however, this was not the case from the late 1970s to end of the 1980s when it declined in importance and was often marginalized in its efforts to deal with the Falklands/Malvinas War and the Central American crisis. Thereafter, the OAS returned to a principal role in hemispheric affairs, largely the result of the end of the Cold War. Since 1989, as indicated by the size of the relevant bibliographical section, the OAS has expanded its activities to include the promotion of democracy, protection of human rights, trade, and development, and the recent fight against corruption.

There are several ways of measuring the relationship between the activity level and importance of the OAS and the output of academic literature on the subject. First, one can note the pattern of neglect by the small number of doctoral dissertations and the lack of scholarly books on the OAS and the inter-American system during certain historical periods.[1] For example, in contrast to the period from 1960 to 1975 when considerable scholarly attention was devoted to the OAS, few dissertations or books were written in any language from the late 1970s until 1988–1989. Second, the renewed attention devoted to the OAS in the late 1980s was preceded by a number of critical works that examined the need for changes in the way the organization functions in the Western Hemisphere. Two critical works by Tom J. Farer, his edited *The Future of the Inter-American System* (1979) and a monograph, *The United States and the Inter-American System: Are There Functions for the Forms?* (1978), set the stage for the expanded attention that would follow in the late 1980s. A book based on numerous interviews (many critical) by Henry H. Han, *Problems and Prospects of the Organization of American States: Perceptions of the Member States' Leaders* (1987), appeared in the late 1980s and was followed by a mixed critical-positive analysis by L. Ronald Scheman, *The Inter-American Dilemma: The Search for Inter-American Cooperation at the Centennial of the Inter-American System* (1988). Celso Rodríguez, the editor of the OAS's *Inter-American Review of Bibliography/Revista de Bibliografía Interamericana,* commissioned a number of articles for a special issue, "The First Century of the Inter-American System," that appeared in 1989. Two favorable and useful compilations published in the 1980s, one by Anthony T. Bryan and the other by Germán Arciniegas, are also included in this section of the bibliography.

The number of publications on the OAS increased dramatically at the beginning of the 1990s. Six books have so far been published, two of them bibliographies. An excellent bibliography is provided in Thomas L. Welch and René Gutiérrez, *The Organization of American States: A Bibliography* (1990). David Scheinen's *The Organization of American States* (1996) is current, comprehensive, and thoroughly annotated. Three of the most recent publications are O. Carlos Stoetzer, *The Organization of American States* (1993); Viron Vaky and Heraldo Muñoz, *The Future of the Organization of American States* (1993); and César Gaviria, *A New Vision of the OAS* (1995), the OAS secretary-general's response to the 1994 Summit of the Americas in Miami.[2] A comprehensive complement to the volumes mentioned above is G. Pope Atkin's *Encyclopedia of the Inter-American System* (1997).

Global and Universal Organizations

This literature is covered in part IV of the bibliography and is extensive, and often critical, dealing mainly with the International Monetary Fund

(IMF) and the World Bank. This is due in large part to the age of these universal organizations—they have been in existence for more than 50 years—and the fact that they have been closely involved with often controversial finance and development issues in the Third World. Two good examples of critical assessments of these international organizations are Morris Miller, *Coping is Not Enough! The International Debt Crisis and the Roles of the World Bank and International Monetary Fund* (1986) and Kevin Danaher, ed. *50 Years is Enough: The Case Against the World Bank and the International Monetary Fund* (1994). Section B 2 covers Latin American and Caribbean activism in the United Nations, starting in the 1960s as a part of the Third World voting bloc. The literature on this subject is vast, but two leading books on their growing influence are Gaston de Prat Gay, *Política Internacional del Grupo Latinoamericano* (1980), and Robert L. Rothstein, *Global Bargaining: UNCTAD and the Quest for a New International Economic Order* (1979).

Latin American/Caribbean Relations with the World

Latin American and Caribbean relations with European, African, Middle East, and Asian organizations are covered in Parts V, VI, and VII of the bibliography. Ties with European organizations are the oldest and have expanded considerably due to the creation of the Institute for European-Latin American Relations (IELAR), an international think tank, by the European Community (EC) in 1985. IELAR is located in Madrid, Spain, and publishes an annual bilingual *Yearbook of European-Latin American Relations* (1994–). Two recent and excellent works are Wolf Grabendorff and Riordan Roett, eds., *Latin America, Western Europe, and the U.S.: Reevaluating the Atlantic Triangle* (1985) and Abraham F. Lowenthal and Gregory F. Treverton, eds., *Latin America in a New World* (1994), which includes a chapter on Latin American-European relations. A relatively new and growing relationship between Latin America and Asia is illustrated with the creation of the Asia-Pacific Economic Cooperation Forum (APEC), where ties with international organizations are expanding. This linkage is examined in Barbara Stallings and Gabriel Székely, eds., *Japan, the United States and Latin America: Toward a Trilateral Relationship in the Western Hemisphere* (1993).

Nongovernmental Organizations (NGOs)

Nongovernmental organizations are important to inter-American relations, but despite their increasing numbers, expanding scope, and importance, they are only a minor part of this book. An important book that indicates the expanding role of NGOs is the recent work edited by Thomas G. Weiss and Leon Gordenker, *NGOs, the UN, and Global Governance* (1996). This is a subject that will no doubt receive growing attention as inter-American organizations realize the importance of nongovernmental organizations. The OAS, for example, now has a formal Working Group that is working on the process of establishing a formal relationship with around 100 NGOs that deal with the environment, democracy, and human rights.

Guides to Professional Journals

Two leading guides to journal articles are *ABC Pol Sci: A Bibliography of Contents, Political Science & Government* (Santa Barbara, CA: ABC-Clio, 1969–) and *HAPI: Hispanic American Periodicals Index* (Los Angeles: University of California, 1970–). The former includes the major international academic journals, numbering over 300, while the latter includes over 200 academic journals published mainly in Latin America. Another valuable source, which stresses articles along with book reviews, is the quarterly *Inter-American Review of Bibliography/Revista Interamericana de Bibliografía* (Washington, D.C.: OAS, 1951–).

The leading academic journals, included in the above guides, are the following: *Caribbean Studies* (University of Puerto Rico Institute of Caribbean Studies at http://www.microstate.com/pub/micros/ics/); *Estudios Internacionales* (Universidad de Chile); *Foro Internacional* (Colegio de México); *Journal of Inter-American Studies and World Affairs* (University of Miami); and *Mundo Nuevo: Revista de Estudios Latinoamericanos* (Universidad Simón Bolívar, Caracas). (The foremost source on all publications, including articles, on Latin America and inter-American relations is the *Handbook of Latin American Studies,* which will be discussed below.) Two especially important guides for articles dealing with international law are the *Index to Legal Periodicals* (New York: H. W. Wilson Co.) and *Index to Foreign Legal Periodicals* (Berkeley: University of California Press). The latter has been available on CD-ROM from Silver Platter and as a commercial on-line service from WESTLAW, beginning with 1984.

Inter-American Organizations and the Internet

Since the bibliographic taxonomy does not include a section on Internet sources, we include them here as another way of accessing resource material on inter-American organizations and inter-American relations. The two leading sources of Internet materials in the United States are the Hispanic Division of the Library of Congress in Washington, D.C., and the Latin American collection at the University of Texas at Austin. The University of Texas at Austin Internet address is http://lanic.utexas.edu/. The Library of Congress' World Wide Web (LC WEB) is a project in progress in general and includes in particular the electronic version of *The Handbook of Latin American Studies,* called HLAS Online. Some current LC WEB offerings include access to LC MARVEL (its Gopher-based campuswide information system) and LOCIS (Library of Congress Information System). The latter's "Foreign Law" file covers journal articles on legal topics, representing primarily Hispanic-speaking countries. Mention should also be made of GLIN (Global Legal Information Network), a link to search the Internet for legal, and some political, material for individual countries. As of May 1996, three Latin American countries had joined GLIN, and five had applied for membership. To access GLIN, click on the following: first, "Government, Congress, and Law" then "Law Library of Congress," followed by GLIN to "The Guide to Law Online."

The articles found in the *Handbook of Latin American Studies* can be an extremely important source of information on Latin America. The *Handbook* has been published annually since 1936 (Austin: University of Texas Press) and has alternated yearly between a volume on the Humanities and one on the Social Sciences. Dolores Moyano Martin has been the editor since 1977. Volumes 1–53 have been available via CD-ROM since 1995. Each volume includes annotated entries for articles, books, monographs, and documents. Humanities volumes are divided into the fields and/or disciplines of Art, History, Literature, Music, Philosophy, and Electronic Resources, while the Social Sciences volumes are divided into Anthropology, Economics, Geography, Government and Politics, International Relations, and Sociology. (Clearly, except for the History section in the former volume, the latter has the most sections relevant for this dictionary.)

It is a relatively easy task to locate articles on HLAS Online. The LC Home Page address is http://lcweb.loc.gov; proceed from this point by clicking on "Research and Collections Services," followed by "Research and References Services." The next step is the "Hispanic Division Reading Room" and then the *Handbook of Latin American Studies.* The database is searchable by full text, author, title, subject, and/or volume number. The topical subject terms, followed by one or more geographical or topical subheadings, are primarily in English. Company or corporate subjects are usually listed in the language of the country in which they are based.

For international organizations located in HLAS Online, search several variants—"Economic Commission for Latin America and the Caribbean," "ECLAC," "Comision Económica para América Latina," "CEPAL"; "Organization of American States," "OAS," "Organización de Estados Americanos," "OEA." Since Vol. 50 of the *HLAS*, the chapters and subsections of the fields/disciplines have each been given a special hierarchical code. By using these codes, a search can be limited to a particular chapter or sub-section. Using the hierarchical tables from a particular volume, click on a discipline. Then click on one of the headings to conduct a search of that particular subsection. (The hierarchical codes for Vols. 52 and 54 on Humanities were available in September 1997.) The search by subject or discipline, chapter or subsection, will indicate all relevant references—articles, books, documents, etc. The *Handbook* cites over 2,000 serial titles (about 5,000 articles) containing information on Latin America.

It is also worth noting that the Hispanic Division's Web Page provides "Selected Links to Additional Hispanic Reading Room Internet Resources." These are "Selected Links to Libraries and Archives," which includes, for example, "Repositories of Primary Sources in Mexico, Central America, and South America"; and "Selected Links to National and International Organizations," including the U.S. Agency for International Development (USAID), Inter-American Development Bank (IADB), Organization of American States (OAS), and the Pan American Health Organization (PAHO).

Notes

1. See Larman C. Wilson's commissioned paper, OAS, General Secretariat, Bureau of Legal Affairs, "The Future of the Inter-American System: A Research Agenda"/"El Sistema Interamericano y su Futuro: Un Plan de Investigación," SG/Ser. D/1–2 (Washington, D.C.: Organization of American States [OAS], 1979).

2. See Larman C. Wilson and David W. Dent, "The United States and the OAS," in *U.S.-Latin American Policymaking: A Reference Handbook,* David W. Dent, ed. (Westport, CT: Greenwood Press, 1995), Chapter 3.

The Bibliography

Contents

I. General

A. International Organizations

Andemicael, B., ed. *Regional International Organization and the United Nations System.* New York: United Nations Institute for Training and Research, 1979.

Archer, Clive. *International Organizations.* 2nd ed. London: Routledge, 1992.

Armstrong, David. *The Rise of the International Organization.* New York: St. Martin's Press, 1989.

Bennett, A. LeRoy. *Historical Dictionary of the United Nations.* Lanham, MD: The Scarecrow Press, 1995.

————. *International Organizations: Principles and Issues.* 4th ed. Englewood Cliffs, NJ: Prentice-Hall, 1988.

Bierzanek, Remigiusz. *Bezpieczénstwo regionalne w systemie.* Warsaw: Wydawnietwo Ministerstwa Obrony Narodowej, 1977.

Butterworth, Robert L. *Moderation from Management: International Organizations and Peace.* Pittsburgh, PA: University of Pittsburgh, 1978.

Claude, Inis L., Jr. *Swords Into Plowshares: The Problems and Progress of International Organizations.* 4th ed. New York: Random House, 1988.

Cox, Robert W., and Harold K. Jacobson, eds. *The Anatomy of Influence: Decision Making in International Organizations.* New Haven, CT: Yale University Press, 1973.

de Cooker, Chris, ed. *International Administration: Law and Management Practices in International Organizations.* New York: United Nations, 1990.

Diehl, Paul F., ed. *The Politics of Global Governance: International Organizations in an Interdependent World.* Boulder, CO: Lynne Rienner, 1996.

————. *The Politics of International Organizations.* Chicago, IL: Dorsey Press, 1989.

Edwards, Michael, and David Hulme, eds. *Beyond the Magic Bullet: NGO Performance and Accountability in the Post–Cold War World.* West Hartford, CT: Kumarian Press, 1996.

Fawcett, Louis, and Andrew Hurrell, eds. *Regionalism in World Politics: Regional Organizations and International Order.* New York: Oxford University Press, 1995.

Feld, Werner J., and Robert S. Jordan, with Leon Hurwitz. *International*

Organizations: A Comparative Approach. 3rd ed. New York: Praeger, 1994.

Figueroa Pla, Uldaricio. *Manual de Organismos Internacionales.* Santiago: Editorial Andrés Bello and Editorial Jurídica de Chile, 1989.

Finkelstein, Lawrence S., ed. *Politics in the United Nations System.* Durham, NC: Duke University Press, 1988.

Goodrich, Leland M., and David A. Kay, eds. *International Organization: Politics and Process.* Madison: University of Wisconsin Press, 1973.

Goodspeed, Stephen S. *The Nature and Function of International Organization.* 2nd ed. New York: Oxford University Press, 1967.

Gregg, Robert W., ed. *International Organization in the Western Hemisphere.* Syracuse, NY: Syracuse University Press, 1968.

Haas, Ernst B. *Why We Still Need the United Nations: The Collective Management of International Conflict.* Berkeley: University of California Press, 1986.

Jacob, Philip E., Axline L. Atherton, and Arthur M. Wallenstein. *The Dynamics of International Organization.* Rev. ed. Homewood, IL: Dorsey Press, 1972.

Jacobson, Harold K. *Networks of Interdependence: International Organizations and the Global Political System.* 2nd ed. New York: Knopf, 1984.

Kapteyn, P.J.G., and Board of Editors. *International Organization and Integration: Functional Organizations and Arrangements.* Vol. II K. Boston, MA: Martinus Nijhoff, 1984.

———. *International Organization and Integration: Organizations Related to the United Nations.* Vol. I B. Boston, MA: Martinus Nijhoff, 1982.

———. *International Organization and Integration: Other Organizations and Arrangements.* Vol. II B. Boston, MA: Martinus Nijhoff, 1983.

Karns, Margaret, and Karen Mingst. *The United States and Multilateral Institutions: Instrumentality and Influence.* New York: Unwin and Unwin, 1990.

Kratochwil, Friedrich V., and Edward D. Mansfield, eds. *International Organization: A Reader.* New York: Harper-Collins, 1994.

Lawson, Ruth C., ed. *International Regional Organizations: Constitutional Foundations.* New York: Praeger, 1962.

Luard, Evan, ed. *The Evolution of International Organizations.* New York: Praeger, 1966.

———. *International Agencies: The Emerging Framework of Interdependence.* Dobbs Ferry, NY: Oceana Publications, 1977.

Lyonette, Louis-Jacques, and Jeanne S. Korman. *Introduction to Inter-*

national Organizations. Dobbs Ferry, NY: Oceana Publications, 1996.

Netherlands Institute for the Law of the Sea, ed. *International Organizations and the Law of the Sea 1994. Documentary Yearbook 1994.* Vol. 10. The Hague: Martinus Nijhoff, 1996.

Nye, Joseph S., ed. *International Regionalism: Readings.* Boston, MA: Little, Brown and Co., 1968.

————. *Peace in Parts: Integration and Conflict in Regional Organizations.* Boston, MA: Little, Brown and Co., 1971.

Owens, Richard. *"The Times" Guide to World Organizations: Their Role and Reach in the New World Order.* London: Times Books, 1996.

Roberts, Adam, and Benedict Kingsbury, eds. *United Nations, Divided World: The UN's Roles in International Relations.* 2nd ed. Oxford: Oxford University Press, 1993.

Salgado, René. "International Economic Organizations." In *U.S.-Latin American Policymaking: A Reference Handbook,* edited by David W. Dent, Westport, CT: 45–63. Greenwood Press, 1995.

Sato, Tetsuo. *Evolving Constitutions of International Organizations.* Cambridge, MA: Kluwer Law International, 1996.

Taylor, Paul. *International Organization in the Modern World: The Regional and the Global Process.* New York: St. Martin's Press, 1993.

————, and A. J. R. Groom. *International Organization: A Conceptual Approach.* London: Frances Pinter Ltd., 1978.

Taylor, Phillip. *Nonstate Actors in International Politics: From Transregional to Substate Organizations.* Boulder, CO: Westview Press, 1984.

U.S. Congress, Committee on Government Operations, United States Senate. *U.S. Participation in International Organizations.* Washington, D.C.: Government Printing Office, 1977.

Vaubel, Roland, and Thomas D. Willett, eds. *The Political Economy of International Organizations: A Public Choice Approach.* Boulder, CO: Westview Press, 1990.

Voitovich, Sergei A. *International Economic Organizations in the International Legal Process.* Boston, MA: Martinus Nijhoff, 1995.

Welch, Thomas. "Introduction to International Organizations." In *Introduction to International Organizations,* edited by Louis-Jacques Lyonette and Jeanne S. Korman, 509–519. Dobbs Ferry, NY: Oceana Publications, 1996.

White, Lyman C. *International Nongovernmental Organizations.* New York: Greenwood Press, 1971.

Wood, Robert, ed. *The Process of International Organization.* New York: Random House, 1971.

Young, Oran R., ed. *The International Political Economy and International Institutions.* 2 vols. Aldershot, UK: Elgar Publishing, 1996.

B. International Law

Akehurst, Michael. *A Modern Introduction to International Law.* 5th ed. Boston, MA: Little, Brown and Co., 1987.

Amerasinghe, C. F. *Principles of the Institutional Law of International Organizations.* New York: Cambridge University Press, 1996.

Beck, Robert J., Anthony Clark Arend, and Robert D. Vander Lugt. *International Rules: Approaches from International Law and International Relations.* New York: Oxford University Press, 1996.

Bernhardt, Rudolph, and Advisory Board, Max Planck Institute for Comparative Public Law and International Law. *Encyclopedia of Public International Law.* 5 vols. Vol. 2, *Decisions of International Courts and Tribunals and International Arbitrations.* Amsterdam and New York: Elsevier Science Publishers, 1988–1990.

Boczek, Boleslaw Adam. *Historical Dictionary of International Tribunals.* Metuchen, NJ: The Scarecrow Press, Inc., 1994.

Boyle, Francis A. *World Politics and International Law.* Durham, NC: Duke University Press, 1988.

Brierly, James L. *The Law of Nations: An Introduction to the Law of Peace.* 6th ed. Revised by H. Waldock. New York: Oxford University Press, 1978.

Burns, Weston, Richard A. Falk, and Anthony A. D'Amato. *International Law and World Order: A Problem-Oriented Coursebook.* 2nd ed. St. Paul, MN: West Publishing Co., 1990.

Caicedo Castilla, José Joaquín. *El Derecho Internacional en el Sistema Interamericano.* Madrid: Centro de Estudios Jurídicos Hispanoamericanos, 1970.

Cançado Trindade, Antônio Augusto. *Princípios do Direito Internacional Contemporâneo.* Brazil: Editora Universidade de Brasília, 1981.

Chen, Lung-chu. *An Introduction to Contemporary International Law: A Policy-Oriented Perspective.* New Haven, CT: Yale University Press, 1989.

Corbett, Percy E. *The Growth of World Law.* Princeton, NJ: Princeton University Press, 1971.

de Visscher, Charles. *Theory and Reality in Public International Law.* Rev. ed. Trans. from 3rd French ed. of 1960. Princeton, NJ: Princeton University Press, 1968.

Deutsch, Karl W., and Stanley Hoffman, eds. *The Relevance of International Law: A Festschrift for Professor Leo Gross.* Cambridge, MA: Schenkman Publishing Co., 1968.

Falk, Richard. *Revitalizing International Law*. Ames, IA: Iowa State University Press, 1989.

————, Friedrich Kratochwill, and Saul H. Mendlovitz, eds. *International Law: A Contemporary Perspective*. Boulder, CO: Westview Press, 1985.

Fenwick, Charles S. *International Law*. 4th ed. New York: Appleton-Century-Crofts, 1965.

Friedmann, Wolfgang. *The Changing Structure of International Law*. New York: Columbia University Press, 1964.

García, Eduardo Augusto. *Manual de Derecho Internacional Público*. Buenos Aires: Ediciones Depalma, 1975.

Higgins, Rosalyn. *Problems and Process: International Law and How We Use It*. New York: Oxford University Press, 1994.

Joyner, Christopher C., ed. *The United Nations and International Law*. 2nd ed. New York: Cambridge University Press, 1997.

Levi, Werner. *Contemporary International Law*. 2nd ed. Boulder, CO: Westview Press, 1990.

Macdonald, R. St. J., and Douglas M. Johnston, eds. *The Structure and Process of International Law: Essays in Legal Philosophy, Doctrine and Theory*. Dordrecht, The Netherlands and Boston, MA: Martinus Nijhoff, 1986.

Martin, Charles E. *Universalism and Regionalism in International Law and Organization*. La Habana: Academia Interamericana de Derecho Comparado e Internacional, 1959.

McDougal, Myres S., Harold D. Lasswell, and Lung-chu Chen. *Human Rights and World Public Order: The Basic Policies of an International Law of Human Dignity*. New Haven, CT: Yale University Press, 1980.

Monroy Cabra, Marco Gerardo. *Manual de Derecho Internacional Público*. Bogotá: Editorial TEMIS Librería, 1982.

Nussbaum, Arthur. *A Concise History of the Law of Nations*. Rev. ed. New York: Macmillan, 1954.

Oliver, Covey T., et al. *Cases and Materials on the International Legal System*. 4th ed. Westbury, NY: Foundation Press, 1994.

Onuf, Nicholas O., ed. *Law-Making in the Global Community*. Durham, NC: Carolina Academic Press, 1982.

Parry, Clive, et al. *Encyclopedic Dictionary of International Law*. Dobbs Ferry, NY: Oceana, 1986.

Rhyne, Charles S. *International Law: The Substance, Processes, Procedures and Institutions for World Peace and Justice*. Washington, D.C.: CLB Publishers, 1971.

Schwarzenberger, Georg, and E. D. Brown. *A Manual of International Law*. 6th ed. 2nd rev. impression. Abington, UK: Professional Books Ltd., 1976 and 1978.

Sepúlveda, César. *Derecho internacional público*. 7th ed. México, D.F.: Editorial Porrúa, 1976.

Shaw, Malcolm N. *International Law*. 3rd ed. Cambridge, UK: Grotius Publications, 1992.

Sheikh, Ahmed. *International Law and International Behavior: A Behavioral Interpretation of Contemporary International Law and Politics*. New York: John Wiley and Sons, 1974.

von Glahn, Gerhard. *Law Among Nations: An Introduction to Public International Law*. 7th ed. New York: Allyn and Bacon, 1995.

C. Inter-American and International Relations

Anderson, Thomas D. *Geopolitics of the Caribbean: Ministates in a Wider World*. New York: Praeger, 1984.

Astiz, Carlos A., ed. *Latin American International Politics: Ambitions, Capabilities and the National Interest of Mexico, Brazil and Argentina*. Notre Dame, IN: University of Notre Dame Press, 1969.

Atkins, G. Pope. *Latin America in the International Political System*. 3rd ed. Boulder, CO: Westview Press, 1995.

———, ed. *South America into the 1990s: Evolving International Relations in a New Era*. Boulder, CO: Westview Press, 1990.

Bailey, Norman A. *Latin America in World Politics*. New York: Walker and Co., 1967.

Bethel, Leslie, and Ian Roxborough, eds. *Latin America Between the Second World War and the Cold War*. New York: Cambridge University Press, 1992.

Biles, Robert E., ed. *Inter-American Relations: The Latin American Perspective*. Boulder, CO: Lynne Rienner, 1988.

Blasier, Cole. *The Giant's Rival: The USSR and Latin America*. rev. ed. Pittsburgh, PA: University of Pittsburgh Press, 1988.

Boersner, Demetrio. *Relaciones internacionales de América Latina. Breve historia*. 4th rev. ed. Caracas: Editorial Nueva Sociedad, 1990.

Braveboy-Wagner, Jacqueline A. *The Caribbean in World Affairs: The Foreign Policies of the English-Speaking States*. Boulder, CO: Westview Press, 1989.

Calvert, Peter. *The International Politics of Latin America*. Manchester, UK: Manchester University Press, 1994.

Cantori, Louis J., and Steven L. Spiegel. *The International Politics of Regions: A Comparative Approach*. 2nd ed. Englewood Cliffs, N.J.: Prentice-Hall, 1980.

Connell-Smith, Gordon. *The Inter-American System*. London: Oxford University Press, 1966.

Coter, Julio and Richard R. Fagen, eds. *Latin America and the United*

States: The Changing Political Realities. Stanford, CA: Stanford University Press, 1974.

Davis, Harold Eugene, John J. Finan, and F. Taylor Peck. *Latin American Diplomatic History: An Introduction.* Baton Rouge: Louisiana State University Press, 1977.

————, Larman C. Wilson, et al. *Latin American Foreign Policies: An Analysis.* Baltimore, MD: Johns Hopkins University Press, 1975.

Dent, David W., ed. *U.S.-Latin American Policymaking: A Reference Handbook.* Westport, CT: Greenwood Press, 1995.

Díaz Albónico, Rodrigo, ed. *Antecedentes, Balance y Perspectivas del Sistema Interamericano.* Santiago: Instituto de Estudios Internacionales, Universidad de Chile, 1978.

Drekonja, Gerhard K. and Juan G. Tokátlian, eds. *Teoría y Práctica de la política exterior Latinoamericana.* Bogotá: Universidad de los Andes, 1983.

Falk, Richard A., and Saul H. Mendlovitz, eds. *Regional Politics and World Order.* San Francisco, CA: Freeman and Co., 1973.

Farer, Tom J., ed. *The Future of the Inter-American System.* New York: Praeger, 1979.

Farell, R. Barry, ed. *América Latina y Canadá frente a la política exterior de los Estados Unidos.* México, D.F.: Fondo de Cultura Económica, 1975.

Ferris, Elizabeth G., and Jennie K. Lincoln, eds. *Latin American Foreign Policies: Global and Regional Dimensions.* Boulder, CO: Westview Press, 1981.

Fontaine, Roger W., and James D. Theberge, eds. *Latin America's New Internationalism: The End of Hemispheric Isolation.* New York: Praeger, 1976.

Gil, Federico G. *Latinoamérica y Estados Unidos.* Madrid: Editorial Tecnos, 1971.

Grabendorff, Wolf, and Riordan Roett, eds. *Latin America, Western Europe, and the United States.* New York: Praeger, 1985.

Grunwald, Joseph, ed. *Latin America and World Economy: A Changing International Order.* Beverly Hills, CA: Sage, 1978.

Haar, Jerry, and Edgar Dosman, eds. *A Dynamic Relationship: Canada's Changing Role in the Americas.* New Brunswick, NJ: Transaction Press, 1994.

Heine, Jorge, and Leslie F. Manigat, eds. *The Caribbean and World Politics: Cross Currents and Cleavages.* New York: Holmes and Meier, 1988.

Helman, Ronald G., and H. Jon Rosenbaum, eds. *Latin America: The Search for a New International Role.* New York: Halsted Press, 1975.

Hughes, G. Philip, and Georges Fauriol, eds. *U.S.-Caribbean Relations into the 21st Century.* Washington, D.C.: Center for Strategic and International Studies, 1995.

Ince, Basil, ed. *Contemporary International Relations of the Caribbean.* St. Augustine, Trinidad: Institute of International Relations, 1979.

Jaguaribe, Hélio. *El nuevo escenario internacional.* México, D.F.: Fondo de Cultura Económica, 1985.

Korzeniewicz, Patricio, and William C. Smith. *Latin America in the World Economy.* Westport, CT: Praeger, 1997.

Kryzanek, Michael J. *U.S.-Latin American Relations.* 3rd ed. Westport, CT: Praeger, 1996.

Lagos Matús, Gustavo, ed. *Las relaciones entre América Latina, Estados Unidos y Europa Occidental.* Santiago, Chile: Editorial Universitaria, 1980.

Lincoln, Jennie K., and Elizabeth G. Ferris, eds. *The Dynamics of Latin American Foreign Policies: Challenges for the 1980s.* Boulder, CO: Westview Press, 1984.

Lindenberg, Klaus, ed. *Latein Amerika: Herrschaft, Gewalt und internationale Abhängigkeit.* Bonn: Verlag Neue Gesellschaft, 1982.

Lowenthal, Abraham F., and Gregory F. Treverton, eds. *Latin America in a New World.* Boulder, CO: Westview Press, 1994.

Mace, Gordon, and Jean-Philippe Thérien, eds. *Foreign Policy and Regionalism in the Americas.* New Brunswick, NJ: Transaction Books, 1996.

Martz, John D., ed. *United States Policy in Latin America: A Quarter Century of Crisis and Challenge, 1961–1986.* Lincoln: University of Nebraska Press, 1988.

Millet, Richard, and W. Marvin Will, eds. *The Restless Caribbean: Changing Patterns of International Relations.* New York: Praeger, 1979.

Muñoz, Heraldo, and Joseph S. Tulchin, eds. *Latin American Nations in World Politics.* 2nd ed. Boulder, CO: Westview Press, 1996.

Parkinson, F. *Latin America, the Cold War, and the World Powers, 1945–1973.* Beverly Hills, CA: Sage, 1974.

Puig, Juan Carlos, ed. *América Latina: políticas exteriores comparadas.* Buenos Aires: Grupo Editor Latinoamericano, 1984.

Rojas Aravena, Francisco, ed. *América Latina y la iniciativa para las Américas.* Santiago de Chile: FLACSO, 1993.

Scheman, L. Ronald. *The Inter-American Dilemma: The Search for Inter-American Cooperation at the Centennial of the Inter-American System.* New York: Praeger, 1988.

El SELA: Presente y futuro de la cooperación económica intralatinoamericana. Buenos Aires: Instituto para la Integración de América Latina, Banco Interamericano de Desarrollo, 1986.

Stallings, Barbara, ed. *Global Change, Regional Response.* New York: Cambridge University Press, 1995.

Tomassini, Luciano, ed. *Relaciones internacionales de la América Latina.* México, D.F.: Fondo de Cultura Económica, 1981.

U.S. Congress. *Inter-American Relations: A Collection of Documents, Legislation, Descriptions of Inter-American Organizations, and Other Material Pertaining to Inter-American Affairs. Report Prepared for the Use of the Committee on Foreign Relations, United States Senate, and Committee on Foreign Affairs, U.S. House of Representatives by the Congressional Research Service, Library of Congress.* 100 Cong., 2nd sess. Washington, D.C.: Government Printing Office, 1989.

Varas, Augusto, ed. *Soviet-Latin American Relations in the 1980s.* New York: Praeger, 1987.

Wallace, Elisabeth. *The British Caribbean: From the Decline of Colonialism to the End of Federation.* Toronto: University of Toronto Press, 1977.

Wiarda, Howard J., ed. *Iberian-Latin American Connection: Implications for U.S. Foreign Policy.* Boulder, CO: Westview Press, 1986.

Williams, Edward J. *The Poltical Themes of Inter-American Relations.* Belmont, CA: Duxbury Press, 1971.

Wilson, Larman C. "Latin America in the World." In *Latin America, Its Problems and Its Promise: A Multidisciplinary Introduction.* 2nd ed, 256–273, edited by Jan Knippers Black. Boulder, CO: Westview Press, 1991.

Wood, Bryce. *The Dismantling of the Good Neighbor Policy.* Austin: University of Texas Press, 1985.

Ziring, Lawrence. *International Relations Dictionary.* Santa Barbara, CA: ABC-CLIO, 1995.

D. Bibliography and Reference

Ali, Sheikh R. *The International Organizations and World Order Dictionary.* Santa Barbara, CA: ABC-CLIO, Inc., 1992.

Arnold, Guy. *Historical Dictionary of Aid and Development Agencies.* Lanham, MD: The Scarecrow Press, Inc., 1996.

Atkins, G. Pope. *Encyclopedia of the Inter-American System.* Westport, CT: Greenwood Press, 1997.

Banks, Arthur S., ed. *Political Handbook of the World, 1995–96.* Binghamton, NY: CSA Publications, 1996.

Bennett, A. LeRoy. *Historical Dictionary of The United Nations.* Lanham, MD: The Scarecrow Press, Inc., 1995.

Bethel, Leslie, ed. *The Cambridge History of Latin America.* Vol. 6,

Latin America since 1930: Economy, Society and Politics and Vol. ll, *Bibliographical Essays*. New York: Cambridge University Press, 1995.

Boczek, Boleslaw Adam. *Historical Dictionary of International Tribunals*. Lanham, MD:The Scarecrow, Inc., Press, 1996.

Calvert, Peter, ed. *Political and Economic Encyclopedia of South America and the Caribbean*. London: Longman Group U.K. Limited, 1991.

Central Intelligence Agency (CIA). *The World Factbook 1995*. Langley, VA: Central Intelligence Agency, 1995.

Colas, Bernard, ed. *Global Economic Co-operation: A Guide to Agreements and Organizations*. 2nd rev. ed. Tokyo: United Nations University Press, 1994.

Collier, Simon, et al., eds. *Cambridge Encyclopedia of Latin America and the Caribbean*. 2nd ed. New York: Cambridge University Press, 1992.

Covington, Paula H., et al., eds. *Latin America and the Caribbean: A Critical Guide to Research Sources*. Westport, CT: Greenwood Press, 1992.

De Conde, Alexander, ed. *Encyclopedia of American Foreign Policy: Studies of the Principal Movements and Idea*. Vol. II. New York: Charles Scribner's Sons, 1978.

Delpar, Helen, ed. *Encyclopedia of Latin America*. New York: McGraw-Hill, Inc., 1974.

Dent, David W., ed. *Handbook of Political Science Research on Latin America: Trends From the 1960s to the 1990s*. Westport, CT: Greenwood Press, 1990.

Europa Publications Ltd. *South America, Central America and the Caribbean 1995*. 5th ed. London: Europa Publications, 1995.

Fenton, Thomas P., and Mary J. Heffron, eds. *Third World Resource Directory, 1994–1995*. New York: Orbis Books, 1994.

Figueroa Pla, Uldaricio. *Manual de Organismos Internacionales*. Santiago: Editorial Andrés Bello and Editorial Jurídica de Chile, 1989.

Finan, John J., and Jack Child, eds. *Latin America: International Relations: A Guide*. Detroit, MI: Gale Research Co., 1981.

Gipson, Carolyn R. *The McGraw-Hill Dictionary of International Trade and Finance*. New York: McGraw-Hill, 1993.

Grow, Michael. *Scholar's Guide to Washington, D.C. for Latin American and Caribbean Studies*. 2nd ed. Washington, D.C.: Smithsonian Institution Press, 1992.

Gunson, Phil, Greg Chamberlain, and Andrew Thompson, eds. *The Dictionary of Contemporary Politics of Latin America and the Caribbean*. New York: Simon and Schuster, 1991.

Hellman, Ronald G., and Beth Kempler Pfannl, eds. *Tinker Guide to*

Latin American and Caribbean Policy and Scholarly Resources in Metropolitan New York. New York: City University of New York, 1988.

Humphreys, Norman K. *Historical Dictionary of the International Monetary Fund.* Metuchen, MD: The Scarecrow Press, Inc., 1993.

Hunter, Brian, ed. *The Statesman's Year-Book 1995.* 132nd ed. New York: St. Martin's Press, 1995.

Institute for European-Latin American Relations. *Handbook for European-Latin American Relations.* 2 vols. Madrid: Institute for European-Latin American Relations, 1993.

Irvin, Linda, ed. *Encyclopedia of Associations: International Organizations.* 25th ed. Detroit, MI: Gale Research Co., 1991.

Janes, Robert W. *Scholar's Guide to Washington, D.C., for Peace and International Security Studies.* Washington, D.C.: The Woodrow Wilson Center Press, 1995.

Jentleson, Bruce W., and Thomas G. Paterson, senior eds. *Encyclopedia of U.S. Foreign Relations.* 4 vols. New York: Oxford University Press, 1997.

Kapteyn, P. J. G., and Board of Editors. *International Organization and Integration: Annotated Basic Documents and Descriptive Directory of International Organizations and Arrangements.* 2nd rev. ed. Boston, MA: Martinus Nijhoff, 1986.

Krieger, Joel, et al. *The Oxford Companion to Politics in the World.* New York: Oxford University Press, 1993.

Kurian, George T., ed. *Encyclopedia of the Third World.* 4th ed. 3 vols. New York: Facts on File, 1992.

Lawson, Edward, ed. *Encyclopedia of Human Rights.* Philadelphia, PA: Taylor and Francis Inc., 1994.

Loroña, Lionel V., ed. *A Bibliography of Latin American and Caribbean Bibliographies 1985–1989: Social Sciences and Humanities.* Metuchen, NJ: The Scarecrow Press, Inc., 1993.

Lux, William. *Historical Dictionary of the British Caribbean.* Metuchen, NJ: The Scarecrow Press, Inc., 1975.

Martin, Dolores Moyano, ed. *Handbook of Latin American Studies.* 2 vols. *Humanities* and *Social Sciences.* [alternating years] Austin: University of Texas Press, 1932–.

Mays, Terry. *Historical Dictionary of Multinational Peacekeeping.* Lanham, MD: The Scarecrow Press, Inc., 1996.

OAS. General Secretariat. Department of Material Resources. *The Directory of Inter-American and Other Associations in the Americas.* Washington, D.C.: OAS, 1986.

Osmanczyk, Edmund Jan, ed. *Encyclopedia of the United Nations and International Agreements.* Philadelphia, PA: Taylor and Francis Inc., 1995.

Owens, Richard. *"The Times" Guide to World Organizations: Their Role and Reach in the New World Order.* London: The Times, 1996.

Plano, Jack C., and Roy Olton, eds. *The International Relations Dictionary.* 4th ed. Santa Barbara, CA: ABC-CLIO, 1988.

Reed Information Services. *The International Yearbook and Statesmen's Who's Who 1995–1996.* 43rd ed. East Grinstead, UK: RIS, 1995.

Rengger, N. J. *Treaties and Alliances of the World.* 5th ed. London: Longman Group U.K. Limited, 1990.

Rosenberg, Jerry M. *Dictionary of International Trade.* New York: John Wiley & Sons, 1994.

Rossi, Ernest E., and Jack C. Plano. *Latin America: A Political Dictionary.* Santa Barbara, CA: ABC-CLIO, 1992.

Schiavone, Giuseppe. *International Organizations: A Dictionary and Directory.* 3rd ed. New York: St. Martin's Press, 1993.

Schraepler, Hans-Albrecht. *Directory of International Organizations.* Baltimore, MD: Georgetown University Press, 1996.

Seymore, Bruce II, ed. *International Affairs Directory of Organizations: The ACCESS Resource Guide.* Santa Barbara, CA: ABC-CLIO, 1992.

Shafritz, Jay M., Phil Williams, and Ronald S. Calinger. *The Dictionary of 20th-Century World Politics.* New York: Henry Holt and Co., 1993.

Tenenbaum, Barbara A., Ed.-in-Chief, et al. *Encyclopedia of Latin American History and Culture.* 5 vols. New York: Scribner and Sons, 1995.

Union of International Associations. *Yearbook of International Organizations, Vol. 1, 1995/96.* Munich, Germany: K.G. Saur, 1996.

Véliz, Claudio, ed. *Latin America and the Caribbean: A Handbook.* London: Anthony Blond, 1968.

Woods, Richard D. *Reference Materials on Latin America in English: The Humanities.* Metuchen, NJ: The Scarecrow Press, Inc., 1980.

II. Regional Organizations

A. The Organization of American States

1. General

a. Bibliographies

Sheinen, David. *The Organization of American States.* International Organizations Series, Vol. II. New Brunswick, NJ: Transaction Publishers, 1996.

Welch, Thomas L., and René Gutiérrez. *The Organization of American States: A Bibliography.* Washington, D.C.: Columbus Memorial Library, OAS, 1990.

b. General

Arciniegas, Germán, ed. *O.E.A.; La Suerte de una Institución Regional.* Bogotá, Colombia: Editorial Planeta, 1985.

Atkins, G. Pope. *Encyclopedia of the Inter-American System.* Westport, CT: Greenwood Press, 1997.

Ball, M. Margaret. *The OAS in Transition.* Durham, NC: Duke University Press, 1969.

Cho, Key Sung. *Organismos interamericanos; Sus antecedentes, estructuras, funciones y perspectivas.* Quito, Ecuador: Ediciones Culturales, 1984.

Connell-Smith, Gordon. *The Inter-American System.* London: Royal Institute of International Affairs, Oxford University Press, 1966.

Díaz Albónico, Rodrigo, ed. *Antecedentes, balance y perspectivas del Sistema Interamericano.* Santiago de Chile: Universidad de Chile, 1977.

Dreier, John C. *The Organization of American States and the Hemisphere Crisis.* New York: Council of Foreign Relations, Harper and Row, 1962.

Fenwick, Charles G. *The Inter-American Regional System.* Washington, D.C.: Kaufmann Printing, 1963.

Fernández-Shaw, Félix Guillermo. *La Organización de los Estados Americanos (O.E.A.); Una nueva visión de América.* 2nd ed. Madrid: Ediciones Cultura Hispánica, 1963.

Gregg, Robert W., ed. *International Organization in the Western Hemisphere.* Syracuse, NY: Syracuse University Press, 1968.

Han, Henry H. *Problems and Prospects of the Organization of American States: Perceptions of the Member States' Leaders.* New York: P. Lang, 1987.

Haverstock, Nathan A. *Organization of American States: The Challenge of the Americas.* New York: Coward-McCann, 1966.

Inter-American Dialogue. *The Inter-American Agenda and Multilateral Governance: The Organization of American States. A Report of the Inter-American Dialogue Study Group on Western Hemisphere Governance.* Washington, D.C.: Inter-American Dialogue, 1997.

Inter-American Institute of International Legal Studies. *The Inter-American System, Its Development and Strengthening.* Dobbs Ferry, NY: Oceana Publications, 1966.

Julien-Laferriere, François. *L'Organisation des Etats Américains.* Paris: Presses Universitaires de France, 1972.

Karen, Ruth. *Neighbors in a New World: The Organization of American States.* Cleveland, OH: World Publishing Co., 1966.

Kutzner, Gerhard. *Die Organisation der Amerikanischen Staaten (OAS).* Hamburg: Hansischer Gildenverlag, Heitmann, 1970.

Manger, William. *Pan America in Crisis: The Future of the OAS.* Washington, D.C.: Public Affairs Press, 1961.

OAS, General Secretariat. *Cumulative Analytical Index of the Volumes of Summaries of the Permanent Council, 1970–1986.* Washington, D.C.: OAS, 1987.

————. *Directory of Inter-American and Other Associations in the Americas.* Washington, D.C.: OAS, 1986.

————. "The First Century of the Inter-American System"/"El Primer Siglo del Sistema Interamericano," Special Issue: *Inter-American Review of Bibliography/Revista Interamericana de Bibliografía* 39, no. 4 (1989).

————. *The Inter-American System Through Treaties, Conventions and Other Documents / El Sistema Interamericano a Través de Tratados, Convenciones y Otros Documentos.* Parts I and II. Washington, D.C.: OAS, 1993.

————. *The OAS and the Evolution of the Inter-American System.* Washington, D.C.: OAS, 1981.

Penna Marinho, Ilmar. *O Funcionamento do Sistema Interamericano dentro de sistema mondial.* Rio de Janeiro: Livararia Freitas Bastos, S.A., 1959.

Scheman, L. Ronald. *The Inter-American Dilemma: The Search for Inter-American Cooperation at the Centennial of the Inter-American System.* New York: Praeger, 1988.

Sepúlveda, César. *El Sistema Interamericano; génesis, integración, decadencia.* México, D.F.: Editorial Porrúa, 1974.

Stoetzer, O. Carlos. *The Organization of American States.* 2nd ed. New York: Praeger, 1993.

Thomas, Ann Van Wynen and A. J. Thomas, Jr. *The Organization of American States.* Dallas, TX: Southern Methodist University Press, 1963.

U.S. Congress, Senate and House of Representatives. *Inter-American Relations: A Collection of Documents, . . ., Description of Inter-American Organizations, and Other Material Pertaining to Inter-American Affairs. Report Prepared for the Use of the Committee on Foreign Relations, United States Senate, and Committee on Foreign Affairs, U.S. House of Representatives by the Congressional Research Staff, Library of Congress,* 100th Cong., 2d sess. Joint Committee Print. Washington, D.C.: U.S. Government Printing Office, 1989.

Zanotti, Isidoro. *Organizacão dos Estados Americanos.* Rio de Janeiro: *Revista do Serviço Público*, 1948.

c. *Individual Countries*

(1) Argentina

Lanús, Juan Archibaldo. *De Chapultepec al Beagle: Política Exterior Argentina, 1945–1980.* Buenos Aires: Emece, 1984.

Milenky, Edward S. *Argentina's Foreign Policies.* Boulder, CO: Westview Press, 1978. Chap. 7. "Multilateral Diplomacy."

Peterson, Harold F. *Argentina and the United States, 1810–1960.* Albany: State University of New York Press, 1964.

Tulchin, Joseph S. *Argentina and the United States: A Conflicted Relationship.* Boston, MA: Twayne Publishers, 1990.

(2) Brazil

Santos, Ralph G. "Brazilian Foreign Policy and the Dominican Crisis: The Impact of History and Events." *Américas* 29 (July 1972): 62–77.

Selcher, Wayne A. *Brazil's Multilateral Relations: Between First and Third Worlds.* Boulder, CO: Westview Press, 1978.

Weis, W. Michael. *Cold Warriors and 'Coups d'etat': Brazilian-American Relations, 1945–1964.* Albuquerque: University of New Mexico Press, 1993.

(3) Canada

Dosman, Edgar J. "Canada and Latin America: the New Look." *International Journal* 47 (Summer 1992): 529–554.

Harbron, John D. *Canada and the Organization of American States.* Toronto: Canadian-American Committee, 1963.

Humphrey, John P. *The Inter-American System: A Canadian View.* Toronto: Macmillan Co. of Canada, 1942.

Rochlin, James. *Discovering the Americas: The Evolution of Canadian Foreign Policy Toward Latin America.* Vancouver: UBC Press, 1994.

Roussin, Marcel. *Le Canada et le système interaméricain.* Ottawa: Editions de l'Université d'Ottawa, 1959.

(4) The Caribbean

Braveboy-Wagner, Jacqueline Anne. *The Caribbean in World Affairs: The Foreign Policies of the English-Speaking States.* Boulder, CO: Westview Press, 1989.

Bryan, Anthony T., ed. *The Organization of American States and the Commonwealth Caribbean: Perspectives on Security, Crisis and Reform.* St. Augustine, Trinidad: Institute of International Relations, 1986.

Glasgow, Roy Arthur. "The Commonwealth Caribbean Countries." In *Latin American Foreign Policies: An Analysis,* edited by Harold E. Davis, and Larman C. Wilson, et al., 178–197. Baltimore, MD: Johns Hopkins University Press, 1975.

Maingot, Anthony P. "National Pursuits and Regional Definitions: The Caribbean as an Interest Area." In *Issues in Caribbean International Relations,* edited by Basil A. Ince, Anthony T. Bryan, Herb Addo, and Ramesh Ramsaran, 309–334. Lanham, MD: University Press of America, 1983.

(5) Central America

LaFebre, Walter. *Inevitable Revolutions: The United States in Central America.* 2nd ed. rev. New York: Norton and Co., 1993. Chapters II. "Maintaining the System," IV. "The Collapse of the System," and VI. "Rearranging the Remains of the System."

Morris, Michael A., and Víctor Millán, eds. *Controlling Latin American Conflicts: Ten Approaches.* Boulder, CO: Westview Press, 1983. Chapters 3. "Controlling Conflict in the Caribbean Basin: National Approaches" and 6. "The Latin American Economic System as a Mechanism to Control Conflicts."

(6) Colombia

Lleras Camargo, Alberto. "Posição da Colombia no Sistema Jurídico Interamericano." *Revista Brasileira de Política Internacional* 4 (March 1961): 5–16.

(7) Mexico

Castañeda, Jorge G. "Pan Americanism and Regionalism: A Mexican View." *International Organization* 10 (August 1956): 373–389.

Corominas, Enrique Venture. *México, Cuba y la OEA.* Buenos Aires: Ediciones Política, Economía y Finanzas, 1965.

Pellicer de Brody, Olga. "México en la OEA." *Foro Internacional* VI (October 1965–March 1966): 228–302.

Zoraida Vázquez, Josefina, and Lorenzo Meyer. *The United States and Mexico.* Chicago, IL: University of Chicago Press, 1985.

(8) United States

Brock, Lothar. *Entwicklungsnationalismus und Kompradorenpolitik; Die Gründung der OAS und die Entwicklung der Abhängigkeit Lateinamerikas von den USA.* Maisenheim am Glan, BRD: Verlag Anton Hain, 1975.

Connell-Smith, Gordon. *The United States and Latin America: An Historical Analysis of Inter-American Relations.* London: Heinemann Educational Books, 1974.

Farer, Tom J. *The United States and the Inter-American System: Are There Functions for the Forms?* St. Paul, MN: American Society of International Law, Studies in Transnational Legal Policy, No. 17, 1978.

Kurth, James R. "The Rise and Decline of the Inter-American System." In *Alternative to Intervention: A New U.S.-Latin American Security Relationship,* edited by Richard J. Bloomfield and Gregory F. Treverton, 9–25. Boulder, CO: Lynne Rienner Publishers, 1990.

Slater, Jerome. *The OAS and United States Foreign Policy.* Athens, OH: Ohio State University Press, 1967.

van Klavern, Alberto. "The United States and the Inter-American Political System." In *Latin American Views of U.S. Policy,* edited by Robert Wesson and Heraldo Muñoz, 20–40. New York: Praeger, 1986.

Wilson, Larman C. "Multilateral Policy and the Organization of American States: Latin American-U.S. Convergence and Divergence." In *Latin American Foreign Policies: An Analysis,* edited by Harold E. Davis, and Larman C. Wilson, et al., 47–84. Baltimore, MD: Johns Hopkins University Press, 1975.

———, and David W. Dent. "The United States and the OAS." In *U.S.-Latin American Policymaking: A Reference Handbook,* edited by David W. Dent, 24–44. Westport, CT: Greenwood Press, 1995.

(9) Venezuela

Cardozo, Hilarión. *Presencia de Venezuela en la OEA; June 1979–Octubre 1982.* Caracas: Ministerio de Relaciones Exteriores, 1982.

Ebel, Roland H., Raymond Taras, and James D. Cochrane. *Political Culture and Foreign Policy in Latin America; Case Studies from the Circum-Caribbean.* Albany: State University of New York, 1991. Chapter 4.

Liss, Sheldon B. *Diplomacy and Dependency: Venezuela, the United States, and the Americas.* Salisbury, NC: Documentary Publications, 1978.

2. Development of the Inter-American System and the Institutionalization of the OAS

a. Evolution of the Inter-American System: from Panamericanism to the OAS

Connell-Smith, Gordon. *The Inter-American System.* London: Royal Institute of International Affairs, Oxford University Press, 1966.

Cuevas Cancino, Francisco M. *Del Congreso de Panamá a la Conferencia de Caracas, 1826–1954; el genio de Bolívar a través de la historia de las relaciones interamericanas.* Caracas, Venezuela: Oficina Central de Información, 1976.

Dupuy, René Jean. *Le Nouveau Panamericanisme; l'evolution du système inter-Américain vers le fédéralisme.* Paris: Editions A. Pedone, 1956.

Fenwick, Charles G. *The Organization of American States: The Inter-American Regional System.* Washington, D.C.: Kaufmann Printing, 1963.

Inman, Samuel G. Edited by Harold E. Davis. *Inter-American Conferences 1826–1954: History and Problems.* Washington, D.C.: University Press of Washington, 1965.

Lleras Camargo, Alberto. *The Organization of American States: An Example for the World.* Lewisburg, PA: Bucknell University Press, 1954.

López Maldonado, Ulpiano. *Del Congreso de Panamá a la Conferencia de Caracas, 1826–1954. El genio de Bolívar a través de la historia de las relaciones interamericanas.* Quito, Ecuador: Imprenta del Ministerio de Educación, 1954.

Moreno Pino, Ismail. *Orígines y evolución del Sistema Interamericano.* México, D.F.: Colección del Archivo Histórico Diplomático Mexicano, Secretaría de Relaciones Exteriores, 1977.

Pike, Frederick B. *FDR's Good Neighbor Policy: Sixty Years of Generally Gentle Chaos.* Austin: University of Texas Press, 1995.

Puig, Juan Carlos. "Evolución histórica de la OEA: las tendencias profundas," *Mundo Nuevo* [Caracas] IX (April–December 1986): 17–175.

Tarragó, Rafael E. *Early U.S.-Hispanic Relations, 1776–1860. An Annotated Bibliography.* Metuchen, NJ: The Scarecrow Press, Inc., 1994.

Yepes, Jesús M. *Del Congreso de Panamá a la Conferencia de Caracas 1826–1954; el genio de Bolívar a través de la historia de las relaciones interamericanas.* Caracas: Talleres de Cromotip, 1955.

b. OAS Charter amendments and reforms and the future of the OAS

Arciniegas, Germán, ed. *O.E.A.; la suerte de una institución regional.* Bogotá, Colombia: Editorial Planeta, 1985.

Atkins, G. Pope. "Mutual Security in the Changing Inter-American System: An Appraisal of OAS Charter and Rio Treaty Revisions." *Military Issues Research Memorandum*, ACN 77029. Carlisle Barracks, PA: US Army War College, 26 July 1977.

Ball, Mary Margaret. "New Format, Old Problems: The Organization of American States Under Revised Charter." *SECOLAS Annals* 3 (March 1972): 24–36.

Betancur, Belisario. "El ideal Americanista y la remodelación de la O.E.A." In *O.E.A.; la suerte de una institución regional,* edited by Germán Arciniegas. Bogotá, Colombia: Editorial Planeta, 1985.

Bloomfield, Richard J., and Gregory Treverton, ed. *Alternative to Intervention: A New U.S.-Latin American Security Relationship.* Boulder, CO: Lynne Reinner Publishers, 1990.

Cho, Key Sung. *La organización de los Estados Americanos; su estructura actual y reformas.* Santiago de Chile: Instituto de Relaciones Internacionales, Universidad de Chile, 1972.

Dreier, John C. "New Wine and Old Bottles: The Changing Inter-American System." *International Organization* 22 (Spring 1968): 477–493.

Farer, Tom J., ed. *The Future of the Inter-American System.* New York: Praeger, 1979.

Feinberg, Richard E. *Summitry in the Americas: A Progress Report.* Washington, D.C.: Institute for International Economics, 1997.

Freitas, José João de Oliveira. *Carta da Organização dos Estados Americanos; Comentario.* Porto Alegre: Sulima, 1973.

Jova, Joseph John. "A Review of the Progress and Problems of the Organization of American States." *U.S. Department of State Bulletin* 65 (13 September 1971): 284–293.

Kunz, Joseph I. "The Bogotá Charter of the Organization of American States." *American Journal of International Law* 42 (1948): 568–589.

Kurth, James R. "The Rise and Decline of the Inter-American System: A U.S. View." In *Alternatives to Intervention: A New U.S.-Latin American Security Relationship,* edited by Richard J. Bloomfield and Gregory F. Treverton, 9–25. Boulder, CO: Lynne Reinner Publishers, 1990.

Llosa, Jorge Guillermo. *La reestructuración del Sistema Interamericano (Carta de la OEA-TIAR); Intervenciones en la Comisión Especial para Estudiar el Sistema Interamericano y Proponer Medidas para su Reestructuración (CEESI).* Lima, Peru: Ministerio de Relaciones Exteriores, 1982.

McComie, Val T. *La reforma de la OEA desde la perspectiva del Caribe de habla inglesa.* Washington, D.C.: OAS, October 1985.

Manger, William. "Reform of the OAS: The 1967 Buenos Aires Protocol of Amendment to the 1948 Charter of Bogotá: An appraisal." *Journal of Inter-American Studies* 10 (January 1968): 1–14.

Molineu, Harold. "The Inter-American System: Searching for a New Framework." *Latin American Research Review* 29 (1994): 215–226.

Monroy Cabra, and Marco Gerardo. *La reforma del Sistema Interamericano.* Bogotá: Pontificia Universidad Católica Javeriana, 1986.

Mora Otero, José A. *From Panama to Punta del Este: Past Experience and Future Prospects, 1956–1968.* Washington, D.C.: OAS, 1968.

Muñoz, Heraldo. "A Latin American View." In *Alternatives to Intervention: A New U.S.-Latin American Security Relationship*, edited by Richard J. Bloomfield and Gregory F. Treverton, 27–37. Boulder, CO: Lynne Reinner Publishers, 1990.

———. "A New OAS for the New Times." In *Latin America in a New World*, edited by Abraham F. Lowenthal and Gregory F. Treverton, 191–202. Boulder, CO: Westview Press, 1994.

Orfila, Alejandro. *The Americas in the 1980's: An Agenda for the Decade Ahead.* Lanham, MD: University Press of America, 1980.

OAS, General Secretariat, Permanent Council. *Charter of the Organization of American States: As Amended by the Protocol of Buenos Aires in 1967, by the Protocol of Cartagena de Indias in 1985 and by the Protocol of Managua in 1993.* OEA/Ser.G CP/INF.3964/96 16 May 1996. Washington, D.C.: OAS, 1996.

———. *An International Partnership in Support of Representative Democracy, Sustainable Development, and Hemispheric Integration.* Washington, D.C.: OAS, 1996.

———. *A New Vision of the OAS.* Washington, D.C.: OAS, April 1995.

———. *Report of the Permanent Council on Amendments to the OAS.* And *Observations by . . . [nine states].* Sixteenth Special Session of the General Assembly on Charter Amendments, December 15, 1992. Washington, D.C.: OAS, 1992.

Orrego Vicuña, Francisco. "La búsqueda de un nuevo papel para la Organización de los Estados Americanos. El Protocolo de Reformas de la Carta de 1985." *Estudios Internacionales* [Santiago, Chile] 20 (January–March 1987): 70–87.

Perina, Rubén. "Is There any Future for the Interamerican System?" *Inter-American Review of Bibliography/Revista Interamericana de Bibliografía* 31, no. 1 (1981): 70–75.

Rodríguez, Celso, ed. "El Primer Siglo del Sistema Interamericano"/ "The First Century of the Inter-American System." Special Issue: *Revista Interamericana de Bibliografía/Inter-American Review of Bibliography* 39, no. 4 (1989).

Roldan Acosta, Eduardo E. "Bibliografía selecta sobre la reestructuración de la O.E.A." *Relaciones Internacionales* [México, D.F.] 4 (January–March 1976): 113–117.

Rosenberg, Robin and Steve Stein. *Advancing the Miami Process: Civil Society and the Summit of the Americas.* Miami, FL: North-Center Press, 1995.

Scheman, L. Ronald. "Institutional Reform in the Organization of American States, 1975–1983: A Case Study in Problems of International Cooperation." *Public Administration and Development* 7 (April–June 1987): 215–236.

Stoetzer, O. Carlos. *The Organization of American States.* 2nd ed. New York: Praeger, 1993. Chapters 7. "The Road toward the Revision of the Charter," 8. "The Revised Charter and the New Structure of the OAS," and 9. "The Last Two Decades and the Protocol of Cartegena de Indias (1970–1991)."

U.S. Congress, House of Representatives. *The Role of the Organization of American States in the 1990s: Hearing before the Subcommittees on Human Rights and International Organizations, and on Western Hemisphere Affairs of the Committee on Foreign Affairs.* Vols. 1 and 2. 100st Cong., 1st and 2nd sessions, July 12, 1989 and May 1, 1990. Washington, D.C.: Government Printing Office, 1989–1990.

Vaky, Viron P., and Heraldo Muñoz. *The Future of the Organization of American States.* New York: Twentieth Century Fund, 1993.

Wilson, Larman C. "The Concept of Collective Economic Security for Development and Contemporary Latin American-U.S. Relations." *Towson State Journal of International Affairs* 12 (Fall 1977): 7–41.

3. The OAS and the United Nations

Canyes, Manuel. *The Organization of American States and the United Nations.* 5th ed. Washington, D.C.: Pan American Union, 1960.

Claude, Inis L., Jr. "The OAS, the U.N., and the United States." *International Conciliation* 547 (March 1964).

Gómez Robledo, Antonio. *Las Naciones Unidas y el Sistema Interamericano; conflictos jurisdiccionales.* México, D.F.: El Colegio de México, 1974.

Herrero de la Fuente, Alberto. *Seguridad colectiva y arreglo pacífico de controversias; dos sistemas en presencia, O.N.U. y O.E.A.* Valladolid, España: Universidad de Valladolid, 1973.

Levin, Aida Luisa. *The Organization of American States and the United Nations: Relations in the Peace and Security Field.* New York: United Nations Institute for Training and Research, 1974.

MacDonald, R. St. John. "The Developing Relationship between Superior and Sub-ordinate Political Bodies at the International Level: A Note on the Experience of the United Nations and the Organization of American States," In *Canadian Yearbook of International Law, II, 1964,* 21–54. Vancouver: University of British Columbia Press, 1965.

Moreno Guerra Luis. *ONU y OEA: Relaciones en el Ámbito del mantenimiento de la paz y la seguridad Internacional.* Quito: Editorial Universitaria, Universidad Central de Ecuador, 1975.
OAS, General Secretariat, General Assembly. *Cooperation between the OAS and the United Nations: Report by the Secretary General to the Twenty-Third General Assembly.* OEA/Ser. P, AG/doc 2930. Washington, D.C.: OAS, May 6, 1993.
Ruda, José M. "Relaciones de la O.E.A. y las N.U. en cuanto al mantenimiento de la paz y la seguridad internacional." *Revista Jurídica de Buenos Aires* I–II (January–June 1961): 15–76.
Scheman, L. Ronald. *The Inter-American Dilemma: The Search for Inter-American Cooperation at the Centennial of the Inter-American System.* New York: Praeger, 1988. Chapter 6. "The OAS and the United Nations: Regionalism Reconsidered."

4. Major Organs and Structure, Secretary-General, Budget and Membership

a. Organs and Structure

Baquero Lazcano, Emilio. *La Unión Panamericana, Actual Secretaría de la O.E.A.; Origin, evolución, régimen actual.* Córdoba, Argentina: Imprenta de la Universidad, 1956.
Canyes, Manuel. *The Meetings of Consultation: Their Origin, Significance and Role in Inter-American Relations.* 3rd ed. Washington, D.C.: OAS, 1966.
Dreier, John C. "The Council of the OAS: Performance and Potential." *Journal of Inter-American Studies* 5 (July 1963): 197–312.
Gannon, Francis X. "The Tenth General Assembly: Optimistic Soundings for the Hemisphere." *Américas* 33 (March 1981): 50–54.
Guerrant, Edward O. "The Council of the Organization of American States: Watchdog of the Hemisphere." *World Affairs Quarterly* V (January 1956): 387–397.
Meek, George. "First General Assembly." *Américas* 23 (June/July 1971): 2–7.
Stoetzer, O. Carlos. *The Organization of American States.* 2nd ed. New York: Praeger, 1993. Chapters 4. "The OAS (1948 through 1967–1970): The Inter-American Conference, the Meeting of Consultation of Ministers of Foreign Affairs, and the Council of the OAS" and 5. "The OAS (1948 through 1967–1970): The Pan American Union."
Vaky, Viron P. "Obstacles and Dilemmas Confronting the OAS" and "Organizational Structure of the OAS." In *The Future of the Organization of American States,* edited by Viron P. Vaky and Heraldo Muñoz, 31–47, 115–118. New York: Twentieth Century Fund, 1993.

b. Secretary-General

Caminos, Hugo, and Roberto Lavalle. "New Departures in the Exercise of Inherent Powers by the UN and OAS Secretaries General: The Central American Situation." *American Journal of International Law* 83 (April 1989): 395–402.

Gómez Berges, Víctor. *Solo al Verdad; historia de las elecciones para secretario general de la Organización de los Estados Americanos en 1975.* Ciudad de Vaticano: Tipografía Poliglota Vaticana, 1985.

Grayson, George W., Jr. "New Leadership for the O.A.S." *Current History* 56 (January 1969): 19–24, 52.

"Opiniones de Ilustrados Internacionalistas Centroamericanos a propósito de la OEA y su Nuevo Secretario General." *Revista Conservadora Pensamiento Centroamericano* 19 (August 1968): 15–32.

Posado, Jaime. "Alberto Lleras y la OEA." *Correo de los Andes* [Bogotá] 33 (August/September 1985): 76–80.

Sims, Winston S. *The Public Role of the Secretary-General of the Organization of American States in Political-Security Matters.* Pittsburgh, PA: University of Pittsburgh Press, 1969.

c. Budget and Finance

OAS, General Secretariat. *The Organization of American States. Report Submitted by the Pan American Union to the Eleventh Inter-American Conference.* Prepared for conference never held. Washington, D.C.: Pan American Union, 1959.

———. *Program-Budget of the Organization for the 1994–95 Biennium 1994 Quotas and Pledges to the Voluntary Funds.* OEA/Ser. P, AG/doc 3033/93, June 11, 1993. Washington, D.C.: OAS, 1993.

Scheman, L. Ronald. "Institutional Reform in the Organization of American States, 1975–1987: A Case Study in Problems of International Cooperation." *Public Administration and Development* 7 (April–June 1987): 215–236.

———. "Rebuilding the OAS: A Program for its Second Century." *Inter-American Review of Bibliography* 39 (1989): 527–534.

d. Membership

Bunker, Ellsworth. "First Special Inter-American Conference Provides for Admission of New Members to Organization of American States." *U.S. Department of State Bulletin* 52 (11 January 1965): 46–49.

Gobbi, Hugo J. *Admisión y Exclusión de Miembros en la OEA.* Buenos Aires: Bibliográfica Omeba, 1966.

Kim, Jung-Gun. "Nonmember Participation in the Organization of American States." *Journal of Inter-American Studies* 10 (April 1968): 194–212.

Scheman, L. Ronald. "Admission of States to the Organization of American States." *American Journal of International Law* 58 (October 1964): 968–974.

5. Collective Security

American Foreign Policy Institute. *Argentina, OAS and Hemisphere Security*. Washington, D.C.: American Foreign Policy Institute, 1979.

Barliant, Ronald. "The OAS Peace and Security System." *Stanford Law Review* 21 (May 1969): 1156–1203.

Bethell, Leslie, and Ian Roxborough, eds. *Latin America Between the Second World War and the Cold War, 1944–1948*. New York: Cambridge University Press, 1992.

Bloomfield, Richard J., and Gregory F. Treverton, eds. "Collective Security in the Americas: New Directions." Appendix in *Alternative to Intervention: A New U.S.-Latin American Security Relationship*. Boulder, CO: Lynne Rienner Publishers, 1990.

Brana-Shute, Gary. "The Regional Security System (RSS)." In *Beyond Praetorianism: The Latin American Military in Transition*, edited by Richard L. Millett and Michael Gold-Biss, 83–101. Boulder, CO: Westview Press, 1996.

Bryan, Anthony T. "Changes in Western Hemispheric Security: A Caribbean Perspective." In *Evolving U.S. Strategy for Latin America and the Caribbean*, edited by L. Erik Kjonnerod. Washington, D.C.: National Defense University Press, 1992.

Buzan, Barry, Ole Waever, and Jaap de Wilde. *Security: A New Framework for Analysis*. Boulder, CO: Lynne Rienner, 1997.

Calvert, Peter, ed. *The Central American Security System: North/South or East/West?* Cambridge, UK: Cambridge University Press, 1988.

Carter, Ashton B., William J. Perry, and John D. Steinbruner. *A New Concept of Cooperative Security*. Washington, D.C.: Brookings Institution, 1992.

Child, Jack. "Present Trends in the Interamerican Security System and the Role of the Rio Treaty." In *Anuario Jurídico Interamericano 1983*, OAS, General Secretariat, 43–82. Washington, D.C.: OAS, 1984.

Damrosch, Lori Fisler, and David J. Scheffer, eds. *Law and Force in the New International Order*. Boulder, CO: Under auspices of American Society of International Law by Westview Press, 1991. Part Two on "Collective Security."

Domb, M. "Defining Economic Aggression in International Law: Possibility of Regional Action by the Organization of American States." *International Law Journal* 11, no. 1 (1978): 85–105.

Downes, Richard. "Security: Emerging Patterns of Security Cooperation in the Western Hemisphere." *North-South Issues* V, no. 1 (1996).

Duggan, Laurence. *The Americas: The Search for Hemisphere Security.* New York: H. Holt and Co., 1949.

Farer, Tom J. "The Role of Regional Collective Arrangements." In *Collective Security in a Changing World,* edited by Thomas G. Weiss, 153–188. Boulder, CO: Lynne Rienner Publishers, 1993.

Fauriol, Georges, ed. *Security in the Americas.* Washington, D.C.: National Defense University Press, 1989.

García Amador, Francisco V. "El TIAR: Génesis, desarrollo y crisis de un sistema regional de seguridad colectiva." In *Anuario Jurídico Interamericano 1983,* OAS, General Secretariat, 3–42. Washington, D.C.: OAS, 1984.

García Muñiz, Humberto, and Betsaida Velez Natal. *Bibliografía militar del Caribe.* Rio Peidras, PR: Center for Historical Investigation, University of Puerto Rico, 1992.

Gómez Robledo, Antonio. "El Protocolo de Reformas al Tratado Interamericano de Asistencia Recíproca." *Foro Internacional* 17 (January/March 1977): 338–357.

———. *La Seguridad colectiva en el Continente Americano.* México, D.F.: Escuela Nacional de Ciencias Políticas y Sociales, Universidad Nacional Autónoma de Mexico, 1960.

Griffith, Ivelaw L. "Caribbean Security: Retrospect and Prospect." *Latin American Research Review* 30, no. 2 (1995): 3–32.

———. *The Quest for Security in the Caribbean: Problems and Promises in Subordinate States.* Armonk, NY: M.E. Sharpe, 1993.

———. "Security for Development: Caribbean-Asia Pacific Regional Mechanisms." In *The Caribbean in the Pacific Century,* edited by Jacqueline Braveboy-Wagner, W. Marvin Will, Dennis J. Gayle, and Ivelaw L. Griffith, 101–126. Boulder, CO: Lynne Rienner Publishers, 1993.

Jagan, Jeddi. *My Fight for Guyana's Freedom.* NY: International Publishers, 1966.

Klepak, H. P., ed. *Canada and Latin American Security.* Laval, Quebec: Meridien, 1993.

Kunz, Josef L. "The Idea of 'Collective Security' in Pan-American Developments." *Western Political Quarterly* 6 (December 1953): 658–679.

Lewis, Gary. "The Prospects for a Regional Security System in the Eastern Caribbean." *Millenium: Journal of International Studies* 15, no. 1 (1986): 73–90.

Llosa, Jorge Guillermo. "La defensa política del continente y la seguridad económica colectiva." In *Anuario Jurídico Interamericano 1983*, OAS, General Secretariat, 83–102. Washington, D.C.: OAS, 1984.

Marchand Stens, Luis. *Sistema Interamericano de Seguridad y de Paz.* Lima: Ediciones Peruanas, 1966.

Mercado Jarrín, Edgardo. *Un sistema de seguridad y defensa sudamericano.* Lima: CEPEI, 1989.

Millett, Richard L., and Michael Gold-Biss. *Beyond Praetorianism: The Latin American Military in Transition.* Coral Gables, FL: North-South Center Press, 1996.

Morris, Michael A. *Caribbean Maritime Security.* London: Macmillan, 1994.

OAS, Consejo Permanente, Comisión sobre Seguridad Hemisférica. *Aporte a un nuevo concepto de seguridad hemisférica y seguridad cooperativa.* Washington, D.C.: OAS, May 1993.

OAS, General Secretariat. *Inter-American Treaty of Reciprocal Assistance: Applications, Volume I 1948–1959; Volume II 1960–1972.* 3rd ed. Washington, D.C.: OAS, 1973.

———. *Volume III 1973–1976.* 3rd ed. Washington, D.C.: OAS, 1977.

———. *Supplement, Part II 1977–1981.* Washington, D.C.: OAS, 1982.

Painter, David S. "Collective Security and the Inter-American System." In *Historical Issues.* Washington, D.C.: Office of the Historian, Bureau of Public Affairs, Department of State Pub. 9511, November 1986.

Perry, William, and Max Primorac. "The Inter-American Security Agenda." *Journal of Inter-American Studies and World Affairs* 36 (Fall 1994): 111–127.

Rodríguez Beruff, Jorge, and Humberto García Muñiz, eds. *Security Problems and Policies in the Post-Cold War Caribbean.* Basingstoke, UK: Macmillan, 1996.

Ronning, C. Neale. *Punta del Este: The Limits of Collective Security in a Troubled Hemisphere.* New York: Carnegie Endowment for International Peace, 1962.

Slater, Jerome. *A Reevaluation of Collective Security: The OAS in Action.* Athens: Ohio State University Press, 1965.

Somavía, Juan, and José Miguel Insulza. *Seguridad democrática regional: Una concepción alternativa.* Caracas: Nueva Sociedad, 1990.

Stark, Jeffery. "Democratization: Rethinking Security in the Americas." *North/South Issues* (September, 1992).

Stoetzer, O. Carlos. *The Organization of American States.* 2nd ed. New York: Praeger, 1993. Chapter 12. "The OAS and Peace and Security."

Varas, Augusto. "From Coercion to Partnership: A New Paradigm for Security Cooperation in the Western Hemisphere." In *The United States and Latin America in the 1990s: Beyond the Cold War*, edited by Jonathan Hartlyn, Lars Schoultz, and Augusto Varas, 46–63. Chapel Hill: University of North Carolina Press, 1992.

Villagrán de León, Francisco. *The OAS and Regional Security.* Washington, D.C.: U.S. Institute of Peace, 1993.

Weiss, Thomas G., ed. *Collective Security in a Changing World.* Boulder, CO: Lynne Rienner Publishers, 1993.

Wilson, Larman C. "The Concept of Collective Economic Security for Development and Contemporary Latin American-U.S. Relations." *Towson State Journal of International Affairs* 12 (Fall 1977): 7–41.

Zacher, Mark W. *International Conflicts and Collective Security, 1946–77: The United Nations, Organization of American States, Organization of African Unity, and Arab League.* New York: Praeger Publishers, 1979. Chapters 1. "Collective Security: Background, Theory and Research Design" and 3. "The Organization of American States and Inter-American Conflicts."

6. Conflict Resolution: Peaceful Settlement and Peacemaking

a. Bibliography

Fermann, Gunnar. *Bibliography on International Peacekeeping.* Dordrecht, The Netherlands: Martinus Nijhoff, 1992.

Jones, Peter. *Peacekeeping: An Annotated Bibliography.* Kingston, ON: Frye, 1989.

Mays, Terry. *Historical Dictionary of Multinational Peacekeeping.* Lanham, MD: The Scarecrow Press, Inc., 1996.

b. General

Barrera Reyes, Arturo. *O.E.A., la Organización de los Estados Americanos: Medios pacíficos para la solución de conflictos interamericanos.* México, D.F.: Universidad Nacional Autónoma de México, 1955.

Brandt, Niels. *Das Interamerikanische Friedensystem; Idee und Wirklichkeit.* Hamburg: Hansischer Gildenverlag, 1971.

Butterworth, Robert L. *Moderation from Management: International Organizations and Peace.* Pittsburgh, PA: Center for International Studies, University of Pittsburgh, 1978. Chap. 4. "Regional Experiences: The Organization of American States."

Gerold, Rainer. *Die Sicherung des Friedens durch die Organisation der Amerikanischen Staaten (OAS).* Berlin: Duncker und Humbolt, 1971.

Krieg, William L. *Peaceful Settlement of Disputes through the Organization of American States: Development and Outlook. Report Pre-*

pared for the U.S. Department of State. Washington, D.C.: Office of External Research, Bureau of Intelligence and Research, 1974.

Lagos, Enrique. "Los nuevos mecanismos procesales para la eficacia de la solución pacífica de las controversias, con particular referencia a la práctica de la O.E.A. en los últimos años." In *Perspectivas del Derecho Internacional Contemporáneo. Experiencias y visión de América Latina.* V. 2, edited by Francisco Orrego Vicuña and J. Irigoin Barrene, 81–93. Santiago de Chile: Instituto de Estudios Internacionales, Universidad de Santiago, 1981.

Martz, Mary Jeanne Reid. "OAS Reform and the Future of Pacific Settlement." *Latin American Research Review* 12, no. 2 (1977): 176–186.

Montgomery, Tommie Sue, ed. *Peacemaking and Democratization in the Western Hemisphere.* Miami, FL: North-South Center Press, 1997.

Pan American Union, Inter-American Peace Committee. *Report of the Inter-American Peace Committee to the Second Special Inter-American Conference on the Activities of the Committee since the Tenth Inter-American Conference 1954–1965.* Washington, D.C.: OAS, 1965.

Pathmanathan, Murugesu. *The Pacific Settlement of Disputes in Regional Organizations: A Comparative Perspective of the OAS, OAU, and ASEAN.* Kuala Lumpur, Malaysia: Antara Book Co., 1978.

Scheman, L. Ronald, and John W. Ford. "The Organization of American States as Mediator." In *International Mediation in Theory and Practice,* edited by Saadia Touval and I. William Zartman, 197–232. Boulder, CO: Westview Press, 1985.

Zelaya Coronado, Jorge L. "Regional Negotiations: OAS Negotiations." In *Multilateral Negotiation and Mediation: Instruments and Methods,* edited by Arthur S. Lall, 17–31. New York: International Peace Academy, Pergamon Press, 1985.

c. The Caribbean

(1) The Dominican Civil War (after U.S. intervention)

Brown-John, C. Lloyd. "Economic Sanctions: The Case of the O.A.S. and the Dominican Republic, 1960–1962." *Caribbean Studies* 15 (July 1975): 73–105.

Carey, John, ed. *The Dominican Republic Crisis 1965: Background Paper and Proceedings of the Ninth Hammarskjöld Forum.* Dobbs Ferry, NY: Published for The Association of the Bar of the City of New York by Oceana Publications, 1967.

Estrella, Julio C. *La revolución dominicana y la crisis de la OEA.* Santo Domingo, RD: Revista AHORA, 1965.

Fulbright, J. William. "The Situation in the Dominican Republic—Compliance with the Law." *Vital Speeches* 31 (October 1, 1965): 747–755.

Gleijeses, Piero. *The Dominican Crisis: The 1965 Constitutionalist Revolt and American Intervention.* Baltimore, MD: Johns Hopkins University Press, 1978.

Jose, James R. *An Inter-American Peace Force within the Framework of the Organization of American States: Advantages, Impediments, Implications.* Metuchen, NJ: The Scarecrow Press, Inc., 1970.

Lowenthal, Abraham F. *The Dominican Intervention.* Cambridge, MA: Harvard University Press, 1972.

Palmer, Bruce, Jr. *Intervention in the Caribbean: The Dominican Crisis of 1965.* Lexington: University of Kentucky Press, 1989.

PAU, General Secretariat, Tenth Meeting of Consultation of Ministers of Foreign Affairs. *Official Documents.* OAS/Ser. F/II.10, 1965–1966. Washington, D.C.: OAS, 1966.

————. *Report of the Secretary-General of the Organization of American States Regarding the Dominican Situation: Activities from April 29, 1965, until the Installment of Provisional Government.* Document 405, November 1, 1965. Washington, D.C.: OAS, 1965.

Schreiber, Anna P., and Philippe S. E. Schreiber. "The Inter-American Commission on Human Rights in the Dominican Crisis." *International Organization* 22 (Winter 1968): 508–529.

Shiv Kumar, Vaidyanathan. *US Interventionism in Latin America: The Dominican Republic and the OAS.* New York: Advent Books, 1987.

Slater, Jerome. *Intervention and Negotiation: The United States and the Dominican Revolution.* New York: Harper & Row, 1970.

————. "The Limits of Legitimation in International Organizations: The Organization of American States and the Dominican Crisis." *International Organization* 23 (Winter 1969): 48–72.

Wilson, Larman C. "Estados Unidos y la guerra civil dominicana." *Foro Internacional* [Mexico City] 8 (October–December, 1967): 155–178.

————. "La intervención de los Estados Unidos de América en el Caribe: la crisis de 1965 en la República Dominicana." *Revista de Política Internacional* [Madrid] 122 (July–August 1972): 37–82.

(2) Haitian Coup and Suppression

Acevedo, Domingo E. "The Haitian Crisis and the OAS Response: A Test of Effectiveness in Protecting Democracy." In *Enforcing Restraint: Collective Intervention in Internal Conflicts*, edited by Lori

Fisler Damrosch, 119–155. New York: Council on Foreign Relations Press, 1993.

Cerna, Cristina. "The Case of Haiti before the Organization of American States." In *Proceedings of the 86th Annual Meeting*, American Society of Inernational Law, 378–383. Washington, D.C.: ASIL, 1992.

"The Diplomacy of the Haiti Crisis." In *Haitian Frustrations: Dilemmas for U.S. Policy: A Report of the CSIS Program,* edited by Georges A. Fauriol, 204–210. Washington, D.C.: Center for Strategic & International Studies, 1995.

Facio, Gonzalo. *The Haitian Crisis Is Testing the Democratic Will of the OAS: Special Report.* Washington, D.C.: Council for Inter-American Security Foundation, 1992.

Fauriol, Georges A. *The Haitian Challenge: U.S. Policy Considerations.* Washington, D.C.: Center for Strategic & International Studies, 1993.

———, and Andrew S. Faiola. "Prelude to Intervention." In *Haitian Frustrations: Dilemmas for U.S. Policy,* edited by Georges A. Fauriol, 103–116. Washington, D.C.: Center for Strategic & International Studies, 1995.

Harvard Center for Population Studies. *Sanctions in Haiti: Crisis in Humanitarian Action.* Cambridge, MA: Program on Humanitarian Security Working Paper Series, November 1993.

Horblitt, Stephen. "Multilateral Policy: The Road toward Reconciliation." In *The Haitian Challenge: U.S. Policy Considerations*, edited by Georges A. Fauriol, 67–80. Washington, D.C.: Center for Strategic and International Studies, 1993.

Martin, Ian. "Haiti: Mangled Multilateralism." *Foreign Policy* 95 (Summer 1994): 72–89.

OAS, Asamblea General. *Cumplimiento de la Resolución AG/Res. 1199 (XXII-0/92) "Cooperación Entre la OEA y los Sistemas de Naciones Unidas. Misión Civil Internacional OEA/ONU en Haiti."* OEA/Ser.P AG/doc.2930/93 add.2 9 junio 1993. Washington, D.C.: OAS, 1993.

———, Permanent Council. *Report of the Secretary General to the Ad Hoc Meeting of Ministers of Foreign Affairs on Haiti.* MRE/doc. 6/93. Washington, D.C.: OAS, June 1993.

———, ———. Ad Hoc Meeting of Ministers of Foreign Affairs. *Support of the Democratic Government of Haiti: Resolution of October 3, 1991* MRE/Res. 1/91 and *Support for Democracy in Haiti: Resolution of Oct. 8, 1991* MRE/Res. 2/91. Washington, D.C.: OAS, October 1991.

Perusse, Roland I. *Haitian Democracy Restored, 1991–1995.* Lanham, MD: University Press of America, 1995.

Pezzullo, Lawrence. "The Challenge of the Negotiation Process." In *Haitian Frustrations: Dilemmas for U.S. Policy,* edited by Georges

A. Fauriol, 98–102. Washington, D.C.: Center for Strategic & International Studies, 1995.

Schulz, Donald E., and Gabriel Marcella. *Reconciling the Irreconcilable: The Troubled Outlook for U.S. Policy toward Haiti.* Carlisle, PA: Strategic Studies Institute, U.S. Army War College, 1994.

Taft-Morales, Maureen. "Haiti: Efforts to Restore President Aristide, 1991–1994." *CRS Report for Congress.* Washington, D.C.: Congressional Research Service, Library of Congress, 1995.

Tardieu, Jerry. *Embargo sur Haiti: les premieres consequences; suggestions pour l'apres-crise.* Port-au-Prince, Haiti: Jerry Tardieu, 1992.

U.S. Atlantic Command. *Operation Uphold Democracy: Joint After Action Report.* Norfolk, VA: U.S. Atlantic Command, June 29, 1995.

U.S. President. *Update of Events in Haiti ('Uphold Democracy'): Communication from the President of the United States Transmitting an Update of Events in Haiti Consistent with the War Powers Resolution to Ensure that the Congress is Kept Fully Informed Regarding Events in Haiti.* Washington, D.C.: Government Printing Office, 1995.

Wilson, Larman C. "The Organization of American States and the Haitian Political Experience." In *The Haitian Challenge: U.S Policy Consideration,* edited by Georges A. Fauriol, 39–48. Washington, D.C.: Center for Strategic & International Studies, 1993.

d. Central America

(1) The Soccer War

Anderson, Thomas P. *The War of the Dispossessed: Honduras and El Salvador, 1969.* Lincoln: University of Nebraska Press, 1981.

Carías, Marco Virgilio, Daniel Slutzky, et al. *La Guerra Inútil. (Análisis socio-económico del conflicto entre Honduras y El Salvador).* Colección Seis. San José, Costa Rica: Editorial Universitaria Centroamericana (EDUCA), 1971. OAS role on pp. 314–318, 154–160, and 331–335.

Martz, Mary Jeanne Reid. *The Central American Soccer War: Historical Patterns and Internal Dynamics of OAS Settlement Procedures.* Athens: Ohio University Center for International Studies, Latin America Program, 1978.

OAS, General Secretariat. *Inter-American Treaty of Reciprocal Assistance: Applications Volume II 1960–1972.* 3rd ed. Washington, D.C.: OAS, 1973, 269–364.

Rowles, James P. *El conflicto Honduras-El Salvador: y el orden Jurídico Internacional (1969).* Colección Seis. San José, CR: Editorial Universitaria Centroamericana, 1980.

(2) The Central American/Contadora Peace Process

Adams, Jan S. *A Foreign Policy in Transition: Moscow's Retreat from Central America and the Caribbean, 1985–1992.* Durham, NC: Duke University Press, 1992.

Arias Sánchez, Oscar. *El camino de la paz.* San José, Costa Rica: Editorial Costa Rica, 1989.

Arnson, Cynthia J. *Crossroads: Congress, the President, and Central America, 1976–1993.* 2nd ed. University Park: Pennsylvania State University Press, 1993.

———. *Negotiating Peace: A Guatemala Conference Report.* Washington, D.C.: Woodrow Wilson International Center for Scholars, June 1996.

Bagley, Bruce. *Contadora and the Diplomacy of Peace in Central America: Vol. I: The United States, Central America, and Contadora; Vol. II: From Contadora to Esquipulas.* Boulder, CO: Westview Press, 1987.

———, Roberto Alvarez and Katherine J. Hagedorn, eds. *Contadora and the Central American Peace Process: Selected Documents.* Vol. I. Boulder, CO and Washington, D.C.: Westview Press and Johns Hopkins University Press, 1985.

———, and Juan G. Tokátlian. *Contadora: The Limits of Negotiation.* Lanham, MD: University Press of America, 1987.

Baranyi, Stephen. *Promoting Peace and Demilitarization in Central America.* Toronto, ON: York University Center for Strategic Studies, 1988.

Blackman, Morris J., William M. Leogrande and Kenneth Sharpe, eds. *Confronting Revolution: Security Through Diplomacy in Central America.* New York: Pantheon, 1986.

Calvert, Peter, ed. *The Central American Security System: North/South or East/West?* Cambridge, UK: Cambridge University Press, 1988.

Canada, House of Commons. *Peace Process in Central America, Minutes of Proceedings*, 27 April 1988, 4 May–29 June 1988.

Cepeda Ulloa, Fernando. *Contadora: Desafío a la diplomacia tradicional.* Bogotá, Colombia: Universidad de los Andes, 1985.

———, and Rodrigo Pardo. *Negociaciones de pacificación en América Central.* San José, CR: FLACSO, 1987.

Child, Jack. *The Central American Peace Process, 1983–1991: Sheathing Swords, Building Confidence.* Boulder, CO: Lynne Rienner Publishers, 1992.

Coleman, Kenneth M., and George C. Herring, eds. *Understanding the Central American Crisis: Sources of Conflict, U.S. Policy, and Options for Peace.* Wilmington, DE: Scholarly Resources Books, 1991.

Dallanegra Pedraza, Luis. *Proceso de desmovilización de la resistencia Nicaragüense.* Buenos Aires: Ministerio de Asuntos Exteriores, 1990.

Durán, Esperanza. "Pacification, Security and Democracy: Contadora's Role in Central America." In *The Central American Security System: North/South or East/West?* Edited by Peter Calvert, 155–176. Cambridge, UK: Cambridge University Press, 1988.

Eguizábal, Cristina, ed. *América Latina y la crisis Centroamericana: En busca de una solución regional.* Buenos Aires: GEL, 1988.

Fagen, Richard, ed. *Forging Peace: The Challenge of Central America.* New York: Basil Blackwell, 1987.

Frohman, Alicia. "De Contadora al Grupo de los Ocho." *Estudios Internacionales* 26 (July1989): 385–427.

———. "Regional Initiatives for Peace and Democracy: The Collective Diplomacy of the Rio Group." In *Collective Responses to Regional Problems: The Case of Latin America and the Caribbean. A Collection of Essays from a Project of the American Academy of Arts and Sciences,* edited by Carl Kaysen, Robert A. Pastor, and Laura W. Reed, 129–141. Cambridge, MA: Committee on International Security Studies, AAAS, 1994.

Gettleman, Marvin E., Patrick Lacefield, Louis Menashe, David Mermelstein, and Ronald Radosh, eds. *El Salvador: Central America in the New Cold War.* New York: Grove Press, 1981.

Goodfellow, William, and James Morrell, "From Contadora to Esquipulas to Sapoá and Beyond." In *Revolution and Counterrevolution in Nicaragua,* edited by Thomas W. Walker, 369–393. Boulder, CO: Westview Press, 1991.

van de Haag, Ernest, and Tom J. Farer. *U.S. Ends and Means in Central America: A Debate.* New York: Plenum, 1988.

Hahn, Walter F., ed. *Central America and the Reagan Doctrine.* Lanham, MD: University Press of America, 1987.

Inter-American Defense Board. *Basic Norms for the Organization and Employment of an Inter-American Peacekeeping Force.* IADB Document T-369, 9 November 1979. Washington, D.C.: IADB, 1979.

Jauberth, H. Rodrigo, Gilberto Castañeda, Jesús Hernández, and Pedro Vuskovic. *The Difficult Triangle: Mexico, Central America, and the United States.* Boulder, CO: Westview Press, 1991.

Jockel, Joseph T. *Canada and International Peacekeeping.* Significant Issues Series, Americas Program. Washington, D.C.: Center for Strategic & International Studies, 1994.

Klepak, H. P. *Security Considerations and Verification of a Central American Arms Regime.* Ottawa: External Affairs, Arms Control and Disarmament Division, 1990.

Kornbluh, Peter. *Nicaragua: The Price of Intervention.* Washington, D.C.: Institute for Policy Studies, 1987.

LaFeber, Walter. *Inevitable Revolutions: The United States and Central America*. 2nd ed. New York: W. W. Norton, 1993.

Lemco, Jonathan. *Canada and the Crisis in Central America*. New York: Praeger, 1991.

Leonard, Thomas M. "Central America, U.S. Policy, and the Crisis of the 1980s: Recent Interpretations." *Latin American Research Review* 31, no. 2 (1996): 194–211.

Maira, Luis. "El Grupo de Contadora y la Paz en Centroamerica." In *Las políticas exteriores latinoamericanas frente a la crisis*. Compiled by Heraldo Muñoz. Buenos Aires: Grupo Editor Latinamericano, 1985.

McNeil, Frank. *War and Peace in Central America*. New York: Charles Scribner's Sons, 1988.

Moore, John N. *The Secret War in Central America: The Sandinista Assault on World Order*. Frederick, MD: University Publications of America, 1987.

Moreno, Dario. *The Struggle for Peace in Central America*. Gainesville: University Press of Florida, 1994.

National Bipartisan Commission on Central America. *Report of the President's National Bipartisan Commission on Central America* [Kissinger Commission Report]. Washington, D.C.: U.S. Government Printing Office, 1984.

OAS, General Assembly. *Report of the Secretary General to the General Assembly on the Situation in Central America, Twentieth Regular Session, June 4, 1990, Asunción, Paraguay*. OEA/Ser. PAG/doc. 2565/90 corr. 17 June 1990. Washington, D.C.: OAS, 1990.

———, Permanent Council. *Report of the Secretary General on the Work and Programs of the CIAV/OEA in Nicaragua*. OEA/Serv.G CP/doc. 22112/90 30 October 1990. Washington, D.C.: OAS, 1990.

Ortega, Daniel. *Combatiendo por la Paz*. México, D.F.: Siglo XXI, 1988.

Pardo-Maurer, Rogelio. *The Contras, 1980–1989; A Special Kind of Politics*. Washington, D.C. and New York: Center for Strategic & International Studies and Praeger, 1990.

Ramírez Ocampo, Augusto. *Contadora: pedagogía para la paz y la democracia*. Bogotá, Colombia: Fondo Rotatorio del Ministerio de Relaciones Exteriores, 1986.

Ratliff, William. "The Reagan Doctrine and the Contras." In *Security in the Americas*, edited by Georges A. Fauriol, 189–208. Washington, D.C.: National Defense University Press, 1989.

Rojas Aravena, Francisco. *Costa Rica: Política exterior y crisis centroamericana*. Heredia, CR: Universidad Nacional, 1990.

Tinoco, Víctor Hugo. *Conflicto y paz: el proceso negociador centroamericano*. México, D.F.: Editorial Mestiza, 1988.

United Nations, International Court of Justice. *Military and Paramilitary Activities in and Against Nicaragua (Nicaragua vs United States of America), Judgement of the Court.* Communique 86/8 of 27 June 1986.

U.S. Congress, House of Representatives, Committee on Foreign Afairs. *The Central American Peace Process: Hearings before the Subcommittee on Western Hemisphere Affairs of the Committee on Foreign Affairs, House of Representatives.* 100th Cong., 1st Sess., October 20 and 21, 1987. Washington, D.C.: U.S. Government Printing Office, 1987.

U.S. Department of State. *Communist Interference in El Salvador* [White Paper on El Salvador]. Washington, D.C.: U.S. Department of State, February 23, 1981.

————. *Negotiations in Central America (Rev. Ed.): Chronology of Key Events, 1981–1987, . . .* Department of State Pub. 9551, Rev. October 1987. Washington, D.C.: U.S. Department of State, 1987.

U.S. Department of State and Department of Defense. *'Revolution Beyond Our Borders': Sandinista Intervention in Central America.* Washington, D.C.: U.S. Department of State, September 1985.

————. *The Soviet-Cuban Connection in Central America and the Caribbean.* Washington, D.C.: U.S. Department of State, March 1985.

Walker, Thomas W., ed. *Reagan versus the Sandinistas: The Undeclared War on Nicaragua.* Boulder, CO: Westview Press, 1987.

Wilson, Larman C. "The Nicaraguan Insurrection and the Delegitimization of Somoza: Intervention and the Role of the OAS and UN." In *Terrorism, Political Violence and World Order,* edited by Henry H. Han, 387–428. Lanham, MD: University Press of America, 1984.

———— and Raúl González Díaz, "UN Peacekeeping in Central America." In *A Crisis of Expectations: UN Peacekeeping in the 1990s,* edited by Ramesh Thakur and Carlyle A. Thayer, 141–158. Boulder, CO: Westview Press, 1995.

(3) Panama Canal Treaties Negotiations

Black, Jan. "The Canal and the Caribbean." In *The Restless Caribbean: Changing Patterns of International Relations,* edited by Richard Millett and W. Marvin Will, 90–102. New York: Praeger Publishers, 1979.

Bray, Wayne D. *The Controversy over a New Canal Treaty between the United States and Panama: A Selective Annotated Bibliography of United States, Panamanian, Colombian, French, and International Organization Sources.* Washington, D.C.: U.S. Government Printing Office, 1976.

Busey, James L. *Panama Canal Report*. Manitou Springs, CO: Juniper Editions, 1978.

Crane, Philip M. *Surrender in Panama: The Case Against the Treaty*. New York: Dale Books, 1978.

Farnsworth, David N., and James W. McKenney. *U.S.-Panama Relations, 1903–1978: A Study in Linkage Politics*. Boulder, CO: Westview Press, 1983.

Habeeb, William Mark, and I. William Zartman. *The Panama Canal Negotiations*. FPI Case Studies No. 1, Foreign Policy Institute, School of Advanced International Studies. Washington, D.C.: Johns Hopkins University, 1986.

Irwin, Wallace, Jr. *Panama: A Great Decision Approaches*. New York: Foreign Policy Association, 1977.

Jorden, William J. *Panama Odyssey*. Austin: University of Texas Press, 1984.

LaFeber, Walter. *The Panama Canal*. New York: Oxford University Press, 1979.

Millett, Richard L., Guest Editor. "Special Issue: The Future of Panama and the Canal." *Journal of Interamerican Studies and World Affairs* 35 (Fall 1993).

Moss, Ambler H., Jr. "The Panama Canal Treaties: How an Era Ended." *Latin America Research Review* 21, no. 3 (1986): 171–178.

Ropp, Steve. "Panama and the Canal." In *Latin America: Its Problems and Its Promise*, edited by Jan Knippers Black, 329–342. Boulder, CO: Westview Press, 1984.

Torrijos Herrera, Omar. *Nuestra Revolución: discursos fundamentales del General Omar Torrijos Herrera, jefe de gobierno de la República de Panamá*. Panama City: Ministerio de Relaciones Exteriores, 1974.

U.S. Department of State. *Selected Documents: Documents Associated With the Panama Canal Treaties*. Washington, D.C.: Department of State, Bureau of Public Affairs, 1977.

(4) Panama: OAS and Elections

Baena Soares, João Clemente. *Profile of a Mandate: Ten Years at the OAS*. Washington, D.C.: OAS, General Secretariat, 1994. Chap. II. "The Strengthening of Democracy."

Cottam, Martha L. *Images and Intervention: U.S. Policies in Latin America*. Pittsburgh, PA: University of Pittsburgh Press, 1994.

Eagleberger, Lawrence S. "The OAS and the Panama Crisis." *U.S. Department of State Bulletin* 29 (November 1989): 67–68.

Horowitz, Susan G. "Indications and Warning Factors." In *Operation Just Cause: The U.S. Intervention in Panama*, edited by Bruce W.

Watson and Peter G. Tsouras, 49–64. Boulder, CO: Westview Press, 1991.

OAS. Meeting [21st] of Consultation of Ministers of Foreign Affairs. *The Serious Crisis in Panama in its International Context*. OEA/Ser.F/II.21 Doc.8/89 rev. 2 17 May 1989. Washington, D.C.: General Secretariat of the OAS, 1989.

OEA. Reunión de Consulta de Ministros de Relaciones Exteriores. *Informe de la Misión Designada por la Vigésimoprimera Reunión de Consulta de Ministros de Relaciones Exteriores*. OEA/Ser.F/11.21 Doc. 56/89 23 agosto 1989. Washington, D.C.: Secretaría General de la OEA, 1989.

Robinson, Linda. *Intervention or Neglect: The United States and Central America Beyond the 1980s*. New York: Council on Foreign Relations, 1991. Chap. 6. "Panama and the United States: From Symbiosis to Festering Crisis."

Scranton, Margaret E. *The Noriega Years: U.S.-Panamanian Relations, 1981–1990*. Boulder, CO: Lynne Rienner Publishers, 1991.

Weeks, John, and Phil Gunson. *Panama: Made in the U.S.A.* London: Latin American Bureau, 1991.

e. South America

(1) South Atlantic War

(a) Bibliography

Argentine Republic. Dirección de Bibliotecas Populares. *Soberanía: contribución bibliográfica a la afirmación de derechos argentinos sobre las Malvinas, islas y sector antártico*. Buenos Aires: Ministerio de Cultura y Educación, 1975.

Etchepareborda, Roberto. "La Bibliografía Reciente sobre la Cuestión Malvinas (Primera Parte) [and] (Segunda Parte)." *Revista Interamericana de Bibliografía/Inter-American Review of Bibliography* 34, no. 1 (1984): 1–52 and no. 2 (1984): 227–288.

Larson, Everette E. "Historic Chronology and Bibliography." In *The Falkland Islands Dispute in International Law and Politics: A Documentary Sourcebook*, edited by Raphael Perl, 59–85, 691–722. New York: Oceana Publications, 1983.

———, comp. "A Selective Listing of Monographs and Government Documents on the Falkland/Malvinas Islands in the Library of Congress," *Hispanic Focus*, No. 1 (May 1982).

Orgill, Andrew. *The Falklands War: Background, Conflict, Aftermath. An Annotated Bibliography*. London: Mansell Publishng, 1993.

Wilson, Larman C. "The Impact of the Falkland/Malvinas Conflict

Upon the Inter-American System, OAS and Rio Treaty: A Selected and Annotated Bibliography." In *Anuario Jurídico Interamericano 1983*, OAS, Secretaría General, Subsecretaría de Asuntos Jurídicos, 295–343. Washington, D.C.: OAS, 1994.

(b) General and other

"América Latina después de las Malvinas" (Special Issue). *Estudios Internacionales* 15, no. 60 (October–December 1982). Articles on impact on regional system and international context by Carlos J. Moneta, Francisco Orrego Vicuña, and Luciano Tomassini; on Brazil by Hélio Jaguaribe and Celso Lafer; and on the U.S. by Jorge A. Sábato and Francisco Orrego Vicuña.

Child, Jack. *Geopolitics and Conflict in South America: Quarrels Among Neighbors*. New York: Praeger Publishers, 1985.

———. "Present Trends in the Interamerican Security System and the Role of the Rio Treaty." In *Anuario Jurídico Interamericano 1983*, OAS, Secretaría General, Subsecretaría de Asuntos Jurídicos, 43–82. Washington, D.C.: OAS, 1984.

———. "War in the South Atlantic." In *United States Policy in Latin America: A Quarter Century of Crisis and Challenge, 1961–1986*, edited by John D. Martz, 202–234. Lincoln: University of Nebraska Press, 1988.

Coll, Alberto R., and Anthony C. Arend, eds. *The Falklands War: Lessons for Strategy, Diplomacy and International Law*. Winchester, MA: Allen and Unwin, 1985.

Dabat, Alejandro, and Luis Lorenzano. *Argentina: The Malvinas and the End of Military Rule*. Trans. by Ralph Johnstone. London: Verso, 1984.

Freedman, Lawrence, and Virginia Gamba-Stonehouse. *Signals of War: The Falklands Conflict of 1982*. London: Faber and Faber, 1990.

Goebel, Julius. *The Struggle for the Falkland Islands: A Study in Legal and Diplomatic History*. New Haven, CT: Yale University Press, 1927. Re-issued in Spanish in Buenos Aires, 1950, in English in 1971 (Port Washington, NY: Kennikat Press), and in 1982 with a new preface and introduction (Aylesbury, Bucks, UK: Hazell Watson and Viney Ltd.).

Gompert, David C. "American Diplomacy and the Haig Mission: An Insider's Perspective." In *The Falklands War: Lessons for Strategy, Diplomacy and International Law*, edited by Alberto R. Coll, and Anthony C. Arend, 106–117. Winchester, MA: Allen and Unwin, 1985.

Haig, Alexander M. *Caveat: Realism, Reagan and Foreign Policy*. New York: Macmillan, 1984.

Hastings, Max, and Simon Jenkins. *The Battle for the Falklands.* New York: W. W. Norton, 1983.

Institut für Iberoamerika-Kunde, Dokumentations-Leitstelle Lateinamerika, Aktueller Informationdienst Lateinamerika. *Der Malwinen/Falkland Konflikt im Spiegal der Lateinamerikanischen Presse/El conflicto Malvinas/Falkland en la prensa latinoamericana.* Hamburg, Germany: Institut für Iberoamerika-Kunde, 1982.

Kinney, Douglas S. *National Interest/National Honor: The Diplomacy of the Falklands Crisis.* New York: Praeger Publishers for Institute for the Study of Diplomacy, Georgetown University, 1990.

Mestre, Tomas. *El Sistema Interamericano y la Guerra de las Malvinas; su mutuo impacto.* Madrid: Instituto de Cuestiones Internacionales, 1984.

OEA. Consejo Permanente. *Acta de la Sesión Protocolar Celebrada el 5 de abril de 1982* [for visit of Argentine Minister of Foreign Affairs Nicanor Costa Mendez]. Washington, D.C.: OEA, 5 abril 1982.

———. *Convocation of the Twentieth Meeting of Consultation of Ministers of Foreign Affairs.* Washington, D.C.: OAS, 21 April 1982.

OEA. Reunión de Consulta de Ministros de Relaciones Exteriores. *Vigésima Reunión de Consulta de Ministros de Relaciones Exteriores, 25 abril 1982—Washington, D.C.: Acta de la Primera Sesión de la Comisión General.* Doc. 20/82, 26 abril 1982 [through] *Sexta Sesión de la Comisión General,* Doc. 81/82 corr. 1, 30 junio 1982.

Oliveri López, Angel M. *Key to an Enigma: British Sources Disprove British Claims to the Falkland/Malvinas Islands.* Boulder, CO: Lynne Rienner Publishers, 1995.

Perera, Srilal. "The OAS and the Inter-American System: History, Law, and Diplomacy." In *The Falklands War: Lessons for Strategy, Diplomacy and International Law,* edited by Alberto R. Coll and Anthony C. Arends, 132–155. Winchester, MA: Allen and Unwin, 1985.

Perina, Rubén M. "The View from Buenos Aires," In Wayne S. Smith, ed. *Toward Resolution? The Falkands/Malvinas Dispute,* 45–60. Boulder, CO: Lynne Rienner, 1991.

Perl, Raphael. *The Falkland Islands Dispute in International Law and Politics: A Documentary Sourcebook.* London, UK: Oceana Publications, 1983.

Quiroga G., Alberto. "El caso de las Malvinas visto desde la perspectiva del Organo de Consulta del TIAR." In *Anuario Jurídico Interamericano 1983,* OAS, Secretaría General, Subsecretaría de Asuntos Jurídicos, 223–293. Washington, D.C.: OAS, 1984.

Smith, Wayne S., ed. *Toward Resolution? The Falklands/Malvinas Dispute.* Boulder, CO: Lynne Rienner, 1991.

Thomas, David. "The View from Whitehall." In *Toward Resolution?*

The Falklands/Malvinas Dispute, edited by Wayne S. Smith, 15–43. Boulder, CO: Lynne Rienner, 1991.

U.S. Congress. House of Representatives. *Latin America and the United States After the Falklands/Malvinas Crisis: Hearings Before the Subcommittee on Inter-American Affairs of the Committee on Foreign Affairs, House of Representatives.* 97th Cong., 2nd Sess. July 20 and August 5, 1982. Washington, D.C.: Government Printing Office, 1982.

7. International Law

a. Bibliography

Beebe, Benjamin R. *Intervention and Counterinsurgency: An Annotated Bibliography of the Small Wars of the United States, 1989–1984.* New York: Garland, 1985.

Wolpin, Miles. *United States Intervention in Latin America: A Selected and Annotated Bibliography.* New York: American Institute for Marxist Studies, 1971.

b. General and Intervention-Nonintervention

Boyle, Francis A. *World Politics and International Law.* Durham, NC: Duke University Press, 1985. Chap. 19. "International Lawlessness in the Caribbean Basin."

Caicedo Castilla, José J. *El derecho internacional en el Sistema Interamericano.* Madrid: Ediciones Cultura Hispánica, 1970.

———. *The Work of the Inter-American Juridical Committee.* Washington, D.C.: OAS, 1964.

Damrosch, Lori Fisler. "Politics Across Borders: Nonintervention and Nonforcible Influence over Political Affairs." *American Journal of International Law* 83 (January 1989): 1–50.

———, and David J. Scheffer, eds. *Law and Force in the New International Order.* Boulder, CO: American Society of International Law by Westview Press, 1991. "Intervention," Part Three, chapters 9–24.

Dawson, Frank G. "Contributions of Lesser Developed Nations to International Law: The Latin American Experience," *Journal of International Law* 13 (Winter 1981): 37–81.

D'Estefano Pisani, Miguel A. "International Law and U.S.-Cuban Relations." In *U.S.-Cuban Relations in the 1990s,* edited by Jorge I. Domínguez and Rafael Hernández, 255–279. Boulder, CO: Westview Press, 1989. [by Cuban Foreign Ministry's legal adviser].

Díaz Albónico, Rodrigo. *Consideraciones sobre el particularismo latin-*

oamericano en derecho internacional. Santiago: Departamento de Estudios Internacionales, Universidad de Chile, 1975.

Dinerstein, Herbert S. *Intervention Against Communism.* Washington, D.C.: Washington Center of Foreign Policy Research, School of Advanced International Studies, Johns Hopkins University, 1967.

Dore, Issak I. "The U.S. Invasion of Grenada: Resurrection of the 'Johnson Doctrine'?" *Stanford Journal of International Law* 20 (1984): 173–189.

Ferguson, Yale H. "Reflections on the Inter-American Principle of Nonintervention: A Search for Meaning in Ambiguity." *Journal of Politics* 32 (August 1970): 628–654.

Forsythe, David P. *The Politics of International Law: U.S. Foreign Policy Reconsidered.* Boulder, CO: Lynne Rienner Publishers, 1990. Chapter III. " 'Covert' Intervention in Nicaragua."

Gordon, Dennis R., and Margaret M. Munro. "The External Dimension of Civil Insurrection: International Organizations and the Nicaraguan Revolution." *Journal of Inter-American Studies and World Affairs* 25 (February 1983): 59–82.

Jacobini, H. B. *A Study of the Philosophy of International Law as Seen in Works of Latin American Writers.* The Hague: Martinus Nijhoff, 1954.

Kane, William E. *Civil Strife in Latin America: A Legal History of U.S. Involvement.* Baltimore, MD: Johns Hopkins University Press, 1972.

Kirkpatrick, Jeane J., and Allan Gerson. "The Reagan Doctrine, Human Rights, and International Law." In *Right v. Might: International Law and the Use of Force,* edited by Louis Henkin, Stanley Hoffmann, Jeane J. Kirkpatrick, Allan Gerson, William D. Rogers, and David J. Scheffer, 9–36. New York: Council on Foreign Relations Book, 1989.

Kryzanek, Michael J. "Intervention and Interventionism." In *U.S.-Latin American Policymaking: A Reference Handbook,* edited by David W. Dent, 397–423. Westport, CT: Greenwood Press, 1995.

———. *Leaders, Leadership and U.S. Foreign Policy Toward Latin America and the Caribbean.* Boulder, CO: Westview Press, 1992. Chapter 8. "Latin American Leaders: Dealing with Intervention."

Levitin, Michael J. "The Law of Force and the Force of Law: Grenada, the Falklands, and Humanitarian Intervention." *Harvard International Law Journal* 27 (Spring 1986): 621–658.

OAS, General Secretariat. *Inter-American Convention on Extradition.* Washington, D.C.: OAS, 1981.

———. Inter-American Juridical Committee. *Contribution of the American Continent to the Principles of International Law that Govern the Responsibility of the State. Opinion prepared in accordance with Resolution[s] . . . of the Tenth Inter-American Conference, . . . of the*

Third Meeting and . . . of the Fourth Meeting of the Inter-American Council of Jurists. Washington, D.C.: OAS, January 1962.

———. ———. *Differences Between Intervention and Collective Action.* Washington, D.C.: OAS, January 1966.

Papermaster, Daniel I. "A Case Study of the Effect of International Law on Foreign Policy Decisionmaking: The United States Intervention in the Dominican Republic in 1965." *Texas International Law Journal* 24, no. 3 (1989): 463–497.

Pearce, Jenny. *Under the Eagle: U.S. Intervention in Central America and the Caribbean.* London: Latin American Bureau, 1982.

Puig, Juan Carlos. *Doctrinas internacionales y autonomía latinoamericana.* Caracas: Instituto de Altos Estudios de América Latina, La Universidad Simón Bolívar, 1980.

———. "El Principio de no intervención en el derecho internacional público interamericano." In *Anuario Jurídico Interamericano 1979,* OAS, Secretaría General, Subsecretaría de Asuntos Jurídicos, 55–87. Washington, D.C.: OAS, 1980.

Reisman, W. Michael, and James E. Baker. *Regulating Covert Action: Practices, Contexts, and Policies of Covert Coercion Abroad in International and American Law.* New Haven, CT: Yale University Press, 1992.

Rikard, David A. "An End to Unilateral U.S. Action in Latin America: A Call for Expanding the Role of the OAS." *Syracuse Journal of International Law and Commerce* 14 (Winter 1987): 273–289.

Rodley, Nigel S. and C. Neale Ronning, eds. *International Law in the Western Hemisphere.* The Hague: Martinus Nijhoff, 1974.

Ronning, C. Neale, ed. *Intervention in Latin America.* New York: Alfred A. Knopf, 1970.

———. *Law and Politics in Inter-American Diplomacy.* New York: John Wiley and Sons, 1963.

Schachter, Oscar. "Authorized Uses of Force by the United Nations and Regional Organizations." In *Law and Force in the New International Order,* edited by Lori Fisler Damrosch and David J. Scheffer, 65–93. Boulder, CO: Westview Press under the auspices of the American Society of International Law, 1991.

Scheffer, David J. "Introduction: The Great Debate of the 1980s." In *Right v. Might: International Law and the Use of Force,* edited by Henkin, Louis, Stanley Hoffmann, Jeane J. Kirkpatrick, Allan Gerson, William D. Rogers and David J. Scheffer, 1–17. New York: Council on Foreign Relations, 1989.

Schraeder, Richard, ed. *Intervention in the 1990s: U.S. Foreign Policy in the Third World.* 3rd ed. Boulder, CO: Westview, 1995.

Seara Vázquez, Modesto. *La política exterior de México; La práctica de México en el derecho internacional.* México, D.F.: Esfinge, 1969.

Stoetzer, O. Carlos. *The Organization of American States.* New York: Praeger Publishers, 1993. Chapter ll. "The OAS and International Law, Human Rights, and Democracy."

Taylor, Philip B. *Law and Politics in Inter-American Diplomacy.* New York: John Wiley and Sons, 1963.

Tercero Castro, David. *Contribución de la O.E.A. al Derecho Internacional.* Guatemala City: Tipografía J. Gallardo, 1955.

Tesón, Fernando R. *Humanitarian Intervention: An Inquiry into Law and Morality.* 2nd ed. Irvington, NY: Transnational Publishers, 1996.

Thomas, Ann van Wynen and A. J. Thomas, Jr. *Non-Intervention: The Law and its Import in the Americas.* Dallas, TX: Southern Methodist University Press, 1956.

Tucker, Robert W., et al. *Intervention and the Reagan Doctrine.* New York: Council on Religion and International Affairs, 1985.

Vincent, R. J. *Nonintervention and International Order.* Princeton, NJ: Princeton University Press, 1974. Chap. Six. "United States Doctrine and Practice."

Weller, Marc, and Ana MacLean, eds. *The Haiti Crisis in International Law.* New York: Cambridge University Press, 1995.

Wilson, Larman C. "The Contemporary Practice of International Law in Central America: Intervention and Non-Intervention." *Towson State Journal of International Affairs* 20 (Spring 1986): 85–105.

―――. "Law and Intervention in the Cuban 'Invasion' of 1961." *Revue de Droit International* [Geneva] 4 (1965): 1–11.

―――. "The Monroe Doctrine, Cold War Anachronism: Cuba and the Dominican Republic." *Journal of Politics* 28 (May 1966): 322–346.

c. U.S. Interventions (Invasions)

(1) U.S. and OECS in Grenada

Beck, Robert. *The Grenada Invasion: Politics, Law, and Foreign Policy.* Boulder, CO: Westview Press, 1993.

Bell, Wendell. "False Prophecy and the Invasion of Grenada." In *The Caribbean After Grenada: Revolution, Conflict, and Democracy*, edited by Scott B. MacDonald, Harald M. Sandstrom, and Paul B. Goodwin, Jr., *69–85.* New York: Praeger Publishers, 1988.

Burrowes, Reynold A. *Revolution and Rescue in Grenada.* Westport, CT: Greenwood Press, 1988.

Curry, W. Frick. "Grenada: Force as First Resort." *International Policy Report.* Washington, D.C.: Center for International Policy, January 1984.

Davidson, Scott. *Grenada: A Study in Politics and the Limits of International Law.* Aldershot, UK: Gower Publishing Co., 1987.

Dieguez, Richard P. "The Grenada Intervention: 'Illegal in Form, Sound as Policy.' " *New York University Journal of International Politics* 16 (Summer 1984): 1167–1204.

Dore, Isaak I. "The U.S. Invasion of Grenada: Resurrection of the 'Johnson Doctrine'?" *Stanford Journal of International Law* 20 (1984): 173–189.

Dunn, Peter M., and Bruce W. Watson, eds. *American Intervention in Grenada: The Implications of Operation 'Urgent Fury.'* Boulder, CO: Westview Press, 1985.

Forsythe, David P. *The Politics of International Law: U.S. Foreign Policy Reconsidered.* Boulder, CO: Westview Press, 1990. Chap. IV. "Overt Intervention in Grenada."

Gerson, Allan. *The Kirkpatrick Mission: Diplomacy Without Apology— America at the United Nations 1981–1985.* New York: The Free Press, 1991. Chap. 13. "Grenada, and the Emergence of a Reagan Doctrine."

Gordon, Edward, Richard B. Bilder, Arthur W. Rovine, and Don Wallace, Jr. "International Law and the United States Action in Grenada: A Report." *The International Lawyer* 18 (Spring 1984): 331–380.

Heine, Jorge, ed. *A Revolution Aborted: The Lessons of Grenada.* Pittsburgh, PA: University of Pittsburgh Press, 1990.

Joyner, Christopher C. "Reflections on the Lawfulness of Invasion." *American Journal of International Law* 78 (January 1984): 131–144.

Karas, Jon M., and Jerald M. Goodman. "The United States Action in Grenada: An Exercise in Realpolitik." *University of Miami Inter-American Law Review* 16 (Spring 1984) 53–108.

Kryzanek, Michael J. "Intervention and Interventionism." In *U.S.-Latin American Policymaking: A Reference Handbook,* edited by David W. Dent, 397–423. Westport, CT: Greenwood Press, 1995.

MacDonald, Scott B., Harald M. Sandstrom and Paul B. Goodwin, Jr., eds. *The Caribbean After Grenada: Revolution, Conflict, and Democracy.* New York: Praeger Publishers, 1988.

Manigat, Leslie. "Grenada: Revolutionary Shockwave, Crisis, and Intervention." In *The Caribbean and World Politics: Cross Currents and Cleavages,* edited by Jorge Heine, and Leslie Manigat, 178–221. New York: Holmes and Meier, 1988.

Moore, John Norton. "Grenada and the International Double Standard." *American Journal of International Law* 78 (January 1984): 145–168.

O'Shaughnessy, Hugh. *Grenada: An Eyewitness Account of the U.S. Invasion and the Caribbean History that Provoked It.* New York: Dodd, Mead, 1984. [British edition is *Grenada: Revolution, Invasion, and Aftermath.* London: Sphere Books, 1984.]

Pastor, Robert A. "The United States and the Grenada Revolution: Who Pushed First and Why?" In Jorge Heine, ed. *A Revolution Aborted: The Lessons of Grenada,* 181–214. Pittsburgh, PA: University of Pittsburgh Press, 1990.

Payne, Anthony. "The Foreign Policy of the People's Revolutionary Government." In Jorge Heine, ed. *A Revolution Aborted: The Lessons of Grenada*, 123–151. Pittsburgh, PA: University of Pittsburgh Press, 1990.

————, Paul K. Sutton, and Tony Thorndike. *Grenada: Revolution and Invasion*. London: Croom Helm, 1984.

Riggs, Ronald M. "The Grenada Intervention: A Legal Analysis." *Military Law Review* 109 (Summer 1985): 1–81.

Schoenhals, Kai, and Richard Melanson. *Revolution and Intervention in Grenada*. Boulder, CO: Westview Press, 1985.

U.S. Department of State and Department of Defense. *Grenada: A Preliminary Report*. Washington, D.C.: Departments of State and Defense, December 16, 1983.

————. *Grenada Documents: An Overview and Selection*. Washington, D.C.: Departments of State and Defense, September 1984.

Valenta, Jiri, and Herbert J. Ellison, eds. *Grenada and Soviet/Cuban Policy: Internal Crisis and U.S./OECS Intervention*. Boulder, CO: Published under the auspices of the Kennan Institute for Advanced Russian Studies, Woodrow Wilson International Center for Scholars, Washington, D.C., and the Program of Soviet and East European Studies, Department of National Security, Naval Postgraduate School, Monterey, CA, by Westview Press, 1986.

Waters, Maurice. "The Law and Politics of a U.S. Intervention: The Case of Grenada." *Peace and Change* 14 (January 1989): 65–105.

Wheeler, Laura. "The Grenada Invasion: Expanding the Scope of Humanitarian Intervention." *Boston College International and Comparative Law Review* 8 (Spring 1985): 413–430.

(2) U.S. and Capture of Noriega in Panama

Berman, Alan. "In Mitigation of Illegality: The U.S. Invasion of Panama." *Kentucky Law Journal* 79, no. 4 (1990–91): 735–800.

Bogus, Carl T. "The Invasion of Panama and the Rule of Law." *International Lawyer* 26 (Fall 1992): 781–787.

Buckley, Kevin. *Panama: The Whole Story*. New York: Simon and Schuster, 1991.

Cottam, Martha L. *Images and Intervention: U.S. Policies in Latin America*. Pittsburgh, PA: University of Pittsburgh Press, 1994. Chap. 6. "The New World Order: Intervention in Post-Cold War Latin America."

D'Amato, Anthony D. "The Invasion of Panama was a Lawful Response to Tyranny." *American Journal of International Law* 84 (April 1990): 516–524.

Donnelly, Thomas, Margaret Roth and Caleb Baker. *Operation Just Cause: The Storming of Panama*. New York: Lexington Books, 1991.

Farer, Tom J. "Panama: Beyond the Charter Paradigm." *American Journal of International Law* 84 (April 1990): 503–515.

Independent Commission of Inquiry on the U.S. Invasion of Panama. *The U.S. Invasion of Panama: The Truth Behind Operation 'Just Cause.'* Boston, MA: South End Press, 1991.

Kryzanek, Michael. "The Grenada Invasion: Approaches to Understanding." In *United States Policy in Latin America: A Decade of Crisis and Challenge, 1981–1991*, edited by John Martz. Lincoln: University of Nebraska Press, 1994.

Levitt, Geoffrey M. "Intervention to Combat Terrorism and Drug Trafficking." In *Law and Force in the New International Order*, edited by Lori Fisler Damrosch and David J. Scheffer, 224–232. Boulder, CO: Published under the auspices of the American Society of International Law by Westview Press, 1991.

Ma, Frances Y. F. "Noriega's Abduction from Panama: Is Military Invasion an Appropriate Substitute for International Extradition?" *Loyola of Los Angeles International and Comparative Law Journal* 13 (June 1991): 925–953.

Nanda, Ved P. "Validity of United States Intervention in Panama under International Law." *American Journal of International Law* 84 (April 1990): 494–503.

Noriega, Manuel, and Peter Eisner. *America's Prisoner: The Memoirs of Manuel Noriega*. Westminster, MD: Random House, 1997.

OAS. Permanent Council. *Serious Events in the Republic of Panama: Resolution 534*. OAS/PC 800/89 22 December 1989. Washington, D.C.: OAS, 1989.

Scranton, Margaret E. *The Noriega Years: U.S.-Panamanian Relations, 1981–1990*. Boulder, CO: Westview Press, 1990.

U.S. Department of State, Bureau of Public Affairs. *Panama: A Just Cause*. Current Policy No. 1240. Washington, D.C.: U.S. Department of State, December 1989.

Watson, Bruce W., and Peter G. Tsouras, eds. *Operation Just Cause: The U.S. Intervention in Panama*. Boulder, CO: Westview Press, 1991.

Woodward, Robert. *The Commanders*. New York: Simon and Schuster, 1991.

8. Democracy and Human Rights

a. Democracy

(1) General

Acosta Romero, Miguel, and Jorge A. Castañeda. *La Observación Internacional de Elecciones*. México, D.F.: Porrúa, 1994.

American University, Washington College of Law, International Legal Studies Program. "Transitions to Democracy and the Rule of Law: Symposium." *The American University Journal of International Law and Policy* 5 (Summer 1990): 965–1086.

Baloyra, Enrique A., ed. *Comparing New Democracies: Transition and Consolidation in Mediterranean Europe and the Southern Cone.* Boulder, CO: Westview Press, 1987.

Betancur, Belisario, ed. "Transición y Perspectivas de la Democracia en Iberoamérica." *Pensamiento Iberoamericano: Revista de Economía Política* 14 (July–December 1988).

Camp, Roderic A., ed. *Democracy in Latin America: Patterns and Cycles.* Wilmington, DE: SR Books, 1996.

Diamond, Larry, Juan J. Linz and Seymour M. Lipset, eds. *Democracy in Developing Countries: Latin America.* Vol. 4. Boulder, CO: Lynne Rienner Publishers, 1989.

Domínguez, Jorge I., and Abraham F. Lowenthal, eds. *Constructing Democratic Governance.* 3 vols. Vol. 1: *Latin America and the Caribbean in the 1990s—Themes and Issues*; Vol. 2: *Mexico, Central America, and the Caribbean in the 1990s*; Vol. 3: *South America in the 1990s.* Baltimore, MD: The Johns Hopkins University Press, 1997.

Griffith, Ivelaw I., and Betty N. Sedoc-Dahlberg, eds. *Democracy and Human Rights in the Caribbean.* Boulder, CO: Westview Press, 1997.

Linz, Juan J., and Alfred Stepan, eds. *The Breakdown of Democratic Regimes: Latin America.* Baltimore, MD: The Johns Hopkins University Press, 1978.

Lipset, Seymour M., ed. *The Encyclopedia of Democracy.* 4 vols. Washington, D.C.: Congressional Quarterly Books, 1995.

Lowenthal, Abraham F. *Exporting Democracy: The United States and Latin America: Case Studies.* Baltimore, MD: The Johns Hopkins University Press, 1991.

Mauro Marini, Ruy. *América Latina: democracia e integración.* Caracas: Editorial Nueva Sociedad, 1993.

Pastor, Robert A., ed. *Democracy in the Americas: Stopping The Pendulum.* New York: Holmes and Meier, 1989.

Pelletier, Stephen R. *Revolution Reassessed: Democracy and the Left in Contemporary Central America.* Armonk, NY: M. E. Sharpe, 1996.

Reilly, Charles A., ed. *New Paths to Democratic Development in Latin America: The Rise of NGO-Municipal Collaboration.* Boulder, CO: Lynne Rienner, 1995.

Uribe Vargas, Diego. *Panamericanismo Democrático, bases para una transformación del sistema continental.* Bogotá: Ediciones Nuevo Signo, 1958.

Wiarda, Howard F. *The Democratic Revolution in Latin America: History, Politics, and U.S. Policy.* New York: Holmes and Meier, 1990.

Zagorsky, Paul. *Democracy vs. National Security: Civil-Military Relations in Latin America.* Boulder, CO: Lynne Rienner, 1992.

(2) Cases and Countries

Acevedo, Domingo E. "The Haitian Crisis and the OAS Response: A Test of the Effectiveness of Protecting Democracy." In *Enforcing Restraint: Collective Intervention in Internal Conflict,* edited by Lori Fisler Damrosch, 119–155. New York: Council on Foreign Relations, 1993.

Arnson, J. Cynthia, and Johanna Mendelson Forman. "Projecting Democracy in Central America: Old Wine, New Bottles?" In *Political Parties and Democracy in Central America,* edited by Louis W. Goodman, William M. Leogrande, and Johanna Mendelson, 237–266. Boulder, CO: Westview Press, 1990.

Blasier, Cole. "Democracy: Dilemmas in Promoting Democracy: Lessons from Grenada, Panama, and Haiti," *North-South Issues* 4, no. 4 (1995).

Bloomfield, Richard J. "Making the Western Hemisphere Safe for Democracy? The OAS Defense of Democracy Regime." *The Washington Quarterly* 17 (Spring 1994): 157–169.

Booth, John A. "Elections and Democracy in Central America: A Framework for Analysis." In *Elections and Democracy in Central America,* edited by John A. Booth and Mitchell A. Seligson, 7–39. Chapel Hill: University of North Carolina Press, 1989.

Carothers, Thomas. *In the Name of Democracy: U.S. Policy toward Latin America in the Reagan Years.* Berkeley: University of California Press, 1991.

Cohn, Elizabeth and Michael J. Nojeim. "Promoting Democracy." In *U.S.-Latin American Policymaking: A Reference Handbook,* edited by David W. Dent, 457–480. Westport, CT: Greenwood Press, 1995.

Dupuy, Alex. *Haiti in the New World Order: The Limits of the Democratic Revolution.* Boulder, CO: Westview Press, 1997.

Facio, Gonzalo. *The Haitian Crisis Is Testing the Democratic Will of the OAS: Special Report.* Washington, D.C.: Council for Inter-American Security, 1992.

Farer, Tom. *Beyond Sovereignty: Collectively Defending Democracy in the Americas.* Baltimore, MD: Johns Hopkins University Press, 1996.

Fauriol, Georges A. "Hunting for Democracy" and "Inventing Democracy: The Elections of 1990." In *The Haitian Challenge: U.S. Policy Considerations,* edited by Georges A. Fauriol, 8–12, 49–66. Washington, D.C.: Center for Strategic and International Studies, 1993.

———. "Reinventing Democracy." In *Haitian Frustrations: Dilemmas for U.S. Policy* edited by George A. Fauriol, 1–6. Washington, D.C.: Center for Strategic and International Studies, 1995.

Inter-American Dialogue. *Advancing Democracy and Human Rights in the Americas: What Role for the OAS? A Conference Report.* Washington, D.C.: Inter-American Dialogue, May 1994.

Hayes, Margaret Daly. "Not What I Say, but What I Do: Latin American Policy in the Reagan Administration." In *United States Policy in Latin America: A Quarter Century of Crisis and Challenge, 1961–1986,* edited by John D. Martz, 98–131. Lincoln: University of Nebraska Press, 1988.

"International Organizations and Democracy." *Journal of Democracy* 4 (July 1993): 3–69. Sections on the OAS by Heraldo Muñoz and Peter Hakim.

Martz, John D. "Democracy and Human Rights." In *The United States and Latin America: Redefining U.S. Purposes in the Post-Cold War Era,* edited by G. Pope Atkins, 43–55. Austin: Lyndon B. Johnson School of Public Affairs, University of Texas, 1992.

———. "Democracy and the Imposition of Values: Definitions and Diplomacy." In *Latin America, the United States, and the Inter-American System,* edited by John D. Martz and Lars Schoultz, 145–171. Boulder, CO: Westview Press, 1980.

Millett, Richard L. "Beyond Sovereignty: International Efforts to Support Latin American Democracy." *Journal of Inter-American Studies* 36 (Fall 1994): 1–23.

OAS. *Democracy and Nicaragua.* Washington, D.C.: OAS, 1987.

———. *Realizing a Vision of Democracy.* Washington, D.C.: OAS, 1989.

———. *Report on the Secretary General's Mission to Guatemala.* MRE/doc 2/93 corr. l; 7 June 1993. Washington, D.C.: OAS, 1993.

———. *Second [Fourth and Fifth] Report on the Observation of the Nicaraguan Electoral Process.* (July 13–Nov. 13, 1989) [Jan. 1–Feb. 15, 1990 and Feb. 16–March 20, 1990].

———. Inter-American Juridical Committee. *Strengthening and Effective Exercise of Democracy.* Report prepared in accordance with Resolution VII of the Fourth Meeting of Consultation of Ministers of Foreign Affairs. Washington, D.C.: OAS, January 1959.

Pastor, Robert A. "The Carter Administration and Latin America: A Test of Principle." In *United States Policy in Latin America: A Quarter Century of Crisis and Challenge, 1961–1986,* edited by John D. Martz, 61–97. Lincoln: University of Nebraska Press, 1988.

Perina, Rubén M. "El Papel de la OEA y la promoción de las políticas Latinoamericanas." In *Integración solidaria: reconstrucción de los sistemas Políticos latinoamericanos,* edited by Raúl Vernal-Mega, et al., 207–213. 2 vols. Caracas: Universidad Simón Bolívar, 1994.

Perusse, Roland I. *Haitian Democracy Restored, 1991–1995*. Lanham, MD: University Press of America, 1995.

Stoetzer, O. Carlos. *The Organization of American States*. New York: Praeger Publishers, 1993. Chap. 11. "The OAS, Human Rights, and Democracy."

Villagrán de León, Francisco. *The OAS and Democratic Development*. Washington, D.C.: U.S. Institute of Peace, 1992.

Williams, Philip J. "Elections and Democratization in Nicaragua: The 1990 Elections in Perspective." *Journal of Inter-American Studies and World Affairs* 23 (Winter 1990): 13–34.

Wilson, Larman C. "Democracy and Human Rights in the Dominican Republic." In *Democracy and Human Rights in the Caribbean*, edited by Ivelaw I. Griffith and Betty Sedoc-Dahlberg, 113–137. Boulder, CO: Westview Press, 1997.

———. "The OAS and Promoting Democracy and Resolving Disputes: Reactivation in the 1990s?" *Inter-American Review of Bibliography/ Revista Interamericana de Bibliografía* 39, no. 4 (1989): 477–499.

b. Human Rights

(1) Bibliographies and Reference

Columbia University, Center for the Study of Human Rights. *Human Rights: A Topical Bibliography*. Boulder, CO: Westview Press, 1983.

Human Rights: An International and Comparative Law Bibliography. Westport, CT: Greenwood Press, 1985.

Lawson, Edward. *Encyclopedia of Human Rights*. 2nd ed. New York: Taylor & Francis, 1995.

Lillich, Richard B., ed. *International Human Rights Instruments: A Compilation*. New York: William S. Hein & Co., 1983 (regularly updated).

Welch, Claude E., ed. "International Human Rights: A Guide to Collection Development." *Choice* 28 (January 1991): 741–747.

Wilson, Richard J. "Researching the Jurisprudence of the Inter-American Commission on Human Rights: A Litigator's Perspective." *The American University Journal of International Law and Policy* 10 (Fall 1994): 1–17.

(2) General

Brown, Peter G., and Douglas MacLean, eds. *Human Rights and U.S. Foreign Policy: Principles and Applications*. Lexington, MA: Lexington Books, 1979.

Buergenthal, Thomas. *International Human Rights in a Nutshell*. St. Paul, MN: West Publishing Co., 1988.

————, and Dinah Shelton. *Protecting Human Rights in the Americas: Cases and Materials*. 4th rev. ed. Strasbourg, Germany: N. P. Engel, 1995.

Cabranes, José A. "The Protection of Human Rights by the Organization of American States." *American Journal of International Law* 62 (October 1968): 889–908.

Cançado Trindade, Antônio A. "The Evolution of the Organisation of American States (OAS) System of Human Rights Protection: an Appraisal." In *German Yearbook of International Law* 25, 498–514. Berlin: Duncker and Humblot, 1982.

————, ed. *The Modern World of Human Rights/El Mundo Moderno de los Derechos Humanos. Essays in honour of Thomas Buergenthal*. San José, CR: Inter-American Institute of Human Rights/Instituto Interamericanos de Derechos Humanos, 1996.

Cohn, Elizabeth. "Human Rights." In *U.S.-Latin American Policymaking: A Reference Handbook*, edited by David W. Dent, 424–456. Westport, CT: Greenwood Press, 1995.

Crahan, Margaret E. "Human Rights and U.S. Foreign Policy: Realism Versus Stereotypes." In *The United States and Latin America in the 1980s: Contending Perspectives on a Decade of Crisis,* edited by Kevin J. Middlebrook and Carlos Rico, 411–451. Pittsburgh, PA: University of Pittsburgh Press, 1986.

Damrosch, Lori Fisler. "Commentary on Collective Military Intervention to Enforce Human Rights." In *Law and Force in the New International Order*, edited by Lori Fisler Damrosch and David J. Scheffer, 215–223. Boulder, CO: Westview Press under the auspices of the American Society of International Law, 1991.

Donnelly, Jack. *International Human Rights*. Boulder, CO: Westview Press, 1993.

Forsythe, David P. *Human Rights and U.S. Foreign Policy: Congress Reconsidered*. Gainesville: University of Florida Press, 1988.

————. "Human Rights, The United States and the Organization of American States." *Human Rights Quarterly* 13, no. 1 (1991): 66–98.

————. *The Internationalization of Human Rights*. Lexington, MA: Lexington Books, 1991. Chap. 4. "Human Rights and the OAS: A Regime Analysis."

Henkin, Alice H., ed. *Honoring Human Rights and Keeping the Peace: Lessons From El Salvador, Cambodia, and Haiti*. Aspen, CO: Aspen Institute, 1995.

Hennelly, Alfred T., and John P. Langan, eds. *Human Rights in the Americas: The Struggle for Consensus*. Washington, D.C.: Georgetown University, 1982.

Hey, Hilde. *Gross Human Rights Violations: A Search for Causes. A Study of Guatemala and Costa Rica.* Dordrecht, The Netherlands: Martinus Nijhoff, 1995.

Kirkpatrick, Jeane J., and Allan Gerson. "The Reagan Doctrine, Human Rights, and International Law." In *Right v. Might: International Law and the Use of Force*, edited by Louis Henkin, Stanley Hoffmann, Jeane J. Kirkpatrick, Allan Gerson, William D. Rogers, and David Scheffer, 19–36. New York: Council on Foreign Relations Book, 1989.

LeBlanc, Lawrence J. *The OAS and the Promotion and Protection of Human Rights.* The Hague, The Netherlands: Martinus Nijhoff, 1977.

Medina Quiroga, Cecelia. *The Battle of Human Rights: Gross, Systematic Violations and the Inter-American System.* Dordrecht, The Netherlands: Martinus Nijhoff, 1988.

Mower, A. Glenn, Jr. *Human Rights and American Foreign Policy: The Carter and Reagan Experiences.* Westport, CT: Greenwood Press, 1987.

———. *Regional Human Rights: A Comparative Study of the West European and Inter-American Systems.* Westport, CT: Greenwood Press, 1991.

Schoultz, Lars. *Human Rights and United States Policy Toward Latin America.* Princeton, NJ: Princeton University Press, 1981.

———. "U.S. Diplomacy and Human Rights in Latin America." In *Latin America, the United States, and the Inter-American System*, edited by John D. Martz and Lars Schoultz, 173–205. Boulder, CO: Westview Press, 1980.

Weston, Burns H., Robin Ann Lukes, and Kelly M. Hnatt. "Regional Human Rights Regimes: A Comparison and Appraisal." *Vanderbilt Journal of Transnational Law* 20 (October 1987): 585–637.

Wilson, Larman C. "Human Rights in United States Foreign Policy: The Rhetoric and the Practice." In *Interaction: Foreign Policy and Public Policy*, edited by Don C. Piper and Ronald J. Terchek, 178–208. Washington, D.C.: American Enterprise Institute, 1983.

(3) Countries, Commission on Human Rights and Court of Human Rights

Buergenthal, Thomas. "The Inter-American Court, Human Rights and the OAS." *Human Rights Law Journal* 7, pts 2–4 (1986): 157–164.

———. "The Inter-American Court of Human Rights." *American Journal of International Law* 76 (April 1982): 231–245.

———. "Judicial Interpretation of the American Human Rights Convention." *Human Rights in the Americas*, OAS, Inter-American Commission on Human Rights, 253–260. Washington, D.C.: OAS, 1984.

Celli, Tulio Bruni. *Report on the Human Rights Situation in Haiti.* Prepared in accordance with Commission on Human Rights resolution 1991/77, docs. E/CN.4/1992/50 31 January 1992 and E/CN/1992/50 Add 1 17 February 1992. Washington, D.C.: OAS, 1992.

Centro de Información, Documentación y Análisis Latinoamericano. *Los derechos humanos, la OEA y Chile*. Caracas: CIDAL, 1976.

Cerna, Christina M. "The Structure and Functioning of the Inter-American Court of Human Rights (1979–1992)." In *British Year Book of International Law (1992)*, 135–229. Oxford: The Clarendon Press, 1993.

Davidson, Scott. *The Inter-American Court of Human Rights*. Dartmouth, MA: Dartmouth University Press, 1992.

Deodhar, Neal S. "First Contentious Cases Before the Inter-American Court of Human Rights." *The American University Journal of International Law and Policy* 3 (Spring 1988): 283–297.

Frost, Lynda E. "The Evolution of the Inter-American Court of Human Rights: Reflections of Present and Former Judges," *Human Rights Quarterly* 14 (May 1992): 171–205.

García-Amador, Francisco V. *La compentencia de la Comisión Interamericana de Derechos Humanos y las obligaciones internacionales de Cuba en la material*. Washington, D.C.: Inter-American Institute, 1984.

Kaplan, Fredy H. "Combating Political Torture in Latin America: An Analysis of the Organization of American States Inter-American Convention to Prevent and Punish Torture." *Brooklyn Journal of International Law* 15, no. 2 (1989): 399–430.

Lawyers Committee for Human Rights. *Critique: Review of the U.S. Department of State Country Reports on Human Rights Practices for 1991*. New York: Lawyers Committee for Human Rights, 1992.

Lockwood, Bert B., Jr. "Advisory Opinions of the Inter-American Court of Human Rights." *Denver Journal of International Law and Policy* 13, nos. 2–3 (Winter 1985): 245–267.

Maynard, Edwin S. "The Bureaucracy and Implementation of U.S. Human Rights Policy." *Human Rights Quarterly* 11 (May 1989): 178–248.

Medina, Cecilia. "The Inter-American Commission on Human Rights and the Inter-American Court of Human Rights: Reflections on a Joint Venture." *Human Rights Quarterly* 12, no. 4 (1990): 439–464.

OAS. Inter-American Commission on Human Rights. *Fourth Report on the Situation of Human Rights in Guatemala*. Washington, D.C.: OAS, 1993.

———. *Handbook of Existing Rules Pertaining to Human Rights in the Inter-American System*. Washington, D.C.: OAS, 1991.

———. *Inter-American Yearbook on Human Rights/Anuario Inter-*

americano de Derechos Humanos 1995. Dordrecht, The Netherlands: Martinus Nijoff and Washington, D.C.: OAS, 1997.

———. *Report on the Situation of Human Rights in Chile.* Washington, D.C.: OAS, 1985.

———. *Report on the Situation of Human Rights in Haiti.* Washington, D.C.: OAS, 1995.

———. *Report on the Situation of Human Rights in the Republic of Nicaragua.* Washington, D.C.: OAS, 1981.

———. *Ten Years of Activities, 1971–1981.* Washington, D.C.: OAS, 1982.

———. *Twenty-Five Years of Struggle for Human Rights in the Americas, 1959–1984.* Washington, D.C.: OAS, 1984.

———. Inter-American Juridical Committee. *Study on the Juridical Relationship Between Respect for Human Rights and the Exercise of Democracy.* Prepared in accordance with [Resolutions] . . . III of the Fifth Meeting of Consultation . . . and . . . XXI of the Fourth Meeting of the Inter-American Council of Jurists. Washington, D.C.: OAS, May 1960.

Padilla, David J. "Inter-American Commission on Human Rights of the Organization of American States: A Case Study." *The American University Journal of International Law and Policy* 9 (Fall 1993): 95–115.

Schreiber, Anna P. *The Inter-American Commission on Human Rights.* Leiden, The Netherlands: A. W. Sijthoff, 1970.

Sepúlveda, César. "The Inter-American Commission on Human Rights (1960–1981)." In *Israel Yearbook on Human Rights*, 46–61. Tel Aviv: Tel Aviv University, 1982.

Servicio Paz y Justicia. *Uruguay: Nunca Más: Human Rights Violations 1972–1985.* Trans. by Elizabeth Hampsten. Philadelphia, PA: Temple University Press, 1992.

Shelton, Dinah. "The Jurisprudence of the Inter-American Court of Human Rights." *The American University Journal of International Law and Policy* 10 (Fall 1994): 333–372.

Stoetzer, O. Carlos. *The Organization of American States.* 2nd ed. New York: Praeger Publishers, 1993. Chapter 11. "The OAS and International Law, Human Rights, and Democracy."

U.S. Department of State. *Country Reports on Human Rights Practices for 1978*—[annual to date]. Washington, D.C.: Government Printing Office, 1978–.

Villagrán-Kramer, Francisco. "Sanciones por violaciones de los derechos humanos." *Curso de Derecho Internacional.* Vol. 19, OAS, Comité Jurídico Interamericano, 63–80. Washington, D.C.: OAS, 1992.

9. Economic Development and the Environment

Browder, John O. "Deforestation and the Environmental Crisis in Latin America." *Latin American Research Review* 30, no. 3 (1995): 123–137.

Collinson, Helen, ed. *Green Guerrillas: Environmental Conflicts and Initiatives in Latin America and the Caribbean—A Reader.* London: Latin America Bureau, 1996.

Dreier, John C., ed. *The Alliance for Progress: Problems and Perspectives.* Baltimore, MD.: Johns Hopkins University Press, 1962.

Gabay, Marcos, and Carlos María Gutiérrez. *Integración latinoamericana? De la Alianza para el Progreso a la OLAS.* Montevideo: Ediciones Cruz del Sur, 1967.

Goodman, David, and Michael Redclift, eds. *Environment and Development in Latin America: The Politics of Sustainability.* Manchester, UK: Manchester University Press, 1991.

Inter-American Development Bank, Environment Committee. *1994 Annual Report on the Environment and Natural Resources.* Washington, D.C.: IADB, 1995.

Levinson, Jerome, and Juan de Onís. *The Alliance that Lost its Way.* Chicago, IL: Quadrangle Books, 1970.

MacDonald, Gordon J., Daniel L. Nielson, and Marc A. Stern. *Latin American Environmental Policy in International Perspective.* Boulder, CO: Westview Press, 1996.

May, Herbert K. *Problems and Prospects of the Alliance for Progress: A Critical Examination.* New York: Praeger, 1968.

Moscoso, Teodoro, "The Will to Economic Development." In *The Alliance for Progress: A Retrospective*, edited by L. Ronald Scheman, 81–87. Westport, CT: Praeger, 1988.

Muñoz, Heraldo, ed. *Environment and Diplomacy in the Americas.* Boulder, CO: Lynne Rienner, 1992.

——— and Robin Rosenberg. *Difficult Liaison: Trade and the Environment in the Americas.* Coral Gables, FL: North-South Center Press, 1993.

OAS. *Alliance for Progress. Official Documents Emanating from the Special Meeting of the Inter-American Economic and Social Council at the Ministerial Level.* Washington, D.C.: OAS, 1961.

———, ESESA. *The Economy of Latin America and the Caribbean: Guidelines for a Comprehensive Approach to the Foreign Debt Problem and Possible Action by the Inter-American System.* Washington, D.C.: OAS, 1986.

———. *The Economy of Latin America and the Caribbean: Analysis and Interpretation Prompted by the Financial Crisis.* Washington, D.C.: OAS, 1984.

OAS, General Secretariat. *Inter-American Program of Action for Environmental Protection.* OEA/Ser P, AG/doc 2769/91, rev. 2 (June 8, 1991).

—. *Hemispheric Cooperation and Integral Development.* Washington, D.C.: OAS, 1982.

—. *Latin America and the Reform of the International Monetary System.* Washington, D.C.: OAS, 1972.

—. *Latin America's Development and the Alliance for Progress.* Washington, D.C.: 1973.

—. *Meeting of Chiefs of State, Punta del Este, Uruguay, April 12– 14, 1967.* Washington, D.C.: OAS, 1967.

—. *The Organization of American States and the Issues of Environment and Development: Draft Report.* OEA/Ser.G, AG/doc. 2834 May 1992. Washington, D.C.: OAS, 1992. Especially chap. 3.

Painter, Michael, and William H. Durham, eds. *The Social Causes of Environmental Destruction in Latin America.* Ann Arbor: University of Michigan Press, 1995.

Prebisch, Raúl. "Economic Aspects of the Alliance for Progress." In *The Alliance for Progress: Problems and Perspectives,* edited by John C. Dreier, 24–65. Baltimore, MD: The Johns Hopkins University Press, 1962.

Roett, Riordan. "The Debt Crisis and Economic Development in Latin America." In *The United States and Latin America in the 1990s: Beyond the Cold War,* edited by Jonathan Hartlyn, Lars Schoultz, and Augusto Varas, 131–151. Chapel Hill, NC.: University of North Carolina Press, 1992.

Rogers, William D. *The Twilight Struggle: The Alliance for Progress and the Politics of Development in Latin America.* New York: Random House, 1967.

Sanz de Santamaría, Carlos. *Revolución silenciosa.* México: Fondo de Cultura Económica, 1971.

Scheman, L. Ronald, ed. *The Alliance for Progress: A Retrospective.* Westport, CT: Praeger, 1988.

Tulchin, Joseph S., with Andrew I. Rudman, eds. *Economic Development and Environmental Protection in Latin America.* Boulder, CO: Westview Press, 1991.

United States Congress. *Survey of the Alliance for Progress.* Compilation of Studies and Hearings of the Subcommittee on American Republics Affairs of the Committee on Foreign Relations. Washington, D.C.: U.S. Government Printing Office, 1969.

10. Cuba

Bermúdez, Colón. *Der Einfluss der Kubanischen Revolution auf Grundlagen und Funktionsfähigkeit des Inter-Amerikanischen Systems.* Berlin: Freie Universität, 1968.

Brenner, Philip. *From Confrontation to Negotiation: U.S. Relations with Cuba.* Boulder, CO: Westview Press, 1988.

Conte Agüero, Luis. *Cuba, la OEA y la fuerza interamericana de paz.* Coral Gables, FL: Service Offset Printers, 1965.

Corominas, Enrique Ventura. *México, Cuba y la OEA.* Buenos Aires: Ediciones Política, Economía y Finanzas, 1965.

Fontaine, Roger W. *On Negotiating with Cuba.* Washington, D.C.: American Enterprise Institute for Public Policy Research, 1975.

Franklin, Jane. *The Cuban Revolution and the United States: A Chronological History.* 2nd ed. Dobbs Ferry, NY: Oceana Press, 1995.

García Amador, Francisco V. *La cuestión Cubana en la OEA y la crisis del sistema interamericano.* Coral Gables, FL: University of Miami, Graduate School of International Studies, 1987.

Jamison, Edwin Alden. "Cuba and the Inter-American System: Exclusion of the Castro Regime from the Organization of American States." *The Americas* 36, no. 3 (January 1980): 317–346.

Krinsky, Michael, and David Golove, eds. *United States Economic Measures Against Cuba: Proceedings in the United Nations and International Law Issues.* Northampton, MA: Aletheia Press, 1993.

Larson, David L. *The 'Cuban Crisis' of 1962: Selected Documents and Chronology.* Boston, MA: Houghton Mifflin Co., 1963.

Mattfeldt, Rudolf. "Monroe-Doktrin, Kuba und OAS." *Aussenpolitik* [Stuttgart] 10, no. 11 (October, 1960): 619–699.

Organization of American States, General Secretariat. *Eighth Meeting of Consultation of Ministers of Foreign Affairs. Serving as Organ of Consultation in Application of the Inter-American Treaty of Reciprocal Assistance.* Punta del Este, Uruguay, January 22–31, 1962. Washington, D.C.: OAS, 1962.

Plank, John, ed. *Cuba and the United States: Long Range Perspectives.* Washington, D.C.: Brookings Institution, 1967.

Ronning, C. Neale. *Punta del Este: The Limits of Collective Security in a Troubled Hemisphere.* New York: Carnegie Endowment for International Peace, 1963.

Szulc, Tad. "Exporting the Cuban Revolution." In *Cuba and the United States: Long Range Perspectives,* edited by John Plank, 69–97. Washington, D.C.: The Brookings Institution, 1967.

Taylor, Maxwell. *Operation ZAPATA: The Ultra-Sensitive Report and Testimony of the Board of Inquiry on the Bay of Pigs.* Frederick, MD: Aletheia Books, 1981.

Tondel, Lyman M., Jr., ed. *The Inter-American Security System and the Cuban Crisis.* Dobbs Ferry, NY: Oceana Publications, 1964.

Welch, Richard E. *Response to Revolution: The United States and the Cuban Revolution, 1959–1961.* Chapel Hill: University of North Carolina Press, 1985.

Whitaker, Arthur P. "Cuba's Intervention in Venezuela: A Test of the OAS." *Orbis* 8 (Autumn 1964): 511–536.

Wilson, Larman C. "International Law and the United States Cuban Quarantine of 1962." *Journal of Inter-American Studies* 7, no. 4 (October, 1965): 485–492.

———. "Multilateral Policy and the Organization of American States: Latin American-U.S. Convergence and Divergence." In *Latin American Foreign Policies: An Analysis,* edited by Harold E. Davis and Larman C. Wilson, et al., 47–84. Baltimore, MD: Johns Hopkins University Press, 1975.

———. "The Settlement of Conflicts within the Framework of Relations between Regional Organizations and the United Nations: The Case of Cuba, 1962–1964." *Netherlands International Law Review* 22, no. 3 (1975): 282–318.

III. Other Regional and Subregional Organizations

A. Common Markets, Developments Banks, Free Trade, and Integration Associations

1. General and Regional

Axline, W. Andrew. *Caribbean Integration.* New York: Nicholas Publishers, 1979.

Baer, Werner, and Melissa H. Birch, eds. *Privatization in Latin America: New Roles for the Public and Private Sectors.* Westport, CT: Greenwood Press Group, 1994.

Barros C., Raymundo, ed. *El momento actual de la cooperación y la integración económica en América Latina.* Santiago: Universidad de Chile, Editorial Universitaria, 1978.

Beretta, Nora, Fernando Lorenzo, and Carlos Paolino. *En el umbral de la integración.* Montevideo, Uruguay: Centro de Investigaciones Económicas; Ediciones de la Banda Oriental, 1991.

Bernal, Richard L. *Paths to the Free Trade Area of the Americas.* Washington, D.C.: Center for Strategic and International Studies, January 15, 1997.

Bizzozero, Lincoln, Klaus Bodemer, and Marcel Vaillant, eds. *Nuevos regionalismos: cooperación o conflicto?* Caracas: Editorial Nueva Sociedad, 1994.

Bouzas, Roberto, and Nora Lustig. *Liberalización comercial e integración regional: de NAFTA a MERCOSUR.* Buenos Aires, Argentina: Facultad Latinoamericana de Ciencias Sociales (FLACSO); Emece Editores, 1992.

Bryan, Anthony T., ed. *The Caribbean: New Dynamics in Trade and Political Economy.* Boulder, CO: Lynne Rienner Publishers, 1995.

————, and Andrés Serbin, eds. *Distant Cousins: The Caribbean-Latin American Relationship.* Boulder, CO: Lynne Rienner Publishers, 1996.

Culpeper, Roy. *Titan or Behemoths?: The Multilateral Banks, Vol 5.* Boulder, CO: Lynne Rienner Publishers, 1995.

Dietz, James. *Latin America's Economic Development: Confronting Crisis.* Boulder, CO: Lynne Rienner, 1995.

Feinberg, Richard, and Ricardo Ffrench-Davis, eds. *Development and External Debt in Latin America: Basis for a New Consensus.* Notre Dame, IN: University of Notre Dame Press, 1988.

Frankel, Jeffrey A. *Regional Trading Blocs in the World Economic System.* Washington, D.C.: Institute for International Economics, 1997.

Frohmann, Alicia. *Cooperación política e integración latinoamericana en los '90.* Santiago, Chile: FLACSO, 1996.

García-Amador, F. V., ed. *Instruments of Economic Integration in Latin America and the Caribbean.* 2 vols. Dobbs Ferry, NY: Oceana Publications, 1975.

Gauhar, Altaf, ed. *Regional Integration: The Latin American Experience.* London: Third World Foundation for Social and Economic Studies, 1985.

Grunwald, Joseph, Miguel S. Wionczek, and Martin Carnoy. *Latin American Economic Integration and U.S. Policy.* Washington, D.C.: Brookings Institution, 1972.

Hufbauer, Gary C., and Jeffrey J. Schott, eds. *Western Hemisphere Economic Integration.* Washington, D.C.: Institute for International Economics, 1994.

Iglesias, Enrique, ed. *The Legacy of Raúl Prebisch.* Westport, CT: Greenwood Press, 1993.

Inter-American Development Bank (IDB) and Economic Commission for Latin America and the Caribbean (ECLAC). *Trade Liberalization in the Western Hemisphere.* Washington, D.C.: IDB/ECLAC, 1995.

Inter-American Institute for International Legal Studies. *Instruments Relating to the Economic Integration of Latin America.* Dobbs Ferry, NY: Oceana Publications, 1968.

Instituto de Relaciones Europeo-Latinoamericanas (IRELA). *Foreign Direct Investment in Developing Countries: The Case of Latin America.* Madrid: IRELA, 1994.

————. *Prospects for the Processes of Sub-Regional Integration in Central and South America.* Madrid: IRELA, 1992.

Kozolchyk, Boris, ed. *Making Free Trade Work in the Americas.* Vol. 1. Irvington, NY: Transnational Juris Publications, 1995.

Lawton, Jorge A., ed. *Privatization Amidst Poverty: Contemporary Challenges in Latin American Political Economy.* Coral Gables, FL: North-South Center Press, 1995.

Mace, Gordon, and Jean-Philippe Thérien, eds. *Foreign Policy and Regionalism in the Americas.* Boulder, CO: Lynne Rienner Publishers, 1996.

McAfee, Kathy. *Storm Signals: Structural Adjustment and Development Alternatives in the Caribbean.* Boston, MA: South End Press, 1995.

Maritano, Nino. *A Latin American Economic Community: History, Policies, and Problems.* Notre Dame, IN: University of Notre Dame Press, 1970.

Nazmi, Nader. *Economc Policy and Stabilization in Latin America.* Armonk, NY: M. E. Sharpe, 1996.

Nishijima, Shoji, and Peter H. Smith, eds. *Cooperation or Rivalry? Regional Integration in the Americas and the Pacific Rim.* Boulder, CO: Westview Press, 1996.

Ocampo López, Javier. *Historia de las ideas de integración de América Latina.* Instituto de Estudios para el Desarrollo y la Integración de América Latina. Serie Fundamentos y doctrina. Vol. 1. Tunja-Boyaca, Colombia: Editorial Bolivariana Internacional, 1981.

Organization of American States, Group of Experts, Inter-American Economic and Social Council. *Hemispheric Cooperation and Integral Development: Report for the General Secretariat.* Washington, D.C.: Organization of American States, 1982.

———, *Hemispheric Cooperation and Integral Development: Report for the OAS Special Assembly.* Rev. ed., 2 vols. Washington, D.C.: Organization of American States, 1986.

———, Trade Unit, Council for Integral Development. *Hacía el libre comercio en las Américas/Toward Free Trade in the Americas.* Washington, D.C.: OAS, 1995.

———, *Trade and Integration Arrangements in the Americas: An Analytical Compendium.* Washington, D.C.: OAS, distribution and release dependent upon approval by all member governments (expected in late 1997).

Rojas Aravena, Francisco, ed. *América Latina y la Initiativa para las Américas.* Santiago: FLACSO, 1993.

Saborio, Sylvia, ed. *The Premise and the Promise: Free Trade in the Americas.* Washington, D.C.: Overseas Development Council and Transaction Publishers, 1992.

Segal, Aaron. *The Politics of Caribbean Economic Integration.* Rio Piedras: University of Puerto Rico, 1968.

"El Sistema Centro-Periferia en Transformación." *Pensamiento Iberoamericano: Revista de Economía Política,* no. 11 (January–June 1987).

Smith, Robert Sidney, et al. *Economic Systems and Public Policy; Essays in Honor of Calvin Bryce Hoover.* Durham, NC: Duke University Press, 1966.

Thorp, Rosemary, and Laurence Whitehead, eds. *Latin American Debt and the Adjustment Crisis*. London: Macmillan, 1987.

Tussie, Diana, and David Glover, eds. *The Developing Countries in World Trade: Policies and Bargaining Strategies*. Boulder, CO: Lynne Rienner Publishers, 1993.

Twentieth Century Fund. *In the Shadow of the Debt: Emerging Issues in Latin America*. New York: Twentieth Century Fund Press, 1992.

United Nations, Economic Commission on Latin America and the Caribbean. *Open Regionalism in Latin America and the Caribbean: Economic Integration as a Contribution to Changing Production Patterns with Social Equity*. Santiago, Chile: ECLAC, 1992.

U.S. Congress, Senate, Committee on Governmental Affairs. *U.S. Participation in the Multilateral Development Banks*. Washington, D.C.: Government Printing Office, 1979.

United States, U.S. International Trade Commission. *U.S. Market Access in Latin America: Recent Liberalization Measures and Remaining Barriers (With a Special Case Study on Chile)*. Washington, D.C.: United States International Trade Commission, 1992.

————. *The Year in Trade 1994: Operation of the Trade Agreements Program*. 46th Report. Washington, D.C.: United States International Trade Commission, 1995.

Weintraub, Sidney. *Caribbean Integration Into the World Economic System*. Washington, D.C.: Center for Strategic and International Studies, 1995.

————. *Integrating the Americas: Shaping Future Trade Policy*. New Brunswick, NJ: Transaction Books, 1994.

————. *Prospects for Hemispheric Trade and Economic Integration*. Washington, D.C.: Center for Strategic and International Studies, 1995.

Williamson, John, ed. *Latin American Adjustment: How Much Has Happened?* Washington, D.C.: Institute for International Economics, 1990.

————. *The Progress of Policy Reform in Latin America*. Washington, D.C.: Institute for International Economics, 1990.

Wionczek, Miguel S. *Latin American Economic Integration: Experiences and Prospects*. New York: Praeger, 1966.

Wish, John R. *Economic Development in Latin America: An Annotated Bibliography*. New York: Praeger, 1965.

a. Inter-American Development Bank

Dell, Sidney. *The Inter-American Bank: A Study in Developing Financing*. New York: Praeger, 1972.

DeWitt, R. Peter, Jr. *The Inter-American Development Bank and Politi-*

cal Influence: With Special Reference to Costa Rica. New York: Praeger, 1977.

Inter-American Development Bank. *Dos décadas al servicio de América Latina: 20 años de actividades.* Washington, D.C.: BID, 1980.

———. *Economic and Social Progress in Latin America.* Washington, DC: Inter-American Development Bank, 1961–. Published annually.

———. *Fifteen Years of Activities: 1960–74.* Washington, D.C.: Inter-American Development Bank, 1974.

———. and Economic Commission for Latin America and the Caribbean (ECLAC). *Trade Liberalization in the Western Hemisphere.* Washington, D.C.: IDB and ECLAC, 1995.

Sánchez, Manuel, and Rossana Corona, eds. *Privatization in Latin America.* Westport, CT: Greenwood Press, 1993.

Syz, John. *International Development Banks.* Dobbs Ferry, NY: Oceana Publications, 1974.

Tussie, Diana. *The Inter-American Development Bank.* Boulder, CO: Lynne Rienner, 1994.

b. Latin American Economic System

Brown, Fortunato. *El SELA y el drama económico latinoamericano.* Caracas: Editora ABCD, 1984.

Díaz Muller, Luis. *El Sistema Económico Latinoamericano: proposiciones para un modelo subregional.* Santiago: Instituto de Estudios Internacionales, Universidad de Chile, 1977.

Latin American Economic System (LAES). *Latin American-U.S. Economic Relations 1982–1983: Latin American Economic System.* Boulder, CO: Westview Press, 1984.

Luddemann, M.K. "SELA, The Latin American Economic System in Action: A Preliminary Assessment of its Performance." Georgetown University Graduate School. Washington, D.C.: Georgetown University, 1979.

Martz, Mary Jeanne Reid. "SELA: The Latin American Economic System 'Ploughing the Seas?' " *Inter-American Economic Affairs* 32 (1979): 33–64.

Pérez, Carlos Andrés, et al. *El SELA: presente y futuro de la cooperación económica intralatinoamérica.* Buenos Aires: Instituto para la Integración de América Latina, Banco Inter-Americano de Desarrollo, 1986.

2. The Caribbean

a. Caribbean Community and Caribbean Free Trade Association

Axline, W. Andrew. *Caribbean Integration: The Politics of Regionalism.* London, U.K.: Frances Pinter; New York: Nichols Publishing Company, 1979.

Beltrán, Luis, and Andrés Serbin, eds. *The Caribe entre Europa y América: evolución y perspectivas.* Caracas, Venezuela: Editorial Nueva Sociedad, 1992.

Bryan, Anthony T., ed. *The Caribbean: New Dynamics in Trade and Political Economy.* Boulder, CO: Lynne Rienner, 1995.

——. "CARICOM: The Caribbean Community in a Post-NAFTA World: Facing the Free Trade Dilemma." *North-South Focus* 1, no. 1 (1994).

Calderón Cruz, Angel, ed. *Problemas del Caribe contemporáneo/Contemporary Caribbean Issues.* Rio Piedras, PR: Instituto de Estudios del Caribe, Universidad de Puerto Rico, 1979.

Caribbean Community. *Annual Report of the Secretary-General of the Caribbean Community.* Georgetown, Guyana: CARICOM Secretariat, 1989–. Published annually.

——. *The Caribbean Community in the 1980s: Report.* Georgetown, Guyana: Caribbean Community Secretariat, 1981.

Chernick, S. E. *The Commonwealth Caribbean: The Integration Experience: Report of a Mission Sent to the Commonwealth Caribbean by the World Bank.* Baltimore, MD: Published for the World Bank by Johns Hopkins University Press, 1978.

Clagett, Helen L. "Bibliography on Economic Integration in Latin America." In Inter-American Institute of International Legal Studies, *Instruments Relating to the Economic Integration of Latin America,* 419–450. Dobbs Ferry, NY: Oceana Publications, 1968.

Comitas, Lambros. *Complete Caribbean, 1900–1975: A Bibliographical Guide to the Scholarly Literature.* Millwood, NY: K.T.O. Press, 1977.

Crassweller, Robert D. *The Caribbean Community: Changing Societies and U.S. Policy.* New York: Published for the Council on Foreign Relations by Praeger, 1972.

Erisman, H. Michael. *Pursuing Postdependency Politics: South-South Relations in the Caribbean.* Boulder, CO: Lynne Rienner Publishers, 1992.

Gómez, María, and Fredic Kayser. *The Caribbean Common Market: Implications for U.S. Business.* Washington, D.C.: U.S. Department of Commerce, International Trade Administration, 1981.

Goslinga, Marian. *A Bibliography of the Caribbean.* Lanham, MD: The Scarecrow Press, Inc., 1996.

Griffith, Winston H. "CARICOM Countries and the Caribbean Basin Initiative." *Latin American Perspectives* 17, no. 1 (Winter, 1990): 33–54.

Hosten-Craig, Jennifer. *The Effect of a North American Free Trade Agreement on the Commonwealth Caribbean.* Lewistown, PA: Mellen Press, 1992.

Instituto de Relaciones Europeo-Latinoamericanas (IRELA). *Foreign*

Direct Investment in Latin America and the Caribbean: An Overview of Flows from Europe, Japan and the United States, 1979–1990. Madrid: IRELA, 1993.

Inter-American Development Bank. *Ten Years of CARICOM: Papers presented at a Seminar sponsored by the Inter-American Development Bank, July 1983.* Washington, D.C.: IADB, 1983.

Klak, Thomas, ed. *Globalization and Neoliberalism: The Caribbean Context.* Lanham, MD: Rowman and Littlefield, 1997.

Lowenthal, David. *The West Indies Federation: Perspectives on a New Nation.* Westport, CT: Greenwood Press, 1976.

———, and Lambros Comitas, eds. *The Aftermath of Sovereignty: West Indian Perspectives.* Garden City, NY: Doubleday, 1973.

Manley, Michael. *Jamaica: Struggle in the Periphery.* London: Readers and Writers, 1982.

Payne, Anthony J. *The Politics of the Caribbean Community, 1961–1979: Regional Integration Amongst New States.* New York: St. Martin's Press, 1980.

Preiswerk, Roy, ed. *Regionalism and the Commonwealth Caribbean. Seminar on the Foreign Policies of Caribbean States.* St. Augustine, Trinidad: Institute of International Relations, University of the West Indies, 1969.

Segal, Aaron. *The Politics of Caribbean Economic Integration.* Rio Piedras: University of Puerto Rico, 1968.

Serbín, Andrés. "The CARICOM States and the Group of Three: A New Partnership Between Latin America and the Non-Hispanic Caribbean." *Journal of Inter-American Studies and World Affairs* 33 (Summer 1991): 53–80.

———. "Towards an Association of Caribbean States: Raising Some Awkward Questions." *Journal of Inter-American Studies and World Affairs* 36 (Winter 1994): 61–90.

———, and Anthony Bryan, eds. *El Caribe hacía el 2000.* Caracas, Venezuela: Editorial Nueva Sociedad, 1991.

———. *El Caribe: zona de paz? Geo-política, integración y seguridad en el Caribe no hispánico.* Caracas, Venezuela: Editorial Nueva Sociedad, 1989.

———. *Vecinos indiferentes? El Caribe de habla inglesa y América Latina.* Caracas, Venezuela: Editorial Nueva Sociedad, 1990.

Summit of the Americas Center, Florida International University. *Association of Caribbean States (ACS).* Miami, FL: Summit of the Americas Publications, 1996.

Vega, Bernardo. *Estudio de las Implicaciones de la Incorporación de la República Dominicana a la Comunidad del Caribe.* Santo Domingo, RD: Fondo para el Avance de las Ciencias Sociales, 1978.

Watson, Hilbourne A. *The Caribbean in the Global Political Economy.* Boulder, CO: Lynne Rienner Publishers, 1994.

————, Guest ed. "Human Resources and Institutional Requirements for Global Adjustments: Strategies for the Caribbean." (Special Issue). *21st Century Policy Review* 2, nos. 1–2 (Spring 1994).

Weintraub, Sidney. *Caribbean Integration into the World Economic System.* Washington, D.C.: Policy Papers on the Americas, Vol. VI, Study 8, CSIS (July 27, 1995).

West Indian Commission. *Overview of the Report of the Indian Commission: A Time for Action.* Black Rock, Barbados: West Indian Commission, 1992.

b. Caribbean Development Bank

Caribbean Development Bank. *CDB Annual Report.* St. Michael, Barbados: CDB, 1970–. Published annually.

————. *The First Twenty Years, 1970–1990.* St. Michael, Barbados: CDB, 1991.

Hardy, Chandra. *The Multilateral Development Banks: Vol. 3, The Caribbean Development Bank.* Boulder, CO: Lynne Rienner, 1995.

Marshall, Ione. *Barbados and the CDB, Background Paper.* St. Michael, Barbados: CDB, August 1992.

Reid, George. *Jamaica's Relations with the CDB 1970–1992.* Kingston: North-South Institute, University of the West Indies, 1995.

St. Rose, Marius. *The CDB as an Instrument for Promoting Economic Cooperation and Development.* St. Michael, Barbados: CDB, July 1990.

3. Central America

a. Central American Common Market

Business International Corporation. *The Central American Common Market: Profits & Problems in an Integrating Economy.* New York: Business International Corporation, 1969.

Cline, William R., and Enrique Delgado. *Economic Integration in Central America.* Washington, D.C.: The Brookings Institution, 1978.

Cochrane, James D. *The Politics of Regional Integration: The Central American Case.* New Orleans, LA: Tulane University, 1969.

Cohen Orantes, Isaac. *Regional Integration in Central America.* Lexington, MA: D.C. Heath Publishers, 1972.

Colombia, Presidencia de la República. *Central America in the Midst of the Whirlwind: Essays on the Crisis and its Alternatives: Proceedings of the International Symposium on Central America and the Capital-*

ization of the Central-American Bank of Economic Integration, Cartagena, Colombia, November 28–30, 1984. Bogotá: The Presidency, 1986.

Costa Rica, Inter-American Development Bank, Instituto Centroamericano de Administración Pública. Temas sobre integración Centroamericana. San José, Costa Rica: ICAP-BID, 1979.

Fagen, Stuart I. Central American Economic Integration: The Politics of Unequal Benefits. Berkeley, CA: Institute of International Studies, University of California Press, 1970.

Fuentes Mohr, Alberto. La creación de un mercado común: apuntes históricos sobre la experiencia de centroamerica. Buenos Aires: Instituto para la Integración de América Latina, B.I.D., 1973.

Gordon, Michael W. Mexico, Central America, Panama, and the Central American Common Market. Dobbs Ferry, NY: Oceana Publications, 1981.

Holbik, Karel, and Philip L. Swan. Trade and Industrialization in the Central American Common Market; The First Decade. Austin: Bureau of Business Research, University of Texas at Austin, 1972.

Irvin, George. Central America: The Future of Economic Integration. Boulder, CO: Westview Press, 1989.

Lizano Fait, Eduardo. Tres ensayos sobre Centroamerica. San José, Costa Rica: FLACSO, 1990.

McClelland, Donald H. The Central American Common Market; Economic Policies, Economic Growth, and Choices for the Future. New York: Praeger, 1972.

Nugent, Jeffrey B. Economic Integration in Central America: Empirical Investigations. Baltimore, MD: Johns Hopkins University Press, 1974.

Ramsett, David E. Regional Integration Development in Central America: A Case Study of the Integration Scheme. New York: Praeger Publishers, 1969.

Royer, Daniel King. The Central American Common Market. Gainesville: University of Florida, 1964.

Schmitter, Philippe C. Autonomy or Dependence as Regional Integration Outcomes: Central America. Research Series No. 17. Berkeley: Institute of International Studies, University of California, 1972.

Shaw, Royce Q. Central America: Regional Integration and National Political Development. Boulder, CO: Westview Press, 1978.

Swan, Philip L. Trade and Industrialization in the Central American Common Market: The First Decade. Austin: Bureau of Business Research, University of Texas at Austin, 1972.

Walter, Ingo, and Hans C. Vitzthum. The Central American Common Market; A Case Study on Economic Integration in Developing Regions. New York: Institute of Finance, New York University, 1967.

Wardlaw, Andrew B. *Achievement and Problems of the Central American Common Market: A Report.* Washington, D.C.: Office of External Research, U.S. Department of State, 1969.

4. South America

a. Andean Group

Barrera, Cristina, Oswaldo Dávila, and Marc Meinardus, eds. *Integración y burocracia. Trabas no arancelarias.* Caracas: Editorial Nueva Sociedad, 1991.

Barros Charlín, Raymundo. *Vigencia y proyección e ALALC y del Pacto Andino.* Santiago: Instituto de Estudios Internacionales, Universidad de Chile, 1976.

Bywater, Marion. *Andean Integration, A New Lease on Life?* London: The Economist Intelligence Unit, 1990.

Díaz Albónico, Rodrigo, ed. *Estabilidad y flexibilidad en el ordenamiento jurídico de ALALC y Pacto Andino.* Santiago: Editorial Universitaria, Universidad de Chile, 1978.

Fontaine, Roger. *The Andean Pact: A Political Analysis.* Beverly Hills, CA: Sage Publications, 1977.

Morawetz, David. *The Andean Group; A Case Study in Economic Integration Among Developing Countries.* Cambridge, MA: Massachusetts Institute of Technology, 1974.

Mytelka, Lynn Krieger. *Regional Development in a Global Economy: The Multinational Corporation, Technology, and Andean Integration.* New Haven, CT: Yale University Press, 1979.

Orrego Vicuña, Francisco. *Cambio y estabilidad en la integración económica: el marco conceptual y la experiencia del Grupo Andino.* Santiago: Instituto de Estudios Internacionales, Universidad de Chile, 1976.

Puyana de Palacios, Alicia. *Economic Integration Among Unequal Partners: The Case of the Andean Group.* New York: Pergamon Press, 1982.

Rioseco Vásquez, Alberto. *El proceso de retiro de Chile del Acuerdo de Cartagena.* Santiago: Instituto de Estudios Internacionales, Universidad de Chile, 1978.

Salgado, Germánico, and Rafael Urriola, eds. *El fin de las barreras. Los empresarios y el Pacto Andino en la década de los 90.* Caracas: Editorial Nueva Sociedad, 1991.

Seidel, Robert Neal. *Toward an Andean Common Market for Science and Technology; Public Policy for Science, Technology and Industrialization in the Andean Group.* Ithaca, NY: Program on Policies for

Science and Technology in Developing Nations, Cornell University, 1974.

United States, General Accounting Office. *U.S. Direct Investment in South America's Andean Common Market: Department of Commerce Report to Congress.* Washington, D.C.: General Accounting Office, 1977.

b. Rio Group

Colombia, Presidencia de la República. *La integración Latinoamericana: El Grupo de Rio, El Grupo Andino, El Grupo de los Tres.* Bogotá: Secretaría de Información y Prensa de la Presidencia de la República, 1995.

Institute for European-Latin American Relations (IELAR but better known by its Spanish acronym, IRELA). "The Group of Eight: A New Regional Actor for Latin America?" *Dossier No. 17.* Madrid: IRELA, 1989.

Yopo H., Boris. "The Rio Group: Decline or Consolidation of the Latin American *Concertación* Policy?" *Journal of Inter-American Studies* 33 (Winter 1991): 27–44.

c. Group of Three

Colombia, Presidencia de la República. *La integración Latinoamericana: El Grupo de Rio, El Grupo Andino, El Grupo de los Tres.* Bogotá: Secretaría de Información y Prensa de la Presidencia de la República, 1995.

Serbin, Andrés and Carlos A. Romero, eds. *El Grupo de los Tres: Aasimetrías y convergencias.* Caracas: Editorial Nueva Sociedad, 1993.

d. Latin American Free Trade Association and Latin American Integration Association

Business International Corporation. *LAFTA; Key to Latin America's 200 Million Consumers.* New York: Business International Corporation, 1966.

Cahaparro Alfonzo, Julio. *ALADI o el nuevo orden de integración regional.* Caracas: I.P. Publications, 1981.

Milenky, Edward S. *The Politics of Regional Organization in Latin America: The Latin American Free Trade Association (LAFTA).* New York: Praeger, 1973.

Rebella, Jorge, and Evelyn Samore. *Gaining a Competitive Edge in Latin America through LAIA.* New York: Business International Corporation, 1988.

Serwiansky, Bernardo. *ALADI: Un nuevo esquema de integración latinoamericana*. 2 vols. Montevideo, Uruguay: Fundación de Cultura Universitaria, 1983.

Wionczec, Miguel. "Latin American Integration and United States Economic Policies." In *International Organization in the Western Hemisphere*, edited by Robert W. Gregg, 91–156. Syracuse, NY: Syracuse University Press, 1968.

e. Southern Cone Common Market

Abreu, Sergio. *MERCOSUR e integración*. Montevideo, Uruguay: Fundación de Cultura Universitaria, 1991.

Baumann, Renato. "Integración y desviación de comercio." *Revista de la Cepal: Naciones Unidas, Comisión Económica para América Latina y el Caribe* 51 (December 1993): 133–48.

Bizzozero, Lincoln. "La relación entre el MERCOSUR y la Comunidad Europea: un nuevo parametro de vinculación?" *Estudios Internacionales* [Chile] 26 (January-March, 1993): 37–56.

Canitrot, Adolfo, et al. *Macroeconomic Conditions and Trade Liberalization*. Washington, D.C.: Inter-American Development Bank; Baltimore, MD: Johns Hopkins University Press, 1993.

Cardenas, Emilio J. "Road to Mercosur." *Latinfinance* 35 (March, 1992): 44–46.

Centro de Economía Internacional (ed.). *Estudios Argentinos para la integración del MERCOSUR*. Buenos Aires: El Centro, 1993.

Chudnovsky, Daniel. "El futuro de la integración hemisférica: El Mercosur y la iniciativa para las Américas." *Desarrollo Económico* [Argentina] 32 (January–March, 1993): 483–511.

Díaz, Eduardo Alberto. "Estratégias empresariales para la integración: el papel de la Universidad en su determinación." *Integración Latinoamericana: Instituto para la Integración de América* 18 (October, 1993): 15–22.

Fairlie Reinoso, Alan. "Crisis, integración y desarrollo en América Latina: la dinámica del Grupo Andino con el MERCOSUR en la década de 1980." *Integración Latinoamericana: Instituto para la Integración de América* 18 (August, 1993): 11–40.

Halperin, Marcelo. "Lealtad competitiva y dilemas de la integración: el caso del MERCOSUR." *Integración Latinoamericana: Instituto para la Integración de América* 17 (November 1992): 36–43.

————. "El reto de la 'nueva' integración: objectivos e instrumentos para la consolidación del MERCOSUR." *Integración Latinoamericana: Instituto para la Integración de América* 17 (January–February 1992): 32–40.

Halperin, Marcelo, et al. *Instrumentos básicos de integración económ-*

ica en América Latina y el Caribe. Buenos Aires: Instituto para la Integración de América Latina, Banco Interamericano de Desarrollo, 1992.

————, and Bill Hinchberger. "Mercosur on the March." *Institutional Investor* 27 (March 1993): 107–112.

Ibarra Pardo, Gabriel. "Políticas de competencia en la integración en América Latina." *Integración Latinoamericana: Instituto para la Integración de América* 18 (September 1993): 45–51.

Lavopa, Jorge H. "La estructura orgánica funcional del MERCOSUR." *Contribuciones: Centro Interdisciplinario de Estudios Sobre el Desarrollo Latinoamericano* [Argentina] 10 (April–June 1993): 19–33.

Manzetti, Luigi. "Political Economy of MERCOSUR." *Journal of Inter-American Studies and World Affairs* 35 (Winter 1993–94): 101–141.

Mayoral, Alejandro. "Armonización de políticas macro en el MERCOSUR." *Contribuciones: Centro Interdisciplinario de Estudios Sobre el Desarrollo Latinoamericano* 10 (April–June 1993): 57–66.

Pastori, Alejandro. "Marché commun du sud: MERCOSUR." *Revue du Marché Commun et de L'Union Européene* 372 (November 1993): 778–784.

Peña, Felix. "MERCOSUR y NAFTA: dos realidades hemisféricas." *Contribuciones: Centro Interdisciplinario de Estudios Sobre el Desarrollo Latinoamericano* 10 (April–June 1993): 95–101.

Purcell, Susan Kaufman, and Riordan Roett, eds. *Brazil Under Cardoso.* Boulder, CO: Lynne Rienner, 1997.

Quartino, Jorge. *Sur, MERCOSUR y después.* Montevideo, Uruguay: Fundación de Cultura Universitaria, 1991.

Rigg, Melissa, and Seymour Goodman. "MERCOSUR: Reconciling Four Disparate Information Technology Policies." *International Information Systems* 1 (July 1992): 73–86.

Rojas Aravena, Francisco. "El cono sur latinoamericano y la iniciativa para las Américas." *Estudios Internacionales* 26 (January–March 1993): 98–122.

Sanguinetti, Julio Maria, Sergio Abreu and Alberto Couriel. *Uruguay y el MERCOSUR.* Montevideo, Uruguay: Editorial Universidad, 1991.

Villamil, J. Antonio. "La actitud de los EE.UU. frente al MERCOSUR." *Contribuciones: Centro Interdisciplinario de Estudios Sobre el Desarrollo Latinoamericano* 10 (April–June 1993): 103–107.

Villanueva, Javier. "La experiencia de la Comunidad Europea: posibles lecciones para el Mercosur." *Contribuciones: Centro Interdisciplinario de Estudios Sobre el Desarrollo Latinoamericano* 9 (April–June 1992): 7–42.

Zelada Castedo, Alberto, "Competencias legales y toma de decisiones en la integración en América Latina." *Integración Latinoamericana:*

Instituto para la Integración de América 18 (December, 1993): 57–75.

5. North America

a. North American Free Trade Agreement

Abbott, Frederick M. *Law and Policy of Regional Integration: The NAFTA and Western Hemispheric Integration in the World Trade Organization System.* Hingham, MA: Kluwer Academic Publishers, 1995.

Baer, M. Delal, and Sidney Weintraub, eds. *The NAFTA Debate: Grappling with Unconventional Trade Issues.* Boulder, CO: Lynne Rienner, 1994.

Baer, M. Delal, Joseph T. Jockel, and Sidney Weintraub, eds. *NAFTA and Sovereignty: Trade-offs for Canada, Mexico, and the United States.* Washington, D.C.: Center for Strategic and International Studies, 1996.

Barry, Donald, Mark O. Dickerson and James D. Gaisford, eds. *Toward a North American Community? Canada, the United States, and Mexico.* Boulder, CO: Westview Press, 1995.

Belous, Richard S., and Jonathan Lemco, eds. *NAFTA as a Model of Development: The Benefits and Costs of Merging High- and Low-Wage Areas.* Stony Brook, NY: State University of New York Press, 1995.

Bongnanno, Mario Frank, and Kathryn J. Ready. *The North American Free Trade Agreement: Labor, Industry, and Government Perspectives.* Westport, CT: Quorum Books, 1993.

Bulmer-Thomas, Victor, Nikki Craske, and Mónica Serrano. *Mexico and the North American Free Trade Agreement: Who Will Benefit?* New York: St. Martin's Press, 1994.

Castañeda, Jorge G. *The Mexican Shock: Its Meaning for the U.S.* New York: W.W. Norton and Co., 1996.

Fatemi, Khosrow. *North American Free Trade Agreement: Opportunities and Challenges.* New York: St Martin's Press, 1993.

Globerman, Steven. *Assessing NAFTA: A Trinational Analysis.* Vancouver, BC: Fraser Institute, 1993.

Grayson, George W. *The North American Free Trade Agreement: Regional Community and the New World Order.* Lanham, MD: University Press of America, 1994.

———. *The North American Free Trade Agreement.* Headline Series No. 299. New York: Foreign Policy Association, 1993.

Green, Roy. *The Enterprise for the Americas Initiative: Issues and Pros-*

336 • BIBLIOGRAPHY

pects for a Free Trade Agreement in the Western Hemisphere. Westport, CT: Praeger, 1993.

Hart, Michael. A North American Free Trade Agreement: The Strategic Implication for Canada. Ottawa: Centre for Trade Policy and Law and the Institute for Research on Public Policy, 1990.

Hoebing, Joyce, Sidney Weintraub, and M. Delal Baer, eds. NAFTA and Sovereignty: Trade Offs for Canada, Mexico, and the United States. Washington, D.C.: Center for Strategic and International Studies, 1996.

Holbein, James R., and Donald J. Musch, eds. NAFTA: Final Text, Summary, Legislative History & Implementation Directory. Dobbs Ferry, NY: Oceana Press, 1994.

Housman, Robert. Reconciling Trade and the Environment: Lessons from the North American Free Trade Agreement. Environment and Trade Series 3. New York: United Nations, UNEP, 1994.

Hufbauer, Gary C., and Jeffrey J. Schott. NAFTA: An Assessment. Rev. ed. Washington, D.C.: Institute for International Economics, 1993.

———. North American Free Trade: Issues and Recommendations. Washington, D.C.: Institute for International Economics, 1992.

Jorge, Antonio, Robert Cruz, and Alicia Díaz. The Enterprise for the Americas Initiative: Its Impact on South Florida. Coral Gables, FL: North-South Center Publications, 1992.

Kozolchyk, Boris, ed. Toward Seamless Borders: Making Free Trade Work in the Americas. Vol. 1. Irvington, NY: Transnational Juris Publications, 1993.

Loeb, Hamilton, et al. North American Free Trade Agreement: Opportunities and Challenges. New York: St. Martin's Press, 1993.

Lustig, Nora, Barry P. Bosworth, and Robert Z. Lawrence, eds. North American Free Trade: Assessing the Impact. Washington, D.C.: The Brookings Institution, 1992.

Marks, Siegfried, ed. Miami Report III: Recommendations for a North American Free Trade Agreement and for Future Hemispheric Trade. Coral Gables, FL: North-South Center Publications, 1992.

Martin, Philip L. Trade and Migration: NAFTA and Agriculture. Washington, D.C.: Institute for International Economics, 1993.

Moss, Ambler H. Assessments of the North American Free Trade Agreement. New Brunswick, NJ: Transaction Publishers, 1993.

O'Hop, Paul A., Jr. "Hemispheric Integration and the Elimination of Legal Obstacles Under a NAFTA-Based System." Harvard International Law Journal 36, no. 1 (Winter, 1995): 127–176.

Orme, William A., Jr. Understanding NAFTA: Mexico, Free Trade, and the New North America. Austin: University of Texas Press, 1996.

Randall, Stephen J., and Herman W. Konrad. NAFTA in Transition. Calgary, BC: University of Calgary Press, 1996.

Riggs, A. R. and Tom Velk. *Beyond NAFTA: An Economic, Political and Sociological Perspective.* Vancouver, BC: Fraser Institute, 1992.

Rochlin, James F. *Redefining Mexican 'Security': Society, State, and Region Under NAFTA.* Boulder, CO: Lynne Rienner, 1997.

Roett, Riordan, ed. *The Mexican Peso Crisis: International Perspectives.* Boulder, CO: Lynne Rienner Publishers, 1996.

Rubin, Seymour J., and Dean C. Alexander, eds. *NAFTA and the Environment.* The Hague, The Netherlands: Kluwer Law International, 1996.

Rugman, Alan M. *Foreign Investment and NAFTA.* Columbia: University of South Carolina Press, 1994.

Schott, Jeffrey J., and Murray G. Smith, eds. *The Canada-United States Trade Agreement: The Global Impact.* Washington, D.C.: Institute for International Economics, 1988.

Suchlicki, Jaime. *Mexico: From Montezuma to NAFTA, Chiapas and Beyond.* New York: Brassey's, 1995.

United States, Congress. *Foreign Policy Implications of the North American Free Trade Agreement (NAFTA) and Legislative Requirements for the Side Agreements: Hearings before the Committee on Foreign Relations.* Washington, D.C.: U.S. Government Printing Office, 1994.

————, ————. *How NAFTA will Affect U.S. Agriculture: Hearing Before the Committee on Agriculture, Nutrition, and Forestry.* United States Senate, 103rd Congress, First Session, September 21, 1993. Washington, D.C.: U.S. Government Printing Office, 1993.

————, ————. *The Impact of the North American Free Trade Agreement on U.S. Jobs and Wages: Hearing Before the Committee on Banking, Housing, and Urban Affairs.* United States Senate, 103rd Congress, First Session, April 22, 1993. Washington, D.C.: U.S. Government Printing Office, 1993.

————. *North American Free Trade Agreement: American Jobs and Environmental Protection: Hearing Before the Subcommittee on International Economic Policy and Trade and on Western Hemisphere Affairs of the Committee on Foreign Affairs.* House of Representatives, 102nd Congress, December 9, 1991. Washington, D.C.: U.S. Government Printing Office, 1992.

————, ————. *North American Free Trade Agreement: Business and Politics in Mexico: Hearing Before the Committee on Small Business, House of Representatives.* House of Representatives, 103rd Congress, First Session, October 27, 1993. Washington, D.C.: U.S. Government Printing Office, 1994.

————. *The North American Free Trade Agreement: Environment and Labor Agreements: Joint Hearing Before the Subcommittees on Economic Policy, Trade, and Environment and Western Hemisphere Affairs of the Committee on Foreign Affairs.* House of Representatives,

103rd Congress, First Session, February 24, 1993. Washington, D.C.: U.S. Government Printing Office, 1993.

————, ————. *NAFTA and Peso Devaluation: A Problem for U.S. Exporters?: Hearing Before the Committee on Small Business.* House of Representatives, 103rd Congress, First Session, May 20, 1993. Washington, D.C.: U.S. Government Printing Office, 1994.

————, ————. *The NAFTA: Report on Environmental Issues.* Washington, D.C.: U.S. Government Printing Office, 1993.

————, ————. *North American Free Trade Agreement, Texts of Agreement, Implementing Bill, Statement of Administrative Action, and Required Supporting Statements: Message from the President of the United States Transmitting North American Free Trade Agreement.* Washington, D.C.: United States Congress, 1993.

————. *Report of the Administration on the North American Free Trade Agreement and Actions Taken in Fulfillment of the May 1, 1991 Commitments.* Washington, D.C.: U.S. Govenment Printing Office.

Weintraub, Sidney. *NAFTA: What Comes Next?* The Washington Papers, No. 166. Westport, CT: Praeger Publishers, 1994.

B. Political and Security Groups

1. Contadora and Support Group, Rio Group

Bagley, Bruce. *Contadora and the Central American Peace Process: Vol. 1, Documents.* Boulder, CO: Westview Press, 1985.

————. *Contadora and the Diplomacy of Peace in Central America.* Boulder, CO: Westview Press, 1987.

Child, Jack. *The Central American Peace Process, 1983–1991: Sheathing Swords, Building Confidence.* Boulder, CO: Lynne Rienner, 1992.

Frohman, Alicia. "De Contadora al Grupo de los Ocho," *Estudios Internacionales* 22 (July 1989): 385–427.

Wilson, Larman C., and Raúl González Díaz, "UN Peacekeeping in Central America." In *A Crisis of Expectations: UN Peacekeeping in the 1990,* edited by Ramesh Thakur and Carlyle A. Thayer, 141–159. Boulder, CO: Westview Press, 1995.

2. Others

Calvert, Peter, ed. *The Central American Security System: North-South or East-West?* Cambridge, U.K.: Cambridge University Press, 1988.

Demas, William. *Towards OECS Political Union: Seize the Time.* St. Michael, Barbados: Caribbean Development Bank, 1987.

Engel, Salo. "The New ODECA." *American Journal of International Law* 60 (October 1966): 806–809.

García Robles, Alfonso. *The Denuclearization of Latin America*. Washington, D.C.: Carnegie Endowment for International Peace, 1967.
García Vilchez, Julio R. *El Parlamento Centroamericano.* Managua, Nicaragua: INESP, 1993.
Gilmore, William. "Legal and Institutional Aspects of the Organization of East Caribbean States." *Review of International Studies* 11 (October 1985): 311–328.
Menon, B. K. "The Organization of Eastern Caribbean States—An Important Milestone in Subregional Integration." *University of Miami Inter-American Law Review* 17, no. 2 (Winter, 1986): 297–311.
Organización de Estados Centroamericanos (ODECA). *ODECA: una organización en marcha.* San Salvador, El Salvador: ODECA, 1967.
Organización Latinoamericana de Solidaridad. *Première conférence de l'organisation latino-américaine de solidarité.* Paris: François Maspero, 1967.
Quester, George H. *Brazil and Latin-American Nuclear Proliferation: An Optimistic View.* ACIS Working Paper No. 17. Los Angeles: Center for International and Strategic Affairs, University of California, 1979.

C. Health

1. Pan American Health Organization

Bustamante, Miguel E. *The Pan American Sanitary Bureau: Half a Century of Health Activities, 1902–1954.* Washington, D.C.: PASB, 1955.
Ferreira, José Roberto, Charles Godue, and María Isabel Rodríguez, eds. *International Health: A North South Debate.* Washington, D.C.: PAHO, 1992.
Halsey, Neal A., and Ciro A. de Quadros, eds. *Recent Advances in Immunization: A Bibliographic Review.* Washington, D.C.: PAHO, 1983.
Paganini, José María. "Current PAHO/WHO Policies and Strategies to Achieve Health for all by the Year 2000—Local Health Systems." In Pan American Health Organization, *Primary Health Care and Local Health Systems in the Caribbean* Washington, D.C.: PAHO, 1989.
Pan American Health Organization. *Basic Principles for Action of the Pan American Health Organization, 1987–1990.* Washington, D.C.: PAHO, 1987.
———. *Facts on Health Progress: Goals in the Charter of Punta del Este.* Washington, D.C.: PAHO, 1968.
———. *Health Planning in Latin America.* Washington, D.C.: PAHO, 1973.
Rodríguez, María Isabel. "The International Health Program of the Pan

American Health Organization." In *International Health: A North South Debate*, edited by José Roberto Ferreira, Charles Godue, and María Isabel Rodríguez, 127–148. Washington, D.C.: PAHO, 1992.

IV. Global and Universal Organizations

A. League of Nations

Edwards, Agustín. *La América Latina y la Liga de las Naciones.* Santiago de Chile: Editorial Universitaria, 1937.

Farcau, Bruce. *The Chaco War: Bolivia and Paraguay, 1932–1935.* Westport, CT: Greenwood Press, 1996.

Honegger, Claude. *Friedliche Streitbeilegung durch Regionale Organisationen; Theorie und Praxis der Friedenssicherungs—Systeme der OAS, der Liga der Arabischen Staaten und der OAU im Vergleich.* Zürich: Schultess, 1983.

Kelchner, Warren H. *Latin American Relations with the League of Nations.* Boston: World Peace Foundation, 1929.

Rout, Leslie B., Jr. *Politics of the Chaco Peace Conference, 1935–1939.* Austin: University of Texas Press, 1970.

Wood, Bryce. "War Termination in Latin America." In "How Wars End," edited by William T. R. Fox, 40–50, *The Annals of the American Academy of Political and Social Science.* Philadelphia, PA: AAPSS, November 1970.

B. United Nations

1. Latin American Development, Trade, and the Environment

a. Economic Commission on Latin America and the Caribbean

Cayuela, José. *ECLAC: 49 Years (1948–1988).* Santiago, Chile: ECLAC, 1988.

Comisión Económica para América Latina. *El pensamiento de la CEPAL.* Santiago, Chile: CEPAL, 1969.

Edwards, J. David. *Criteria for an Effective International Organization: The Case of ECLA.* Occasional Paper 8. Muscatine, IA: The Stanley Foundation, 1975.

Fontaine, Pierre-Michel. *Functionalism and Regionalism in the United Nations: The Economic Commission for Latin America.* Santiago, Chile: ECLA, 1975.

Guzmán, Gabriel. *El desarrollo latinoamericano y la CEPAL.* Barcelona, España: Planeta, 1976.

Solís, Leopold. *Raúl Prebisch at ECLA: Years of Creative Intellectual Effort.* Occasional Paper of the International Center for Economic Growth. San Francisco, CA: ICS Press, 1988.

b. General Agreement on Tariffs and Trade and the World Trade Organization

Hoekman, Bernard, and Michel Kostecki. *Political Economy of the World Trading System.* New York: St. Martin's Press, 1996.

Jackson, John H. *The World Trading System.* Cambridge, MA: MIT Press, 1989.

Jackson, John H., and Alan Sykes. *Implementing the Uruguay Round.* New York: Oxford University Press, 1997.

Low, Patrick. *Trading Free: The GATT and U.S. Trade Policy.* New York: The Twentieth Century Fund Press, 1993.

Preeg, Ernest H. *Traders in a Brave New World.* Chicago, IL: University of Chicago Press, 1996.

Qureski, Asif H. *The World Trade Organization: Implementing International Trade Norms.* Manchester, UK: Manchester University Press, 1996.

Schott, Jeffrey J., ed. *Free Trade Areas and U.S. Trade Policy.* Washington, D.C.: Institute for International Economics, 1989.

UN World Trade Organization. *Regionalism and the World Trading System.* Geneva: WTO, 1995.

c. International Bank for Reconstruction and Development

Ayres, Robert L. *Banking on the Poor: The World Bank and World Poverty.* Cambridge, MA: Massachusetts Institute of Technology Press, 1983.

Brown, Bartram. *The United States and the Politicization of the World Bank: Issues of International Law and Policy.* London: Kegan Paul International, 1992.

Camps, Miriam, and Catherine Gwin. *Collective Management: The Reform of Global Economic Organizations.* New York: McGraw-Hill, 1981.

Caulfield, Catherine. *Masters of Illusion: The World Bank and the Poverty of Nations.* New York: Henry Holt, 1997.

Clark, William. *From Three Worlds: Memoirs.* London: Sidgwick & Jackson, 1986.

Clausen, A.W. *The Development Challenge of the Eighties: A.W. Clausen at the World Bank: Major Policy Addresses, 1981–1986.* Washington, D.C.: World Bank, 1986.

Danaher, Kevin, ed. *50 Years is Enough: the Case Against the World*

Bank and the International Monetary Fund. Boston, MA: South End Press, 1994.

De Vires, Barend A. *Remaking the World Bank*. Lanham, MD: Seven Locks Press, 1987.

Feinberg, Richard E. *Between Two Worlds: The World Bank's Next Decade*. New Brunswick, NJ: Transaction Books, 1985.

———, et al. *Adjustment Crisis in the Third World*. New Brunswick, NJ: Transaction Books, 1984.

Fried, Edward R., and Henry Owen. *The Future Role of the World Bank: Addresses by Robert S. McNamara, George P. Schultz, Edward R. Fried, R. T. McNamara, David Rockefeller, Manfred Lahnstein, A.W. Clausen*. Presented at a Conference at the Brookings Institution on January 7, 1982. Washington, D.C.: Brookings Institution, 1982.

George, Susan, and Fabrizio Sabelli. *Faith and Credit: The World Bank's Secular Empire*. Washington, D.C.: Institute for Policy Studies, 1994.

Gwin, Catherine. *U.S. Relations with the World Bank, 1945–92*. Washington, D.C.: Occasional Paper of The Brookings Institution, 1994.

Krueger, Anne O., et al. *Aid and Development*. Baltimore, MD: Johns Hopkins University Press, 1989.

Mason, Edward Sagendorph. *The World Bank Since Bretton Woods: The Origins, Policies, Operations, and Impact of the International Bank for Reconstruction and Development and the Other Members of the World Bank Group: The International Finance Corporation, the International Development Association [and] the International Centre for Settlement of Investment Disputes*. Washington, D.C.: Brookings Institution, 1973.

McNamara, Robert S. *The McNamara Years at the World Bank: Major Policy Addresses of Robert S. McNamara, 1968–1981: With Forewards by Helmut Schmidt and Leopold Senghor*. Baltimore, MD: Johns Hopkins University Press, 1981.

Miller, Morris. *Coping is Not Enough! The International Debt Crisis and the Roles of the World Bank and International Monetary Fund*. Homewood, IL: Dow Jones-Irwin, 1986.

Morse, Elliott R. *Implementing Rural Development Projects: Lessons from AID and World Bank Experiences*. Boulder, CO: Westview Press, 1985.

OAS, General Secretariat, Inter-American Committee on the Alliance for Progress. *Latin America and the Reform of the International Monetary System*. Washington, D.C.: OAS, 1972.

Oliver, Robert W. *George Woods and the World Bank*. Boulder, CO: Lynne Rienner Publishers, 1994.

Paul, Samuel. *Community Participation in Development Projects: The World Bank Experience*. Washington, D.C.: World Bank, 1987.

Payer, Cheryl. *The World Bank: A Critical Analysis.* New York: Monthly Review Press, 1982.

Please, Stanley. *The Hobbled Giant: Essays on The World Bank.* Boulder, CO: Westview Press, 1984.

Salda, Anne C. M. *The World Bank.* Vol. 9 in Reference Works series. New Brunswick, NJ: Transaction Press, 1995.

Shihata, Ibrahim F. I. *The World Bank Inspection Panel.* Washington, D.C.: World Bank, 1995.

Ul Haq, Mahab, Richard Jolly, Paul Streeten, and Khadija Haq. *The UN and the Bretton Woods Institutions.* New York: St. Martin's Press, 1995.

United Nations, UNCTAD. *Proceedings of G-24 Conference* Vol. IV. New York: UN, 1994. Sections on "Relations Between the IMF, the World Bank and Developing Countries"; "The Regional Development Banks and the World Bank"; and "The Developing Countries' Influence within the International Financial System."

Van De Laar, A. J. M. *The World Bank and the Poor.* Boston, MA: Martinus Nijhoff, 1980.

Weiss, Charles, and Nicholas Jequier. *Technology, Finance and Development: An Analysis of the World Bank as a Technological Institution.* Lexington, MA: Lexington Books, 1984.

World Bank. *Country Economics Department, International Bank for Reconstruction and Development.* Washington, D.C.: World Bank, 1989.

———. *The World Bank Annual Report.* Washington, D.C.: International Bank for Reconstruction and Development, 1982–. Published annually.

———. *The World Bank Economic Review.* Washington, D.C.: World Bank, 1986–. Published annually.

———. *The World Bank Group in the Americas.* Washington, D.C.: World Bank, 1974.

d. International Monetary Fund

Budhoo, Davison. *Enough is Enough (Letter of Resignation to the International Monetary Fund).* New York: Apex Press, 1990.

Chossudovsky, Michel. *The Globalization of Poverty: Impacts of IMF and World Bank Reforms.* London: Zed Books, 1996.

Ghai, Dharam, ed. *The IMF and the South: The Social Impact of Crisis and Adjustment.* London: Zed Books, 1991.

Gold, Joseph. *The IMF and International Law.* London: Kluwer Law International, 1996.

Humphreys, Norman K. *Historical Dictionary of the International Monetary Fund.* Lanham, MD: The Scarecrow Press, Inc., 1996.

International Monetary Fund. *Directory: Members, Quotas, Governors, Voting Power, Executive Board, Officers.* Washington, D.C.: IMF, 1994.

―――. IMF Staff Country Reports. *Argentina: Recent Economic Developments.* Washington, D.C.: IMF, 1995. There is such a report on many members each year but on all members every few years.

Lister, Frederick A. *Decision-Making Strategies for International Organizations: The IMF Model.* Denver, CO: Monograph Series in World Affairs, Graduate School of International Studies, University of Denver, 1984.

Salda, Anne C. M. *The International Monetary Fund.* Vol. 4 in Reference Works series. New Brunswick, NJ: Transaction Press, 1992.

Spraos, John. *IMF Conditionality: Ineffectual, Inefficient, Mistargeted.* Essays in International Finance, No. 166. Princeton, NJ: Department of Economics, Princeton University, 1986.

de Vries, Margaret G. *The IMF in a Changing World 1945–85.* Washington, D.C.: IMF, 1986.

―――. *The International Monetary Fund, 1972–78: Co-operation on Trial.* Vols. I–III. Washington, D.C.: IMF, 1985.

―――. *The International Monetary Fund, 1966–71: The System Under Stress.* Vols. I–II. Washington, D.C.: IMF, 1976.

Williamson, John F. *IMF Conditionality.* Washington, D.C.: Institute for International Economics, 1983.

―――. *The Lending Policies of the International Monetary Fund.* Washington, D.C.: Institute for International Economics, August, 1982.

e. United Nations Development Program

Alesina, Alberto, and Roberto Perotti. "The Political Economy of Growth: A Critical Survey of the Recent Literature." *World Bank Economic Review* 8, no. 3 (1994): 351–371.

Birdsall, Nancy. "Social Development is Economic Development." *Policy Research Working Paper 1123.* Washington, D.C.: World Bank, 1993.

Grupo de Rio. "Buenos Aires' Declaration on the Fulfillment of the Commitments of the World Summit for Social Development." Buenos Aires: Grupo de Rio, 1995.

Streeten, Paul, with Shahid Javed Burki, Mahbub ul Haq, Norman Hicks, and Frances Stewart. *First Things First: Meeting Basic Needs in the Developing Countries.* New York: Oxford University Press, 1981.

United Nations, UN Development Programme. *Donor Organizations and Participatory Development.* New York: UNDP, 1995.

———. *Generation, Portrait of the United Nations Development Programme.* New York: UNDP, 1985.

———. *Human Development Report.* New York: UNDP, 1990–. Published annually.

———. *PROGRESS REPORT. Progress Against Poverty: A Report on Activities Since Copenhagen.* New York: UNDP, 1996.

World Bank. *World Development Report.* New York: Oxford University Press, 1988–. Published annually.

———. "Task Force on the Enabling Environment for Economic and Social Development: Draft Terms of Reference." Washington, D.C.: World Bank, 1996.

f. United Nations Environmental Program

Bartlett, Robert V., et al. *International Organizations and Environmental Policy.* Westport, CT: Greenwood Press, 1995.

Birnie, Patricia. "The UN and the Environment." In *United Nations, Divided World: The UN's Roles in International Relations,* 2nd ed., edited by Adam Roberts and Benedict Kingsbury, 327–383. Oxford, UK: Clarendon Press, 1993.

Choucri, Nazli, ed. *Global Accord: Environmental Challenges and International Responses.* Cambridge, MA: MIT Press, 1994.

Commission to Study the Organization of Peace. *The United Nations and the Human Environment.* New York: CSOP, April 1972.

Eblen, Ruth A., and William R. Eblen. *The Encyclopedia of the Environment.* Burlington, MA: Houghton Mifflin Co., 1994.

Handl, Gunther, ed. *Yearbook of International Environmental Law.* Vol. 5. Cary, NC: Oxford University Press, 1996. Chapters on Oceans (IV), International Commons/Areas Beyond National Jurisdiction (VII), and Country/ Regional Reports (X).

Hurrell, Andrew, and Benedict Kingsbury, eds. *The International Politics of the Environment: Actors, Interests, and Institutions.* Cary, NC: Oxford University Press, 1992.

MacDonald, Gordon J., Daniel L. Nielson, and Marc A. Stern, eds. *Latin American Environmental Policy in International Perspective.* Boulder, CO: Westview Press, 1996.

Sands, Philippe. *Principles of International Environmental Law I [and] II.* Manchester, UK: Manchester University Press, 1995. Part 3 includes "Oceans and Seas: Global" and "Regional"; Part 2 includes "The Polar Regions"; Part 11 includes "The Antarctic."

Trolldalen, Jon Martin. *International Environmental Conflict Resolution: The Role of the United Nations.* Washington, D.C.: National Institute for Dispute Resolution, 1995.

Tulchin, Joseph S., with Andrew I. Rudman, eds. *Economic Development and Environmental Protection in Latin America*. Boulder, CO: Lynne Rienner Publishers, 1991.

United Nations, UN Environmental Programme. *Agenda 21—Earth Summit The United Nations Programme of Action from Rio*. New York: UN Publications, 1993.

————. *Countries of Latin America and the Caribbean and the Action Plan for the Environment: A Strategy for Living*. New York: UN Publications, 1993.

————. *Global Partnership for Environment and Development: A Guide to Agenda 21, The Post Rio Edition*. New York: UN Publications, 1993.

————. *UNEP's New Way Forward: Environmental Law and Sustainable Development*. New York: UN Publications, 1996.

United Nations, UN Environmental Programme, Regional Office for Latin America. *The Countries of Latin America and the Caribbean and the Action Plan for the Environment: A Strategy for Living*. Mexico, D.F.: UNEP, ROLAC, 1991.

————. *Derecho internacional ambiental regional. Serie de Legislación Ambiental*, no. 2. México, D.F.: UNEP, ROLAC, 1993.

————. *General en América Latina y el Caribe. Serie de Legislación Ambiental*, no. 1. México, D.F.: UNEP, ROLAC, 1992.

————. *Green Production: Toward an Environmental Rationality*. New York: Guilford Publishing Group, 1994.

————. *Situación actual del derecho internacional ambiental en América Latina y el Caribe. Serie de Documentos Sobre Derecho Ambiental*, no. 2. Mexico, D.F.: UNEP, ROLAC, 1993.

————. *United Nations Yearbook on the Environment*. New York: UN, 1993–. Published annually.

Young, Oran R., and Gail Osherenko, eds. *Polar Politics: Creating International Environmental Regimes*. Ithaca, NY: Cornell University Press, 1993.

2. Latin American and Caribbean Politics in the United Nations

a. General

Houston, John A. *Latin America in the United Nations*. New York: Carnegie Endowment for International Peace, 1956.

Hovet, Thomas, Jr. *Bloc Politics in the United Nations*. Cambridge, MA: Harvard University Press, 1960.

de Prat Gay, Gastón. *Politica internacional del Grupo Latinoamericano*. Buenos Aires: Abeledo-Perrot, 1980.

b. *United Nations Conference on Trade and Development, New International Economic Order, and Charter on the Economic Rights and Duties of States*

(1) Bibliographies

Hoskins, Linus A. *The New International Economic Order: A Bibliographic Handbook.* Washington, D.C.: University Press of America, 1983.

Serrato Combe, Marcela. "Bibliografia seleccionada de obras recientes sobre nuevo orden internacional y diálogo norte-sur." *Foro Internacional* 28 (October–December 1977): 373–384.

(2) General

Castañeda, Jorge, et al. *Derecho económico internacional. Análisis jurídico de la Carta de Derechos y Deberes Económicos de los Estados.* México, D.F.: Fondo de Cultura Económica, 1976.

Ffrench-Davis, Ricardo, and Ernesto Tironi, eds. *Hacía un Nuevo Orden Económico Internacional: Temas prioritarios para América Latina.* México, D.F.: Fondo de Cultura Económica, 1981.

Henkin, Louis. *How Nations Behave: Law and Foreign Policy.* 2nd ed. New York: Columbia University Press for Council on Foreign Relations, 1979. Chapters 6. "The Third World" and 10. "The Politics of Economics: The New International Economic Order."

Hurrell, Andrew. "Latin America in the New World Order: A Regional Bloc of the Americas?" *International Affairs* [UK] 68 (January 1992): 121–139.

König, Wolfgang. "América Latina y un Nuevo Orden Económico Internacional," In "Nuevo Orden Internacional" (Special Issue), edited by Manuel Felguerez, Carlos Mérida, Sebastián y Renata Schussheim, 225–240. *Nueva Política* [México, D.F.] 1, no. 4 (October–March, 1977).

Nye, Joseph S. "UNCTAD: Poor Nations' Pressure Group." In *The Anatomy of Influence: Decision Making in International Organization,* edited by Robert W. Cox and Harold K. Jacobson, 334–370. New Haven, CT: Yale University Press, 1973.

Rothstein, Robert L. *Global Bargaining: UNCTAD and the Quest for a New International Economic Order.* Princeton, NJ: Princeton University Press, 1979.

Sandstrom, Harold M. "The New International Economic Order and the Caribbean: The External/Internal Nexus." In *The Restless Caribbean: Changing Patterns of International Relations,* edited by Richard Millett and W. Marvin Will, 71–80. New York: Praeger Publishers, 1979.

Sauvant, Karl P., and Hajo Hasenpflug, eds. *The New International Economic Order: Confrontation or Cooperation between North and South?* Boulder, CO: Westview Press, 1978.

Wilson, Larman C. "The Caribbean States and International Organization: The United Nations, Organization of American States, and Inter-American Development Bank." In *The Restless Caribbean: Changing Patterns of International Relations,* edited by Richard Millett and W. Marvin Will, 266–283. New York: Praeger Publishers, 1979.

Zammit Cutajar, M. *UNCTAD and the South-North Dialogue: the First Twenty Years.* New York: Pergamon Press, 1985.

c. United Nations, Third Conference on the Law of the Sea

(1) Bibliographies

Székely, Alberto. *Bibliography on Latin America and the Law of the Sea.* Kingston: Law of the Sea Institute, University of Rhode Island, 1976.

United Nations. *The Law of the Sea: A Bibliography on the Law of the Sea 1968–1988.* New York: UN, 1992.

(2) General

Burke, W. Scott and Frank S. Brokaw. "Ideology and the Law of the Sea." In *Law of the Sea: U.S. Policy Dilemma,* edited by Bernard Oxman, David D. Caron, and Charles L. O. Buderi, 43–58. San Francisco, CA: Institute for Contemporary Studies, 1983.

Churchill, Robin R., and A. V. Rowe. *The Law of the Sea.* 2nd ed. Manchester, UK: Manchester University Press, 1988.

Comisión Permanente del Pacífico Sur. "El nuevo derecho del mar," *Pacífico Sur* [Lima], Número Especial (1978).

Ewell, Judith. "The Caribbean and the Law of the Sea: New Occasion for Discord." In *The Restless Caribbean: Changing Patterns of International Relations*, edited by Ricard Millett and W. Marvin Will, 81–89. New York: Praeger Publishers, 1979.

García-Amador, Francisco F. *América Latina y el derecho del mar.* Santiago: Instituto de Estudios Internacionales, Universidad de Chile, 1976.

Hagen, Virginia M. *The Latin American-United States Fishing Rights Controversy: Dilemma for United States Foreign Policy (1969–1971).* Washington, D.C.: Congressional Research Service, Library of Congress, 1971.

Henkin, Louis. *How Nations Behave: Law and Foreign Policy.* 2nd ed. New York: Columbia University Press for the Council on Foreign Relations, 1979. Chapter 11. "Remaking the Law of the Sea."

Hjertonsson, Karin. *The New Law of the Sea: Influence of the Latin American States on Recent Developments of the Law of the Sea.* Leiden, The Netherlands: Sijthoff, 1973.

Knight, Gary. *The Law of the Sea: Cases, Documents and Readings.* Baton Rouge, LA: Claitor's Publishing Division, 1980.

Larson, David L. *Major Issues of the Law of the Sea.* Durham, NH: University of New Hampshire, 1976.

Miles, Edward. "The Structure and Effects of the Decision Process in the Seabed Committee and the Third United Nations Conference on the Law of the Sea." In "Restructuring Ocean Regimes: Implications of the Third United Nations Conference on the Law of the Sea" (Special Issue), edited by Edward Miles, 159–234. *International Organization* 31, no. 2 (Spring 1977).

Morris, Michael. "Influence and Innovation in the Law of the Sea: Latin America and Africa." *Ocean Development and International Law Journal* 7, no. 1/2 (1979): 1–25.

Organization of American States, Inter-American Juridical Committee. *Opinion on the Breadth of the Territorial Sea.* OEA/Ser.I/VJ.2 (English) CIJ-80. Washington, D.C.: OAS, 1966.

Orrego Vicuña, Francisco. *Exclusive Economic Zone: A Latin American Perspective.* Boulder, CO: Westview Press, 1984.

Oxnam, Bernard H. "Recent Developments in the Law of the Sea," *San Diego Law Review*, Vols. 11–20 (1974–1983). An annual progress report and summary of the proceedings of the Third UN Law of the Sea Conference, 1973–1982.

Pohl, Reynaldo Galindo. "Latin America's Influence and Role in the Third Conference on the Law of the Sea." *Ocean Development and International Law Journal* 7, no. 1/2 (1979): 65–88.

United Nations, General Assembly. *The Law of the Sea: Report of the Secretary General.* Doc. A/48/527, 10 Nov. 1993. New York: UN, 1993.

United States, Department of State. *The US Proposals for Amendments to the Draft Convention of the Law of the Sea.* Washington, D.C.: Department of State, 1981.

Van Dyke, Vernon, ed. *Consensus and Confrontation: The United States and the Law of the Sea Convention.* Honolulu: University of Hawaii, 1984.

Zacklin, Ralph, ed. *The Changing Law of the Sea: Western Hemisphere Perspectives.* Leiden, The Netherlands: Sijthoff, 1974.

3. Conflict Resolution and Peacekeeping

a. General

Boutros-Ghali, Boutros. *Agenda for Peace: Preventive Diplomacy, Peacemaking and Peace-keeping.* New York: UN, 1992.

Chayes, Abram, and Antonia Handler Chayes, eds. *Preventing Conflict in the Post-Communist World: Mobilizing International and Regional Organizations.* Washington, D.C.: Brookings Institution, 1996.

Crocker, Chester A., and Fen Osler Hampson, with Pamela Aall, eds. *Managing Global Chaos: Sources of and Responses to International Conflict.* Washington, D.C.: United States Institute of Peace Press, 1996.

Daniel, Donald C. F., and Bradd C. Hayes. *Securing Observance of U.N. Mandates Through the Employment of Military Forces.* Occasional Paper Series 9:OP:3. Notre Dame, IN: Joan B. Kroc Institute for International Peace Studies, University of Notre Dame, 1995.

Durch, William J., ed. *The Evolution of UN Peacekeeping: Case Studies and Comparative Analysis.* New York: St. Martin's Press, 1993. Part Five is on "Peacekeeping in the Western Hemisphere."

————, and Barry M. Blechman. *Keeping the Peace: The United Nations in the Emerging World Order.* Washington, D.C.: Henry L. Stimson Center, 1992.

Franck, Thomas M., and Georg Nolte. "The Good Offices Function of the UN Secretary-General." In *United Nations, Divided World: The UN's Roles in International Relations*, 2nd ed., edited by Adam Roberts and Benedict Kingsbury, 143–182. Oxford, UK: The Clarendon Press, 1993.

Howard, Michael. "The Historical Development of the UN's Role in International Security." In *United Nations, Divided World: The UN's Roles in International Relations*, 2nd ed., edited by Adam Roberts and Benedict Kingsbury, 63–80. Oxford, UK: The Clarendon Press, 1993.

Mokhtari, Fariborz L., ed. *Peacemaking, Peacekeeping and Coalition Warfare: The Future Role of the United Nations. Proceedings of a Conference Cosponsored by National Defense University and Norwich University.* Washington, D.C.: National Defense University Press, 1995.

Morphet, Sally. "UN Peacekeeping and Election-Monitoring." In *In United Nations, Divided World: The UN's Roles in International Relations*, 2nd ed., edited by Adam Roberts and Benedict Kingsbury, 183–239. Oxford, UK: The Clarendon Press, 1993.

Norton, Augustus R., and Thomas G. Weiss. "UN Peacekeepers: Soldiers with a Difference." *Headline Series*, No. 292 (Spring 1990).

Pérez de Cuéllar, Javier. "The Role of the UN Secretary-General." *United Nations, Divided World: The UN's Roles in International Relations*, 2nd ed., edited by Adam Roberts and Benedict Kingsbury, 125–142. Oxford, UK: The Clarendon Press, 1993.

Rikhye, Indar Jit, and Kjell Skjelsback, eds. *The United Nations and*

Peacekeeping: Results, Limitations and Prospects—The Lessons of 40 Years of Experience. New York: St. Martin's Press, 1990.

United Nations. *The Blue Helmets: A Review of United Nations Peace-Keeping.* 2nd ed. New York: United Nations, 1990.

———, United Nations Institute for Training and Research. *The United Nations and the Maintenance of International Peace and Security.* Dordrecht, The Netherlands: Martinus Nijhoff, 1987.

Urquhart, Brian. "The UN and International Security after the Cold War." In *United Nations, Divided World: The UN's Roles in International Relations,* 2nd ed., edited by Adam Roberts and Benedict Kingsbury, 81–103. Oxford, UK: The Clarendon Press, 1993.

Weiss, Thomas G., ed. *The United Nations and Civil Wars.* Boulder, CO: Lynne Rienner Publishers, 1995.

White, N. D. *Keeping the Peace: The United Nations and the Maintenance of International Peace and Security.* Manchester, UK: University of Manchester Press, 1993.

b. Security Council and Secretary-General

(1) Cuban Missile Crisis

Butterworth, Robert L. *Managing Interstate Conflict, 1945–1974: Data with Synopses.* Pittsburgh, PA: University Center for International Studies, University of Pittsburgh, 1976. Synopsis #206.

Chayes, Abram. *The Cuban Missile Crisis: International Crises and the Role of Law.* New York: Oxford University Press under the auspices of the American Society of International Law, 1974. Chap. V. "Law as Organization: The O.A.S. and the U.N."

Foreign Policy Association. *The Cuban Crisis: A Documentary Record.* Headline Series No. 157 (January–February 1963).

Harrelson, Max. *Fires All Around the Horizon: The U.N.'s Uphill Battle to Preserve the Peace.* New York: Praeger Publishers, 1989. Chap. 15. "The Bay of Pigs and the Cuban Missile Crisis."

James, Alan. *Peacekeeping in International Politics.* New York: St. Martin's Press, 1990. Sec.D.

Krinsky, Michael, and David Golove, eds. *United States Economic Measures Against Cuba: Proceedings in the United Nations and International Law Issues.* Northampton, MA: Aletheia Press, 1993.

Larson, David E., ed. *The 'Cuban Crisis' of 1962: Selected Documents and Chronology.* Boston, MA: Houghton Mifflin Co., 1963.

(2) The Dominican Civil War and U.S. Intervention: UN S-G's DOMREP

Butterworth, Robert L. *Managing Interstate Conflict, 1945–1974: Data with Synopses.* Pittsburgh, PA: University of Pittsburgh, 1976. Synopses #250, 251, 252.

Claude, Inis L., Jr. "The OAS, the UN and the United States," *International Conciliation*. No. 547 (March 1964).

Harrelson, Max. *Fires All Around the Horizon: The U.N.'s Uphill Battle to Preserve the Peace*. New York: Praeger Publishers, 1989. Chap. 20. "On the Use of Force: The Dominican Republic and Czechoslovakia."

James, Alan. *Peacekeeping in International Politics*. New York: St. Martin's Press, 1990. Sec. J.

Morphet, Sally. "UN Peacekeeping and Election-Monitoring." In *United Nations, Divided World: The UN's Roles in International Relations*. 2nd ed., edited by Adam Roberts and Benedict Kingsbury, 195–197. Oxford, UK: The Clarendon Press, 1993.

United Nations. *The Blue Helmets: A Review of United Nations Peace-Keeping*. 2nd ed. NY: UN, 1990. Chapter X. "Representative of the Secretary-General in the Dominican Republic."

(3) Falkland-Malvinas / South Atlantic War

Arend, Anthony C. "The Falklands War and the Failure of the International Legal Community." In *The Falklands War: Lessons for Strategy, Diplomacy, and International Law*, edited by Alberto R. Coll and Anthony C. Arend, 52–64. Boston, MA: Allen and Unwin, 1985.

Claude, Inis L., Jr. "UN Efforts at Settlement of the Falkland Islands Crisis." In *The Falklands War: Lessons for Strategy, Diplomacy, and International Law*, edited by Alberto R. Coll and Anthony C. Arend, 118–131. Boston, MA: Allen and Unwin, 1985.

Coll, Alberto R. and Anthony C. Arend, eds. *The Falklands War: Lessons for Strategy, Diplomacy, and International Law*. Boston, MA: Allen and Unwin, 1985.

Franck, Thomas M., and Georg Nolte. "The Good Offices Function of the UN Secretary-General." In *United Nations, Divided World: The UN's Roles in International Relations*, 2nd ed., edited by Adam Roberts and Benedict Kingsbury, 158–159. Oxford, UK: The Clarendon Press, 1993.

Gerson, Allan. *The Kirkpatrick Mission: Diplomacy Without Apology— America at the United Nations 1981–1985*. New York: The Free Press, 1991. Chapter 8. " 'Malvinas, Malvinas': The Falklands Crisis."

de la Guardia, Ernesto. "La Cuestión de las Islas Malvinas en las Naciones Unidas." In *Anuario Jurídico Interamericano 1986*, OEA, Secretaría General, 97–140. Washington, D.C.: OEA, 1987.

James, Alan. *Peacekeeping in International Politics*. NY: St. Martin's Press, 1990. Sec. H.

(4) Central American Peace Process

Franck, Thomas M., and Georg Nolte. "The Good Offices Function of the UN Secretary-General." In *United Nations, Divided World: The UN's Roles in International Relations.* 2nd ed., edited by Adam Roberts and Benedict Kingsbury, 152–155. Oxford, UK: Oxford University Press, 1993.

James, Alan. *Peacekeeping in International Politics.* New York: St. Martin's Press, 1990. Sec. L.

Johnstone, Ian. *Rights and Reconciliation: UN Strategies in El Salvador.* New York: International Peace Academy, 1995.

Montgomery, Tommie Sue. "Peace: The United Nations and Peacemaking in El Salvador," *North-South Issues* IV, no. 3 (1995).

Morphet, Sally. "UN Peacekeeping and Election-Monitoring." In *United Nations, Divided World: The UN's Roles in International Relations.* 2nd ed., edited by Adam Roberts and Benedict Kingsbury, 216–219. Oxford, UK: Oxford University Press, 1993.

United Nations. *The Blue Helmets: A Review of United Nations Peace-Keeping.* 2nd ed. New York: UN, 1990. Chapter XVIII. "UN Observer Group in Central America."

United Nations. *The United Nations and El Salvador, 1990–1995.* New York: UN, 1995.

(5) Haitian Coup and Suppression

UN. General Assembly. *Interim Report of the International Civilian Mission to Haiti [established by the UN and OAS] for the Period 9 February–31 May 1993.* A/47/960 3 June 1993.

UN. *Governors Island Agreement.* New York: UN, July 1993.

UN. *The United Nations and Haiti, 1990–1996.* New York: UN, 1996.

U.S. Congressional Research Service, Library of Congress. *Haiti: Efforts to Restore President Aristide, 1991–1994.* Prepared by Maureen Taft-Morales. Washington, D.C.: CRS, May 11, 1995.

———. *CRS Report for Congress: Haiti: U.N. Security Council Resolutions, Texts and Votes—1993–1994.* Prepared by Marjorie Ann Browne. Washington, D.C.: CRS, August 25, 1994.

c. International Court of Justice

(1) General

Bodie, Thomas J. *Politics and the Emergence of an Activist International Court of Justice.* Westport, CT: Praeger Publishers, 1995.

Damrosch, Lori Fisler, ed. *The International Court of Justice at a Crossroads*. Dobbs Ferry, NY: Transnational Publishers, 1987.

Rodríguez Cedeno, Victor. *La Corte Internacional de Justicia: un mecanismo de solución de controversias*. Caracas: Tierra de Gracia Editores, 1993.

Rosenne, Shabtai. *The Law and Practice of the International Court of Justice*. 2nd rev. ed. Dordrecht, The Netherlands: Nijhoff, 1985.

UN. *World Court—What it is and How it Works*. 4th ed. New York: UN, 1990.

(2) Case Concerning Military and Paramilitary Activities In and Against Nicaragua *(Nic. v. U.S.)*, 1986 I.C.J.

Carty, Anthony. "Intervention and the Limits of International Law." In *Political Theory, International Relations, and the Ethics of Intervention*, edited by Ian Forbes and Mark Hoffman, 32–42. London, UK: St. Martin's Press, 1993.

Chayes, Abram. "Nicaragua, The United States, and the World Court." *Columbia Law Review* 85, no. 7 (1985): 1445–1482.

Gerson, Allan. *The Kirkpatrick Mission: Diplomacy Without Apology—America at the United Nations 1981–1985*. New York: The Free Press, 1991. Chap. 16. "The Last Illusion: The International Court of Justice."

Highet, Keith. "Evidence, the Court, and the Nicaragua Case." *American Journal of International Law* 81 (January 1987): 1–56.

Maier, Harold G., ed. "Appraisals of the ICJ's Decision: Nicaragua v. United States (Merits)." *American Journal of International Law* 78 (January 1984): 77–183.

Rosenne, Shabtai. *Intervention in the International Court of Justice*. Dordrecht, The Netherlands: Martinus Nijhoff, 1993.

Schwebel, Stephen M. [U.S. member of ICJ]. "Indirect Aggression in the International Court." In *Law and Force in the New International Order*, edited by Lori Fisler Damrosch, 298–303. Boulder, CO: Westview Press, 1991.

C. Nonaligned Movement

Jackson, Richard L. *The Non-Aligned Movement, the UN and the Superpowers*. New York: Praeger Publishers, 1983.

Jankowitsch, Odette, and Karl P. Sauvant. *The Third World Without Superpowers: The Collected Documents of the Non-Aligned Countries*. 12 vols. Dobbs Ferry, NY: Oceana Publishers, 1978–1993.

Willetts, Peter. *The Non-Aligned Movement*. New York: Nichols, 1978.

V. Latin American and European Organizations

A. Europe, European Community, and Latin America and the Caribbean

1. General

Borón, Atilio, and Alberto van Klaveren, eds. *América Latina y Europa Occidental en el umbral del siglo XXI.* Santiago, Chile: PNUD/ CEPAL Proyecto de Cooperación con los Servicios Exteriores de América Latina, 1989.

CEPAL, *The Economic Relations of Latin America With Europe.* Santiago, Chile: CEPAL [Economic Commision for Latin America], 1980.

Coffey, Peter, and L. Lago de Correa, eds. *The EEC and Brazil.* London: Pinter, 1988.

————, and Miguel Wionczek, eds. *The EEC and Mexico.* Dordrecht, The Netherlands: Martinus Nijhoff, 1987.

Durán, Esperanza. *Mexico's Relations with the European Community.* Working Paper 33. Madrid, Spain: IRELA, 1992.

Freres, Christian L., ed. *European Union Bilateral Development Assistance for Latin America.* Madrid: Asociación de Investigación y Especialización sobre Temas Iberoamericanos (AIETI), 1997.

Freres, Christian L., Alberto van Klaveren, and Guadalupe Ruiz-Giménez. "Europa y América Latina: La Búsqueda de Nuevas Formas de Cooperación." *Síntesis* 18 (September/December): 91–178.

Friscia, A. Blake, and Françoise Simon. "The Economic Relationship Between Europe and Latin America." In *Europe and Latin America in the World Economy,* edited by Susan Kaufman Purcell and Françoise Simon, 5–37. Boulder, CO: Lynne Rienner Publishers, 1995.

Grabendorff, Wolf. "Germany and Latin America." In *Europe and Latin America in the World Economy,* edited by Susan Kaufman Purcell and Françoise Simon, 85–112. Boulder, CO: Lynne Rienner Publishers, 1995.

————, and Riordan Roett, eds. *Latin America, Western Europe, and the U.S.: Reevaluating the Atlantic Triangle.* New York: Praeger, 1985.

Heine, Jorge, and Leslie F. Manigat, eds. *The Caribbean and World Politics: Cross-Currents and Cleavages.* New York: Holmes and Meier, 1986.

Lagos Matús, Gustavo, ed. *Las relaciones entre América Latina, Estados Unidos, y Europa Occidental.* Santiago, Chile: Universidad de Chile, 1979.

MacDonald, Scott B., and Albert L. Gastmann. "Grenada, the Caribbean Basin, and the European Economic Community." In *The Carib-*

bean after Grenada: Revolution, Conflict, and Democracy, edited by Scott B. MacDonald, Harald M. Sandstrom, and Paul B. Goodwin, Jr., 229–250. New York: Praeger, 1988.

Mower, Alfred Glenn, Jr. *The European Community and Latin America: A Case Study in Global Role Expansion.* Westport, CT: Greenwood Press, 1982.

Oxford Analytica. *Latin America in Perspective.* Boston, MA: Houghton Mifflin Co. 1991. Chap. 18. "Latin America and Western Europe."

Purcell, Susan Kaufman, and Françoise Simon, eds. *Europe and Latin America in the World Economy.* Boulder, CO: Lynne Rienner Publishers, 1995.

Rosenberg, Robin L. *Spain and Central America: Democracy and Foreign Policy.* New York: Greenwood Press, 1992.

Roy, Joaquín, ed. *The Reconstruction of Central America: The Role of the European Community.* Coral Gables, FL: University of Miami, North-South Center, 1992.

Schumacher, Edward. "Spain and Latin America: The Resurgence of a Special Relationship." In *Europe and Latin America in the World Economy*, edited by Susan Kaufman Purcell and Françoise Simon, 113–137. Boulder, CO: Lynne Rienner Publishers, 1995.

Simon, Françoise, and Susan Kaufman Purcell. "The Impact of Regional Integration on European-Latin American Relations." In *Europe and Latin America in the World Economy*, edited by Susan Kaufman Purcell and Françoise Simon, 39–84. Boulder, CO: Lynne Rienner Publishers, 1995.

Sutton, Paul, ed. *Europe and the Caribbean.* London: Macmillan, 1991.

Twitchett, Carol Cosgrove. *A Framework for Development: The EEC and the ACP.* London: Allen & Unwin, 1981.

van Klaveren, Alberto. "Europe and Latin America in the 1990s." In *Latin America in a New World,* edited by Abraham F. Lowenthal and Gregory F. Treverton, 81–104. Boulder, CO: Westview Press, 1994.

2. European Community Commission

Instituto de Relaciones Europeo-Latinoamericanas (IRELA). *The Andean Group and the European Union: Forging Stronger Links?* DOS 47. Madrid, Spain: IRELA, 1993.

———. *Anuario de las relaciones europeo-latinoamericanas, 1993.* Madrid: IRELA, 1994.

———. *Europe and Latin America: A Partnership for Action.* Madrid: IRELA, 1994.

———. *The European Union and MERCOSUR: Towards a New Economic Relationship?* Madrid: IRELA, 1996.

————. *The European Union and the Rio Group: The Biregional Agenda 1990–1995*. Madrid: IRELA, 1996.

————. *Handbook for European-Latin American Relations* Vol. I. European Institutions. Vol. II. Latin American and Caribbean Institutions. Madrid: IRELA, 1994.

————. *The Latin American Parliament and its Relations with the European Union*. Madrid: IRELA, 1995.

————. *Las relaciones entre el GRAN y el MERCOSUR: ¿hacía un espacio económico integrado en América del Sur?* Madrid: IRELA, 1995.

————. *Prospects for the Processes of Sub-regional Integration in Central and South America*. Madrid: IRELA, 1992.

————. *Ten Years of the San José Process: Review of 10 Years of European-Central American Relations*. Madrid: IRELA, 1994.

————. *Yearbook of European-Latin American Relations, 1994*. Madrid, Spain: IRELA 1995.

Wolf, Ulrike. *Bibliography of Western European-Latin American Relations*. Working Paper No. 1. Madrid: IRELA, 1986.

VI. Latin American–African and –Middle Eastern Organizations

A. General

Bahbah, Bishara. *Israel and Latin America: The Military Connection*. New York: St. Martin's Press, 1986.

Fernández, Damían J., ed. *Central America and the Middle East: The Internationalization of the Crises*. Gainesville: University of Florida Press, 1990.

Hunter, Jane. *No Simple Proxy: Israel in Central America*. Washington, D.C.: Washington Middle East Associates, 1987.

Kaufman, Edy, Yoram Shapira, and Joel Barromi. *Israeli-Latin American Relations*. New Brunswick, NJ: Transaction Books, 1979.

Marshall, Jonathan, Peter Dale Scott, and Jane Hunter. *The Iran-Contra Connection: Secret Teams and Covert Operations in the Reagan Era*. Boston, MA: South End Press, 1987.

Shearman, Peter, and Phil Williams, eds. *The Superpowers, Central America, and the Middle East*. London: Brassey's Defence Publishers, 1988.

B. Organization of Petroleum Exporting Countries

Ahrari, Mohammed E. *OPEC: The Failing Giant*. Lexington: University Press of Kentucky, 1986.

Rabe, Stephen G. *The Road to OPEC: United States Relations with Venezuela, 1919–1976.* Austin: University of Texas Press, 1982.

Sampson, Anthony. *The Seven Sisters: The Great Oil Companies and the World They Made.* London: Coronet, 1980.

VII. Latin American and Asian Organizations

A. Asian-Pacific Economic Cooperation Forum and Association of Southeast Asian Nations

CEPAL, *La evolución económica del Japón y su impacto en América Latina.* Santiago, Chile: CEPAL, 1988.

Elton, Charlotte. "Panama and Japan: The Role of the Panama Canal." In *Japan, the United States, and Latin America: Toward a Trilateral Relationship in the Western Hemisphere,* edited by Barbara Stallings and Gabriel Székely, 210–228. Baltimore, MD: The Johns Hopkins University Press, 1993.

Pathmanathan, Murugesu. *The Pacific Settlement of Disputes in Regional Organizations: A Comparative Perspective of the OAS, OAU, and ASEAN.* Kuala Lumpur, Malaysia: Antara Book Co., 1978.

Purcell, Susan K., and Robert Immerman, eds. *Japan and Latin America in the New Global Order.* Boulder, CO: Lynne Rienner Publishers, 1992.

Stallings, Barbara. "The Reluctant Giant: Japan and the Latin American Debt Crisis." *Journal of Latin American Studies* [UK] 22 (February 1990): 1–30.

Stallings, Barbara, and Gabriel Székely, eds. *Japan, the United States, and Latin America: Toward a Trilateral Relationship in the Western Hemisphere.* Baltimore, MD: The Johns Hopkins University Press, 1993.

Székely, Gabriel, ed. *Manufacturing Across Borders and Oceans: Japan, the United States, and Mexico.* San Diego, CA: Center for U.S.-Mexican Studies, University of California at San Diego, 1991.

―――. "Mexico's New International Strategy: Looking East and North." In *Japan, the United States, and Latin America: Toward a Trilateral Relationship in the Western Hemisphere,* edited by Barbara Stallings and Gabriel Székely, 149–170. Baltimore, MD: The Johns Hopkins University Press, 1993.

Torres, Ernani T. "Brazil-Japan Relations: From Fever to Chill." In *Japan, the United States, and Latin America: Toward a Trilateral Relationship in the Western Hemisphere,* edited by Barbara Stallings and Gabriel Székely, 125–148. Baltimore, MD: The Johns Hopkins University Press, 1993.

VIII. Non-Governmental Organizations

A. General

Bebbington, Anthony, and Graham Thiele, eds. *Non-Governmental Organizations and the State in Latin America*. London: Routledge, 1993.

Carroll, Thomas F. *Intermediary NGOs: The Supporting Link in Grassroots Development*. West Hartford, CT: Kumerian Press, 1992.

Fisher, Julie. *The Road from Rio: Sustainable Development and the Nongovernmental Organizations in the Third World*. Westport, CT: Praeger Publishers, 1993.

Instituto Brasileiro de Analises Sociais e Econômicas (IBASE). *Desenvolvimento, Cooperação Internacional e as ONGs*. Rio de Janeiro: IBASE, 1992.

Livezey, Lowell W. *Nongovernmental Organizations and the Ideas of Human Rights*. Princeton, NJ: Princeton University Press, 1988.

Nelson, Paul. *The World Bank and NGOs: The Limits of Apolitical Development*. New York: St. Martin's Press, 1995.

Organization of American States, Consejo Permanente, Comisión de Asuntos Jurídicos y Politicos, Grupo de Trabajo para estudiar la posibilidad de otorgar status en la OEA a los organismos no gubernamentales (ONG). *Organismos no Gubernamentales con los cuales la Organización de los Estados Americanos ha Establecido Relaciones de Cooperación*. OEA/Ser.G CP/CAJP—962/94 1 septiembre 1994. Washington, D.C.: OAS, 1994.

Reilly, Charles A., ed. *New Paths to Democratic Development in Latin America: The Rise of NGO-Municipal Collaboration*. Boulder, CO: Lynne Rienner Publishers, 1995.

Smith, Brian H. "Non-Governmental Organisations in International Development: Trends and Future Research Priorities." *Voluntas* [Manchester, UK] 4, no. 2 (1993): 301–325.

Weiss, Thomas G., and Leon Gordenker, eds. *NGOs, the UN, and Global Governance*. Boulder, CO: Lynne Rienner, 1996.

Willetts, Peter. *Pressure Groups in the International System: The Transnational Relations of Issue-Oriented Non-Government Organizations*. London: Frances Pinter, 1982.

About the Authors

LARMAN C. WILSON (B.A., Nebraska State College; M.A. and Ph.D., University of Maryland) is professor emeritus of international relations at American University, Washington, D.C. He was awarded fellowships at The Hague Academy's Centre for Studies and Research in International Law and International Relations (1974) and the OAS's Inter-American Juridical Committee's Course on International Law (1976). The coauthor of two earlier books (one on U.S.-Caribbean relations and the other on inter-American relations), he is the author of the following recent chapters: "The Organization of American States and the Haitian Political Experience," in Georges A. Fauriol, ed., *The Haitian Challenge: U.S. Foreign Policy Considerations* (CSIS, 1993); "Latin America in the World," in Jan K. Black, ed., *Latin America, Its Problems and its Promise* (2nd ed., Westview, 1992); (with David W. Dent), "The United States and the OAS," in David W. Dent, ed., *U.S.-Latin American Policymaking: A Reference Handbook* (Greenwood, 1995); and "Democracy and Human Rights in the Dominican Republic," in Ivelaw I. Griffith and Betty N. Sedoc-Dahlberg, eds., *Democracy and Human Rights in the Caribbean* (Westview, 1997).

DAVID W. DENT (B.A. and M.A., San Diego State University; Ph.D., University of Minnesota) is professor of political science at Towson University (formerly Towson State University) in Baltimore. He is the editor of the *Handbook of Political Science Research on Latin America: Trends from the 1960s to the 1990s* (Greenwood, 1990) and *U.S.-Latin American Policymaking: A Reference Handbook* (Greenwood, 1995) and the author of "Recent Trends in Political Science Research on Latin America," *Latin American Research Review* (1986), as well as several articles in *Comparative Political Studies* and the *Journal of Latin American Studies* and chapters in the *Encyclopedia of Political Systems and Parties*. He has prepared university students to participate in the Model Organization of American States since 1980, and for the past twenty-two years he has served as a contributing editor for the *Handbook of Latin American Studies*.

361